ɫemerciements

e tiens à remercier Agnès Berbinau, Fabien Grenèche, Patrick et Francine Moffett t Jean-François Sené pour leurs suggestions et leurs encouragements.

Pour Adèle et Camille

2 How To Be British Collection © LGP, Brighton, www.lgpcards.com ; **23** LES HUMANOIDES .SSOCIES SAS, Paris ; **110** DAILY EXPRESS ; **144** BIS/Ph. Eileen Tweedy © Archives Larbor ; **45** Printed by permission of The Norman Rockwell Family Agency © 1943 The Norman Rockwell amily Entities ; **149** BIS/Ph. Eileen Tweedy © Archives Larbor ; **152** Science & Society Picture ibrary, Londres ; **153** AKG- images, Paris ; **154** ORANGE UK Plc ; **155** Bartle Bogle Hegarty/Black evi's/Photo Alan Brooking ; **156** Mc Cann, Hong Kong/Cathay Pacific ; **158** Kevin Kallaugher ; **159** evin Kallaugher ; **281** BRIDGEMAN-GIRAUDON ; **347** CORBIS/Bettmann/© Adagp, Paris 2007 :s autres documents sont la propriété de l'auteur.

ination éditoriale : Christine Asin
n : Séverine Martineau
ɔtion graphique de l'intérieur et de la couverture : Courant d'idées
raphie et schémas : Légendes cartographie
n page : Alinéa
tion : Lucile Germaine
:aphie : Maryse Hubert

n, 2007 – 25 avenue Pierre de Coubertin 75211 PARIS CEDEX 13
78-2-09-160423-7

Angl

The Guide

Françoise Grellet
Agrégée d'anglais,
professeur au lycée Henri IV à Paris

Coor
Éditi
Conc
Carto
Mise
Fabri
Icono

© Nat
ISBN:

AVANT-PROPOS

POURQUOI CE GUIDE ?

Le but de ce guide est de fournir aux élèves et aux étudiants un ouvrage de référence et d'accompagnement. Les manuels sont en priorité conçus comme des supports du travail de classe, et l'on n'y trouve conseils de méthode et apports culturels qu'au hasard des textes. Par ailleurs, les élèves ne gardent que rarement leurs manuels à la fin de l'année.

Pendant la première année des études supérieures, ces méthodes et connaissances culturelles sont souvent considérées comme acquises, l'enseignement devenant alors plus spécialisé.

Le but de ce guide est donc de fournir en un même livre les principaux outils et méthodes nécessaires de la fin du second cycle au début des études supérieures. Ce n'est pas un manuel de classe, mais un livre de référence.

QUELLES RÉFÉRENCES ?

→ Des outils :

Comment lire les chiffres, précis grammatical, précis phonologique

→ Des méthodes :

Comment écrire une lettre, faire un essai ou un récit, comment analyser un document iconographique, un article de journal, un texte de fiction, comment traduire un texte...

→ Des références :

Précis culturel

QUELLE UTILISATION ?

Ce guide peut être utilisé parallèlement à n'importe quel manuel ou cours. L'étudiant pourra y vérifier un point de grammaire, y trouver des conseils méthodologiques pour le résumé, l'essai ou la traduction qu'il a à faire, ou bien s'y référer pour consulter une carte ou vérifier un point de civilisation, par exemple comment un président américain est élu.

La langue utilisée dans le texte est parfois le français (pour donner des conseils de méthode), parfois l'anglais (dans la partie culturelle, par exemple, car les termes doivent être connus en anglais). Quand il s'agit d'anglais, la plupart des termes difficiles ont été traduits, soit à l'aide de notes, soit directement dans le texte pour que la non connaissance de certains mots ne soit pas un obstacle à l'apprentissage. Par ailleurs, la traduction des mots difficiles sur la page peut aider l'étudiant à se rappeler plus facilement du sens de ces mots.

Chacun des chapitres ou fiches est suivi de courts exercices auto-correctifs qui permettront à l'étudiant d'appliquer ce qu'il a appris et de s'auto-corriger. Les corrigés des exercices se trouvent en fin d'ouvrage.

Sommaire

I Communiquer

I. Les règles propres à certains genres

II. Quelques notions

III. Quelques fonctions de communication

IV. Chiffres et mesures

II Analyser

I. Documents écrits

V DÉCOUVRIR LA CULTURE

I COMMUNIQUER

I LES RÈGLES PROPRES À CERTAINS GENRES

1. ÉCRIRE UNE LETTRE

Même à l'époque du téléphone et du courrier électronique, il est constamment nécessaire d'écrire des lettres, qu'il s'agisse de lettres personnelles envoyées à sa famille ou ses amis (pour remercier ou inviter, par exemple) ou de lettres officielles ou commerciales (pour réserver une place, pour réclamer, pour faire une commande). Voici quelques conseils concernant la présentation des lettres et les expressions les plus courantes qui vous seront utiles pour ces deux types de lettres.

Lettres personnelles

1 25 Richmond Road
Kingston upon Thames
TW 54 AJD

2 5 November 1992

3 Dear John

4 Thank you very much for ....
....

5 Looking forward to seeing you soon.

6 Love

7 Jennifer

1 Votre adresse complète

2 La date. Elle peut s'écrire de différentes façons :

→ *Saturday, 5 (th) November (,)* 1992

→ *November 5 (th) (,)* 1992

→ *5.11.92*

Attention ! En anglais américain, le mois est mentionné en premier lorsque vous vous écrivez la date en chiffres :

→ 11.5.92 = November 5th, 1992 (US)
= 11th May, 1992 (GB)

On omet souvent l'année dans les lettres personnelles.

❸ La salutation/❻ La formule de fin de lettre

Ces expressions diffèrent en fonction de la personne à qui vous écrivez :

	Salutation	Formule de fin de lettre
Langue plus soignée	Dear Mrs Jones	Yours sincerely Sincerely yours Yours truly
Langue plus familière	Dear John My dear John My dearest John	(Yours) affectionately Your affectionate nephew With kind regards Best wishes Yours (ever) Love Lots of love/Much love

❹ La partie principale de la lettre. Voici quelques expressions courantes qui peuvent vous permettre de commencer votre lettre :

→ *Thank you for your last letter.../Many thanks for...*
→ *I'm sorry I haven't written earlier but...*
→ *I'm writing to tell you.../wish you.../apologize for...*
→ *I thought I would send you a few lines/drop you a line to...*

> Dear Philip,
>
> I may as well come straight to the point. I've had what I believe is called a poison-pen letter from Euphoria, an anonymous letter. It says you are having an affair with Morris Zapp's daughter. I know it's not true but please write at once and tell me that it isn't. I keep bursting into tears and can't tell anybody why.
>
> Love,
>
> Hilary
>
> ▲ **David Lodge,** *Changing Places*.© Agence Hoffman.

❺ On utilise la plupart du temps une dernière phrase qui sert de lien entre la partie principale de la lettre et la formule de fin de lettre. On y mentionne généralement le futur (plans, attente d'une réponse, visite future...).

→ *I am looking forward to seeing you all soon.../to hearing from you...*
(look forward to + V + -ing = attendre avec impatience)
→ *My regards to your parents.*

- *We both hope you can come.../hope these arrangements will suit you...*
- *I hope everything is going well for you at the moment.*
- *Thanking you in anticipation* (en vous remerciant à l'avance)
- *See you soon.* (plus familier : à bientôt)
- *I wish you were here.*
- *Don't hesitate to contact me if there is anything I can do.*
- *I'll write again soon.*

7 Votre signature.

Lettres officielles et commerciales

1 20 Spring Road
Liverpool LR 3 9OG
13 June 1993

2 13 June 1993

3 Your reference: XDF / 453

4 Elizabeth Hotel
37 Eccleston Square
Victoria, London SW1V 1PB

5 Dear Sir

6 I am writing to confirm ....
....
....
....

7 I am looking forward to hearing from you.

8 Yours Sincerely,

9 John Gardener.
JOHN GARDENER

1 Votre adresse complète.

2 La date (mêmes remarques que pour les lettres personnelles, mais il ne faut pas oublier de mentionner l'année.)

3 La référence, s'il y en a une.

4 Le nom et l'adresse de la personne ou de l'entreprise à qui vous écrivez.

5 La salutation (suivie ou non d'une virgule).

8 La formule de fin de lettre :

	Salutation	Formule de fin de lettre
Style plus guindé	*Dear Sir* *Dear Madam* (si vous ne connaissez pas le nom de la personne à qui vous écrivez)	*Yours faithfully*
Style plus neutre	*Dear Mr/Mrs/Miss/ Ms Smith* (si vous connaissez le nom de la personne à qui vous écrivez)	*Yours sincerely* *Sincerely Yours*

Notez que *Ms* s'emploie pour une femme lorsque l'on préfère ne pas employer *Mrs* ou *Miss*.

6 La partie principale de la lettre. Voici quelques expressions souvent utilisées dans les lettres officielles :

- *Thank you for your letter of + date*
- *In reply to your letter…* (En réponse à votre lettre…)
- *I am writing to tell you…/ask you…/inform you…/inquire about…/concerning…*
- *I wish to draw your attention to…* (J'aimerais attirer votre attention sur…)
- *I should be grateful if you would send me…/tell me…*
- *I would appreciate it if you could…*
- *With reference to your advertisement in* The Times*…/for a secretary…*
- *I should like to apply for the position/job of…*
- *We are pleased to…/We regret to inform you that…*

7 La « formule de conclusion » comme dans les lettres personnelles. Voici quelques possibilités :

- *I look forward to hearing from you.* (dans l'attente de votre réponse)
- *We would be most grateful if you could settle this matter.*
  (Je vous serais reconnaissant de bien vouloir régler cette question…)
- *I should be glad to come for an interview at any time that would suit you.*
- *Thanking you in anticipation* (Je vous remercie à l'avance.)

9 Votre signature. Dans une lettre officielle, il est préférable d'écrire son nom en majuscules sous la signature.

Lettres de motivation

Une lettre de motivation accompagne votre CV lorsque vous postulez pour un emploi ou un stage. Voici quelques conseils pour écrire ce type de lettre.
N'écrivez pas votre lettre à la main. Respectez les mêmes conseils de présentation que pour une lettre officielle. Essayez de connaître le nom de la personne responsable et de lui adresser directement la lettre (*Dear Mrs Dawkins/Yours sincerely*).
Sinon, adressez votre lettre au *Personnel Department* et commencez par *Dear Sir* ou *Madam*, pour terminer également par *Yours sincerely*.
Le corps de la lettre comprend souvent quatre parties.

1 Qui vous êtes (rapidement puisque vous envoyez également votre CV) et pourquoi vous écrivez cette lettre.
- *I have just graduated from...* (Je viens d'obtenir mon diplôme de...)
- *I am a second-year student at...* (Je suis en seconde année à...)
- *As a history student at..., I am particularly interested in....* (Étudiant en histoire à..., je m'intéresse tout particulièrement à...)
- *I would like to apply for a summer job in your bank.*
- *I am looking for a position as... in your organization/company.*
- *I am interested in the position you advertised in* The Times *on January 3rd* (Je suis intéressé par le poste mentionné dans votre annonce du...)
- *I am answering your ad for a waiter in the October 18th* Times. (Je vous écris car je suis intéressé par le poste de serveur mentionné dans votre annonce du...)

2 Pourquoi ce travail vous intéresse.
- *I have always been interested in...*
- *When I studied at... I had the opportunity to...* (Lorsque j'ai étudié à..., j'ai eu l'occasion de...)
- *I like dealing with people...* (J'aime le contact avec les autres...)
- *I am keen to work in the field of...* (Je tiens beaucoup à travailler dans le domaine...)

3 Votre expérience : pourquoi vous pensez être qualifié pour ce travail.
- *I think my knowledge of Russian could prove useful for your business.*
- *I already have two years of experience in working with children...*
- *Working late/hard/long hours... is not a problem for me.*

4 Un paragraphe de conclusion.
- *I enclose my CV...* (Vous trouverez ci-joint mon CV.)
- *I will take the liberty of phoning/calling (US) you later next month to discuss the possibility of an interview.* (Je me permettrai de vous téléphoner...)
- *I will be in London next month and can come for an interview at any time convenient for you.*
- *You can reach me at the above telephone number.*
- *I look forward to hearing from you.*
- *Thank you (in advance) for your consideration.*

exercices

1 Corrigez la lettre écrite par cet étudiant :

2 Complétez la lettre que Pierre a écrite à Mrs Sheila Smith.

33 rue Blanche
75008 Paris

5 May 2003

....

My cousin, Leslie Norman, has told me that you could put me up for a few days if I went to Edinburgh next summer. I want to .... your kind offer. I have always wanted to visit Scotland, and this would be an ideal way of doing so. I hope ....

....

....

3 Alan Green veut poser sa candidature pour un travail d'été à la bibliothèque de Reading. Les différentes parties de sa lettre sont dans le désordre. Remettez-les en ordre.

(1) *I hope you will consider my application and would be very pleased to come for an interview whenever it is convenient for you.*

(2) *I enclose my CV, which will show you that I have indeed already worked a little in my school library.*

(3) *Alan Green 22 Oakview Crescent, Basingstoke*

(4) *I look forward to hearing from you.*

(5) *I am writing in response to your advertisement of March 20th in* The Reading Gazette.

(6) *The Librarian Reading Public Library*

(7) *Dear Sir*

(8) *My reason for applying is that I have always been interested in books and spend a lot of time in libraries.*

(9) *I would be happy to send you any other details you may require.*

(10) *Yours faithfully,*

(11) *I would like to apply for the summer job of assistant in your library.*

4 Traduisez les phrases suivantes en ayant recours à des expressions anglaises équivalentes mentionnées dans ce chapitre.

(1) Je vous serais reconnaissant de bien vouloir m'envoyer votre nouveau catalogue.

(2) Dans l'attente de votre réponse.

(3) Je me réfère à votre annonce dans l'*Independent* et vous serais reconnaissant de bien vouloir m'envoyer des précisions supplémentaires.

(4) Veuillez trouver ci-joint la liste des prix que vous nous avez demandée.

(5) Nous vous embrassons tous les deux. Mes amitiés à votre père.

2. ÉCRIRE UN COURRIER ÉLECTRONIQUE

Les courriers électroniques (e-mails) ont beaucoup de points communs avec les lettres mais sont écrits dans un registre plus familier, dans une langue plus proche de la langue orale.

On peut par exemple y utiliser :

1 Des abréviations, qui permettent d'écrire plus rapidement, ce qui est important dans les forums de conversation (*chat rooms*). Certaines abréviations sont couramment utilisées :

→ *iow = in other words ; asap = as soon as possible ; yr = your*

2 Des orthographes phonétiques, par exemple : u = you

3 Des majuscules, pour mettre l'accent sur un ou plusieurs mots.

→ *Congratulations ! What a FANTASTIC result !*

4 Des *'SMILEYS'* (ou *'EMOTICONS'*), qui permettent de transmettre des sentiments à l'aide de quelques touches du clavier de l'ordinateur.

→ :) = *happiness (smiling)*

> **Attention !**
> Il ne faut utiliser ces procédés que si le message est très informel.

Voici l'exemple d'une lettre plus neutre :

Dear Peter

Thank your for your mail. I'm fine, but I had a bad cold last Wednesday, and couldn't make it to[1] the restaurant. Wld you be free next Wednesday? Same place, same time?

Don't forget to take yr diary.

Hope to see you then,

Love,

Ann

1. **make it to**: get to, reach

- On pourrait avoir *"Hello Peter"* ou *"Hi Peter"* dans une langue plus familière, ou simplement *Peter*.
- Abréviations :
  Wld = would ***yr = your***
- Omission du sujet *(I hope to see…)*. On pourrait aussi dire *"All the best"*.

exercices

1 Récrivez les abréviations qui suivent en anglais standard.

1. C U There : ……………………………………
2. 2 morrow : ……………………………………
3. GR 8 ! : ……………………………………
4. U want 2 ? ……………………………………
5. C U B 4 5 ……………………………………
6. wb home ! : ……………………………………
7. b4 U go : ……………………………………
8. nxt wk : ……………………………………
9. How r things with u ? ……………………………………
10. What r u up 2 now ? ……………………………………

2 Faites correspondre 'smileys' et émotions.

1. :)	A. Angelic
2. >:(	B. Clowning
3. :D	C. Crying
4. :O	D. Feeling separate
5. :-|	E. Frowning
6. ;)	F. Happy
7. :*)	G. Indifferent
8. :-(	H. Laughing
9. :-<	I. Pouting[2]
10. :'	J. Very angry
11. :-[	K. Very sad
12. |-O	L. Wanting to hug[3]
13. O:-)	M. Winking, joking[4]
14. []	N. Yawning[5]
15.][	O. Yelling

2. **pout :** *faire la moue.* 3. **hug :** *serrer dans ses bras.* 4. **wink :** *faire un clin d'œil.* **joke :** *plaisanter.* 5. **yawn :** *bailler.*

3. ÉCRIRE UNE PAGE DE JOURNAL INTIME

Les journaux intimes sont d'ordinaire écrits dans un style informel, ce qui explique pourquoi on y trouve beaucoup d'ellipses et de formes contractées.

Principales ellipses :
- le verbe to be : *Meeting cancelled tomorrow.* (= *is cancelled*)
- le pronom sujet première personne (*I/we*) : *Need to write more about this.* (= *I need to write more about this.*)
- certains articles et déterminants : *Left car at the garage.* (= *I left the car…*)
- abréviations : *K. coming for dinner.* (= *Kim*)

Voici un exemple tiré d'un roman :

C. today accused of having stolen a football from gym. Teacher called up, asked if I'd seen it in the house. I said no, but would search the house. Did not find it. Have no doubt C. did steal it, maybe passed it on to some boy who doesn't even go to Brunswick School. This evening C. was evasive, angrily says he is being falsely accused. B. and I on the fence[1] whether we should offer to pay for football. B. ashamed, says let it ride[2] till we know something definite. Too bad C. starts out so soon on wrong foot.

P. Highsmith, *Edith's Diary*, Bloomsbury Publishing.

1. **To be on the fence :** *ne pas avoir pris position.*
2. **Let it ride :** *attends, laisse courir.*

Notez que l'on utilise la même langue elliptique pour écrire de courts messages ou des cartes postales.

Carte postale

Dear Penny, Spending a week in Cyprus. The weather is beautiful and the site gorgeous. Wish you were here. See you next week. Love Lilian	Penny Waller 12 Crescent Road Guildford GU 56 4 TD

Message

Left car at the garage. Will be home late. Phil

exercices

1 Récrivez les phrases suivantes dans le style d'un journal intime.

(a) I've decided to keep a diary. I will write in it everything that happens to me and Jonathan.

(b) Tuesday. I was awoken at 6 a.m. by a loud noise at the door. First I thought it might be the police after what happened last night, then I realized it was Juliet.

2 Lisez cet extrait du journal de Pepys, écrit en 1665, l'année où la peste (*the plague*) **s'est déclarée à Londres. Puis récrivez les passages elliptiques ou peu cohérents du point de vue temporel afin de transformer ce texte en récit.**

10 June. Lay long in bed; and then up and at the office all the morning. At noon dined at home, and then to the office, busy all the afternoon. In the evening home to supper, and there to my great trouble hear that the plague is come into the City (though it hath[1] these three or four weeks since its beginning been wholly out of the City); but where should it begin but in my good friend and neighbour's, Dr Burnett in Fanchurch Street – which in both points troubles me mightily[2]. To the office to finish my letters, and then home to bed – being troubled at the sickness…

1. **hath :** has.
2. **mightily :** very much.

4. Écrire un CV

Un Curriculum Vitae (CV en anglais britannique), *Résumé* en anglais américain ['rezjumei] informe un employeur sur vos diplômes, votre carrière, votre vie personnelle. Il doit être aussi clair que possible dans sa présentation. Voici un exemple classique de CV. Vous trouverez sur la page suivante un certain nombre de conseils et variantes pour chacune des rubriques.

Florence BELAIR
7, rue des Moulins
78000 Versailles
France
Home : 00 33 1 46 87 45 56
Mobile : 06 76 55 39 75
Email : flobel@wanadoo.fr

PERSONAL DETAILS

Nationality : French

Date of birth : 4 March 1981

Marital status : Married, 2005.

WORK EXPERIENCE

2004-2005 : Public Relations Officer at Banque Populaire. Liaise with customers and deal with complaints.

July 2004: Holiday job at Caisse d'Épargne (a savings bank) : secretarial work

August 2003: Holiday job as a cashier in a supermarket (Monoprix)

EDUCATION & QUALIFICATIONS

2004: Maîtrise (equivalent to MA) in Economics from Université de Paris I, Paris, France.

2003: Licence (equivalent to BA) in Economics from Université de Paris I, Paris, France.
1999: Baccalauréat (equivalent to A Levels), ES section (specialized in economics)
1992- 1999 : Lycée Hoche, Versailles

SKILLS

Driving licence : Full
Fluent English
Good command of Spanish.
First Aid Certificate.

INTERESTS AND ACTIVITIES

Skiing, handball
Playing the violin
Cooking
Volunteer help for a local youth club.

References available

THE HEADING

Votre nom, adresse, numéro de téléphone et E-mail en haut de la page, centré.
N'oubliez pas de faire précéder votre numéro de téléphone par l'indicatif de la France (0033 + 1 pour un numéro en 01 par exemple) pour que l'on puisse vous joindre de l'étranger.

PERSONAL DETAILS

Marital status : Single, divorced, separated
L'indication de la situation familiale n'est pas obligatoire.

WORK EXPERIENCE

Il est plus courant d'opter pour un ordre chronologique inversé (en commençant par ce qui est plus récent).
On peut mentionner les emplois de vacances tels que *waiter*, *cashier* (caissier), *operator* (standardiste), *holiday camp counsellor (GB) / counselor (US)* (moniteur de colonie de vacances)...

EDUCATION & QUALIFICATIONS

Indiquez vos diplômes français et un équivalent entre parenthèses.

- Baccalauréat *(equivalent to A Levels (GB)/High School Diploma (US))*
- Licence *(equivalent to BA)*
- Mastère *(equivalent to MA)*
- DESS *(One-year post-graduate diploma)*

→ DEA *(First year of PhD)*
→ Doctorat *(PhD)*
→ *Gained admission to HEC, ENS, X School of Management...*

SKILLS

Basic/Good knowledge of computers and word-processing
Lorsque vous décrivez votre niveau linguistique, vous pouvez dire :
Bilingual French – English
Fluent English
Good command of English
Working knowledge of English (votre niveau d'anglais vous permet de travailler).

INTERESTS AND ACTIVITIES

Mentionnez les sports que vous pratiquez *(skiing, cycling, mountaineering/hiking...)*, vos hobbies *(painting, playing the cello...)*.
Toute activité bénévole *(Volunteer work for the National Trust, for a school, a charity...)* sera appréciée.

exercice

Écrivez votre propre CV.

5. Écrire un récit

Lorsque vous écrivez une lettre ou un journal intime, lorsque vous racontez une anecdote, vous êtes conduits à faire un récit, à raconter une histoire. Il n'existe pas de règles d'écriture propres à ce genre, où l'on se contente le plus souvent de suivre l'ordre chronologique des évènements. Mais il est essentiel de bien maîtriser un certain nombre de points.

1 – Les temps

La plupart des récits racontent des faits passés et se font donc au *simple past*. Mais vous pourrez utiliser le *present tense* pour parler du moment de l'écriture (*I remember* dans l'exemple qui suit) et le *past perfect* pour parler d'un moment antérieur à celui du récit, souvent pour expliquer les évènements (*she had written* dans l'exemple qui suit).

exemple

The first thing I remember about that day is the surprise, or rather the look of puzzlement, on my mother's face when she opened the letter as I came down for breakfast. A few weeks earlier, she had written to Uncle Jeremy in Australia, and when I saw the stamps on the blue envelope, I assumed that the letter came from him...

Parfois, on pourra contraster *simple past* et *past + -ing*, si une action ponctuelle ❶ s'inscrit au milieu d'une situation ou action qui dure ❷.

exemple

I was listening to the radio (❷) *when I heard the doorbell.* (❶)

Mais attention : un résumé de film ou de livre se fait la plupart du temps au présent.

exemple

The novel is set in London during the war. The main characters are Ruth, a painter, and Cyril, her friend, with whom she shares a flat....

2 – La chronologie

Pour raconter une histoire vous aurez également besoin d'adverbes et de mots de liaison temporels. Reportez-vous pour cela à la partie « Développement chronologique ».

3 – Rapporter des paroles

Vous pourrez aussi avoir besoin de rapporter les paroles de quelqu'un. Vous pourrez le faire de plusieurs façons.

Si les paroles que vous voulez rapporter sont :
MY MOTHER : I don't understand. Someone's telling me that my brother Jeremy has disappeared !

Vous pouvez :

❶ Résumer ces paroles :
→ *My mother said someone was writing to tell her that her brother had disappeared.*

❷ Utiliser le style indirect :
→ *My mother said that she did not understand. That someone was telling her that her brother Jeremy had disappeared.*
(Pour plus de détails, voir « Le discours indirect », p. 250, dans la partie grammaire.)

❸ Citer les paroles au style direct. (Vous utiliserez alors des verbes tels que *say, cry, answer, complain*... pour introduire ces paroles.)
→ *"I don't understand", my mother said. "Someone's telling me that my brother Jeremy has disappeared !"*

P. 44 (PONCTUATION DU DIALOGUE)

Voici par exemple le début d'une nouvelle d'Alan Sillitoe. Notez l'utilisation de **marqueurs temporels**, du *past perfect* pour des explications par « retour en arrière » et des **paroles citées au style direct** et introduites par le verbe *"call"*.

Enoch's parents parted in a singular way. He was eight years of age **at the time**.

It happened **one morning after** he **had gone** to school, so that he didn't know anything about it **till** coming home in the evening.

Jack Boden got up as usual **at seven o'clock**, and his wife, who was Enoch's mother, set a breakfast of bacon and egg before him. They never said much, and spoke even less **on this particular morning** because both were solidly lost in their separate thoughts which, unknown to each other, they were at last intending to act on.

Instead of getting a bus to his foundry[1], Jack boarded one for the city centre. He sought out a public lavatory where, for the price of a penny, he was able to draw off his overalls, and emerge with them under his arm. They were wrapped in the brown paper which he **had put** into his pocket **before** leaving the house, as he **called** from the kitchen: **'So long, love. See you this afternoon.'**

Now wearing a reasonable suit, he walked to the railway station. There he met René, who had in her two suitcases a few of his possessions that he **had given to** her during clandestine meetings over the past fortnight. Having worked in the same factory, they **had**, as many others who were employed there saw, **fallen in love**. René wasn't married, so there seemed nothing to stop her going away with him.

Adapted from Enoch's Two Letters in *Men, Women and Children*, by **Alan Sillitoe, W.H. Allen & Co. Ltd**.

1. **foundry:** *fonderie (usine).*

exercices

1 Retrouvez l'ordre des différentes parties de ce récit. (Le narrateur s'appelle Bateman.)

A. Then an accident happened.

B. He passed difficult moments, but he could not deny that Edward was worthy of his good fortune, and, anxious that nothing should spoil the friendship he so greatly valued, he took care never by a hint to reveal his own feelings.

C. They had both known her when she was a child and they long-legged boys, but for two years she had been in Europe to finish her education and it was with a surprised delight that they renewed acquaintance[2] with the lovely girl who returned.

D. It had all begun long ago when he and Edward Barnard, still at college, had met Isabel Longstaffe at the tea-party given to introduce her to society.

E. Her only answer was to throw her arms round his neck and burst into tears.

F. Both of them fell desperately in love with her, but Bateman saw quickly that she had eyes only for Edward, and, devoted to his friend, he resigned himself to the role of confidant.

G. He came home one night, told his wife he was ruined, and after dinner, going into his study, shot himself.

H. In six months the young couple were engaged.

I. They had to wait a year. Bateman remembered the winter at the end of which Isabel and Edward were to be married, a winter of dances and theatre-parties and of informal gaieties at which he, the constant third, was always present. He loved her no less because she would shortly be his friend's wife; her smile, a gay word she said to him, the confidence[3] of her affection, never ceased to delight him; and he congratulated himself, somewhat complacently[4], because he did not envy their happiness.

J. A great bank failed, there was a panic on the exchange, and Edward Barnard's father found himself a ruined man.

K. But they were very young and Isabel's father decided that they should not marry at least till Edward graduated[5].

L. A week later, Edward Barnard, with a tired, white face, went to Isabel and asked her to release[6] him.

Adapted from **W.S. Maugham**, The Fall of Edward Barnard, *Collected Short Stories*, 1951, William Heinemmann.

2. to renew acquaintance with: *renouer connaissance avec.*
3. confidence: *confiance.*
4. complacently: *avec suffisance.*
5. graduate: get one's university diploma.
6. release him: tell him they would not marry.

The right order is: ....

2 Voici la première page d'une bande dessinée. Lisez-la, puis étudiez la façon dont elle a été transformée en récit.

(1) Complétez le passage avec les marqueurs temporels donnés ci-dessous dans le désordre.

a few minutes later – already – as – immediatly – meanwhile – that morning – then

(2) Surlignez:

– en orange les paroles rapportées au style direct;

– en rouge les paroles rapportées au style indirect;

– en vert les pensées rapportées ou résumées au style indirect;

– en bleu le résumé des paroles.

▲ Dupuy et Berberian, Monsieur Jean, t. 1, *L'amour, la concierge*, Les Humanoïdes associés.

When Monsieur Jean opened his fridge ...., he discovered that it was practically empty. He mentally made a list of all he needed to buy – coffee, sugar, pizza, camembert –, wondered if there was anything else he had forgotten, and left his flat. .... he was going down the stairs, he met his concierge, Madame Colin, and they greeted each other.

"Go ahead! I'm such a slowpoke!", she said to him, motioning to him to pass her on the stairs, ... commenting on the energy and youth of Monsieur Jean, who was .... down the steps, whistling. ...., he was in the supermarket, filling his shopping trolley with a variety of food. .... just behind him, a young woman was explaining to someone that she was doing a survey on the eating habits of people under 35 and wondering if she could ask them a few questions. Monsieur Jean turned round, looked at the pretty blonde, and .... fell in love.

6. Écrire un résumé

Il est important de savoir faire un résumé, non seulement parce qu'il s'agit d'un exercice qui vous sera demandé à de nombreux examens et concours, mais aussi parce que, quel que soit votre métier, vous aurez souvent à transmettre par écrit à quelqu'un d'autre les idées principales d'un document.
Les points qui suivent sont essentiels pour faire un bon résumé.

1 La longueur du résumé.
Un résumé fait d'ordinaire environ un tiers de la longueur du texte de départ. Lorsqu'on vous demande de faire un résumé lors d'un examen, le nombre de mots demandé est spécifié. Assurez-vous très vite que vous avez une idée de ce que représente la longueur demandée. Vous n'aurez plus ainsi qu'à faire des changements mineurs au dernier moment. On accepte d'ordinaire une marge de différence de 10 % par rapport au nombre de mots demandé.

2 Le point de vue
Le point de vue doit rester celui de l'auteur du document d'origine. On ne rapporte donc pas ce qui est dit au style indirect (*the author of the article says that…*), mais on imagine ce que l'auteur du document aurait pu écrire, de façon plus concise.

3 Un résumé doit être objectif. On ne donne pas son opinion, mais on résume le texte de façon neutre et objective.

4 L'organisation du résumé
Pour rendre compte des idées essentielles du texte, il y a deux possibilités :
– si le texte est bien construit, on peut suivre l'organisation du texte de départ ;
– si le texte est répétitif et mal organisé, le résumé sera plus clair s'il ne suit pas l'ordre du texte.
Le résumé final doit être clair et bien articulé.

5 La langue
Le résumé doit être fait en vos propres termes et ne doit pas juxtaposer une suite de phrases ou d'expressions du texte. Utilisez des mots de liaison et des propositions relatives. N'employez pas de formes contractées.

6 La méthode
Lisez le texte plusieurs fois pour en comprendre le sens général ainsi que les idées essentielles. Puis :
– repérez l'organisation du texte ;
– soulignez les phrases essentielles du texte qui résument l'information (*topic sentences*) et les mots-clés du texte.
Puis reformulez ces idées et rédigez le résumé.

exemple

Lisez le texte suivant, sur le mouvement non-violent de Martin Luther King contre la ségrégation aux États-Unis, et notez la façon dont la structure du texte et ses phrases et mots-clés ont été repérés. C'est là l'étape qui doit précéder tout résumé.

King and non-violent resistance

In leading the mass assault on racial barriers, King preached non-violent resistance to unjust laws. It was a doctrine he derived from the teachings of Christianity and the historical examples of civil disobedience in Gandhi's struggle for India's independence and in Thoreau's protest against the Mexican War. King's tactics surfaced first in Montgomery, Alabama, where a black woman, Rosa Parks, was arrested in December 1955 ~~for refusing to give up~~ her seat in the white section of a bus. Led by King, the city's black people engaged in a massive bus boycott. After a year, the bus company agreed to desegregate its facilities[1]. From Montgomery, the movement spread to Greensboro, North Carolina, where black college students staged a "sit-in[2]" at a drugstore lunch counter to protest discrimination in places of public accommodation[3]. This passive resistance tactic caught on quickly, and subsequent "sit-ins" resulted in the desegregation of hundreds of public places throughout the South.

King's organization, the Southern Christian Leadership Conference (SCLC) was joined in peaceful resistance by the Congress of Racial Equality (CORE) and the Student Non-Violent Coordinating Committee (SNCC). The non-violent phase of the civil rights drive reached a peak[4] in the summer of 1964, when thousands of black and white students converged on the South from all over the nation to register prospective back voters and organize new bi-racial groups, such as the Mississippi Freedom Democratic Party. At this point, the goal of the movement was integration of black people into white society. Blacks and whites worked together, organized together, marched together, even died together, in pursuit of that goal.

▲ *The Shaping of America*, Curry, Sproat & Cramer, Holt, Rinehart & Winston.

Structure

The title/first sentence sum up the subject.

1. 3 **influences** on King's movement
   - Christianity
   - Gandhi
   - Thoreau
2. **Chronology** of events from 1955 to 1964 + link-words eg. First
   - The beginnings
   - Growth of the movement (a list)
3. The **aim** of the movement at its peak.

1. **facilities :** *lieux, installations.*
2. **sit-in :** *protestation en restant assis quelque part.*
3. **accommodation :** place to stay or live in.
4. **reach a peak :** *culminer.*

exercice

L'article de journal qui suit devait être résumé en environ 125 mots. Voici quatre résumés, tous de longueur acceptable. Décidez lequel est le meilleur et dites pourquoi vous avez rejeté les trois autres (il peut y avoir plusieurs raisons pour chacun des résumés).

Cut-price private schools to open
Geraldine Hackett
Education Correspondent

A CORPORATION based in Dubai plans to shake up Britain's education establishment by opening the country's largest chain of independent schools.

Global Educational Management Systems (Gems) was founded by Sunny Varkey, an Indian businessman who has made a fortune by providing private healthcare and education in the United Arab Emirates and other parts of the Gulf.

It wants to own 50 schools throughout Britain within 10 years and could fill the gap between poorly regarded state education and costly and selective private schools.

Fees[1] at Gems schools will be lower than average and there will be no entrance tests. Simon Cummins, the company's director of schools, said: "We have done the research and we know there are parents disillusioned with state education who would opt for independent education if they could afford it."

The project, unveiled this weekend, could herald the biggest expansion of private education since the Labour government moved against direct grant schools in the 1970s. Then, more than 100 schools with reputations for high academic achievement moved to the private sector.

The plan is being backed by some of the best-known names in education. The company's advisory board includes Mike Tomlinson, the former head of Ofsted, Professor Sir Gareth Roberts, Whitehall's most trusted adviser on higher education, and James Sabben-Clare, a former headmaster of Winchester College.

Varkey, whose two sons were educated at Winchester, already runs 30 private schools around the world. He started the business after he inherited a private school in Dubai.

Gems has already bought two schools in Britain — Bury Lawn in Milton Keynes, Buckinghamshire, and Sherborne House, a preparatory school in Chandlers Ford, Hampshire. It has promised parents that £1m will be spent at each school on improving facilities[2] and standards.

The company wants all its schools to be within easy distance of big cities. It hopes to buy about 25 existing schools and build a further 25 by the end of the decade.

"It will depend on the area, but we will be trying to pitch[3] fees at between £5,000 and £6,000 a year," Cummins said last week.

Established independent schools are unlikely to welcome the move. Growing demand for private education has enabled them to increase their fees far ahead of the rate of inflation and the Office of Fair Trading is conducting an inquiry into allegations of fee-fixing cartels after an investigation by *The Sunday Times*.

The Times, September 21, 2003.

1. **fees :** *frais de scolarité.*
2. **facilities :** *les lieux, les locaux.*
3. **pitch :** *fixer, déterminer.*

Meilleur résumé : …

Résumés rejetés :

Résumés n°	Informations fausses	Langue et style	Information non essentielle	Résumé non objectif

1. Gems is a Dubai company which already owns two independent schools in Buckinghamshire and Hampshire and hopes to open several more, particularly near big cities. Its aim is to expand private education in Britain, just as the Labour government decided to do in the 1970s. With more schools to choose from (Gems might open up to 50 schools in the next decade), parents will be tempted to move to private education. Their fees will be between £5,000 and £6,000 a year, but growing demand for private education may lead them to increase these fees. Many well-known people in education, such as professors and headmasters, have backed the project.

2. Global Educational Management Systems plans to open Britain's largest chain of independent schools. It wants to fill the gap between state education and private education. Fees will be low and pupils will have no entrance exam. It will be the largest expansion in private education since the 1970s. Many influential people back the plan. Gems already owns two schools in Britain and hopes to open about 50. Most of the schools will be close to large cities. Fees will be between £5,000 and £6,000. Other independent schools will not appreciate this project : growing demand for private education means that they have been able to increase their fees freely.

3. A Dubai company, Global Educational Management Systems (Gems), plans to open several private schools in Britain. With fees under £6,000 a year and with no entrance exams, the schools would be aimed at parents disillusioned with state education, yet unable to get their children accepted in a more selective system or to afford the high cost of most independent schools. Gems's founder, Sunny Varkey, who already runs private schools all around the world, hopes to open 50 schools in the next decade, which would mean the largest increase in private education in 30 years. The idea is supported by many influential people in the field of education, although most independent schools are bound to condemn a plan which can only undermine their present control over prices.

4. At last parents will be able to have more choice regarding their children's education. If Gems (Global Educational Management Systems) have their own way, they will create some 50 independent schools in the next decade. What is new and interesting about the project is that it is aimed at parents who do not care for the low standards of state education, yet cannot afford the very high prices of most private schools. With fees ranging from £5,000 to £6,000 a year, many middle-class parents will welcome this new opportunity. Another clear advantage will be the absence of an elitist entrance exam, which means that the schools will be open to all children, whatever their abilities.

7. Écrire un essai

Un essai est un court développement personnel sur un sujet donné. On peut parfois vous demander de respecter une longueur correspondant à un certain nombre de mots.

I – Les différentes parties d'un essai

1 Une introduction

Vous expliquez les termes du sujet ou replacez le problème dans son contexte. Vous pouvez également introduire le sujet en partant d'un exemple, d'une anecdote, ou d'une réflexion générale, pour revenir au sujet ensuite et présenter le problème qu'il pose. Annoncez ensuite la structure de votre essai.

2 L'argumentation

La structure de votre argumentation dépendra bien sûr du sujet dont vous traitez. Par exemple :

– Arguments pour ; arguments contre ; synthèse.
– Liste d'exemples dont vous tirerez des conclusions.
– Faits ; causes ; conséquences.

N'oubliez pas qu'il est toujours préférable de commencer par des arguments qui ne sont pas les vôtres pour passer ensuite à votre propre point de vue.
Consacrez un paragraphe (séparé des autres par un interligne) pour chaque partie ou point principal.

Les paragraphes
Mentionnez l'idée principale au début de chaque paragraphe, puis développez cette idée à l'aide d'arguments, d'explications et d'exemples.

exemple

Voici un paragraphe-type dans un essai sur les téléphones portables (*mobile phones*).

> People are increasingly using their mobile phones at work too ❶. Many argue that they are more accessible this way, for instance when they have to leave the office to talk to their colleagues or get a cup of coffee ❷. Others feel that the line is more private – those who call not having to go through their secretaries ❸. For some, it is also a status symbol ❹. Getting many calls is, they believe, a mark of their own importance in the eyes of their colleagues ❺. Whatever the original reason for using mobile phones, it may well be that their use has become an addiction which, like all addictions, is very difficult to regulate ❻.

❶ **Phrase-clé (*topic sentence*), qui résume l'idée principale du paragraphe.**

❷ **Premier exemple.**

❸ **Deuxième exemple.**

❹ **Troisième exemple.**

❺ **Développement/explication du troisième exemple.**

❻ **Conclusion du paragraphe et introduction d'une nouvelle idée avec *regulate* (idée de réglementation) qui pourrait, par exemple, être développée au paragraphe suivant.**

3 Une conclusion
Elle doit résumer les points principaux ainsi que votre opinion, souvent en la nuançant. Elle peut ouvrir le débat sur un thème plus général ou sur l'avenir.

2 – COMMENT PRÉPARER VOTRE ESSAI

■ Réfléchissez au sujet et assurez vous que vous avez bien compris la question posée. N'essayez surtout pas de tirer le sujet vers un autre sujet, déjà traité ; vous risqueriez alors un hors sujet. Soulignez les mots clés et pesez bien chacun des termes utilisés.
■ Notez ensuite toutes les idées et arguments qui vous viennent en tête, de même que des exemples, illustrations, ou oeuvres que vous pouvez citer. Cette phase du travail doit vous conduire à définir votre position personnelle.

■ Organisez ensuite ces idées et arguments en plusieurs groupes.
■ Décidez quelle sera la structure de votre essai.
■ Écrivez un plan rapide où vous classerez vos différentes idées dans chaque partie. N'oubliez pas de réfléchir à de courtes introduction et conclusion.
■ Commencez à rédiger. Si la longueur vous est imposée, sachez que l'on accepte d'ordinaire une marge de 10 %. Dès que vous avez écrit une première partie, vérifiez la longueur pour vous assurer que vous êtes à peu près dans les normes. Vous pourrez ensuite affiner votre texte pour aboutir au nombre de mots souhaité.

3 – La langue

■ Vos paragraphes et vos idées doivent s'enchaîner de façon :
– logique : utilisez des mots de liaison pour souligner les articulations principales de votre essai ;
– mais naturelle : trop de mots de liaison peuvent donner une impression de maladresse et d'artificialité.
■ Votre langue doit être aussi riche que possible et éviter les répétitions et les mots trop vagues.

Voici un certain nombre d'expressions qui vous aideront aux différents stades de votre essai.

Writing essays: words and expressions

■ To start with…
What I'd like to talk/write about/say… is…
First (of all)… / To begin with…/First and foremost…/In the first place…/For a start…
As an introduction/By way of introduction, I will say that…
The point at issue here is… *(Le point/la question soulevé(e) ici…)*
A great deal has been said/written about…

■ To organize your points
Firstly…/Secondly…/Thirdly…
First of all…/Another point…/Finally…
First…/Then…/Next…/Furthermore/Besides/In addition…

■ To give your opinion
In my view/to my mind/in my opinion/for my part…
From my point of view…
It seems to me that…
My point/feeling/view is that…
As far as I am concerned, I think/believe…

As far as I can see...

Personally, I think/believe...

What I mean is that...

What strikes me is that...

I (don't) share this view...

I can't help thinking that... *(Je ne peux m'empêcher de penser que...)*

I believe that.../I am convinced that.../I have the impression that.../It seems to me that...

It's my contention that...

■ **To justify your opinion & give arguments**

It should be pointed out that...

It is important to note/consider/remember that...

We must bear in mind that... *(Il ne faut pas oublier que...)*

We must take into account the fact that... *(Nous devons tenir compte du fait que...)*

It is clear/obvious/self-evident that...

We must not overlook the fact/forget that... *(N'oublions pas que.. / Ne négligeons pas de...)*

Actually/as a matter of fact/in fact...

Moreover.../Besides.../What's more.../In addition....

The problem is not to..., but to...

It is often argued that... but I believe... *(On dit souvent que...)*

Contrary to what people often say/think...

No matter what people say, I keep thinking that...

Another reason why... is that...

Another argument in favour of.../against... is...

Another factor explaining... is that...

On the one hand... On the other hand... *(D'un côté... de l'autre...)*

■ **To introduce a new idea or argument**

What I want to add is that...

Besides/moreover/in addition/furthermore/what's more/on top of that.....

Indeed + proposition (*introduit une confirmation*: He never agreed with his parents, indeed he was in open rebellion against them.)

This raises another problem... *(Cela soulève un autre problème...)*

Not to mention (*Sans parler de*: They have a flat in London and two country houses, not to mention a cottage in Wales.)

As well as (*De même que*: As well as creating jobs, it would have the advantage of improving infrastructures.)

Nor (= and not) : They were not rich. Nor were they happy. *(Notez l'inversion.)*

Not only (+ *proposition avec inversion*), but + *proposition*. Not only are they poor, but they are in poor health as well.)

Similarly (+ *proposition*)

The difficulty with this argument is that (+ *proposition*)

■ To insist

I do think/feel/believe that...

I cannot stress this point enough. *(Je ne peux pas insister assez sur ce point.)*

The one and only way of solving the problem is...

There's no escaping the fact that... *(Il est indéniable que...)*

■ To give examples

For instance.../for example...

This is clear in the case of...

notably *(notamment)*

This is reflected in...

Consider the case of...

One of the most striking/interesting/bizarre... examples is...

To be more precise...

History provides numerous examples of...

→ e.g. : to introduce an example you give. (The use of public transportation, e.g. trains or buses, is a way of saving energy. *Ici* e.g. *introduit deux exemples de transports publics.*)

→ i.e. : to introduce a reformulation (= that is to say). (I'll give you £10 if you mow the lawn, and twice as much, i.e. £20, if you do it immediately. *Dans cette phrase* i.e. *explique, reformule* twice as much.)

■ To quote someone's words

According to...

As X wrote,....

And, to quote X's words... *(pour citer les paroles de...)*

■ To make deductions

Therefore/And so...

As a result/Consequently...

The upshot is that... *(Le résultat, c'est que...)*

This shows that...

The lesson to be drawn from these examples is that...

All this points to the fact that...

Given these facts...

■ Transitions

Now let us consider...

If we now turn to...

As to.../As for *(quant à)*

Another point we need to consider...

■ To reformulate

To put it differently/more simply....

What I mean is...

Or rather...

In other words...

■ To express reservation

Of course/Why not/I suppose so...... but...

Of course/Yes, but it depends on/what....

Yes/Of course, as long as... *(tant que...)*, if.../provided... *(à condition que)*

..., but I would not go so far as to say that... *(mais je n'irais pas jusqu'à dire que...)*

This is true, but up to a point. *(jusqu'à un certain point)*

However, we should not forget that...

■ To sum up

To sum up/In short/In a word/In brief.../Finally...

To cut a long story short...

To put it briefly...

In a nutshell.../To put it in a nutshell... *(En un mot...)*

What it all boils down to is... *(Cela revient à dire que...)*

All things considered.../All in all...

After due consideration... *(Après mûre réflexion...)*

When all is said and done...

If one weighs the pros and cons... *(Si l'on pèse le pour et le contre...)*

■ To conclude

Last but not least,... *(Le dernier point, mais ce n'est pas le moindre...)*

Finally/Lastly/In conclusion/To conclude/As a conclusion/In the end...

The lesson we can learn is that...

I'll wind up by saying that... *(Je terminerai en disant que...)*

What we can say in conclusion is that...

We can conclude by saying...

Voici, à titre d'exemple, un court *leader* (éditorial) de *The Economist*, dont la structure et les articulations ont été soulignées pour vous. Ce n'est pas un essai mais le journaliste répond en fait à la question : *Is the government right to want to liberalise gambling* (les jeux d'argent)*?*, ce qui pourrait être le sujet d'un essai.

exemple

The British government's sensible plan to liberalise gambling is being vilified[1] from all sides

LOCKING up foreign terror suspects indefinitely without trial causes barely a stir[2]. Breaking a promise to replace the House of Lords with a democratically-elected second chamber leads to a few mutterings[3] from civil libertarians. **But** let the British government suggest that people should be able to gamble a little more freely and the wrath[4] of the nation's press descends on it in equal measure from both right and left.

Introduction :
– exemples de décisions ou lois graves n'ayant pas été critiquées.
– Articulation (But) : le projet de loi sur le jeu entraîne des protestations.
→ Le journaliste est clairement en faveur du projet gouvernemental.

Britain's gambling laws date from the 1960s. Things have changed a little since then, which is **one reason** why the government thought the existing laws could do with a little updating[5]. **Another** is that they are silly. Casinos, for instance, are for members only ; and punters[6] must join up 24 hours before they are allowed to place a bet.

1) Le point de vue du gouvernement
ses raisons :
1. *things have changed*
2. *silly laws*

The new gambling bill[7], published on October 19th, would get rid of that rule. It would also allow casinos to set up anywhere, rather than in a few restricted areas, would permit much bigger ones than are allowed under the current legislation and would leave it up to councils to decide where casinos could be built.

Ses nouvelles propositions :
1. *set up anywhere*
2. *bigger casinos*
3. *decisions taken by councils*

The opposition to these plans seems motivated by, **on the one hand**, right-wing paternalism (the peasants must be protected against their mental and moral weakness) and, **on the other**, left-wing Methodism[8] (if it's fun it's bad). This unusual alliance has loosed[9] some powerful prose against the government. « […] this Government is sacrificing the most weak and vulnerable to the high priests of gambling, » thundered the *Daily Mail*. Even the right-wing *Sun*, Britain's biggest-selling tabloid, has taken against the idea. […]

2) Les critiques du projet
(deux critiques principales)
1. *Paternalism*
2. *Methodism*

Exemples de critiques dans la presse

Liberalisation's opponents[10] base their case on **four arguments**. **First**, they say, there is no demand for it. Surveys show that Britons think there is quite enough gambling avail-

Les arguments des critiques

able already. **Well**, if people are as unenthusiastic about the reality of more gambling as they are at the prospect of it, that's fine: casinos will be set up, people will stay at home playing Scrabble, and the casinos will close down.

But that argument does not sit comfortably with[11] **the second one**, which depends on the idea of looming[12] social Armageddon[13]. Liberalising the industry, according to this line, will lead to much more gambling, and thus radically increase the number of gambling addicts. **That seems unlikely**. If people want to gamble, they already can. Joining a casino doesn't take much effort, and those who are both desperate to gamble and too lazy to sign up (which sounds like a smallish group) can always waste their money on the internet. **Anyway**, in most areas of life, society accepts that the pleasure of the many is worth the problems of the few. Most people (in non-Muslim countries, at least) believe that drinking alcohol should be allowed even if a small minority is alcoholic.

The third argument is that the bill will allow big business – and American big business, horrors – to take over the gambling industry. That may well be right. [...] **But** they are likely to dominate the industry anyway, since they are more efficient and offer better services to customers. If big business takes over, gamblers are likely to enjoy themselves more.

The fourth argument is that the spread of huge casinos will dramatically change the nature of some of the seaside towns where they are expected to set up. Blackpool could become like Las Vegas. Some people may indeed regard that as a threat. **Others**, especially those who have spent much time in Blackpool, may think it an excellent idea.

The Economist, Oct 21, 2004.

1. **vilified:** criticised.
2. **causes barely a stir:** *n'a guère eu de retentissement.*
3. **mutterings:** protests.
4. **wrath:** anger.
5. **to update:** *mettre à jour.*
6. **punters:** gamblers.
7. **a bill:** *un projet de loi.*
8. **Methodism:** the Methodist Church stresses personal and social morality.
9. **loosed:** *causer, déclencher.*
10. **opponents:** those who are against.
11. **sit comfortably with:** be compatible with.
12. **looming:** approaching.
13. **Armageddon:** the last battle between the forces of good and evil.

(chacun des arguments est expliqué, puis réfuté) :

1. no demand for gambling
But (Well) : then the casinos will close and there is no problem.

2. it will lead to more gambling
But : it probably will not.
And (second reason to refute the argument) : we accept such risks in other fields.

3. It will allow big business to take over.
But : it will happen anyway.

4. It will change the aspect of the cities where there are casinos
But : in some of these cities, it might be a good thing

exercices

1 L'introduction

Voici quelques façons de commencer un essai :

(1) partir de la définition du mot-clé

(2) partir d'une question

(3) donner quelques exemples ou une anecdote pour illustrer le problème

(4) expliquer rapidement le contexte historique de la question

(5) partir d'un proverbe ou d'un dicton

(6) partir de données ou de statistiques

• **Lesquelles de ces possibilités sont utilisées dans les débuts d'articles et d'éditoriaux qui suivent ?**

A. So you think your home is small ? One night recently…
(*The New York Times*, February 11, 2006)

B. Jetta is eleven months old, with big eyes, a few pearly teeth – and a tiny index finger that can already operate electronic entertainment devices.
(*The New York Times*, January 21, 2006, an article about educational toys for children.)

C. The art of the state of the union address[1] is to rouse the faithful, deflect[2] critics and identify a problem for which your administration is not to blame, but which you will selflessly combat. President Putin's contribution to the genre…
(*The New York Times*, May 20, 2006, an article about President Putin's state of the union speech)

1. **state of the union address :** *discours annuel d'un chef d'État sur la situation du pays.* 2. **deflect critics :** *faire taire les critiques.*

D. Some weeks nothing happens ; some weeks change history.
(*The New York Times*, March 26, 2006)

E. Not so many years ago, nuclear energy was a villain to environmentalists, who feared the potential for catastrophic accidents and long-term radiation contamination. But this is a new era…
(*The New York Times*, May 27, 2006, an article about the renewed interest in nuclear power.)

2 La conclusion

Elle doit résumer les idées de votre essai, puis ouvrir sur d'autres perspectives, qui peuvent être :

(1) une mise en garde ou un vœu

(2) une prédiction

(3) une question

(4) une prise de position claire

• **Lesquelles de ces possibilités sont utilisées dans les conclusions d'articles et d'éditoriaux qui suivent ?**

A. With the sun finally setting on the hopes for Doha, there may be very dark times ahead for trade.
(*The Economist*, July 24, 2006, an article about the failure of the Doha trade talks that were supposed to help poor countries.)

B. These are mightily complicated areas, but the United States has always had a genius for translating the highfalutin'[1] talk of the American Dream into practical policies, such as the GI Bill, a scholarship scheme for returning troops after the second world war. The country needs another burst of practical idealism. It is still the model the rest of the world is following.
(*The Economist*, June 15, 2006, an article about inequality in the United States.)

1. **highfalutin':** *prétentieux.*

C. On that crucial issue, Mr. Bush is leaving a legacy that he and America can be proud of.
(*The New York Times*, May 20, 2006, an article about President Bush's policy regarding prostitution.)

3 Les phrases du paragraphe qui suit sont données dans le désordre. Le paragraphe est extrait d'un éditorial qui montre les bénéfices que les pays les plus pauvres pourraient tirer d'un usage plus étendu des téléphones portables. Le paragraphe est consacré à la raison principale pour laquelle ils sont encore peu utilisés, leur coût.

• **Lisez les phrases.**
• **Retrouvez l'ordre logique de leur présentation.**

A. So the first step in promoting the adoption of mobile phones, say operators in developing countries, is to reduce the cost of the handsets.

B. There is already talk of prices falling below $30 next year.

C. Several such schemes are under way: in particular, several operators in developing countries have joined together to aggregate their buying power, and Motorola, the world's second-largest handset-maker, has agreed to supply up to 6m handsets for less than $40 each.

D. The primary obstacle to wider adoption is the cost of handsets.

E. In the developing world, in contrast, a $50 handset would account for 14 % of the annual income of someone earning $1 a day.

F. In the rich world, these typically cost around $200 (though most pay less than this thanks to subsidies from network operators), or less than 1 % of the average income per person.

• **Faites correspondre chaque phrase et sa fonction dans l'argumentation, également présentée ci-dessous dans le désordre.**

(1) Consequence of these experiments.

(2) Examples of such experiments being carried out.

(3) Explanation of the word 'cost'(1) in richer countries

(5) Explanation of the word 'cost'(2) in poorer countries.

(5) Logical solution to the problem.

(6) Topic sentence

4 **L'article qui suit pourrait être un essai répondant à la question qui est donnée en titre. Lisez l'article et complétez le tableau qui suit pour montrer quels paragraphes et quels mots de liaison correspondent à la structure du texte.**

SHOULD THE STATE TELL US WHAT TO EAT AND DRINK?

ANTHONY DANIELS

The British do not eat, so much as graze ruminantly on a diet of corn-starch, fats and salt

1. Anyone who, in an honest spirit of enquiry, has watched the British eat and drink will have been appalled[1] at the sight. A large part of the population has become simultaneously gluttonous and undiscriminating: or rather it chooses terrible things to consume and terrible ways of consuming them. And, increasingly, it has the physique to prove it.

2. How far should the Government be responsible for the health consequences of its own population's lack of taste and self-control? How far should it attempt to rein in[2] those companies that profit from encouraging the idle and foolish to consume junk food[3] and alcopops[4]? Should the state be nanny[5] or indifferent bystander[6]?

3. There is no simple principle of political philosophy that will answer the question, that makes the Government responsible either for everything or responsible for nothing. Almost no one, for example, would deny that the Government had the right, indeed the obligation, to limit the sale of alcohol; no one believes that alcohol should be sold everywhere, to anyone of whatever age, at any time.

4. We expect the Government to protect us from adulteration[7] and outright poisoning. In the 19th century, for example, arsenic regularly found its way into chocolates, beer and other commodities. But the harm done by the couch potato[8]'s diet[9] is less clear-cut: I am often startled by the blooming health and gargantuan size of those who have been brought up on a diet of junk. Nevertheless, the evidence seems to be that the sugary fatty, salty products of the prepared food industry are bad for the health, at least long-term.

5. The question boils down[10], at least partly, to one of efficacy rather than one of fundamental philosophical principle. Will the Government's envisaged advertising bans[11] make much difference? Personally, I rather doubt it, but I cannot work myself up into a lather of indignation[12] against them on the grounds that they threaten our fundamental liberties. Moreover, I might be wrong, and the Government might be right: the proof of the pudding, to coin a phrase, will be in the eating[13].

6. We should not overlook[14] far deeper and more revealing aspects of the national diet, however. Most people prefer not to think about these, because they reveal a society in a state of profound decomposition. Britain is the most littered[15] country in Europe. Why is this? If you examine the national litter, as I do wherever I walk, you discover that is composed mainly of the wrappings of junk and fast food. The British eat on the street to a degree almost unknown anywhere else.

7. But why should this be? A sociologist told me that half of British households no longer have a dining table, and this certainly accords with my experience of my adolescent and young adult patients, many of whom have never in their lives known what it is to eat a meal at a table with someone else. They have been taught, and have learnt, to eat when and where they feel like it: and, as the monstrous regiment of nibblers[16] shows, they feel like it now and always.

8. Households in which there are no dining tables are also households in which not much in the way of cooking fresh ingredients goes on. The micro-wave is the cooker, the saucepan, the casserole, dish, the entire batterie de cuisine in fact. And everyone in the household eats not as a social activity, but almost furtively. Meals are nasty, British, solitary and short.

9. In other words, one of the most elementary but important and enjoyable of all social activities, eating together, is now closed to a considerable proportion of the population. It does not eat, so much as graze[17] ruminantly on a diet of cornstarch[18], fats[19] and salt.

If I am right, adorning packages with little symbols to alert consumers to their relative healthiness or unhealthiness, will not make much difference. Convenience and immediate gratification are more powerful attractions than is maturity-onset diabetes 20, 30 or 40 years later a deterrent[20]. It is a mistake to suppose that what people need to live healthily is yet more information. In fact, family structure and stability is much more important than information about the nutritional quality of cheese-and-kipper-flavoured crisps.

10. Another problem, not likely to be solved by the Government's proposals, is the habit of mothers, developed in recent decades, of asking young children what they would like to eat. This has the effect not of increasing the child's repertoire, but of limiting it. The result is that huge numbers of young adults now eat like children. And the habit of asking children what they would like to eat is itself the result of a sentimental and trashy[21] notion of childhood.

11. There is no doubt that we are now the fattest, greediest, most slovenly and least discriminating people in Europe. You see fat people in France, but far fewer than here, and when they are fat they are also less fat. There are far fewer fat people even in Germany, where overeating is not unknown. And the logical connections of our eating habit with our way of life, including our family life, presents us with a most unflattering picture of contemporary Britain.

The Writer is a doctor.

▲ *The Independent*, November 16. 2004.

1. **appalled :** horrified. 2. **rein in :** restrain, control. 3. **junk food :** food with low nutritional value. 4. **alcopops :** *boissons gazeuses alcoolisées.* 5. **nanny :** protective, like a nurse. 6. **bystander :** a mere spectator, who does not intervene. 7. **adulteration :** falsification. 8. **couch potato :** a lazy young person, who spends a lot of time watching television. 9. **diet :** the type of food you eat. 10. **boils down to :** *revient à, se résume à.* 11. **advertising bans :** *interdictions de publicité.* 12. **work myself up into a lather of indignation :** become indignant. 13. **the proof of the pudding is in the eating : a proverb :** *la qualité se révèle à l'usage.* 14. **overlook :** *oublier, négliger.* 15. **littered :** full of litter *(ordures, détritus)*. 16. **nibblers :** *grignoteurs.* 17. **graze :** *brouter.* 18. **cornstarch :** *farine de maïs.* 19. **fats :** *matières grasses.* 20. **a deterrent :** *un effet de dissuasion.* 21. **trashy :** poor, worthless.

Structure	Paragraph numbers	Link words & articulations
Introduction • The situation in Britain • The question it leads us to ask ourselves **Part I : Can the problem be solved politically ?** • The government has a duty to protect us, but it is not so obvious in the case of our diet. • → The journalist is neither for nor against government measures. The only thing which matters is what will work. **Part II : The real problem = eating habits** • Example of litter : we don't eat at home but on the streets. • A meal is no longer a social activity around the dining-room table. • → People do not need more information, but more of a family structure. • Asking children what they want to eat reduces variety. **Conclusion** • The resulting situation		

8. COMMUNIQUER PAR TÉLÉPHONE

Souvenez-vous tout d'abord que lorsqu'on lit un numéro de téléphone, on lit chaque chiffre séparément. 976 56 43 se lit « *nine seven six five six four three* ».

Voici deux courtes conversations où vous trouverez les expressions les plus courantes.

Hullo, could I speak to Julia please ?
Who's calling please ?
This is Simon Bell.
Hold on please, I'll get her.
[...]
Hello Simon, Julia here.
Julia ? How are you ? Look, I know you're busy and I won't keep you. It's just that I can't find Paul Winter's telephone number and I need to speak to him. It's rather urgent.
Hold on, will you ? I've got it somewhere... Here you are : it's 788 56 49.
Thank you, Julia. Look, why don't we have a drink together soon ?
I'd love to. But I'm going away for two weeks. Ring me when I'm back and we'll arrange something.
Lovely ! And thanks again. Bye !
Bye Simon !

Lorsque vous appelez quelqu'un, attention à la différence : *Is THAT Paul ?* (*THAT* renvoie à la personne à qui vous parlez) *THIS is Jim speaking.* (*THIS* renvoie à vous-même.)

Si la personne à qui vous voulez parler n'est pas là, celle qui répond peut vous dire *Can I take a message for her ?* Ou *Try ringing back after 5.*

Si vous tombez sur un répondeur, vous entendrez un message du type : *This is 453 45 46. I'm sorry I'm not a home at the moment. Please leave a message after the tone/beep, and I will get back to you as soon as I can. Thank you !*

Britark, can I help you ?
Could you put me through to Mr Fielding please ?
Mr Fielding... yes, that's extension 211. Hold on and I'll put you through...
[...]
Who's calling please ?
James Watts. Is that John Fielding ?
No, this is Mr Fielding's secretary. I'm sorry, but Mr Fielding is away at the moment. Can he call you back ?
Yes, of course. My name is James Watts and I wanted to speak to Mr Fielding about the furniture contract for Wellings. Mr Fielding knows my number and I'll be in the office until 6.
Thank you Mr Watts. I'll make sure Mr Fielding rings you back.
Thank you.

Si vous connaissez déjà le poste, vous pouvez dire : *Can you give me extension 211 ?* (le poste 211)

La standardiste aurait pu répondre *Sorry to keep you waiting but the line is engaged* (la ligne est occupée). Ou *There's no reply. Can you ring back later ?*

Vous pouvez aussi dire *I'll call back in a couple of hours.*

↗ exercices

1 Faites correspondre les phrases et leur traduction.

1. *Can I have directory enquiries?*
2. *Don't hang up.*
3. *Hold the line, please.*
4. *I can't get through.*
5. *I'll put you through.*
6. *Is that Sarah?*
7. *It's engaged (GB)/busy (US).*
8. *Sorry, wrong number.*
9. *Speak after the tone.*
10. *There's no reply.*
11. *This is Sarah.*
12. *We've been cut off.*
13. *We've got a crossed line.*
14. *Who (shall I say) is calling?*
15. *Who's speaking?*

A. Ça ne répond pas.
B. C'est de la part de qui ?
C. C'est occupé.
D. C'est Sarah à l'appareil.
E. C'est Sarah à l'appareil ?
F. Il y a quelqu'un d'autre sur la ligne.
G. Je n'arrive pas à avoir le numéro.
H. Je vous le/la passe.
I. Ne quittez pas.
J. Ne raccrochez pas.
K. Nous avons été coupés.
L. Parlez après le bip sonore.
M. Puis-je avoir les renseignements ?
N. Qui est à l'appareil ?
O. Vous faites erreur de numéro.

The phone rings.

HALLY *(To the telephone.)* Hello, Mom… No, everything is okay here. Just doing my homework… What's your news ?…. You've what ? *(Pause. He takes the receiver away from his ear for a few seconds…. Hally places the receiver back to his ear.)* Yes, I'm still here. Oh, well, I give up now. Why did you do it, Mom ?…. Well, I just hope you know what you've let us in for.[1] *(Loudly.)* I said I hope you know what you've let us in for ! It's the end of the peace and quiet we've been having. *(Softly.)* Where is he ? *(Normal voice.)* He can't hear us from in there. But for God's sake, Mom, what happened ? I told you to be firm with him… Then you and the nurses should have held him down, taken his crutches[2] away… I know only too well he's my father !

▲ **Athol Fugard**, *Master Harold and the Boys*, 1982, Selected Plays, 1987, O.U.P.

1. **what you've let us in for :** *dans quelle situation tu nous mets.*
2. **crutches :** *béquilles.*

2 Voici des messages ou des phrases que vous pourriez entendre au téléphone. Complétez ces phrases avec les mots donnés ci-dessous.

tone – hold on – try – press – mobile – voicemail

1. This is John Bank's …
2. Can you … while I get him?
3. For enquiries about prices, … 2.
4. Please leave your message after the …
5. I'm leaving right now. Can you call me back on my … in ten minutes?
6. I'm sorry I'm not at home at the moment. Please … again later.

9. PONCTUER CORRECTEMENT

Voici quelques règles de ponctuation qu'il est nécessaire de connaître si vous voulez que votre texte soit clair et facile à comprendre.

Signe	Nom	Utilisation
.	*full stop* (GB) *period* (US)	– À la fin des phrases – Dans les abréviations, lorsque la dernière lettre de l'abréviation n'est pas la dernière lettre du mot. Ex : *Mr* (sans point), mais *Fr.* (French → suivi d'un point). – Dans les chiffres, avant les décimales : 64.2 % (GB) → 64,2 % (Fr.)
,	*comma*	– Entre les différents termes d'une énumération (mais la virgule n'est pas nécessaire avant le dernier terme, introduit par *and*). *Buy carrots, oranges, bananas (,) and lemons.* – Avant les relatives non déterminatives. *The man, who was about 35, had a very long beard.* – Pour séparer les groupes de trois chiffres : 7, 453 (GB) → 7.453 (Fr.) – Pour séparer les adverbes, les appositions, les propositions, les exclamations du reste de la phrase. *Strangely enough, this turned out to be true. Surprised, she looked up.* – Pour introduire le discours direct : *But she cried, "Don't touch me!"*
;	*semicolon*	Pour séparer deux propositions principales qui sont liées par le sens. (On pourrait aussi employer un point.) *He was feeling sleepy; when he saw a motel, he decided to stop.*
:	*colon*	Pour introduire une liste ou une explication. *It'll be fantastic: good food, swimming, long walks.*

-	***hyphen***	– Dans les mots composés : *a red-haired girl* – Pour lier plusieurs mots entre eux et leur donner le statut d'un seul mot : *She gave me her I-told-you-so smile.*
—	***dash***	Pour introduire une pause dans la structure ou pour les appositions. *She was so very young – only fourteen – to find herself alone in a big city.*
. . .	***dots***	– Pour indiquer qu'une énumération pourrait continuer. *I like the English romantic poets : Keats, Shelley, Coleridge...*
()	***brackets***	Pour ajouter une information (surtout dans un style journalistique). *Philip Strange was born in Muncie (Indiana).*
[]	***square brackets***	S'emploie souvent pour signaler qu'un passage a été coupé : [...]
' '	***single quotation marks or quotes*** *(more informal)* ***or inverted commas*** *(GB)*	Pour encadrer une citation (= *a quote*). *George once called her 'an old cow', and she's never forgiven him.*
" "	***double quotation marks***	Pour rapporter le style direct. Notez la différence entre la ponctuation d'un dialogue en français (guillemets au début et à la fin du dialogue ; tirets avant chaque nouvelle réplique) et en anglais (pas de tirets, mais des guillemets qui encadrent les paroles et non les verbes d'assertion tels que *he said*) : En sortant de la boulangerie, il rencontra Pierre. « Pierre, comment vas-tu ?, dit-il. Cela fait des mois que je ne t'ai pas vu ! – Oui, j'étais en voyage. – Depuis décembre ? – Oui, mon entreprise a crée une succursale à Nice, et c'est moi qui m'en suis occupé. » *Coming out of the bakery, he met Pierre.* *"Hello, Pierre, how are you?" he said. "I haven't seen you for months."* *"Yes, I was away travelling."* *"Since December?"* *"Yes, my firm is opening a branch in Nice, and I've been in charge of it all."*
"	***ditto marks***	= idem
?	***question mark***	À la fin d'une phrase interrogative.

!	*exclamation mark*	À la fin d'une phrase exclamative ou à la fin de certains impératifs.
'	*apostrophe*	– Dans les génitifs : *John's book* – Dans les formes contractées : *They're all gone.* (= They are…)
*	*asterisk*	
/	***slash*** or ***stroke*** or ***solidus*** or ***slant***	
aaaaa	*italics*	– Pour citer un mot étranger, latin. As Dumas said, if you want to get to the bottom of things, *cherchez la femme*. – Pour insister sur certains mots : I didn't do it, *John* did. (In this example, *John* is ***italicized***.)
AAAA	*capital letters*	– Au début des noms propres, des titres, des noms géographiques… comme en français, mais également pour les adjectifs dérivés de ces noms. *An Italian tenor* – Au début des noms de mois, de vacances, de jours de la semaine : *Monday/February/Easter* – Dans les titres de livres, de films, de magazines. Notez qu'en anglais, TOUS les mots prennent la majuscule, sauf les mots grammaticaux, comme articles et conjonctions. *For Whom the Bell Tolls* (In this example, For, Whom, Bell and Tolls are **capitalized**.)
aaaaa	***bold type*** or ***bold face***	Dans les gros titres de journaux. **WOMAN KILLED BY LIGHTNING** (In this example, the whole title is **emboldened**.)

exercices

1 Les phrases ou les expressions qui suivent contiennent toutes des fautes de ponctuation. Corrigez-les.

That is other peoples money. ....

20% OFF ALL CD's ....

FOURTH FLOOR : CHILDRENS' TOYS ....

Mr Blair replied : "It is the right moment for those of us in the Conservative Party, as well as on these benches, who believe passionately that Britain's place is at the centre of Europe decision-making, to make our case."

The Independent, April 21. 04.

2 Expliquez la différence entre les deux phrases de chaque groupe.

(1) The people there, who saw the film, all loved it.
The people there who saw the film all loved it.

(2) The teacher said her student was always late.
The teacher, said her student, was always late.

(3) I'll invite John and his two brothers, Phil and Tom.
I'll invite John and his two brothers, Phil, and Tom.

(4) We'll ask those who haven't made up their minds[1] to come.
We'll ask those who haven't made up their minds, to come.

1. **to make up one's mind:** *se décider.*

3 Ponctuez la phrase qui suit.

charles the first walked and talked half an hour after his head was cut off

▲ *Eats, Shoots & Leaves*, by Lynne (Profile Books, 2003)..

4 Les signes de ponctuation qui suivent manquent dans ce passage. Retrouvez-les.

6 capital letters; 2 commas; 2 full stops; 2 hyphens.

a 50 year old school bus driver was arrested after driving so erratically that police were flooded with calls from motorists terrified children phoned their parents on their mobiles as they were driven home from school in cirencester to stroud gloucester on tuesday

▲ *The Times*, March 5, 2004.

5 Faites le même exercice avec le passage suivant.

13 capital letters; 1 set (=group of two) of inverted commas; 5 commas; 4 full stops; 1 exclamation mark; 2 apostrophes; 1 hyphen.

look here it's no good said my dad

we were in the car on the way back to london my father had just collected me and my trunk[2] from the expensive girls school that i attended he had also just sat through parents day in the course of which i was presented with the latin prize the english essay prize and the prize for the girl who had done best in a levels

▲ Adapted from M. Furlong.

2. **trunk:** *malle.*

II QUELQUES NOTIONS

1. DÉVELOPPEMENT CHRONOLOGIQUE

P. 82 (DATES ET RÉFÉRENCES TEMPORELLES)

Voici un certain nombre de mots de liaison, adverbes et expressions qui sont essentiels pour décrire un développement chronologique.

- Pour parler d'un passé lointain
  In the old days, in those days, formerly (il y a longtemps, autrefois, jadis)
- Pour parler d'un passé proche
  Recently, lately (récemment)
- Pour parler du moment présent ou de son époque
  Now, at present, nowadays, these days, currently, in this time and age (actuellement, à notre époque), *currently, at the moment, for the time being* (en ce moment, pour l'instant).
  In those days: passé lointain
  In these days: l'époque de celui qui parle.

Attention! *Presently* est un faux-ami qui signifie « bientôt ».

- Pour parler d'un futur proche
  Presently, shortly, soon (bientôt)
- Pour parler d'un futur plus lointain
  Later (on) (plus tard)
- Pour introduire les différents points d'une chronologie
  First (Tout d'abord)
  Then (ensuite ou alors)
  Afterwards (Ensuite)
  Some time (a short time/two hours/a few months...) later (... plus tard)
  After a while (au bout d'un moment)
  Eventually (finalement)
- Pour situer une action dans le temps
  As (au moment où) + proposition: *As he entered the room, the phone rang.*
  While (tandis que) + proposition: *She caught the flu while she was on holiday in Scotland.*
  When (quand) + proposition: *I'll tell you all about it when we meet.*
  Whenever (chaque fois que) + proposition: *Whenever he leaves, I cry.*
  Meanwhile/in the meantime (pendant ce temps) + virgule + proposition: *Why don't you go and get some bread? Meanwhile, I'll lay the table.*

Since (depuis) + point de départ d'une action : *We've known him since 1999. He had played the violin since he was nine.*
For (depuis) + durée : *He played the violin for two years, then gave up. He's been living there for three years.*
During + période dans laquelle s'inscrit l'action : *He stayed with us during the holidays/the summer/the train strike.*

Until/till (jusqu'à) + nom ou proposition : *You can watch TV till 11 o'clock. He walked until he was too tired to go on.*
So far + virgule (jusqu'à présent) : *So far, we haven't had any complaints.*
From... to (de... à...) : *You will work in the shop from 9 to 5 (/ from July to September).*
Not... yet (pas encore) : *They have not written yet. He is not sixteen yet.*
Still (encore) : *Of course, it's cold : we're still in winter.*
By (pas plus tard que, dernière limite) : *We must hand in our essays by the end of the week.*
Only (pas plus tard que, pour annoncer un exemple) : *Only yesterday, he asked me for money again.*

As soon as/the moment (dès que) + proposition : *Give me a ring as soon as he comes in. (Give me a ring the moment he comes in.)*
No sooner + inversion... *than* (à peine... que) : *No sooner had she opened the door than she heard the telephone ring.*
Hardly + inversion... *when* (à peine... que...) : *Hardly had she left the station when she remembered she had left her bag in the train.*

N'oubliez pas d'utiliser le temps approprié :
• Le *simple past* pour un fait passé, révolu, situé dans le temps.
→ *I lived there for ten years, between 1980 and 1990. We went to the cinema last night.* (Ce qui correspond le plus souvent à un passé composé en français : Hier, nous sommes allés...)
• Le *past perfect* lorsqu'il y a antériorité par rapport à un fait passé.
→ *When I met my wife, she had known Philip for two years.*
• Le *present perfect* pour une activité, un état qui a débuté dans le passé mais est encore vrai ou dont on envisage les conséquences présentes :
→ *We have been married for three years.* Nous sommes mariés depuis trois ans.

exercices

1 Complétez les phrases qui suivent avec le mot ou l'expression qui convient :
so far – formerly – for – as soon as – since – meanwhile – until – still – during – yet – no sooner – soon

(1) I cannot buy the flat ... I know if they have accepted me for the job.

(2) ... was she out of hospital than she started to ride horses again.

(3) ..., we've always found excellent bed & breakfasts.

(4) ..., it used to take a whole day to go from Paris to London by train.

(5) I'm getting a computer tomorrow, so I'll ... be able to send you e-mails.

(6) Sheila has taken the children to the seaside for a week. ..., I'm working ten hours a day at the office: it's not fair!

(7) We always went to Switzerland ... the Easter holidays, but we haven't been there ... I was sixteen.

(8) ... I heard about the accident, I volunteered to come and help.

(9) I'm not ... eighteen, so I can't drive.

(10) I haven't been to Germany ... several years, but I can ... understand German quite easily.

2 Choisissez entre *since*, *for* et *during* devant les expressions qui suivent.

(a) ... the schoolyear (b) ... two years (c) ... eleven days

(d) ... my birthday (e) ... we met (f) ... last Monday

3 Traduisez.

(1) Il faut qu'il reçoive le livre avant la fin du mois.

(2) Hier soir, j'ai travaillé jusqu'à une heure du matin.

(3) Pierre ne nous a pas encore donné sa réponse.

(4) Ils vivent à Londres depuis qu'ils se sont mariés.

(5) Nous irons faire du ski pendant qu'elle sera à New York. Elle nous rejoindra plus tard.

(6) Elle ne fut pas plus tôt descendue du train qu'elle s'aperçut que c'était la mauvaise gare.

4 Voici une chronologie de la vie de Marie Stuart (voir p. 50)**.**
Utilisez cette chronologie pour compléter le résumé de sa vie, à l'aide des mots et expressions donnés ci-dessous dans le désordre. Attention, certains d'entre eux peuvent être utilisés plusieurs fois.

for – than – soon – from – as soon as – to – no sooner – two years later – later – then – when/after – when – since – until

... the dramatic events of her youth ... the tragedy of her death, Mary Stuart's life has always had great popular appeal. ... was she born ... her father died, an event which made her Queen of Scotland. ... afterwards, her mother sent her to France, where she was educated ... the age of sixteen. It was ... that she married Francis, the French dauphin. One year ... , the dauphin's father having died, she became queen of France. She was to hold this position ... a few months only, as her husband died at the end of that year. ... , Mary returned to Scotland, where she was much admired at court. She remained in Scotland ... seven years, during which time she married the earl of Darnley (their son was ... to become King James I, who succeeded Elizabeth I on the throne of England), then, ... he was murdered, married the earl of Bothwell. These events led the Scottish nobility into deposing her. Mary ... turned to Elizabeth I, her cousin and the Queen of England, for help. But Elizabeth kept her in prison ... the next 19 years, although she lived in relative luxury. But ... Mary conspired to have Elizabeth assassinated, the queen decided to have her killed. She was executed in 1587, never having gone back to her native Scotland ... 1568. ... Schiller wrote a play inspired by Marie Stuart's life in 1800, she had already been dead ... 213 years.

1542	Birth of Mary Stuart. Her parents are James V of Scotland and Marie de Guise. Death of her father. Becomes Queen of Scotland. Sent to France to be educated there.
1558	Marries the French dauphin.
1559	Becomes Queen of France. Death of her husband.
1561	Returns to Scotland.
1565	Marries the Earl[1] of Darnley.
1566	The Earl of Darnley is murdered.
1567	Marries the Earl of Bothwell. Deposition in favour of her one-year-old son by Darnley.
1568	Goes to England to ask Elizabeth I for help. Imprisoned.
1586	Tried[2] for planning to assassinate Elizabeth.
1587	Executed.
1800	Schiller writes *Maria Stuart*, a play about her life.

1. **an earl :** *un comte.*
2. **to try :** *juger.*

2. Développement logique

1 – CAUSE

- *As/since/because* + proposition : *As/since/because he is eighteen, he can now vote.* (Puisque)
- *For* + proposition/*V* + *ing* (pas en début de phrase, mais après la principale) : *He was punished for he had lied/for lying.* (car, pour avoir)
- *Because of/due to/owing to/thanks to* + nom : *Because of the snow, all trains will be delayed today.* (en raison de, à cause de)
- *On account of* + nom : *Schools were closed, on account of the bad weather.* (à cause de)
- *The reason why* + proposition : *The reason why he phoned is that he wants more money.* (La raison pour laquelle…)
- Participe présent : *Being lazy, I love to get up late.* (Étant paresseux…)
- *The floods caused/led to a lot of damage.* (ont entraîné)
- *The report triggered (off)/sparked off a controversy in the press.* (a déclenché)
- *This situation can be attributed to/can be explained by/can be put down to/was the result of… the new immigration policies.* (est due à/vient de/résulte de)

2 – CONSÉQUENCE

- *Consequently,/as a result,/as a consequence,/therefore,/accordingly,/that's why/so (that)/thus* (ainsi) + proposition. (Donc/en conséquence/C'est pourquoi…)
  My car has broken down, so that's why we'll have to go by train.
- *Thus/therefore* + *V* + *ing* : *They left the windows open, thus creating a draught.* (ce qui a causé/causant donc/causant ainsi un courant d'air)
- *Hence* + nom : *He was not dressed for the occasion, hence his embarrassment.* (d'où)
- *What it means is that…* : *My secretary is away with a cold. What it means is that I have to do all the typing and phoning myself.* (Ce qui signifie que…)
- *And of course, it follows that he'll lose his job as well.* (il s'ensuit que)
- *The heat wave resulted in many deaths.* (a conduit à)
- *Many deaths resulted from the heat wave.* (provinrent de)
- *The bad weather caused many people to take their cars.* (a fait que/a poussé…)
- *He's late : he must have missed his train.* (il a dû)
- *He left ten minutes ago : he can't have arrived yet.* (Il ne peut pas être déjà arrivé.)

3 – BUT

- *To/in order (not) to/so as (not) to* + infinitif. *He ran to catch his bus. Don't be too harsh, so as not to discourage her.* (afin de/pour)
- *So that* + *might/could/should* : *I gave him some money so that he might buy a few books.* (pour que)
- *The purpose of the talk was to…/The talk was meant to… tell students about the danger of drugs.* (Le but de la conférence/… avait pour but de…)
- *They ran after the thief in an effort/in an attempt to stop him.* (pour essayer de…)

4 – CONCESSION

- *Although/though/even though/while/even if/in spite of the fact that* + proposition : *Although he was right, he should not have spoken out so forcefully.* (Bien que + subjonctif, même si…)
  We had a wonderful time, in spite of the fact that it rained.
- *Despite/in spite of* + nom : *He won the race, despite his injury.* (malgré)
- *Though*, à la fin d'une proposition, après une virgule : *I haven't heard from him. He had promised to keep in touch, though.* (pourtant)
- *All the same*, au début d'une proposition, suivi d'une virgule : *The film was too long. All the same, we all enjoyed it.* (malgré cela),
- *However, still, yet, nevertheless* + proposition : *Anne finds her job boring. Still, it's better than nothing.* (Cependant)
- Adjectif + *though/as* + proposition ou *however* + adjectif + proposition : *Intelligent though he may be, he will have to work hard to pass the exam. However intelligent he may be, he will have to work hard to pass the exam.* (Aussi intelligent qu'il soit…/Il a beau être intelligent…)
- *For all* + nom : *For all his diplomas, he hasn't found a job yet.* (malgré)
- *No matter* + *where/how/what/when* + proposition : *No matter what you say, he won't like it.* (peu importe)
- *Whatever/Wherever/Whoever/However…* + proposition : *Wherever you go* (où que vous alliez…), *you will find the same problem. However good their pay offer* (Quelque intéressante que soit…), *I will not accept the job.*
- *You may be right, but I still think that's the wrong decision.* (Vous avez peut-être raison, mais…)
- *It may be so, but it's difficult to accept.* (Peut-être, mais…)
- *That's all very well, but who's going to pay ?* (Certes, mais..)

5 – CONDITION

- *If* + proposition : *If I see her, I'll tell her.*
  Notez la différence entre :
  – *If you come, I will give you the keys.* (réelle possibilité : Si vous venez, je vous donnerai les clés.)
  – *If you came, I would give you the keys.* (moins probable, plus hypothétique : Si vous veniez, je vous donnerais...)
  – *If you had come, I would have given you the keys.* (pour parler de quelque chose qui aurait pu se produire dans le passé, mais ne s'est pas produit : Si vous étiez venu, je vous aurais donné...)
- *As long as/so long as/on condition that/provided that/providing that* + proposition : *They won't hear you, so long as you keep quiet.* (pourvu que, du moment que)
- *Unless* + proposition : *We'll have a picnic tomorrow, unless it rains.* (à moins que)
- *If not/otherwise, or else* + proposition : *Take a coat, or else you'll be cold after dusk.* (sinon)
- *Suppose/Supposing* + proposition : *Supposing it rains, what could we do then ?* (Et si.../En supposant que...)
- *In case* + proposition : *Take her telephone number in case you get lost.* (au cas où)

6 – CONTRAST

- *But* + proposition : *I want to go, but I haven't got the money.* (mais)
- *On the contrary* + virgule + proposition : *He is not miserly ; on the contrary, he can be quite generous.* (au contraire)
- *Instead* + virgule + proposition : *Instead, English pupils wear uniforms.* (Au lieu de cela)
- *Unlike* (à la différence de)/*contrary to* (contrairement à) + nom : *Contrary to popular belief, you should never put butter on a burn. Unlike her sister, she is shy and quiet.*
- *While/whereas*, pour introduire une affirmation qui contraste avec la précédente, mais dont la structure est semblable : *I love skiing, while he prefers biking.* (alors que)
- *Instead of* + *V* + *ing* : *Instead of watching TV, you'd better do your homework.* (au lieu de)
- *On the one hand..., on the other hand...* : *On the one hand, he wants to earn more, on the other hand, he's too lazy to try harder.* (D'un côté... de l'autre)
- *This is very different from...* : *this is a very different book from the one you are talking about.* (tout à fait différent)
- *As opposed to such ideas, there is...* (à l'opposé)

7 – ALTERNATIVES

- *You can neither smoke nor eat in the library.* (ni... ni...)
- *You can either drive or take the train.* (ou... ou...)
- *In both cases/in either case, it will take you several hours to get there.* (dans les deux cas/d'une façon ou d'une autre)
- *In neither case will you get there in time for the start of the conference.* (ni d'une manière, ni de l'autre)Notez l'inversion après neither en début de phrase.

8 – COMPARAISON

- *Like/unlike* + nom : *This car is almost like a Rolls-Royce !* (comme)
  Unlike their neighbours, they have no flowers in their garden. (Contrairement à)
- *As* + proposition : *It happened exactly as I said it would.* (comme)
  Attention ! *As* + nom = en tant que. *As your teacher, I can tell you that...* (Étant votre professeur, je peux vous dire que...)
- *As... as... : This film is as good as you said it would be.* (aussi... que)
- *As if/as though* + prétérit : *Try to behave as if you knew nothing.* (comme si)
- *In the same way/similarly* + virgule + proposition : *You must not talk in the library. Similarly, you mustn't eat or drink there.* (De même)
- *The same as/different from/similar to* + nom : *His book is not the same as mine/is different from mine.* (le même que/différent de)
- *By comparison* + virgule + proposition : *John is very tall. By comparison, I look like a pygmy.* (par comparaison)
- *Compared with.../In comparison with.../In contrast with...* + nom : *In comparison with France, flats are more expensive in England.* (en comparaison/par opposition à)
- *They're poles apart/worlds apart.* (très différents, aux antipodes l'un de l'autre)

exercices

1 Associez les propositions des 2 colonnes pour obtenir des phrases complètes et logiques.

1. Although he looks ill	A. all trains will be late.
2. Cold though it is,	B. but he's fine.
3. Due to the heavy snowfall	C. don't open the door to anyone.
4. He may look tired	D. he's never felt better.
5. I turned the heater down	E. I like sleeping with my window open.

6. I'll never find the solution
7. It took me three days to solve the problem,
8. She has lots of diplomas,
9. She's not stupid,
10. There is a lot of fog,
11. Unless you see it's your uncle
12. Whoever calls when I'm out,

F. nor does she lack common sense.
G. not to mention her perfect knowledge of Spanish.
H. so that I might sleep better.
I. tell them I'll be back by ten.
J. therefore some planes may be cancelled.
K. unless I'm given more time.
L. while the computer did it in a few seconds.

2 Complétez les phrases qui suivent avec les mots de liaison donnés ci-dessous dans le désordre.

unlike – as a result – instead of – though – in case – as though – neither – although – so that – provided that – in spite of – because of

(1) You can go to the cinema … you are back by ten o'clock.
(2) Don't forget to take a warm jumper … it gets cold.
(3) He behaved … he did not know me.
(4) … her sister, she has no gift for languages.
(5) He felt … like swimming nor like reading.
(6) Ill … he was, he managed to get up and go to work.
(7) … the heavy rain, the road is closed.
(8) I asked for an appointment … I might explain my problem to the boss.
(9) My watch is slow; … I missed the bus.
(10) … the doctor's advice, he got up and walked in the rain.
(11) It's a very good second hand car … it cost very little.
(12) … turning right, you turned left: that's why we got lost!

3 Faites des phrases complètes à partir des notes qui suivent et en utilisant les mots de liaison ou instructions donnés entre parenthèses.

(1) Rain → picnic outside (in spite of)
(2) Wear proper clothes → They'll let you in (provided)
(3) Sarah : fair ; her mother : dark-haired (unlike)
(4) John broke his leg : no school for a week (*participe présent*)
(5) Don't smoke/don't use your cell phone in this cinema (neither… nor)
(6) John always made faces → nicknamed Monkey (hence)
(7) I want him to ring me at all times → I bought him a cell phone (so that)
(8) Don't fly/take the train (instead of)

3. Description spatiale

Pour décrire des rapports dans l'espace, il est essentiel de bien connaître la valeur des prépositions. Elles ont en effet un sens bien précis en anglais.

P. 141 (DÉCRIRE ET ANALYSER UN DOCUMENT ICONOGRAPHIQUE)

Légende : X = absence de mouvement → = mouvement

PAR RAPPORT À UN POINT

→ • *to*

•X *at*

• → *away from*

• X *away from* / *far from* / *at a distance from*

past / by

(corner) *at* / *in*

→/ *at* (aggressive movement)

PAR RAPPORT À UNE LIGNE

on (to) — *on* — *off* — *across over* — *along*

PAR RAPPORT À UNE SURFACE

on (to) — *on* — *off* — *off* — *across over* — *through*

Notez la différence :

He jumped onto the floor

He jumped on the floor

PAR RAPPORT À UN PLUS GRAND ESPACE OU UN VOLUME

into — *in / inside* — *out of* — *out of / outside* — *through*

Notez la différence :

They danced into the sitting room

They danced in the sitting room

RAPPORTS ENTRE DIFFÉRENTES PERSONNES OU CHOSES

over

Relations verticales

under

above

Pas nécessairement à la verticale

below

Objets se touchant

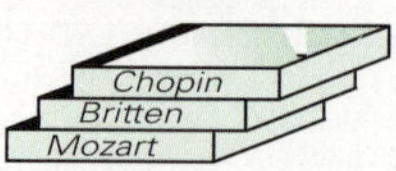

Chopin is ***on top (top of)*** *Britten*

Mozart is ***under (neath) / beneath*** *Britten*

Proximité

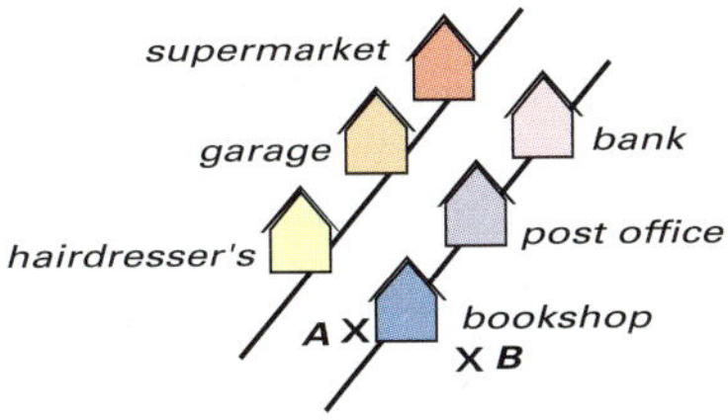

*These places are **near / close to** each other.*
*The supermarket is **next to / by / beside** the garage.*
*The bookshop is **opposite / across the road from** the hairdresser's.*
***A** is in **front of / outside** the bookshop.*
***B** is **behind** it.*
*The garage is **between** the supermarket and the hairdresser's.*

Choses qui se touchent

*Sitting with his back **to / against** the tree.*

Distance : *here > **(a)round** here > **beyond** a certain point.*

Attention aux prépositions utilisées dans les adresses :

– *At* + numéro :
She lives at number 6.
She lives at 6 Belsize Street.

– *In* + nom de rue :
She lives in Sloane Avenue / Chester Street.
(Mais on emploie *on* en anglais américain.)

– *On* + étage
She lives on the third floor.

Between + deux éléments : *I was sitting between John and Mary.*
Among + plusieurs éléments : *I felt lost among all those strangers.*
A place is in the north/south/west/east of a country. (London is in the south of England.)
A place is north/south/west/east of another one. (England is west of France.)
A place is close to/near…
It is in the vicinity of…
It is on the outskirts of…/in the surroundings of…
We're going southward. (vers le sud)
You need to go further away/west to see such landscapes.
Our house is a mile and a half from the pub.
HERE = where you are ≠ THERE = further away
She lives within two miles of the city centre (à moins de trois kilomètres)
Yesterday we walked as far as the river. (jusqu'à – pour une distance)

↗ exercices

1 Associez verbes et particules afin de décrire chacune des positions ou mouvements du chat.

The cat		under	
	is walking	over	the tree
	is jumping	behind	the house
	is sitting	along	the road
		into	the roof
		through	the mouse
		on	the hedge
		away from	
		round	
		to	
		across	
		onto	

2 Traduisez les phrases suivantes.

1. Il a plongé du bateau dans l'eau.
2. Longe le jardin public, passe devant la banque et la pharmacie : tu trouveras ma maison sur la droite.
3. Notre hôtel était en face de l'opéra, à moins de cent mètres de la gare, mais à deux kilomètres du musée.
4. Elle habite au troisième étage du 3, rue du Lac.
5. Le voleur traversa la haie, puis le jardin, fit le tour de la maison en courant, puis descendit les marches qui menaient à la cave.

III QUELQUES FONCTIONS DE COMMUNICATION

Vous trouverez ici des expressions utiles dans des situations de communication courantes. Elles sont à chaque fois classées en trois catégories, en fonction de leur registre : *informal* (familier), *standard* (neutre, correct) et *formal* (langue soignée.)

I. SOCIALIZING

SAYING HELLO/GOODBYE

Informal	Standard	Formal
Hi/Hello, Simon ! Bye ! See you ! So long ! (US) *(Salut !/À plus !)*	Good morning/afternoon/evening, John ! Goodbye ! Have a nice day ! I'd better go. I must be on my way. *(Il faut que je parte.)* See you later ! *(À tout à l'heure !)* See you soon ! *(À bientôt !)*	 I wish you good night. It was a pleasure to meet you !

INTRODUCING SOMEONE (Faire des présentations)

Informal	Standard	Formal
Hello !/Hi ! I'm John. This is Elaine. How're you doing ? *(Comment ça va ?)*	I'm Sheila. This is my friend Mike. You know Mike, don't you ? Let me introduce myself : I'm Fiona. How are things with you ? How do you do ? (*Enchanté* – The answer is the same.) Pleased to meet you. *(Ravi de faire votre connaissance.)*	 May I introduce you to Mr Johnson ? *(Puis-je vous présenter…)* I'd like you to meet Mrs Bennett.

ASKING FOR INFORMATION

Informal	Standard	Formal
Any idea where there's a pub around here ?	Could you tell me what the time is ? Do you know where I can find a bank ? I'd like to know if you have some of these new stamps, please.	Would you be kind enough to tell me how to get to the city hall ? *(Auriez-vous l'amabilité de me dire…)*

	Excuse me, can you give me the time?	Would you happen to know where I can find a post-office around here? *(Sauriez-vous par hasard où…)*

INSTRUCTIONS AND ORDERS

Informal and standard	Formal
Imperatives Open the door…/Wash your hands… Don't forget your keys… Do make sure you have your keys. Never leave a young child alone in a kitchen. Remember to/Don't forget to give us your e-mail address. Always lock the door when you leave. Avoid driving when there is snow. *(Évitez de…/Il est préférable de ne pas…)* Keep turning right. Make sure the windows are closed! *(Assure-toi que.. /Vérifie bien que…)* You should not go out with your cold. I want you to finish the job by six p.m. Will you (please) stop talking! *(Je vous prie de vous taire./Voulez-vous bien vous taire!)* Boots must be left in the hall. Students may not write their names on papers. *(Il est interdit d'écrire son nom…)* You have to be more careful in future. *(Il vous faudra désormais faire plus attention.)*	You are to report to the headmaster's office at 5 o'clock. *(Vous devez vous présenter chez le proviseur…)* Please be kind enough to ring for a taxi. *(Auriez-vous la bonté d'appeler un taxi?)*

REQUESTS (Demandes)

Informal	Standard	Formal
Is it OK if I come? *(D'accord si…?)*	Can/Could you please be quieter? May I borrow your pen for a second? I wonder if you could get that box up there for me? I'd like a cup of tea, please. Come upstairs, won't you? Would you like to leave your umbrella here?	Would you mind switching off the light? *(Cela vous dérangerait-il d'éteindre…)* Would you be so kind as to help me with this suitcase? *(Auriez-vous l'obligeance de…)*

	Why don't you sit down? I beg your pardon, can you say that again? (when you want someone to repeat what he/she said.)	Would you object if we borrowed the car? *(Verriez-vous un inconvénient à ce que...)* We would be much obliged if you could let us use your telephone. *(Nous vous serions très reconnaissants si...)* Visitors are requested to bring their invitations. (written) *(Prière de se munir de l'invitation.)*

INVITING

Informal	Standard	Formal
	Would you like to come over for lunch tomorrow? Won't you join us? *(Vous voulez vous joindre à nous?)* Shall we all go to Brighton for the weekend? Why don't you come with us? What about a cup of tea? *(Tu veux.../Et si on...)*	We would be delighted if you would/could spend a few days with us in Wales next month. *(Nous serions ravis si...)*

OFFERING

Informal	Standard	Formal
Want a hand? *(Tu veux un coup de main?)*	Shall I give you a hand? *(Veux-tu que je t'aide?)* Can I lend you a hand? Can I do anything for you? Let me carry this for you. *(Laisse-moi porter...)* Can you manage on your own? *(Est-ce que vous y arriverez tout seul?)* Would you like me to phone them? Can I be of any assistance/help? *(Puis-je vous aider?)*	

ACCEPTING/REFUSING

Informal	Standard	Formal
Fine! OK. Sure. All right.	I'd love to. That's a good idea. With pleasure. That's very kind of you. We'll look forward to it. *(Nous nous en réjouissons à l'avance.)*	I will come with great pleasure. I shall be very glad to be there.
Don't bother! *(Pas la peine.)* No way! *(Pas question!)* Forget it! Out of the question! Get lost! *(Va te faire voir!)*	No, thanks. (It's very kind of you, but) I'm afraid I can't. I'm sorry, but I can't. It's out of the question! He's unwilling/reluctant to commit himself. *(Il ne tient pas/hésite à s'engager.)* I won't go there again! I refuse to go with them. He has no intention of accepting.	I would love to accept your kind invitation, but unfortunately… I truly regret not being able to meet you.

THANKING

Informal	Standard	Formal
Thanks! Thanks for coming!	Thank you for the lovely meal. Thank you ever so much! It was very nice/kind of you. The answer is often: You're welcome! *(Il n'y a pas de quoi.)*	Our most sincere thanks for your invitation. We are very grateful to you for helping Tom when he was in Bath. I wish to express my gratitude for your help when we moved in. (written) *(Permettez-moi de vous exprimer toute ma reconnaissance pour…)*

CONGRATULATIONS (Félicitations)

Informal	Standard	Formal
Well done! *(Bravo!)* Super! *(Formidable!)* Great!	Congratulations! That was terrific/excellent/great!	Allow me to congratulate you on your promotion. *(Permettez-moi de vous féliciter pour…)*

Apologizing/granting forgiveness (Excuses/Accepter des excuses)

Informal	Standard	Formal
Sorry ! *(Désolé !)* Oops, sorry !	I am (terribly/so) sorry ! I am sorry I left without a word. I do apologize. Please, forgive me (for not telling you). I did not mean to sound so critical. I regret what I said. *Ne confondez pas :* Forgive me/I'm sorry… (to say you are sorry for something you have done) Excuse me (to try and get someone's attention : Excuse me, could you pass me the salt please ?)	I do beg your pardon. *(Je vous prie de m'excuser.)* I would like to apologize for what I said. *(Veuillez m'excuser…)* Please accept my apologies.
Forget it. No problem. That's O.K. *(Ce n'est rien./ Pas de mal.)*	Don't worry. Don't mention it. *(Je vous en prie.)* It doesn't matter. No ill feelings. *(Sans rancune !)* No offence taken. *(Il n'y a pas de mal.)* It's all right. No harm done.	It's of no importance. *(Ce n'est pas grave.)*

exercices

1 *Instructions and orders*

Voici une recette de gâteau au chocolat. Complétez-la avec les verbes donnés dans le désordre :

mix – beat – bake – heat up – add – pour – take off.

In a saucepan, … gently :
– 200g chocolate
– 1 large spoonful of water
– 80g butter (one third of a 250g pack)

When the chocolate has melted and the mixture is smooth, … the heat and … :
– 6 large spoonfuls of sugar
– 2 and a half large spoonfuls of flour
– 3 egg yolks

… the whites until they are firm and … into the chocolate mixture.

… into a baking dish and … for 20 minutes (no more) in a pre-heated oven (Number 6).

② *Instructions and orders*

Vous logez à *Canterbury*, dans *Queens Avenue* (entouré, à gauche dans le plan ci-dessous). Un ami vous a donné des indications pour le rejoindre en ville. Où vous mènent-elles ?

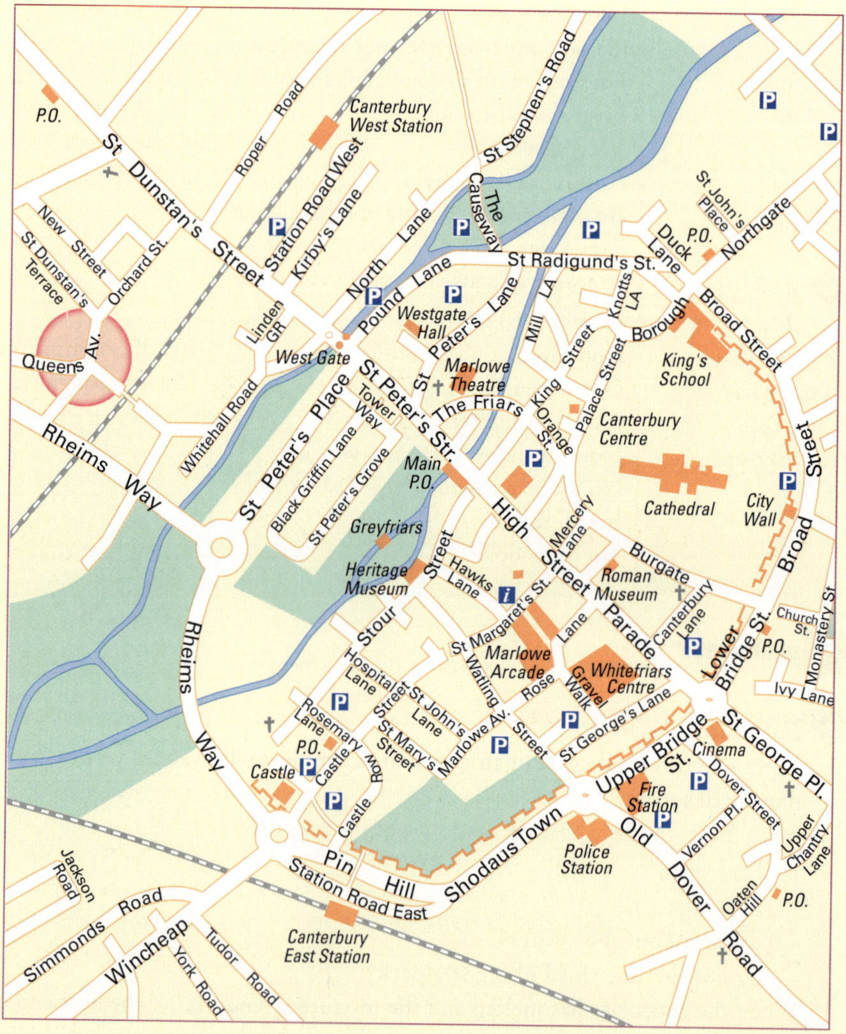

Leave Queens Avenue and go over the railway bridge. Turn left and follow the river until you reach a main road. Turn right over the river : you are at West Gate. Go straight on and turn left at the Post Office. Go straight on and follow the street, which turns right, then left. You will find … immediately on your right.

3 *Requests – Inviting – Refusing*

Récrivez les phrases en commençant par les amorces qui vous sont données.

1. I'd be much obliged if you could lend me the record.
I wonder …
May I …
2. What about a drink before supper?
Shall we …
Why …
3. I'm sorry, but I can't come to the wedding.
I'd love to …
I regret …

4 *Apologizing – Introducing someone – Inviting*

Traduisez les phrases suivantes.

1. « Je suis absolument navrée : j'ai oublié le livre.
– Ce n'est pas grave. »
2. « Je me présente : je m'appelle André.
– Enchanté. »
3. « Et si vous veniez passer le week-end chez nous en Normandie ?
– Avec plaisir. C'est très gentil de votre part. »

2. Emotions

Intention & determination

Informal	Standard	Formal
I'll go to India some day, that's for sure. *(Ça ne fait aucun doute.)* I'm gonna tell him what I think. *(J'vais…)*	We're thinking of having another child. I have a good mind to give it all up. *(J'ai bien envie de…)* I'm going to buy that record. He is bent on buying that car. *(Il est bien décidé à…)* I plan/want/mean/intend to move to New York. She's set her heart on visiting China. *(Elle veut à tout prix…)* She really means to write a detective story. *(Elle a vraiment l'intention de…)*	Do you really intend to sell your flat? *(Avez-vous vraiment l'intention de…)* We propose to visit them in August. *(Nous comptons leur rendre visite…)* He's contemplating a move to Norwich. *(Il envisage d'aller habiter…)*

	I'm buying that dress, whether they like it or not. I've made up my mind to resign. *(J'ai décidé de…)* I've decided to talk to her. I'm determined not to give in. *(Je suis bien résolu à…)* I'm sure he did it deliberately. *(… il l'a fait exprès.)* His plan is to sell his car and buy a motorbike. There's no turning back now. *(C'est décidé./Impossible de revenir en arrière.)* Sorry, I didn't mean it! *(Je ne l'ai pas fait exprès.)*	We had every (/no) intention of trying to dissuade her. *(Nous comptions bien…)* We insist on speaking to him. *(Nous tenons absolument à…)*

DESIRE & WISHES, HOPE

Informal	**Standard**	**Formal**
I'd give my back teeth to go with him! *(Je donnerais n'importe quoi/tout l'or du monde pour…)*	I'd like to/love to/want to see the film. I don't feel like going to the cinema. *(Je n'ai pas envie de…)* I can't wait to meet him! *(Je meurs d'envie de…)* I'm dying for a hot bath! I'm dying to tell her what I think of her. What I really want is a cup of tea. I dream of spending a few days there. I wish I were rich. *(Si seulement j'étais riche !)* If only I could meet him! I wouldn't mind living in a house like that. *(Cela me dirait bien de vivre…)* With any luck, we'll be in time for the plane. *(Avec un peu de chance…)* But all this is wishful thinking! *(Tu prends tes désirs pour la réalité.)* I look forward to meeting you. *(Je suis impatiente de…)*	My dearest wish is to have them settle here. May they always have good health! *(Puissent-ils toujours…)* My sincere good wishes for your recovery. (written) *(Tous mes meilleurs vœux pour votre rétablissement.)* More literary: That was a luxury she had always craved for (or: hankered after/ longed for) *(un luxe dont elle avait toujours rêvé.)*

	I hope it will be all right. I hope to be an actress one day. We can now see the light at the end of the tunnel. *(entrevoir la lumière au bout du tunnel.)* We're all right now, touch wood. *(touchons du bois.)* I hope you'll win: I'll keep my fingers crossed. *(croiser les doigts.)*	I sincerely hope you will visit us soon.

LIKES/SATISFACTION – DISLIKES/DISSATISFACTION

Informal	Standard	Formal
Great! *(Super!)* It was really cool! It was incredible! She's mad/crazy about that singer! She's into tap-dancing. *(Son truc, c'est les claquettes.)* She's nuts over him. *(Elle est dingue de…)*	I (don't) enjoy/like/love skating. I do like this piece of music. What I really like/enjoy is skiing. I'm (not) fond of ice-cream. John is (not) keen on gardening. *(n'est pas passionné par…)* I've never seen anything like it! How/Isn't that nice/lovely/interesting…! It's so original. It's really worth reading. *(… vaut la peine d'être lu.)* They say what's great about the house is that it is near the beach. She's a jazz addict/enthusiast.	I find his plays absolutely fascinating.
The evening was a bore! *(rasoir)* I'm sick of her! *(J'en ai assez/marre de…)* James makes me sick! Yuk! *(Beurk!)* Ugh! *(Pouah!)*	I don't care for science-fiction. *(Je n'aime pas beaucoup/… ne me dit rien.)* I detest such people. I'm not very keen on card games. Playing board games is not my cup of tea. *(Ce n'est pas à mon goût/pas mon genre.)* I hate/can't stand/can't bear/loathe fools. *(déteste/ne peux pas supporter…)* I hate/can't stand/can't bear/loathe doing the washing up/to do… It was all very disappointing. *(C'était très décevant.)*	

	It was a waste of time and money. *(Nous avons perdu notre temps et notre argent.)* How/Isn't that boring/awful...! It was horrendous/awful/disgusting! *(épouvantable)*	

PREFERENCES

Informal	Standard	Formal
	I'd (= I would) rather (not) give him the money. I'd rather you stayed at home. I would prefer to stay at home. I would as soon read a good book. *(Je préfèrerais...)* I prefer cats to dogs. I prefer skating to cycling. I like reading better than writing. I would rather stay at home than go for a walk. This job would suit me better. *(me conviendrait mieux)* What I like best is going to the opera.	

INDIFFERENCE

Informal	Standard	Formal
So what? *(Bon et alors?)* Who cares? *(Qu'est-ce que ça peut bien faire?)* I don't give a damn (about it). *(Je m'en fous!)* I couldn't care less. *(Je m'en fiche!)*	Why not? It doesn't matter. I don't mind (doing it). *(Cela m'est égal de...)* I don't feel concerned. It's all the same to me. *(Cela m'est égal.)* I've nothing against modern art, but it leaves me cold.. *(Ça me laisse froid.)* I'm not terribly keen on science-fiction. I have no preference at all./no preference either way. It doesn't make any difference to me. *(Ça n'a pas d'importance pour moi.)*	I have little interest in the matter.

DISAPPOINTMENT & REGRET

Informal	Standard	Formal
Too bad! *(Dommage !)* Oh heck! *(Zut !)* Why the devil did I say that ? *(Pourquoi diable ai-je dit cela ?)* I could kick myself. *(Je me donnerais des gifles.)* I put my foot in it. *(J'ai fait une gaffe.)*	I'm so sorry! Oh, dear! I'm (terribly) sorry I said that. What a pity/shame! *(Quel dommage !)* It is so disappointing! *(Comme c'est décevant !)* The play was a real disappointment. I wish I had never mentioned it. *(Je n'aurais jamais dû le mentionner.)* Why on earth did I marry him? *(Pourquoi donc… ?)* Next time, we'll be more careful. If I had known, I would not have invited her. *(Si j'avais su…)* If only I had stayed at home! Why didn't I ask him first? I should have told her the truth! *(J'aurais dû…)*	We are very disappointed with your results. I regret writing those words. Had I known, I would have been more careful. We regret to inform you that your appointment has been cancelled. (written)

DESPAIR (Désespoir)

Informal	Standard	Formal
I give up! What's the point? *(À quoi bon ?)* I really feel down. *(J'ai le cafard.)* I've made a mess of things. *(J'ai tout bousillé.)*	It's quite hopeless! *(C'est désespérant !)* It's no use keeping on trying! *(À quoi bon s'acharner ?)* I can't go on like that. What (on earth) am I going to do?	

JOY

Informal	Standard	Formal
Wow! *(Fantastique !)*	It's fantastic/wonderful/brilliant! I'm so glad! I'm feeling on top of the world. *(Je suis aux anges, au 7e ciel.)* He is as pleased as Punch to have a grandson. *(Il est heureux comme un roi)*	We are all positively delighted! *(Nous sommes tous extrêmement heureux…)*

Surprise & incredulity

Informal	Standard	Formal
Wow! *(Waouh!)* Gosh! *(Ça alors!)* Crikey! *(Mince alors!)* Really? Are you mad? No kidding! *(Sans blague!)* That's a bit thick! *(C'est un peu fort.)* Don't give me that! *(À d'autres!)*	What a surprise! What terrible/fantastic news! How extraordinary/strange/amazing/ awful/astounding... (that he should have said that)! Well, I never! *(Ça alors!)* You don't say! *(Je n'en reviens pas!)* Oh my God! That's not possible! Fancy her saying that! *(Qui aurait cru qu'elle dirait cela?)* I can't believe it! You must be joking! *(Vous voulez rire!)* You're pulling my leg. *(Vous vous moquez de moi.)* You can't be serious! *(Ce n'est pas possible!)* It can't be true! I must be dreaming! *(Je rêve!)* I was flabbergasted/dumbfounded. *(J'ai été sidéré.)* He couldn't believe his eyes/ears.	Good gracious! *(Mon Dieu!)* Good Lord! To my amazement, she burst into tears. *(À ma stupéfaction...)* I did not know what to make of it. *(Je ne savais pas qu'en penser.)* I thought my eyes/ears were deceiving me. *(Je n'en croyais pas mes yeux/mes oreilles.)* Who would have imagined they would react this way? *(Qui aurait pensé...)*

Fear

Informal	Standard	Formal
I was scared stiff/scared to death/scared out of my wits. *(J'avais la frousse./ Je n'en menais pas large.)* It was spooky! *(Ça donnait froid dans le dos!)*	I was afraid/terrified/frightened/ scared (of snakes). The film was spine-chilling. *(...un film à vous glacer le sang.)* Darkness gives me the shivers. *(... me donne le frisson.)* The sound made my blood run cold. *(Ce bruit me glaça le sang.)* The dark house made my flesh creep. *(... me donnait la chair de poule.)* I was shaking like a leaf. *(Je tremblais comme une feuille.)*	I did not move, lest (or: for fear) he should hear me. *(... de peur qu'il ne m'entende.)* I'm anxious about the result of the election. *(Je crains beaucoup...)*

Reproach & anger

Informal	Standard	Formal
You're the limit! *(Tu exagères !)* It makes me sick! *(Ça me dégoûte !)* I'm sick of your lies! I'm fed up with your tantrums! *(J'en ai assez/marre de tes crises.)* Rubbish! *(C'est absurde !/Ça n'a pas de sens !)*	Why didn't you tell me? How could you do that? Couldn't you have told us earlier? How dare you speak to me like that! *(Comment osez-vous…)* I'd rather you stopped phoning at such hours ! *(Je préférerais que tu cesses…)* Did you have to do it this way? *(Tu ne pouvais pas faire ça autrement ?)* Look what you've done! Who do you think you are? *(Pour qui te prends-tu ?)* You should know better at your age ! *(À ton âge, tu devrais avoir un peu plus de bon sens !)* Can't you see it's wrong to do that? You might have warned me. That's the last straw! *(C'est le comble !)* I've had more than enough of your language ! *(J'en ai par-dessus la tête…)* I'm not going to put up with/bear such behaviour! *(Je ne supporterai pas un tel comportement !)* I wish you wouldn't leave such a mess in your room! *(Tu ne peux donc pas ranger ta chambre !)*	You might at least have told your mother! *(Tu aurais au moins pu…)* He is to blame for spoiling the evening. *(C'est par sa faute que la soirée a été gâchée.)*

Complaining (Se plaindre)

Informal	Standard	Formal
Look, I've had enough of this. This is the limit ! *(Ça dépasse les bornes !)* Enough is enough ! *(Ça suffit comme ça !)* I'm fed up with your excuses ! *(J'en ai assez/marre de…)*	I think it's a shame to behave like this. *(Quelle honte de…)* This has gone too far ! *(Ça dépasse les limites !)* I'd like to know what you're going to do about it. *(J'aimerais savoir ce que vous comptez faire.)* It's high time she apologized. *(Il est grand temps/il serait temps qu'elle …)*	I'm sorry, but this is not what I expected. *(Je suis désolé, mais ce n'est pas ce que j'attendais.)* I would like to know what you intend to do about it.

	I'm not going to put up with such language! *(Je ne supporterai pas…)* How dare you speak to me in such a way? *(Comment osez-vous…)*	

Worry (Inquiétude)

Informal	Standard	Formal
I was worried sick. *(J'en étais malade d'inquiétude.)* I was dead worried. *(terriblement inquiet)* Jane is worried to death about her mother. *(folle d'inquiétude)*	This is rather/quite worrying. *(assez inquiétant)* We're rather concerned about her future. *(assez inquiets)* The worrying thing is that he seems to have lost interest in everything.	I feel very anxious about the results. *(Les résultats m'inquiètent beaucoup.)*

Reassurance

Informal	Standard	Formal
Take it easy! *(Ne vous en faites pas !)* Cheer up! *(Courage !)*	Don't worry! Never mind! *(Ça n'a pas d'importance !)* There's nothing to worry about. There's no cause for alarm. *(Il n'y a pas de raison de s'inquiéter.)* Everything will be fine/all right.	

Sympathy (Compassion)

Informal	Standard	Formal
Hard luck! *(Pas de chance !)*	How unfortunate! *(Quelle déveine !)* How awful for you! *(Comme c'est affreux pour vous !)* It breaks my heart to see the way she looks. *(Cela me fait mal au coeur de la voir…)* That must have been dreadful for you. *(Cela a dû être terrible…)* That was all you needed! *(Il ne vous manquait plus que cela.)*	My heart goes out to you in these difficult moments. *(Je suis de tout coeur avec vous…)*

Relief (Soulagement)

Informal	Standard	Formal
It was a close call! *(On l'a échappé belle.)*	Thank God he's now better! We had a narrow escape! *(On l'a échappé belle.)* It takes a weight off my mind. *(Cela m'ôte un poids…)*	It is such a relief to know he has found a job. *(Quel soulagement de savoir que…)*

Approval/admiration & disapproval (Approbation/Admiration/Désapprobation)

Informal	Standard	Formal
Well done! *(Bravo!)* Brilliant! *(Parfait!)* Great! *(Formidable!)* Super! Smashing!	Very good! Excellent! This is great news! What a good idea!/How wonderful! This is just/exactly what I needed. You did exactly the right thing. It was the wisest thing to do. *(C'était la voix de la sagesse.)* I'll certainly support your campaign. *(Je vais soutenir…)* What a tremendous/fantastic/ excellent/lovely idea! She looked so confident/smart…! That's some car! *(Voilà ce que j'appelle une voiture!)*	I very much approve of your decision. *(J'approuve totalement votre décision.)* We can only praise your own good work. *(Nous ne pouvons que louer…)* Your new house is absolutely delightful/ magnificent!
It won't do! *(Impossible!)* It's not on! *(Ça va pas?)* He's dead against it. *(Il est totalement contre.)*	I think it's wrong to think that there are easy solutions. I can't see the point of learning this. *(Je ne vois pas l'intérêt de…)* I don't care much for coffee. *(Je n'aime pas beaucoup…)* I don't think much of his idea. *(À mon avis, son idée ne vaut pas grand chose.)* What a stupid/unrealistic/view! He is upset/displeased/uneasy about their decision. He protested against their behaviour. It's scandalous/awful/shocking!	I resent being made to feel like a fool. *(Je n'apprécie pas qu'on me ridiculise.)* I strongly disapprove of such views. *(Je suis tout à fait contre…/ Je trouve inadmissible)* He objects to his son working so late. *(Il s'oppose à ce que…)* Such behaviour is a downright disgrace. *(… est un vrai scandale.)*

exercices

1 **Faites correspondre les réponses aux exclamations et l'émotion qu'elles expriment.**

A. **I've just learnt the prize went to Amy Philips!**

1. What a shame!
2. I wish it had gone to Jane.
3. That's fantastic!
4. I can't wait to see her reaction.
5. Isn't that nice for her!
6. Who cares?
7. Well, I never!
8. How stupid! I wish the jury would show more common sense.
9. Don't worry! I'm sure it'll be you next time.
10. Good. That certainly takes a weight off my mind.

a. desire, impatience.
b. relief
c. surprise
d. indifference
e. disappointment
f. joy
g. reassurance, consolation
h. anger
i. satisfaction
j. regret

B. **Look at my new car!**

1. That's some car!
2. If only I could have one like this!
3. When I earn more, I mean to buy just the same.
4. I so love Rolls-Royces!
5. A bike would suit me better.
6. You can't be serious!
7. Did you have to spend all your money on a car?
8. Thank God you did not buy a plane!

a. preference
b. incredulity
c. admiration
d. liking
e. intention
f. relief
g. wish
h. reproach

2 **Traduisez les phrases suivantes.**

1. Ce type de jazz ne me fait ni chaud ni froid.
2. Ca, c'est incroyable !
3. C'est étrange qu'il n'ait pas appelé.
4. Il meurt d'envie de te raconter ce qui s'est passé.
5. Je déteste me lever tôt.
6. Si j'avais su, je serais venu en train.
7. Je préférerais aller au théâtre, si cela ne t'ennuie pas.
8. Il a gagné 500 livres à la loterie et est absolument ravi !

3. Mental activity

Ability/capability/inability/incapability

(Capacités/Incompétence/Aptitudes/Inaptitude)

Informal	Standard	Formal
He made it! *(Ça y est !/Il a réussi.)* He didn't make it. He's got what it takes! *(C'est pas le talent qui lui manque !)*	Can you fix this broken lamp? *(Pouvez-vous réparer…)* I can't reach it! *(Je n'arrive pas à l'atteindre.)* Do you know how to use this digital camera? I was (un)able to open the bottle. She is (in)capable of lying to us. He is proficient in German. *(Il parle allemand couramment.)* He has a gift for chemistry. *(Il est doué en…)* She has a good grasp/knowledge of Italian. *(Elle a une solide connaissance…)* When it comes to chess, he's second to none. *(Il n'a pas son pareil.)*	You must be able to use a computer in this job. *(Vous devez savoir utiliser…)* He is qualified to work as a lifeguard. *(Il a les compétences/les conditions requises pour…)*
I'm rotten at chemistry. *(nul)* I'm a dead loss ! *(nul)*	It's difficult/impossible/easy for me to do it. Did you manage to clean it? *(As-tu réussi à…)* Did you succeed in starting the engine? He failed to reach the summit. *(Il n'a pas réussi à…)* I'm quite incapable of using a computer. I'm hopeless at maths! *(Je suis nul en…)*	

Obligation

Informal	Standard	Formal
	I was forced/obliged to pay for another ticket. I had to take the train instead.	She was made/compelled to apologize. *(Il lui fallut s'excuser.)*

	I must work harder. The teacher made me write the essay all over again. I need to borrow some money. You are supposed to be there by 9. a.m. (*Vous êtes censés être là…*) They are expected/required to arrive on time. (*Ils doivent arriver à l'heure.*) You've got to see that play: it's a must! (*C'est une pièce à voir absolument.*) They had no choice but to pay. (*Vous n'avez pas le choix, il vous faut payer.*) It is your duty to help your family. (*C'est votre devoir…*) Absence of obligation: You don't have to answer. (*Vous n'êtes pas obligé de…*) You needn't write. It is not necessary for them to book beforehand. You won't need to take an umbrella. (*Vous n'aurez pas besoin de…*	You are to report to the headmaster this afternoon. (*Vous devez vous présenter…*)

Asking for/giving/refusing… permission

Informal	Standard	Formal
Is it okay if I take your bike?	Can I watch that film tonight? Am I allowed to take the car? Do you mind if I smoke? (*Ça ne vous ennuie pas que…*) Is it all right if I make myself a cup of tea? (*Ça va si…*)	May I open the window? (*Puis-je…*) Do you think I could ring him now? Do you mind my leaving early? Would you object/mind if I smoked in here? (*Verriez-vous une objection à ce que…*) Do we have your permission to use the boat?
Sure! (*D'accord!*) Fine! (*D'accord!/O.K.*) No problem! (*Bien sûr.*) Go ahead! (*Allez-y.*) Feel free! (*Allez-y.*)	Certainly. Of course, you can/may. You can/are allowed to/have the right to bring your own pets. I'll let you stay if you are quiet.	You may go out if you have finished
No way! (*Pas question!*) Forget about it! (*Pas question!*)	(I'm sorry, but) you can't swim here. I'm afraid that won't be possible. Don't smoke in here. I don't want you to swim here.	

	I won't let you go out in this weather. You are not allowed to drink alcohol here. You are not supposed to bring food in here. *(Vous n'êtes pas censés…)* You mustn't touch the paintings. I forbid you to marry him ! *(Je t'interdis…)*	your homework. You are entitled to bring a dictionary. *(Vous êtes autorisés à…)* You may not touch the books. *(Vous n'avez pas le droit de…)* You are not to walk on the grass. Such language will not be tolerated here. Smoking is not permitted here. Roller-skating is prohibited here. *(est interdit)*

SUGGESTIONS & ADVICE (Suggestions/Conseils)

Informal	Standard	Formal
(Do you) fancy a drink ? *(As-tu envie de…)* Fancy taking the car ? *(Tu veux prendre la voiture ?)* Go for it ! *(N'hésite pas !/Vas-y !)*	How/What about going to the cinema ? *(Et si on…)* And if we took the bus ? Suppose we invited him ? Why don't we forget about it ? Let's have a drink. Do you care for a drink ? *(Voulez-vous boire quelque chose ?)* Why not join them ? Shall we invite them ? I wonder if they'd let us in without a ticket ? *(Je me demande s'ils nous laisseraient entrer…)* I think we should hurry. It's (high) time you had a flat of your own. *(Il est grand temps que tu aies…)* You ought to/could go and see him. *(Tu devrais…)* You'd better give her a ring. *(Tu ferais mieux de…)* Take my advice and forget about it. *(Suivez mon conseil et…)*	Let me make a suggestion. *(Permettez-moi de suggérer…)* If I may make a suggestion… *(Si je peux me permettre de suggérer…)* You would be wise to write a letter of apology. *(Il serait sage que…)* I suggest you write a letter to complain. I advise you to write to your M.P. *(Je vous conseille…)*

	If I were you, I'd apologize. *(À votre place…)* You could always write to him. *(Vous avez toujours la possibilité de…)* The best course seems to be to wait and do nothing. *(La meilleure solution semble être…)*	

PERSUASION (see also Suggestions and Advice)

Informal	Standard	Formal
	They persuaded me to go cycling with them. They dissuaded me from seeing the film. She talked him into buying her the coat. I talked him out of complaining to the director. *(Je l'ai dissuadé de se plaindre auprès…)* The men were threatened into accepting. *(Ils les obligèrent à accepter en les menaçant.)* I made him do his homework. *(Je lui ai fait faire…)* They had the gardener mend the fence. *(Ils firent réparer la clôture par le jardinier.)*	

AGREEMENT & DISAGREEMENT (Accord/Désaccord)

Informal	Standard	Formal
All right by me. *(D'accord.)* You bet! *(Tu parles!)* Okay. Oh, sure. No problem. Right you are!	I couldn't agree more. *(Tout à fait d'accord.)* I think it's a very good idea. I quite/totally agree. That's true. How true! *(C'est bien vrai.)* You're quite right. I'll go along with that. *(Je suis d'accord/je te suis sur ce point.)* Absolutely. (Precisely./Exactly.)	I do support your proposal. *(Je suis tout à fait en faveur de…)* I cannot but agree with you. *(Je ne peux qu'être d'accord…)* I (don't) share your views on the matter. *(Je ne partage pas votre opinion…)*

	So + Auxiliary + pronoun (So do I. *Moi aussi.*) Neither + Auxiliary + pronoun (Neither do I. *Moi non plus.*) There's no doubt about it. *(Cela ne fait aucun doute.)* Of course (not). *(Bien sûr... Bien sûr que non...)*	I concur with the journalist when he says that. *(Je suis d'accord...)*
Rubbish! *(Ça n'a pas de sens!)* Nonsense! Forget it! *(Pas question!)* No way! Over my dead body! *(Jamais de la vie!)* Not on your life! You must be out of your mind! *(Tu es fou ou quoi?)*	Yes, up to a point. *(dans une certaine mesure)* I tend to disagree > I don't agree. > I (totally) disagree. I don't think so. You're joking! *(Vous plaisantez!)* You can't be serious. *(Vous voulez rire.)* Surely, you can see that it wouldn't work. *(Mais vous devez tout de même bien voir...)* We don't see eye to eye on this matter. *(Nous n'avons pas le même point de vue.)* I take a different view of the matter. *(Je ne vois pas les choses de la même façon.)* Quite, but what about the cost? *(Bien sûr, mais...)* I can't go along with you on this question. *(Je ne vous suis pas...)* You can't possibly believe he's sincere! I fail to see how it would work. *(Je ne vois pas comment...)* I think that's wrong.	Surely, you can't expect me to believe he'll be elected? *(Vous ne voulez tout de même pas me faire croire...)* It could be objected that it will cost too much. *(On pourrait objecter que...)* I do object to this proposal. *(Je suis contre...)* I beg to differ. *(Permettez-moi de ne pas être de votre avis.)*

GIVING ONE'S OPINION

Informal	Standard	Formal
I guess it's a good idea. *(Je crois que...)*	Personally, I think she's right. *(Quant à moi...)* As far as I am concerned, it's over. *(En ce qui me concerne...)* I think/believe/reckon it's a good point. In my opinion/In my view, it won't last. *(À mon avis...)*	From my point of view... *(De mon point de vue...)*

	To my mind, it's got to stop. If you ask me, I think it's too expensive. *(Si tu veux mon avis…)* I can't help thinking that we've forgotten something. *(Je ne peux pas m'empêcher de penser…)* The way I see it, he's gone too far. *(Pour moi…)* I'd say that he's around thirty. *(Je dirais que…)* I'm convinced that it won't work. *(Je suis convaincu…)*	

FROM UNCERTAINTY TO CERTAINTY (Incertitude/Certitude)

Informal	Standard	Formal
I guess it's too late. *(J'imagine…)*	I doubt that he will ever forgive her. *(Je doute qu'il…)* He has probably forgotten. He may/could/might come back late tonight. *(Il se peut/se pourrait qu'il…)* It's difficult to say whether he likes it or not We could well meet them there. *(Il se pourrait bien que…)* Perhaps/Maybe he will phone. I wonder if/whether it will work. I have a feeling they have other plans. *(J'ai comme l'impression…)*	
	I suppose he will resign. He should be back soon. *(Il ne devrait pas tarder.)* He will probably be home late. He's likely/unlikely to succeed. *(Il a de grandes chances/peu de chances de réussir.)* It looks as if it's going to rain. *(On dirait que…)* There's every sign that things are going to change. *(Tout semble indiquer…)*	They are likely to oppose the motion. *(Ils vont probablement voter contre la motion.)*

	The odds are that he will resign. *(Il y a de fortes chances pour que…)*	
It's a dead cert ! *(C'est sûr et certain.)*	I'm sure/certain that he never phoned. No doubt he will mention it to you. *(Sans doute…)* I could have sworn that it was him I saw. *(J'aurais juré que…)* They're 100 % sure of it. We are confident that he'll succeed. *(Nous sommes persuadés qu'il réussira…)* She's convinced that he lied. *(Elle est convaincue…)* It goes without saying that she'll accept. *(Il va sans dire que…)* He can't be thirty already ! He must be thirty by now. He is bound to/sure to accept. *(Il est sûr qu'il va…)*	It is undeniably true that he's too ill to go on. *(Il est indéniable que…)* He was undeniably angry. *(Il est incontestable qu'il était…)*

exercices

1 *Ability – capability – obligation*

Le *Countryside Code* est un ensemble de conseils et de règles pour respecter l'environnement à la campagne. Voici quelques passages de ce code de bonne conduite. Complétez-les avec l'un des modaux ou expressions qui suivent, à la forme qui convient.

(may/can/be entitled to/must/may not/be careful not to/do not have to)

1. By law you … control your dog so that it does not disturb or scare farm animals or wildlife.
2. You … put your dog on a lead *(une laisse)* on public paths, as long as it is under close control.
3. Farmers … destroy a dog that injures or worries their animal.
4. At certain times, dogs … be allowed on some areas of land or … need to be kept on a lead. You … also find more about these rules from www.countrysideaccess.gov.uk
5. Fires … be as devastating to wildlife and habitats as they are to people and property – so … drop a match or smouldering *(mal éteinte, qui fume)* cigarette at any time of the year.

6. By law, cyclists … give way to walkers and horse-riders.
7. A farmer will normally leave a gate closed to keep livestock in, but … sometimes leave it open so that they … reach food and water. Leave gates as you find them.

2 Traduisez les phrases suivantes.

1. A-t-il les qualifications nécessaires pour être chauffeur de taxi ?
2. Je partage tout à fait votre opinion sur ce point.
3. Il est difficile de dire si elle a raison ou non.
4. Je ne pouvais pas m'empêcher d'avoir l'impression qu'il devait y avoir quelqu'un caché dans la maison.
5. L'enfant réussit à convaincre sa mère de lui acheter le jouet.

IV CHIFFRES ET MESURES

1. DATES ET RÉFÉRENCES TEMPORELLES

P. 47 (DÉVELOPPEMENT CHRONOLOGIQUE)

DATES

Les dates se lisent par groupes de deux chiffres :

→ 1874 (lire : *eighteen seventy-four*)
→ 1993 (lire : *nineteen ninety-three*)
→ 2005 (lire : *two thousand and five*), 2018 (lire : *twenty eighteen*)

In 2006

→ *She flew over* **on** *June 3 (or : 3 June, or 3rd June or June 3rd). On prononce : June the third/the third of June.* (Lorsqu'on prononce des dates, on utilise l'article devant le nombre ordinal : *the fifth of August, January the twenty-second*).
→ *On March 9, 2002, they got married.* (On prononce : *March the ninth, two thousand and two.*)

Notez la différence entre la façon dont les Anglais et les Américains écrivent les dates :

→ 10/4/2005 = *April 10th* en anglais britannique
October 4th en anglais américain
→ *The Jazz Age is a term which applies to the 1920s in America. (the 1920s = from 1920 to 1929)*

→ *The early thirties (from 1930 to 1933:* le début des années 30)
→ *The mid thirties (from 1934 to 1936:* au milieu des années 30)
→ *The late thirties (from 1937 to 1939:* à la fin des années 30)

Quand une date est précédée de c. (= *circa*), cela signifie « environ ».
→ *This church was built c. 1240.*

Après une date, *AD* = *Anno Domini (after the birth of Christ)*, alors que *BC* = *Before Christ.* On peut employer *CE* (*Common Era*) au lieu de *AD* pour éviter toute référence religieuse.

RÉFÉRENCES TEMPORELLES

■ Quand ?

On Monday, on Friday, on July 17th. (On + jour de la semaine ou date)
On Tuesdays = every Tuesday
On Tuesday = this coming Tuesday
On Wednesday afternoons = every Wednesday afternoon
In the morning, in the afternoon, in October, in winter
At night, at dawn, at lunchtime, at weekends, at Christmas
This morning, yesterday afternoon, tomorrow night

■ À quelle heure ?

2.15 peut se lire : *a quarter past two/two fifteen*
6.30 peut se lire : *half past six/six thirty*
6.40 peut se lire : *twenty to seven/six forty*
Pour distinguer matin et après-midi (dans des horaires, textes officiels), on peut employer a.m. (matin) et p.m. (après-midi) : *The museum opens at 10 a.m. and closes at 5.30 p.m.*
She arrived at eight o'clock.
We have a class from 9 to 10. 30.
We have a class in three hours/in ten minutes.
Come back by five to two as you have an appointment at two. (= pas plus tard que deux heures moins cinq.)
It is nearly six, just before six, coming up to six. (presque 6 heures)
It is about six. (environ 6 heures)
It is just after six, just gone six. (un peu après 6 heures)

■ Pendant combien de temps ?

He stayed with us for two months/three years/half an hour. (*for* + heures, mois, années...)
He stayed with us during the holidays/the summer/the train strike. (*during* + période)

■ Depuis combien de temps ?

Since + point de départ précis dans le passé *For* + durée	+ *present perfect* ou *past perfect* dans la principale

I've been working on this essay for two weeks. (Je travaille à cet essai depuis 15 jours.)
They had been living in London for two years when I met them last year.
(Ils habitaient Londres depuis deux ans quand je les ai rencontrés l'an dernier.)
They've given up using the car since they had their accident.
(Ils ont cessé de prendre la voiture depuis leur accident.)

■ **Combien de fois (fréquence) ?**
She rings twice a day/three times a day.
He visits us every two years. (tous les deux ans)
She seldom goes to New York. (rarement)
We meet for lunch every now and then/once in a while (de temps en temps).

■ **Il y a combien de temps ?**
He bought a new bike two months ago. (durée + *ago*)
He had sold his piano a year before. (durée + *before*)

■ **Quelques adverbes**
In the old days, in those days, formerly (il y a longtemps, autrefois)
Recently, lately (récemment)
These days, nowadays, in this time and age (actuellement, à notre époque)
Currently, at the moment, for the time being (en ce moment, pour l'instant)
Presently, shortly, soon (bientôt)
Later (on) (plus tard)

■ **Quelques structures**
No sooner + inversion… *than* : *No sooner had she opened the door than she heard the telephone ring.* (À peine avait-elle ouvert la porte qu'elle entendit le téléphone sonner.)
Hardly + inversion… *when* : *Hardly had she left the station when she remembered she had left her bag in the train.* (À peine avait-elle quitté la gare qu'elle se souvint avoir oublié son sac dans le train.)

↗ exercices

1 Complétez les phrases qui suivent avec des prépositions.

1. We always go to the country … the weekend.
2. … Saturdays, we always invite friends … the evening.
3. It is very cold … dawn, but it becomes warmer … the afternoon.
4. … those days people used pencils and ink, but … this time and age, everyone uses computers.
5. Shall we meet … lunchtime or … the afternoon ?

6. … 5 … 6 I have a piano lesson, but I'll be home … 6.30.
7. The meat has been in the oven … 40 minutes now. Do you think it's cooked?
8. I haven't been to the Opera … last July.
9. He was born … July 6th, 1986, … seven o'clock … the morning.

2 Complétez les phrases pour obtenir des phrases de sens équivalent.

1. It happened around 1985. It happened in the … .
2. Every Tuesday night I go to the gym. On … I go to the gym.
3. Hardly had he said the words when the audience burst out laughing. No sooner … .
4. When they became engaged in 2001, they had known each other for two years. When they became engaged in 2001, they had known each other since … .
5. It happened in 1998. It happened in … .

3 Lisez à haute voix cet extrait d'une encyclopédie.

bank holiday A public holiday in Britain. In 1871, John Lubbock (1834-1913) introduced an act which obliged the Bank of England and other banks to close on a number of days, which became public holidays. A number of days were added over the years, bringing the total to eight. In Northern Ireland two more days are recognized: St Patrick's Day (March 17) and the commemoration of the Battle of the Boyne (July 12). In 2004 there was talk of adding other public holidays, to bring Britain in line with the rest of Europe, which has an average of 11 bank holidays.

Bank Holidays

	England & Wales	Scotland	Northern Ireland
January 1	•	•	•
January 2		•	
March 17			•
Good Friday	•	•	•
Easter Monday	•		
First Monday, May	•	•	•
Last Monday, May	•	•	•
July 12			•
First Monday, August		•	
Last Monday, August	•		•
December 25	•	•	•
December 26	•	•	•

If a bank holiday falls on a Saturday or Sunday, the next working day becomes the holiday.

Le tableau est extrait de : Bamber Gascoigne, *Encyclopedia of Britain*, Macmillan, 1994.

2. Mesures

Le système métrique n'est pas utilisé aux États-Unis. Il l'est en revanche de plus en plus en Grande Bretagne, mais lorsque les Anglais parlent de la taille et souvent du poids, ils continuent à préférer l'ancien système. Il est donc nécessaire de connaître ce système, dit imperial, ne serait-ce que pour comprendre ou traduire un texte plus ancien où les mesures sont exprimées en *miles*, *pounds* ou *pints*.

Système impérial	Système métrique
Linear measures (mesures de longueur)	
1 inch (un pouce)	= *2,54 cm* (se lit *centimetres*)
1 foot (un pied)	= *30,48 cm*
1 yard = 3 feet	= *91,44 cm*
1 mile	= *1,609 km* (se lit *kilometres*)
Height (taille)	
He's five foot four. (five foot four inches)	= *1m 62*
He's five foot six.	= *1m 70*
Square measures (mesures de superficie)	
1 in² (se lit *one square inch*)	= *6,45 cm²* (se lit *square centimetres*)
1 yd² (se lit *one square yard*)	= *8361 cm²*
1 square mile	= *2,6 km²* (se lit *square kilometres*)
1 acre = 4,840 square yards	= *4046.86 m²* (se lit *square metres*)
2.471 acres	= *1 hectare*
Cubic measures (mesures de volume)	
1 ft³ (se lit *one cubic foot*)	On parle de *cubic centimetres*
1 yd³ (se lit *one cubic yard*)	et de *cubic metres.*
Capacity	
1 pt (se lit *one pint*)	= *0,57 litre* (GB) ou *0,473 litre* (US)
1 qt (se lit *one quart*) = *2 pints*	
1 g/gal (se lit *one gallon*) = *4 quarts*	
Weight (poids)	
1 oz (se lit *an ounce*) (une once)	= *28,349 grammes* (ou *grams*)
1 lb (se lit *one pound*) (une livre) = *16 ounces*	= *453,59 grammes* (ou *grams*)
1 st (se lit *one stone*) = *14 pounds*	= *6,348 kilogrammes*
1 ton = 2,240 lb.	*1 tonne = 1000 kg*
She weighs 10 stone.	= *63 kilos*
(*Stone* dans ce sens est invariable).	
He weighs 95 pounds.	= *43 kilos*
Temperatures	
32° Fahrenheit	= *0° centigrade*
212° Fahrenheit	= *100° centigrade*

Notez bien les expressions suivantes pour parler de mesures :
The wall is 2 yards high/long. The river is 2 feet deep. The lawn is 3 yards wide/across.
Mais : *a five-foot high wall. A three-mile long path* (*Foot* et *mile* font partie d'un groupe qui a fonction d'adjectif et sont donc invariables.)

TEMPÉRATURES

Pour convertir les Fahrenheit en centigrades : enlever 32 et multiplier par 5/9.

exemple 74°F = 59-32 x 5/9 = 23°C

Weather reports from around the world

	°C	°F	Wthr		°C	°F	Wthr		°C	°F	Wthr
Ajaccio	31	88	s	Florence	36	97	s	Munich	31	88	s
Algiers	33	91	f	Frankfurt	32	90	s	Nairobi	19	66	c
Amsterdam	30	86	s	Geneva	29	84	th	Naples	31	88	s
Anchorage	14	57	r	Gibraltar	22	72	f	New Delhi	26	79	th
Athens	33	91	s	Hamburg	29	84	s	New Orleans	26	79	r
Atlanta	30	86	c	Hong Kong	31	88	sh	New York	29	84	c
B Aires	17	63	f	Honolulu	29	84	c	Nice	30	86	s
Barcelona	32	90	s	Innsbruck	31	88	s	Oslo	26	79	s
Belgrade	32	90	s	Istanbul	29	84	s	Paris	34	93	s
Berlin	30	86	s	Jerusalem	30	86	s	Perth	18	64	f
Bermuda	24	75	sh	Jo'burg	21	70	s	Prague	31	88	s
Biarritz	26	79	c	Karachi	31	88	fg	Reykjavik	11	52	dr
Bombay	30	86	f	Kiev	26	79	s	Rio de Jan.	19	66	f
Bordeaux	29	79	sh	Kingston	32	90	f	Rome	31	88	s
Boston	30	86	f	Lima	21	70	f	Sarajevo	26	79	f
Brisbane	22	72	s	Lisbon	22	72	s	Singapore	32	90	f
Brussels	31	88	s	London	30	86	s	Stockholm	25	77	s
Budapest	33	91	f	Los Angeles	27	81	f	Strasbourg	28	82	s
Cairo	32	90	s	Luxembourg	33	91	s	Sydney	15	59	sh
Calcutta	33	91	r	Madrid	33	91	s	Tel Aviv	30	86	s
Calgary	27	81	s	Majorca	34	93	s	Tokyo	31	88	s
Cape Town	14	57	c	Malaga	27	81	f	Toronto	30	86	s
Casablanca	26	79	s	Malta	30	86	s	Tunis	33	91	s
Chicago	31	88	c	Mecca	39	102	s	Valencia	33	91	s
Corfu	33	91	s	Melbourne	15	59	s	Vancouver	24	75	f
Dakar	30	86	s	Mexico City	22	72	f	Venice	33	91	s
Dallas	33	91	s	Miami	32	90	s	Vienna	31	88	s
Darwin	26	79	s	Milan	32	90	s	Warsaw	30	86	s
Dhaka	30	86	r	Montreal	24	75	th	Washington	27	81	c
Dublin	23	73	s	Moscow	24	75	c	Zurich	28	82	s

▲ The Guardian, July 27, 2006.

BRITISH AND AMERICAN CURRENCIES

Aux États-Unis, la devise est le *dollar*. Il contient 100 *cents*. Il y a des pièces de 5 *cents* (= *nickels*), de 10 *cents* (= *dimes*) et de 25 *cents* (= *quarters*).

En Grande-Bretagne, la devise est la livre (*the pound*). Elle comprend 100 *pence*. Dans l'ancien système (avant 1971), une livre comprenait 240 *pence*. Il y avait 20 *shillings* dans une livre, et 12 *pence* dans un *shilling*. Un florin équivalait à deux *shillings*. Il existait aussi une pièce d'un *half-crown* qui valait 2 *shillings* et 6 *pence*. En République d'Irlande, la devise est l'euro.

Sizes

Women's clothes			Men's clothes		
USA	EUROPEAN	UK	USA	EUROPEAN	UK
8	38	10	32	42	32
10	40	12	34	44	34
12	42	14	36	46	36
14	44	16	38	48	38
16	46	18	40	50	40
18	48	20	42	52	42
20	50	22	44	54	44

Women's shoes			Men's shoes		
USA	EUROPEAN	UK	USA	EUROPEAN	UK
4	35		6	38	
5	36		7	40	
6	37		8	41	
7	38		9	43	
8	39		10	44	
9	40		11	45	
10	41		12	46	

exercice

Traduisez en faisant les conversions nécessaires.

1. Mix 80 oz of dark chocolate and a quarter of a pint of cream.
2. If you are five foot tall and weigh 13 stone, then you are overweight !
3. Tomorrow, temperatures will be in the low 50s, but might reach 60°F in Cornwall.
4. Go on for about two miles, then turn right into the steep path leading up to the church. You are 1,200 feet up and the view is spectacular.

3. Chiffres

Âge

Mary is twenty-two (years old). Or : Mary is twenty-two years of age.
A boy of eight.
A forty-six year old man. (Notez bien que *'year'* est au singulier puisqu'il fait partie d'une expression qui fonctionne comme adjectif.)

The over sixties/the under eighteens (= l'ensemble de ceux qui ont plus de 60 ans/moins de 18 ans)
A woman in her thirties. (*between 30 and 39*)
He is in his early thirties. (*between 30 and 35*)
She is in her late sixties. (*between 65 and 69*)
A man in his mid-seventies. (*around 75*)
A boy still in his teens. (*between 10 and 19*)

CHIFFRES

100 se lit *a hundred* ou *one hundred.*
1,000 se lit a *thousand* ou *one thousand.*
1,562 se lit : *one thousand, five hundred and sixty-two.*
(Lorsque *hundred, thousand, million…* sont précédés d'un nombre ou d'un adjectif, ils sont invariables (*two hundred women, several thousand inhabitants* MAIS *millions of voters, hundreds of children*).
23,560,000 people (= 23 560 000 en français, sans virgule) se lit : *twenty three million five hundred and sixty thousand people.*

→ A billion = un million de millions en anglais britannique
= mille millions en anglais américain

6.71 (= 6,71 en français) se lit *six point seven one* (on prononce chaque chiffre des décimales séparément).
→ Notez l'utilisation du point en anglais à la place de la virgule en français.
→ Au delà de 1 l'expression devient un pluriel en anglais : 1.33 miles

3.61 % (se lit : *three point six one per cent*)
1/2 se lit *a half* ou *one half*
2/3 se lit *two-thirds*
3/4 se lit *three quarters*
1/8 se lit *an eighth*
6 1/2 se lit *six and a half*
I got 7/20 in German ! se lit *seven out of twenty*
Three in ten of the students come from abroad.

→ On utilise les chiffres ordinaux lorsqu'on lit les noms de souverains.
Elizabeth II se lit *Elizabeth the second.*
George III se lit *George the third.*

LE CHIFFRE 0

- dans un nombre : *nought* – *11. 03* se lit : *eleven point nought three*, mais 0 peut aussi se lire comme la lettre « o ».)
- dans des mesures ou notes : *zero*
- températures : 6° (se lit : *six degrees above zero*)

- dans un numéro de téléphone : o (comme la lettre) – *01 23 66 78* (se lit o *one two three double six seven eight.*)
- au tennis : *love – He's won* 6-0 6-0. (se lit *six love*)
- dans les autres sports : *nil – Scotland beat Wales five* 5-0. (se lit *five nil*)

Numéros de téléphone

Chaque numéro est prononcé séparément : 01 43 22 78 se lit o *one four three two two seven eight.*

Additions, divisions, soustractions, multiplications

$2 + 5 = 7$ se lit *two plus (and) five is (equals) seven.*
$9 - 3 = 6$ se lit : *nine minus three is (equals) six.*
$10 \div 5 = 2$ se lit : *ten divided by five is (equals)* two.
$4 \times 4 = 16$ se lit : *four times four (four multiplied by four) is (equals) sixteen*
$x > 3$ se lit : *x is greater than 3.*
$x \leqslant 3$ se lit : *x is greater than or equal to three.*
$x < 3$ se lit : *x is less than 3.*
x^2 se lit : *x squared.*
x^3 se lit : *x cubed.*
x^5 se lit : *x to the power of five.*

Statistiques

Between 2000 and 2003.../Over a period of two years.../
...figures rose/grew/increased/went up/sky-rocketed BY 10 %/ / FROM 10 % TO 20 %.
...figures fell/decreased/went down/dropped/plummeted BY 5,000/from 3,000 to 2,000.
There was an increase/decrease IN sales.
It was an increase OF 12 %.
(Notez la différence : *AN increase OF.../to increase BY...*)

The figure is half as high as it was last year. (deux fois moins élevé)
The figure is twice/three times/ten times.. as high as it was in 1998.
There are three times as many inhabitants in this town as there were 50 years ago.
There is four times as much pollution in this town as there was 50 years ago.
Between 1995 and 1998, it increased twofold (= it doubled)/threefold (= it tripled), tenfold (it was multiplied by 10).

Statistics can be presented in a table (un tableau), *in a pie chart* (un camembert), *in a graph* (un graphique) *or in a map.*

Quelques adverbes...

The figure is hardly, scarcely, barely higher than last year. (à peine)
The figure is dramatically, significantly, markedly, substantially higher than last year.

exercices

1 Lisez à haute voix les phrases qui suivent.

(1) In that country, some 1, 581, 000 people – or 11.2 % of the population – live on less than $1 a day.

(2) Our new postal code is 75005 and the telephone number 01 43 77 02.

(3) In maths, I got a 15/20, a 16/20 and a 6/20, so that I was given 12.33 for the whole term.

(4) (Heard on BBC radio) Last night, Italy beat Spain 3-2 in Milan and John Kilman beat the European record with a time of 21.2 seconds.

(5) 72 × 13 = 935

(6) 9682 − 650 = 9032

(7) 7068 ÷ 42 = 168.28

(8) 651 is an odd number; 76 is an even number.

2 Lisez à haute voix l'extrait suivant du *Financial Times*.

NUMBERS TALK SIMON BRISCOE

A woman's world

→ Women make up 12 per cent of the members in the world's 176 parliaments – up from 7 per cent in 61 parliaments in 1955

→ 11 out of 180 countries are headed by a woman

→ 70m girls and 60m boys are growing up without education

→ Two-thirds of the 850m illiterate people in the world are women – they outnumber males in every region of the world

→ The female illiteracy rate is 30 per cent worldwide but just over 60 per cent in Southern Asia and 55 per cent in Arab states

→ At least one in three women are married before they are 20 years old in three out of five countries in Southern Asia, and in 11 out of 30 countries in sub-Saharan Africa

→ One in three managerial and administrative jobs is filled by women in the developed world compared with one in seven in Africa and Asia

→ Women receive one-third of earned income

→ Two-thirds of women in developing countries work in agriculture compared to 7 per cent in developed countries

The Financial Times, February 22-3, 2003.

3 Faites correspondre les courbes et les phrases.

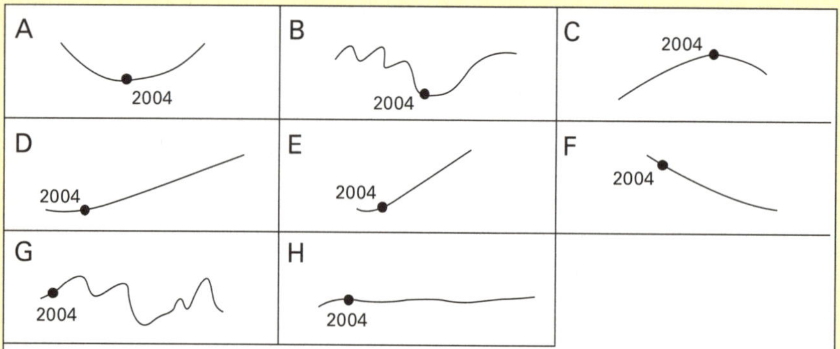

1. Exportations reached a peak in 2004.
2. Exportations stagnated / remained stable after 2004.
3. Exportations fluctuated after 2004.
4. Exportations picked up after 2004.
5. Exportations reached an all-time low in 2004.
6. Exportations soared after 2004.
7. Exportations plummeted (plunged) after 2004.
8. Exportations rose steadily after 2004.

4 Regardez les statistiques ci-dessous concernant le droit de vote (*franchise*) en Grande-Bretagne, et complétez les phrases qui suivent.

Date	Electors (% of the population over 20)	
1831	5.0	1832 : First Reform Act
1832	7.1	
1864	9.0	1867 : Second Reform Act
1868	16.4	
1883	18.0	
1886	28.5	
1914	30.0	1918 : Representation of the People Act
1921	74.0	(universal male suffrage ; women over 30 can vote)
1927	74.0	1928 : Women over 21 can vote.
1931	96.9	

(1) Between 1864 and 1883, the number of electors increased …
(2) The figure for 1931 is more than … as it was in 1914.
(3) Between 1831 and 1832, the number of electors … … 5.0 … 7.1.
(4) Between 1832 and 1931, the number of electors rose … more than 10 %.
(5) … a period of six years, the figure remained stable.

5 Traduisez les phrases suivantes.

(1) La dépression a touché la plupart des Américains pendant les années 30.

(2) C'est gratuit pour les moins de quatorze ans.

(3) Elle doit avoir dans les 45 ans, mais elle ne fait pas son âge.

(4) S'il a une mère de 36 ans, il ne peut pas en avoir 35 !

II Analyser

I Documents écrits

1. De la lecture à l'analyse

Voici quelques réflexes essentiels lorsque vous lisez un texte, que ce soit pour le plaisir, pour l'analyser ou pour le traduire.

1 – Le sens global du texte

1 Déterminez la nature du document que vous allez lire. S'agit-il d'une lettre, d'un poème, d'un passage de roman, d'un article de journal, d'un extrait de pièce de théâtre ? La mise en page *(the layout)*, les photos, le titre du journal et/ou du texte, le nom de l'auteur, la date de publication doivent vous aider : ne négligez donc pas tous ces indices, qui peuvent vous permettre d'anticiper le contenu du texte.

2 Lisez le texte une ou deux fois. Cette première lecture doit vous permettre de comprendre le texte globalement et de répondre assez généralement aux questions qui suivent (même si toutes les questions ne s'appliquent pas à tous les textes).
→ *WHO?* (Qui sont les personnages principaux du texte ? Combien sont-ils ? Quel est le rapport entre eux ? Qui est le narrateur ?)
→ *WHAT?* (Que se passe-t-il dans le texte ? Comment pouvez-vous résumer l'action, les événements ou le message ?)
→ *WHERE?* (Où la scène se passe-t-elle ? Y a-t-il plusieurs lieux ? Le lieu est-il important ou non ?)
→ *WHEN?* (Quand la scène se passe-t-elle ? Quand le texte a-t-il été écrit ? Ces deux temps sont-ils les mêmes ?)
→ *WHY?* (Comment pouvez-vous expliquer les événements ou les actions des personnages ?)

À ce stade, vous devez également avoir une idée générale de l'organisation du texte. S'agit-il d'une organisation logique ? chronologique ? autre ? Quels sont les mots de liaison qui soulignent cette organisation ?

Cette approche globale du sens doit vous donner un cadre qui aidera une deuxième lecture, plus approfondie et nécessaire pour toute analyse.

2 – Apprendre à inférer

On peut certes lire un texte en s'arrêtant à chaque fois que l'on trouve un mot difficile afin de regarder son sens dans un dictionnaire. Mais lire un texte long de cette façon risque fort d'être vite décourageant. Il faut donc apprendre à inférer, c'est-à-dire à deviner le sens global des mots inconnus. Ceci vous permettra non seulement de lire plus vite, mais aussi de réfléchir à la valeur des mots. Vous pourrez ainsi n'avoir recours au dictionnaire que lorsque le sens d'un mot qui semble important vous échappe totalement ou lorsque vous cherchez un sens précis.

Comment inférer ?

- Déterminez tout d'abord la catégorie grammaticale du mot (adjectif, verbe, nom, adverbe…).
- Demandez-vous si la formation du mot peut vous aider (y a-t-il un suffixe ? est-ce un nom ou un adjectif composé ?).

P. 245-248 (LA DÉRIVATION)

- Regardez le contexte du mot (la phrase, le paragraphe, la structure logique du texte), afin de faire une déduction logique quant à son sens.

Dans la phrase qui suit, imaginons que vous ne connaissiez pas le sens des trois mots en caractères gras.

exemple

> OBESITY
> British **waistlines** are expanding so fast that three quarters of the population could suffer the ill effects of excess weight within 10 to 15 years, and obesity could **overtake** smoking as Britain's single biggest **preventable** killer.

1 ***waistlines*** : il s'agit d'un nom, au pluriel. Il est formé de *waist* + *line*. Si vous connaissez le mot *waist*, vous avez compris le sens de *waistline*. Sinon, il vous reste la possibilité de réfléchir grâce au contexte : qu'est-ce qui peut s'élargir, augmenter quand on prend du poids ? Ceci doit vous conduire au sens : taille, tour de taille, ligne.

2 ***overtake*** : il s'agit d'un verbe, qui apparaît ici après un modal sous sa forme de base verbale. Sa formation, à l'aide du préfixe *over*, peut vous suggérer l'idée de quelque chose en trop, d'un dépassement, sens que l'on trouve, par exemple dans le verbe *overflow* (déborder). Quant au contexte, il vous montre que l'obésité pourrait bientôt tuer encore plus que la cigarette. Ceci vous conduit au sens de « passer devant la cigarette (comme cause de mortalité) ».

3 ***preventable*** : il s'agit d'un adjectif, qui qualifie *killer*. C'est ici la formation du mot qui peut le mieux vous aider à comprendre son sens : *prevent* + suffixe *able*, qui indique la possibilité (*eatable* = *eat* + *able* = qui peut être mangé, mangeable, comestible). *To prevent* signifie empêcher. *Preventable*, c'est donc qui peut être empêché, évitable.

Vous pouvez ainsi déduire le sens global d'un bon nombre de mots du texte.

3 – Apprendre à repérer

Lorsque vous êtes confrontés à des phrases complexes, il vous faut repérer les éléments essentiels de cette phrase, c'est à dire **le sujet, le verbe principal et le complément**. Soulignez-les, puis repérez les propositions **relatives**, circonstancielles, **concessives**, etc. Une telle habitude facilitera considérablement votre lecture.

exemple

> Yet Queen Elizabeth II, who celebrates her birthday on April 21st, attracts almost no hostility from mainstream politicians or the press, despite being born into a job that is subsidized, extravagant and seems largely pointless.
>
> *The Economist*, April 22, 2006.

N'oubliez pas également que dans un groupe nominal le nom vient en dernier, souvent précédé de plusieurs adjectifs. Recherchez donc en priorité le nom pour comprendre l'expression. L'expression *these unfair new American immigration laws* décrit avant tout des lois (*laws*). Puis en lisant de droite à gauche vous pouvez préciser le sens : des lois sur l'immigration, des lois qui sont américaines, qui viennent d'être votées, qui ne sont pas justes (*unfair*).

4 – Lecture rapide et lecture continue

Une compréhension globale et superficielle du texte est parfois suffisante, par exemple, pour des activités de *scanning* et de *skimming*.
– *scanning* (= lecture rapide d'un texte pour y trouver une information spécifique)
– *skimming* (= lecture rapide d'un texte pour se faire une idée de son contenu)

Ces deux activités vous obligent à lire vite, en repérant mentalement les mots-clés et les phrases-clés du texte. Elles mettent donc en œuvre des compétences qui vous seront également utiles lors d'une lecture suivie, celle d'une nouvelle ou d'un roman par exemple. En effet, il est nécessaire pour ce type de lecture, de ne pas s'arrêter, de ne pas se bloquer devant un mot inconnu, mais de se raccrocher au contraire à ce qui est connu dans le paragraphe pour comprendre le sens du texte et continuer à lire. Plus on lit ainsi, plus le sens des mots s'affine peu à peu et plus la syntaxe vous devient familière.

5 – Lecture plus approfondie

Il est souvent impossible de s'en tenir à une compréhension globale du texte, tout particulièrement lorsque votre travail doit déboucher sur une analyse du texte. Vous devez alors relire le texte plusieurs fois afin de bien comprendre son organisation et son sens. Votre lecture doit maintenant être critique, aidée par un repérage des éléments importants du texte. C'est à ce stade qu'il est nécessaire de souligner, de surligner et d'entourer, à l'aide de couleurs différentes, les éléments signifiants du texte.

Par exemple :

→ Mettez en valeur la structure du texte, et demandez-vous en quoi elle est intéressante.
→ Étudiez le point de vue.
→ Repérez les champs lexicaux et les réseaux d'images : ils doivent vous aider à comprendre le sens profond du texte, surtout lorsqu'il s'agit d'un texte littéraire.
→ Si vous travaillez sur un article de journal, faites un repérage de tous les mots ou effets rhétoriques qui peuvent vous aider à percevoir le point de vue et le parti pris du journaliste.

Les parties qui suivent (Article de journal, Fiction, Poésie, Théâtre) vous donneront plus de détails sur cette partie du travail.

Cette étape est essentielle avant que vous ne puissiez organiser vos idées en un commentaire.

exercices

1 Lisez l'article de journal qui suit une première fois, sans vous attarder sur les mots que vous ne comprenez pas, puis répondez aux questions.

'Marry the man we chose, or you are dead to us'

To her parents, Jasvinder Sanghera has been dead for more than 20 years. At 15 she escaped from an upstairs window to escape an arranged marriage and a family obsessed with honour. "When I was 14 my family showed me a photograph of a Sikh man and I was told that this was the man I was going to marry," she told *The Times*. "They told me that if I didn't do it I would be dishonouring my family."
Despite begging her parents, originally from the Punjab region in India, not to force her to marry the stranger, they announced plans to fly her to Germany for the wedding.
"I ran away to Newcastle. I contacted my parents and told them that I wanted to return, hoping that they would have realised that it was a definite no to the marriage. My mum said, 'If you come back you marry the person we have proposed for you or you are dead in our eyes'."
It was only when her elder sister, Robina, committed suicide after being trapped in an arranged marriage that she had limited contact with her parents. Ms Sanghera, now 39, has dedicated her life to tackling honour crimes in the Asian community. She was named hero of the month in *Marie Claire* magazine and received *The Times* and Natwest Community Enterprise Award for her work for disadvantaged people. The mother of three now lives in Derby.

▲ *The Times*, December 7, 2004.

- WHO?
- AGE?
  Now:
  Then:
- WHERE?
- WHEN?
- WHAT?
- WHY?

2 **Inférez le sens des mots en gras dans le passage qui suit.**

(The passage takes place in Malaysia, in a far-away British station, where the two British representatives hate each other.)

After this Mr Warburton **seldom** saw Cooper, and never spoke to him. He read his *Times* every morning, did his work at the office, took his exercise, dressed for dinner, dined, and sat by the river smoking his cheroot. If by chance he ran across Cooper he **cut him dead**. Each, though never for a moment unconscious of the **propinquity**, acted as though the other did not exist. Time did nothing to **assuage** their animosity. They watched one another's actions and each knew what the other did. [...] At the beginning of the year Cooper **went down with** fever, and when Mr Warburton caught sight of him again he was surprised to see how thin he had grown. He looked ill and **worn**. The solitude, so much more unnatural because it was due to no necessity, was getting on his nerves. It was getting on Mr Warburton's too, and often he could not sleep at night. He lay awake **brooding**. Cooper was drinking heavily and surely the breaking point was near, but in his dealings with the natives he took care to do nothing that might expose him to his chief's **rebuke**. They fought a grim and silent battle with one another. It was a test of endurance. The months passed, and neither gave sign of weakening. They were like men **dwelling** in regions of eternal night, and their souls were oppressed with the knowledge that never would the day **dawn** for them.

W.S. Somerset Maugham, The Outstation, *The Complete Short Stories*, 1951; AP Watt Ltd.

seldom: ☐ perhaps ☐ rarely ☐ often ☐ always
cut him dead: ☐ did not see him ☐ did not speak to him ☐ killed him ☐ pretended not to see him
propinquity: ☐ proposition ☐ proximity ☐ difference ☐ similarity
assuage: ☐ reduce ☐ increase ☐ change ☐ help
went down with: ☐ stopped having ☐ left with ☐ was ill with ☐ stopped working because of

worn: ☐ excited ☐ very tired ☐ irritated ☐ angry
brooding: ☐ dreaming ☐ reading ☐ having dark thoughts ☐ hoping
rebuke: ☐ interest ☐ consideration ☐ thanks ☐ reprimand
dwelling: ☐ sleeping ☐ forgetting ☐ living ☐ remembering
dawn: ☐ decide ☐ disappear ☐ end ☐ appear

3 **Un certain nombre de mots ont été enlevés dans le texte qui suit. Pouvez-vous retrouver ces mots ou des mots de sens équivalent ? Cet exercice doit vous montrer que même lorsqu'un mot sur dix environ est enlevé (ou est inconnu), vous pouvez tout de même comprendre le sens global d'un texte.**

Freak storm leaves a trail of destruction, with streets closed and trains cancelled, report Alan Hamilton and Steve Bird

Shop fronts blown out, roofs (1) clean off, trees crashing, firefighters and ambulance crews (2) the damage and the injured. This was Birmingham (3) after 3pm yesterday.

It was not a terrorist (4) that struck the Moseley and Kings Heath areas, (5) of the city centre, in the (6) of a thunderstorm; it was a small but (7) tornado.

Within ten minutes it was all over, but the freak (8) left a trail of damage and so many (9) that paramedics had to set up an emergency triage (10) at the scene. At least a dozen (11) were taken to hospital, although only one was (12) to be seriously injured. More than 50 ambulance (13) responded to a huge number of emergency (14).

Streets were closed and trains, (15) to negotiate excessive water on the tracks, (16). For a few frightening minutes the air was (17) with flying debris. Children spoke of being lifted off their (18).

▲ *The Times*, Friday July 29, 2005.

(1) ....
(2) ....
(3) ....
(4) ....
(5) ....
(6) ....
(7) ....
(8) ....
(9) ....
(10) ....
(11) ....
(12) ....
(13) ....
(14) ....
(15) ....
(16) ....
(17) ....
(18) ....

4 Lisez rapidement les petits articles qui suivent et choisissez le titre qui résume le mieux l'information principale.

For every woman who dies in a so-called honour killing, there are1,000 living in fear of attack, District Judge Marilyn Mornington, chairman of a conference on the problem, said in Leeds. About 12 women a year in the UK are thought to die in honour killings. Ms Mornington called for a law to outlaw forced marriages.

▲ *The Independent*, July 21, 2006.

A. Call for law on forced marriages
B. Forced marriages to be banned
C. 1,000 women fear being attacked

An endangered Bolivian squirrel monkey which was stolen from a zoo has been found safe and well. The monkey, named SpongeBob, was found playing with children in Clapham, south London. He was stolen two days earlier from Chessington World of Adventures.

▲ *The Independent*, July 21, 2006.

A. Monkey stolen from zoo
B. Rare monkey recaptured
C. Squirrel monkey found playing with children

Berlin A stuntman drowned while trying to escape from a car that he had driven into a canal during the making of a German television film. The man, aged 39, was supposed to climb free as the car sank. Divers pulled him out and paramedics tried to revive him. Work on the film was suspended. (AP)

▲ *The Independent*, July 21, 2006.

A. A difficult escape
B. TV stunt death
C. TV film suspended

A scientist died from carbon monoxide poisoning as he stirred a large batch of marmalade on a stove, his brother said yesterday. Keith Turnbull, 61, a biochemist, collapsed in the kitchen of his home near Wark, Northumberland, in December last year. An inquest in Hexham last week recorded a verdict of accidental death. His dog Cleugh also died in the accident.

▲ *The Independent*, April 6, 2004.

A. Scientist dies during experiment
B. Scientist dies making marmalade
C. Carbon monoxide in marmalade

A burglar who stole a parrot from a pet shop was traced after it bit him, leaving a trail of blood from which police took his DNA. Tristan Maidment, 23, took Micky the macaw, described as a "miserable old git" by its owner. Maidment admitted burglary and animal cruelty at Frome magistrates court in Somerset.

The Independent, July 21, 2006.

A. Parrot bites man
B. Parrot's DNA helps police
C. Stolen parrot helps police

2. Analyser un article de journal

1 – Comment lire un article

■ **Avant de lire l'article :** utilisez tous les éléments autres que le texte pour vous renseigner sur l'article.

• Regardez le nom du journal ou du magazine. Est-il britannique ? américain ? Est-ce un journal d'information sérieux, est-il politiquement tendancieux ? Est-ce un quotidien, un hebdomadaire, un mensuel ? Quand l'article a-t-il été publié ? La date est-elle importante ?

• Regardez le titre de l'article. Vous aide-t-il à comprendre son contenu ? Contient-il un jeu de mot *(a pun)* ou une allusion culturelle ?

• L'article est-il accompagné d'une illustration (photo, dessin humoristique) ? Est-ce que la photo ou la légende *(the caption)* du dessin vous aident à comprendre le sujet de l'article ?

■ **Le gros titre *(the headline)*.**

Les gros titres ont un double but :
– donner au lecteur une idée du contenu de l'article ;
– faire en sorte très souvent qu'on ait envie de lire l'article (en utilisant l'humour, le suspense ou d'autres éléments accrocheurs).

Les gros titres peuvent être difficiles à comprendre. N'oubliez pas que :
– Ils contiennent souvent des passifs (qui permettent de ne pas mentionner l'agent ou la source de l'information).
→ *DOCTOR IS STRUCK OFF* (*strike off* : radier quelqu'un d'une profession)
– On y utilise souvent le présent, même pour parler de faits passés. Comparez, par exemple, le titre qui suit et la première phrase de l'article :
→ *BOY DIES IN ISRAELI RAID A 14-year-old was killed yesterday when…*

– Les articles et l'auxiliaire *to be* sont souvent omis.

→ *FIRST GM FIELDS TO BE PLANTED* = *The first GM fields are to be planted.* (GM = *genetically modified* = « OMG »). Notez l'utilisation de « *be to* » (*are to be planted*) pour parler d'un événement prévu.

– Ils sont souvent formés d'une série de noms, et il faut donc chercher à comprendre leur rapport. Il est souvent nécessaire de partir du dernier nom, puis de considérer ceux qui précèdent (et qui ont donc valeur d'adjectifs).

→ *SNIFFER DOG HUNT FOR CHARLOTTE* = *hunt by sniffer dog* (chien renifleur)

– Ils contiennent souvent des allusions et jeux de mots, particulièrement dans les magazines.

→ SHEIKH-UP

Il s'agit d'un article sur les souverains du Golfe (*Sheikhs*), et sur le fait que plusieurs d'entre eux sont récemment morts, d'où le jeu de mot, puisque *a shake up* c'est une réorganisation, un remaniement.

Le titre est souvent suivi d'un chapeau (*a lead-in*), qui résume l'information principale du texte. Dans l'article cité plus haut, le chapeau qui suit le titre est *Monarchs of the Gulf have been proving mortal.*

■ Le premier paragraphe.

La plupart des premiers paragraphes :
– résument l'information principale
– ou donnent un exemple qui illustre l'idée principale de l'article.
L'une de ces deux méthodes est-elle utilisée dans l'article que vous étudiez ?

Après avoir lu le titre et le premier paragraphe, vous devriez donc connaître le sujet de l'article et son idée principale.

■ Le reste de l'article.

Le reste de l'article donne des exemples ainsi que des informations et arguments supplémentaires.

Étudiez ensuite la façon dont l'article est organisé. Soulignez les mots de liaison et les mots clés qui révèlent cette organisation.

exemple Voici la façon dont un article est organisé.

→ **Le titre :**
– résume l'information principale de l'article ;
– mais est amusant car la question reflète une certaine incrédulité : New York et politesse sont des mots qui ne vont pas ensemble. D'où le contraste entre les deux parties du titre et la surprise qu'apporte le mot *mandate*.

→ **Le premier paragraphe** résume l'opinion générale : les New-Yorkais sont peu polis, et donne 4 exemples de grossièreté.

→ **Les deux paragraphes suivants** (introduits par *BUT*) annoncent l'adoption de lois pour lutter contre la grossièreté et donnent trois exemples (sports/voiture/métro).

Polite Behavior in New York? New Laws Mandate[1] It

By Winnie Hu

NEW YORK — New Yorkers are known to throw things onto the field during baseball games at Yankee Stadium. They boo their own mayor at parades. Some refuse to surrender their seats to pregnant women on the subway, while others cut in line and never apologize.

But somehow a city whose residents have long been scorned for churlish[2] behavior is being praised for adopting rules and laws that govern personal conduct, making New York an unlikely model for legislating courtesy and decorum.

From tighter restrictions on sports fans and car alarms to a new, $50 fine on subway riders who rest their feet on a seat, New York's efforts to curb everyday annoyances and foster more civility among its residents have increasingly been studied far from home.

When Boston and San Francisco law-makers considered silencing cellphones in their theaters, they, too, looked to New York, which imposed a $50 fine in 2003 on callers who brazenly dial up during movies, concerts and Broadway shows.

And when community groups sought new ways to fight graffiti, they saw that New York passed a law in January making building owners responsible for cleaning up after the vandals.

Under Mayor Michael R. Bloomberg, the city has increasingly focused on social policies once thought to be beyond the realm of government. Mr. Bloomberg was largely responsible for the city's smoking ban in bars, restaurants and night-clubs. He also overhauled[3] the city's noise code for the first time in three decades, taking aim at loud nightclubs, barking dogs and even a staple of summer, the ice cream truck.

The crackdowns have left others wondering if the metropolis once known as Fun City is fun no more. "It sounds like your City Council is getting really uptight[4]," said Aaron Peskin, a member of the San Francisco Board of Supervisors. "It all seems a little overwrought[5]."

Letitia Baldrige, the White House social secretary during the Kennedy years, was happy to hear about the effort. "Most people just seem to ignore common sense and common courtesy so it does have to be legislated," she said. "To have this happen in New York is going to inspire a lot of other people, I cannot applaud it enough."

▲ *The New York Times*, in *Le Monde*, 22 Avril, 2006.

1. **mandate:** *rendre obligatoire.*
2. **churlish:** *grossier*.
3. **overhaul:** *réviser, remanier.*
4. **uptight:** *too conventional.*
5. **overwrought:** *overdone.*

→ **Les deux paragraphes suivants** développent l'idée introduite dans le second paragraphe : New York est devenu un *model*.

– exemple de Boston et de San Francisco

– exemple des *community groups* (associations de résidents)

→ **Le paragraphe qui suit** explique le contexte historique et la politique du maire, Michael R. Bloomberg.

→ **Les deux derniers paragraphes** présentent des opinions : contre (avant-dernier paragraphe) ; pour (dernier paragraphe).

■ Le but de l'article

• L'article est-il neutre ou à sensation ?
• Est-il objectif (son but étant d'informer le lecteur) ou tendancieux, non objectif (*biased*) ? S'il est tendancieux, quel point de vue le journaliste défend-il ?
• Quels mots, quels éléments vous permettent-ils de dire que le journaliste n'est pas objectif ? (Utilisation de mots dépréciatifs ou indûment flatteurs, insinuations, mots vagues pour éviter de citer la source de son information...)
• Pour quel type de lecteurs le journaliste écrit-il ? (cultivés ? D'une tendance politique bien précise ?

■ Votre opinion

Si l'article est objectif, présente-t-il les faits de façon claire ? Est-il complet et détaillé ? Laisse-t-il plusieurs questions sans réponse ? Si l'article n'est pas objectif, le trouvez-vous convaincant ? Le journaliste a-t-il atteint son but ?

2 – COMMENT FAIRE UN COMMENTAIRE D'ARTICLE

Il se fait en cinq étapes principales :

■ **1.** Introduction
– Expliquez la source de l'article, la nature de cette source (par exemple journal pro-conservateurs ou pro-travaillistes), la date à laquelle il a été publié.
– Cet article s'inscrit-il dans une controverse, un mouvement d'idées, une tendance, un contexte particulier... à l'époque où il a été écrit ?
– Présentez les grandes lignes de votre plan.

■ **2.** Utilisez les pages 102 à 105 ci-dessus pour présenter l'article et résumer son contenu. Un résumé doit être neutre et objectif. Ne donnez pas votre opinion dans cette première partie du commentaire. Vous devez simplement chercher à donner à celui qui vous lit ou vous écoute une idée bien claire du contenu de l'article.

■ **3.** Après avoir présenté l'article, analysez-le. Expliquez le but du journaliste, la façon dont il présente l'information, son objectivité ou son manque d'objectivité, le type de lecteurs pour lequel il/elle écrit. Justifiez votre opinion le plus souvent possible en citant le texte.

■ **4.** Discutez l'article, c'est-à-dire commentez la méthode utilisée par le journaliste et la question dont il parle. Trouvez-vous l'article convaincant ? Le journaliste a-t-il laissé de côté des aspects importants de la question ? Êtes-vous d'accord avec son point de vue ? Afin d'expliquer votre opinion, donnez d'autres exemples en utilisant ce que vous savez du contexte social ou culturel.

■ **5.** Conclusion
Résumez les grands points de votre commentaire puis ouvrez le débat sur un point plus large à l'aide d'une question par exemple.

exercices

Les gros titres

1 Quels mots ont-ils été omis dans les gros titres suivants ?

LONGEST MARRIAGE IN WORLD (*The Times*, July 22, 2006)

PARENTS TO PAY FOR THEIR CHILDREN'S SINS (*The Times*, July 21, 2006)

EX-BUTLER JAILED (*The Scotsman*, July 28, 2006)

BROTHERS HELD OVER BOMBAY TRAIN BLASTS (*The Times*, July 28, 2006)

2 À l'aide de phrases complètes, récrivez les gros titres suivants pour expliquer leur sens.

TORIES AT 13-YEAR HIGH, POLL SHOWS (*The Guardian*, July 27, 2006)

OLYMPIC MEDALS THIEF LOCKED UP (*The Scotsman*, July 28, 2006)

GREECE TRANSFIXED BY BOY MURDER CASE (*The Times*, July 28, 2006)

CYCLE NUMBERPLATE PLANS TO CATCH LAWLESS RIDERS
(*The Times*, July 28, 2006)

BLAIR IN CONFLICT CEASEFIRE HOPE (*The Times*, July 28, 2006)
(About the conflict between Israel and Lebanon)

3 Quels jeux de mots ou allusions culturelles les titres suivants contiennent-ils ?

LEONARDO WAS DRIVEN TO INVENT THE CAR (*The Times*, April 24, 2004)

TOWER OF BABEL (*The Economist*, March 11, 2006)
(An article about too much talk and not enough done in the building of the Freedom Tower, America's tallest building, which is to replace the destroyed World Trade Center in New York.)

LAW AND DISORDER (*The Economist*, April 29, 2006)

4 Choisissez le titre le mieux approprié à chaque article.

1. BERLIN A German soccer club is to open a cemetery next to its stadium so devoted fans can rest in peace beside their favourite team. Hamburg SV [...] plans the graveyard 50 ft from the main entrance. The club's deputy chairman Christian Reichert, said: "For many people, it's important to be close to the club after their lives are over. The cemetery will look like a small, open stadium."

▲ *The Independent*, July 21, 2006.

(a) A CEMETERY LIKE A STADIUM
(b) NEW CEMETERY TO OPEN
(c) A CEMETERY FOR SOCCER FANS

2. More than 20 workers at B & Q's store in Clacton, Essex, were taken to hospital yesterday after becoming ill following a spillage of formic acid. Two people were detained in hospital after developing breathing problems. The store was closed for the day.

▲ *The Observer*, July 23, 2006.

(a) 20 WORKERS IN HOSPITAL
(b) ACID SPILL AFFECTS WORKERS
(c) ESSEX STORE CLOSED

3. A dog which saved the lives of two sailors in the Second World War was yesterday posthumously awarded the equivalent of the animals'George Cross. Bamse the St Bernard received the PDSA gold medal for gallantry and devotion.

▲ *The Observer*, July 23, 2006.

(a) DOG SAVES SAILORS
(b) WAR DOG RECEIVES MEDAL
(c) DEVOTED ST BERNARD

L'organisation

5 **Read the article quickly, and try to understand its global meaning.**

THE QUEEN AT 80

Revolution postponed

Why the monarchy is stronger today than ten years ago

For most of its history, Britain's monarchy has attracted a healthy amount of criticism and satire. Kings have repeatedly been lampooned[1] as lazy, ineffectual, greedy, vain or stupid. When King George IV, who was thought to possess most of these vices, died in 1930, the *Times* reckoned that "there never was an individual less regretted by his fellow creatures than this deceased king." Yet Queen Elizabeth II, who celebrates her birthday on April 21st, attracts almost no hostility from mainstream politicians or the press, despite being born into a job that is subsidised, extravagant and seems largely pointless. To mark the event, the BBC even broadcast a laudatory documentary showing a hard-working queen busily representing the nation to itself, which is what monarchists argue the institution is for.

Compare the fortunes of the monarchy with those of another established institution with an ambient role, the Church of England, and it becomes clear that the royal family is doing rather well. It has recovered from a Princess Diana–fuelled dip in the late 1990s: polls show that more people now think the monarchy will be around in ten years time. Yet attendance at Church of England services has continued to decline. Why is the queen prospering while the Church (outside its cathedrals and evangelical movement) languishes?

One reason is that the monarchy thrives[2] on indifference, while the Church is hurt by it. That might sound odd, given that evidence of interest in the royal family is everywhere: over a million people turned out in London for the queen's golden jubilee; dreary books about royals easily outsell ones about elected politicians; and the young royal princes fill the newspapers. But this fascination does not run very deep. According to one poll, only 10% of people aged between 16 and 24 think the monarchy is important to their lives. But because the royal family is the monopoly provider of a something trivial, it hardly seems worth opposing. The Church, by contrast, offers a vital service to its 1.7 m members – spiritual succour – and operates in a competitive confessional market where dissatisfied Christians can shop around. Indifference is thus a threat.

A second reason is that the queen's avoidance of controversy (she never expresses political views) and of the press has reinforced the institution she embodies. She never gives interviews, modelling her media strategy on that of her mother, who gave an interview in 1923 but apparently did not enjoy the experience and kept quiet for the rest of her life. (This was probably wise: Cecil Beaton's diaries describe her as "a marshmallow[3] made on a welding machine[4]".) One executive of a tabloid newspaper argues that this has enhanced the queen's mystique, comparing her with other celebrities who risk irritating their audience through over-exposure. The Church, on the other hand, cannot avoid damaging controversies even when it wants to, as the divisive row over ordaining gay priests reveals.

Third, the monarchy has benefited from a decline in party allegiance and a dilution of ideology in British politics that has not similarly helped the Church. Vigorous anti-monarchism was associated with the hard left, and has atrophied with it. Britain has only one sizeable anti-monarchy club these days – Republic, which has a thousand members – yet when the Prince of Wales had marital problems in the 1870s, 84 were founded.

Vernon Bogdanor, of Oxford University, argues that the decline of party allegiance has also increased the appeal of a non-partisan head of state. The same is not true for the Church. While the Conservative Party had 2.5m members (as it did at its peak), the notion that the Church was the Tory party at prayer did not imply empty pews. Now the Conservatives have only around 250,000 members, it does. Game, set and match to the Windsors.

▲ *The Economist*, April 22, 2006.

1. **lampooned:** attacked.
2. **thrives:** prospers.
3. **marshmallow:** *guimauve.*
4. **a welding machine:** *un chalumeau.*

– Which of the following best sums up the main idea of the article?
  - the subject (above the title)
  - the title
  - the lead-in
  - the first sentence
– What is the monarchy compared with throughout the article?
– Which of the two institutions has been more successful recently?

6 The following table represents the structure of the article and highlights its link words. Read the article a second time and fill in the table, giving titles to the two parts and short summaries of each part and sub-part.

I. ....

1. ....

Yet ....

2. ....

Yet ....

II. ....

1. ....

by contrast ....

2. ....

on the other hand ....

3. ....

the same is not true ....

L'objectivité

7 Les gros titres qui suivent sont-ils objectifs (*objective*) ou non (*biased*) ? Dans le second cas, soulignez les mots qui expliquent votre point de vue.

a. MAN IN COURT OVER TERRORISM LINK (*The Observer*, July 23, 2006)

b. THE SUMMIT FAILS. WAR RAGES (*The Guardian*, July 27, 2006)

c. PRINCE HURRY MANIAC[1] DRIVER (*The Sun*, July 29, 2006)

d. PROTEST IN DUBLIN OVER MIDDLE EAST CONFLICT (*The Guardian*, July 29, 2006)

e. RUMSFELD MUST QUIT OVER ABUSE (*The Observer*, April 9, 2004)

1. **maniac:** behaving wildly, mad.

Voici une première page du *Daily Express* (April 23, 2004)

DAILY EXPRESS

The World's Greatest Newspaper

FRIDAY APRIL 23, 2004 40p

Britain backs the crusading Daily Express

SPECIAL REPORT: PAGES 4,5,6 & 7
EXPRESS OPINION: PAGE 12
MICHAEL HOWARD: PAGE 13

93%

AGREE WE HAVE ALL HAD ENOUGH OF TONY BLAIR

Paul Thomas

DAILY EXPRESS — WHY THE DAILY EXPRESS IS TAKING THE HISTORIC DECISION TO BACK THE CONSERVATIVES — ENOUGH IS ENOUGH, MR BLAIR

By Kirsty Walker
Political Correspondent

BRITAIN yesterday gave the Daily Express its full backing over our historic decision to tell Tony Blair that enough is enough.

An overwhelming 93 per cent of the public gave their thumbs-up to our campaign – splashed on the front page yesterday – to back the Tories and dump Labour at the next general election.

Our phone lines were red hot as thousands of people rang in with a tidal wave of support. The poll is yet more evidence that the British public is sick of Labour's spin and deception.

FULL STORY: PAGE 5

EXCLUSIVE
And guess who's still running the Number 10 spin factory. Yes, the 'retired' bully boy of politics, Alastair Campbell. He's at it again SEE PAGE 4

(Le 22 avril 2004, le *Daily Express* avait pris la décision de cesser de soutenir le parti travailliste de Tony Blair et de soutenir désormais le parti conservateur.)

List all the points which show bias and lack of objectivity.

1. The main picture
   – Who is the man in red?
   – What does the cross on his shield (*bouclier*) represent?
   – What does he carry at the end of his spear (*lance*)?
2. The main headline
   – What about its size?
   – What do you think of the figure (93 %)?
3. Which word is not objective in the headline?

Commenter un article

9 Les points suivants doivent vous guider dans votre commentaire

1. **Before you read the article**

The following article was published in *The New York Times*, and reproduced in the French newspaper *Le Monde* (in its weekly selection from *The New York Times*) on May 2, 2004.

– How reliable are these two newspapers? What kind of article do you expect?
– What about the headline?
– Why is the date of publication important?

A Common Culture (From the U.S.A.) Is Binding Europeans Ever Closer

By ALAN RIDING

PARIS – As 10 countries enter the European Union, it is not so much economic weight or political tradition that has earned them the right to join the regional bloc. Rather, it is a certain cultural identity forged by Christianity and a common artistic heritage. In one crucial sense, then, the lingua franca of this expanded Europe remains that of Shakespeare, Leonardo, Mozart and other giants of the past.

Turn to the contemporary arts, however, and a different picture emerges. Here the union's old and new members alike know surprisingly little about one another's artistic inventiveness today. Creative life may be flourishing in widely different ways across Europe, but the most common cultural link across the region now is a devotion to American popular culture in the form of movies, television and music. In a Europe committed to seeking "ever closer union", where a dozen countries already share a currency, culture seems to be lagging behind. Even as Europeans visit one another's cities and beaches more than ever, national self-obsessions prevail in new offerings in the arts.

After Word War II, American popular culture spread across borders. In response Europeans have tried to reinforce national and regional identities, to hold onto their languages, foods and folkloric traditions. But given the option of American-style entertainment, they show little interest in one another's arts. European artistic endeavors that do manage to cross borders today reach few people.

In movies European artists know whom to blame. The region's movie industries constantly bemoan the power of Hollywood, which for the most part leaves local films less than 15 percent of the box office even in cinephile countries like Italy and Germany.

Three decades after the wellsprings of Fellini, Bergman and Truffaut, Europeans now rarely choose to see one another's films. In 2002, a good year for French cinema, 50 percent of the box office went to American movies and 35 percent to French movies, but only 4.9 percent to British films, 0.8 percent to German and 0.2 percent to Italian. And in Spain last year, Hollywood had 67 percent of the movie market, Spain 15.8 percent, Britain 5.7 percent, France 2.6 percent and Germany just 1.2 percent.

The failure of Europe's contemporary arts to enter the mainstream may help explain the abundance of the more rarefied arts festivals in the region, not only the film jamborees of Cannes, Venice and Berlin but also myriad dance and music festivals. (Dance and music, not requiring words or translation, are more exportable). Similarly, summer theater festivals in Edinburgh and Avignon, France, invite productions from throughout Europe, yet few shows that are not local become commercial hits. In 1996 Yasmina Reza's "Art" was the first play by a living French writer to reach London's West End in 40 years.

There is a similar phenomenon in the visual arts. Europe's museums may be crowded, yet many Europeans would struggle to name the leading living artists of France (Christian Boltanski, Annette Messager, Sophie Calle) or Spain (Antoni Tápies, Miquel Barceló) or Germany (Sigmar Polke, Georg Baselitz, Anselm Kiefer). Even Lucian Freud, generally considered Britain's greatest living painter, speaks little to Continental Europeans.

In the case of books, "Harry Potter" is everywhere, but best-seller lists in Europe are generally dominated by national authors. A few have a European audience, like Italy's Umberto Eco, Germany's Günter Grass and recently Spain's Carlos Ruiz Zafón. But most non-national best sellers come from popular American writers, currently Dan Brown with "The Da Vinci Code," but also frequently John Grisham and Patricia Cornwell or recently Michael Moore.

More surprisingly, while often modeled after American sounds, even European pop music rarely crosses the region's borders, as if Europeans were accustomed to lyrics in English but not in other languages. The Rolling Stones can fill stadiums across the region, but no Continental rock group could do so outside its own country. And France's love for its aging rock star Johnny Hallyday still mystifies other Europeans.

Does this separateness matter? Perhaps it represents the cultural diversity that Europeans continue to covet. Yet if Europeans remain focused on the riches of the past and ignore one another's contemporary work, there may also be a price to pay. As Europe moves toward an "ever closer union" unless it also communicates culturally, popular taste will become ever more American.

▲ *The New York Times*, May 2, 2004.

2. Read the article and answer the following questions to make sure you have understood it.

– Which two paragraphs best sum up the main idea of the article?

– This idea is that:

1. There is no common European cultural heritage & identity
2. European countries have no contemporary art culture.
3. European countries know more about American than about European contemporary culture.

– What is the organisation of the article?

☐ chronological ☐ logical ☐ thesis + examples

– In what order are the following subjects mentioned: the theatre & music/the cinema/literature/pop music/painting?

– Find the key sentence or the key phrase of each paragraph.

1 ....
2 ....
3 ....
4 ....
5 ....
6 ....
7 ....
8 ....
9 ....
10 ....

3. Looking at the article critically.
Here are some of the points you might consider:
– Is the journalist biased? Why or why not?
– Do you agree with his view of European culture?
– What is the journalist's conclusion? Does he think it would be a good thing if Europe became more Americanized? Do you agree with him?
– American culture is linked to the idea of a "popular" culture. Why? Isn't the real difference between popular and intellectual cultures?

3. ANALYSER UN TEXTE LITTÉRAIRE

1 – QUELQUES TERMES LITTÉRAIRES

Effets rhétoriques

Retrouvez à quels termes littéraires correspondent les exemples qui suivent.

1 And I will love thee still, my Dear
Till a'(= all) the seas gang (= go) dry. (R. Burns)
2 I wandered lonely as a cloud
That floats on high o'er (= over) vales and hills (Wordsworth)
3 Give us this day our daily bread. (part of the Lord's prayer)
4 A terrible beauty (Yeats)
5 Love's fire heats water, water cools not love. (Shakespeare, Sonnet 154)
6 All the world's a stage (As You Like It)
7 He rarely speaks the truth. (to mean: He often lies.)
8 a pair of ragged claws (= a crab) T.S. Eliot
9 to spend a penny (= to go to the toilets)
10 Cowards die many times before their deaths. (Shakespeare)
11 Ring out, wild bells!
12 We shall go on to the end, we shall fight in France, we shall fight on the seas and oceans, we shall fight with growing confidence and growing strength in the air, we shall defend our Island, whatever the cost may be, we shall fight on the beaches, we shall fight on the landing grounds, we shall fight in the fields and in the streets, we shall fight in the hills… (W. Churchill)

Termes littéraires	Exemples
Metaphor: identifying two things or ideas by using a word which stands for *(représente)* another one. ex. Night's candles (= the stars)	
Simile: a clearly expressed comparison between two things (usually introduced by as or like). ex. My love is like a red, red rose…	
Metonymy: using, instead of a word, a term closely associated with it. ex. 10 Downing Street (= the British Prime Minister)	
Synecdoche: a type of metonymy, in which you use the part for the whole. ex. Many hands make light work. (in this proverb, hands = people)	
Hyperbole: exaggeration ex. All the perfumes of Arabia will not sweeten this little hand. (*Macbeth*)	
Apostrophe: addressing an absent person, a personified thing or abstraction directly, as if they were there. ex. Oh, gods!	
Anaphora: repetition of words at the beginning of phrases or clauses. ex. in the fields, in the lanes, in the woods	
Oxymoron: contradictory terms placed next to each other ex. sweet grief	
Paradox: a statement which may seem contradictory, but which contains some truth. e.g. Ignorance is strength	
Chiasmus: repetition of words in reverse order (abba) ex. Flowers are lovely, love is flowerlike. (Coleridge)	
Understatement, litotes: representing something as less than it is (*litote*) ex. I don't care much for him. (for: I hate him.)	
Euphemism: A form of understatement: using a weak or vague expression so as not to mention something offending or taboo. ex. to pass away = to die	

2 – Pour enrichir vos commentaires

Voici une liste d'expressions qui vous permettront de ne pas toujours utiliser les mêmes termes dans vos commentaires.

Commentaries: words and expressions

■ **Show**

The poet **explores** the theme of rejection…
The narrator **draws attention to** the character's situation…
The use of the link-word **signals** a change…
What this use of imagery **reveals** is…
The character's use of such words **denotes** anxiety…
In the first stanza, the poet **depicts** the village and its inhabitants…
Shakespeare's **portrayal** of human passions…
Their dialogue **throws/casts/sheds light upon** what happened in the past…

■ **Is about**

The author has chosen to **focus on** an incident…
The novel **deals with** married life…
This essay **tackles** the problem of divorce…
The story **hinges round** the revelation that…
The last paragraph **treats of** the consequences…

■ **Express**

The slow rhythm **conveys** a sense of peace…
The long sentences **contribute to** a feeling of harmony…
With his use of irony, the narrator **voices** his criticism of…
The broken up rhythm **suggests** emotion…
The sight of the house **evokes** a sense of wonder in him…

■ **Emphasize**

The structure of the text **lays/puts/places the emphasis on**…
The syntax **heightens** the feeling of…
The repetition **highlights** the contrast…
The sinister setting **intensifies** the sense of fear…
The narrator **stresses** the character's isolation…
The theme is **underlined** (*souligné*) by the use of…

■ **Echo**

The poem shows the **influence of**…
The name of the character is **taken from**…
This expression is an allusion to Byron's *Don Juan*…
The setting **recalls** (*rappelle*) Poe's *The Fall of the House of Usher*…
The story **reminds us of** the plot of Gothic novels…
There are many biblical **references**…

■ Contrast

The scene stands **in (sharp) contrast to** the preceding one...
The passage **is built on a contrast between** life and death...
There is **a gap between** the syntax **and** the message...
This **disparity between** words **and** meaning...

■ Criticize

Sinclair Lewis **condemns** hypocrisy...
This essay is **an attack on** intolerance...
Orwell **objects to** the way language is used to....
The author's **satire is directed at**...
The author **mocks**.../**ridicules**...

■ Use

By **employing** such a point of view...
The author **makes constant use of** water imagery...
The narrator then **adopts** an ironic tone...
The author **has recourse to** several devices to underline his point.

■ The reader's response

The plot **appeals to** our love of mystery...
The characters **arouse** our sympathy...
This method **compels** (forces) the reader to be alert...
We **identify with** the heroine...
The heroine's **predicament** (= difficult situation) **excites** our pity...

exercice

Les extraits suivants contiennent-ils des *similes* ou des *metaphors*?

(a) As I walked out one evening,
Walking down Bristol Street,
The crowds upon the pavements
Were crowds of harvest wheat. (Auden)

(b) Shall I compare thee[1] to a summer's day?
Thou[2] art more lovely and more temperate. (W. Shakespeare)

(c) This antique, solid, weather-worn, yet imposing front had a somewhat incommunicative character. It was the mask, not the face of the house. It had heavy lids, but no eyes... (H. James)

(d) O, beware, my lord, of jealousy!
It is the green-eyed monster, which doth[4] mock
The meat it feeds on. (W. Shakespeare)

(e) An omnibus across the bridge
Crawls like a yellow butterfly,
And, here and there, a passer-by
Shows like a little restless midge[4]. (O. Wilde)

1. **thee:** you. 2. **thou:** you. 3. **doth:** does. 4. **midge:** a very small insect.

4. Analyser un texte de fiction

Quelques mots essentiels :
the plot *(l'intrigue)* or the story-line
The events move towards **a climax** *(point culminant)*
The characters (stress on the first syllable)
One can **break** the passage **down into** several parts.
The second part begins **at** line 20.

Questions et repérages

Voici quelques-unes des questions que vous devez vous poser lorsque vous analysez un texte de fiction.

1 What kind of passage?

Is it a dialogue, a narrative, or both?
What sort of novel does it come from? A detective story? A psychological novel?....

The main fictional genres

Allegory: A text in which the characters and actions have a further meaning outside the text.
Apprenticeship novel: A novel which shows the development and education of a character, from childhood to adulthood, as he goes through various experiences and spiritual crises. It emphasizes the influence of the early years upon later behaviour and the gradual discovery of a philosophy of life.
Autobiography: A personal account of one's own life. The emphasis is on introspection and the development of personality.
Detective story: A novel or story in which a detective finds out who committed a crime.
Diary: A journal in which personal and intimate details are recorded day by day.
Dystopia: Like a utopia, it describes an imaginary world, but instead of being perfect, it is evil or absurd and reveals some dangerous tendencies in our own society.
Epistolary novel: A novel told through an exchange of letters between different characters.

Fable: A short tale with a moral. The characters are usually animals or objects and the action often includes supernatural elements.
Gothic novel: Set among a wild scenery, in haunted castles and ruined abbeys full of dungeons (*cachots*) and hidden passages, the Gothic novel presents innocent girls and dark villains involved in a melodramatic tale of suspense, mystery and terror.
Historical novel: A novel set in the past and describing the settings, manners and society of that age.
Journal: A day by day relation of events and personal reactions to them.
Novel: A long, fictitious prose narrative.
Picaresque novel: The genre derives from the 16th century Spanish form which described the adventures of a picaro, a clever young man of low birth who despises honour and morality and tries to make his fortune through wit rather than industry. The plot is loose and episodic.
Science-fiction: Narratives taking place in the future, on other planets, or in worlds regulated by different scientific laws.
Short story: Shorter than the novel in length, the short story usually focuses on a short episode or on a moment of crisis or revelation. It is meant to be read at one sitting and is therefore compact.
Thriller: An exciting story, often about crime or espionage.
Utopia: A type of fiction describing an ideal imaginary world.

2 Who?

Who are the main characters?
What is the relationship between them? If necessary, draw a simple diagram to explain this relationship (family relationship, love, hatred, anger, jealousy, etc.)
Describe each of them: age, social class, language, ideas, personality…
Are they flat or round characters? (Flat characters represent one single idea; round characters are more complex and capable of development).

3 The structure of the text

Is the development chronological, logical?
Underline the link-words and the tenses used to justify your point.
What are the main parts or movements in the passage?

4 What?

How can you sum up what happens in the passage?

5 Time

At what time does the story take place?
At what time was it written?
Is the development strictly chronological?

Are there any flashbacks (*retour à des évènements antérieurs*) or flashforwards (*annonce d'évènements futurs*) in the passage?
Are all moments treated in the same way, or are some described in detail, possibly with a dialogue (which slows up the action), and others summarized (which speeds up the action)?
Why are the events told in such a way? What is the effect?
Study the use of tenses in the passage.

6 Point of view

Who tells the story? Is it:
– a first-person narrator who tells us what (s)he can see and think – but no more?
– an omniscient narrator who knows everything about past, future and what goes on in the minds of all the characters?
Is the narrator a character in the story? Is it an outside narrator?

What is the effect of such a point of view?

Remember that:
– An internal point of view (internal focalization) allows you to see things through the eyes of one character, so that you feel closer to him/her. But you only see the other characters and the events through the eyes of that character, you have a limited point of view.
– With an external point of view, the characters seem more distant from you, but more can be explained to you. A narrator who sees everything, like a god, is called an omniscient narrator.

7 How is the story told?

How are the characters'words reported? Are they summarised? Do you have direct speech, reported speech? free indirect speech?

Le style direct et le style indirect

Style direct

On cite les mots exacts de la personne. Ex. *"Don't forget to give John a ring", she said.* Notez que l'on n'utilise pas de tirets en anglais au début de chaque réplique, mais des guillemets, sauf pour le verbe d'assertion. P. 44

Style indirect

Les mots sont rapportés plus tard. Ex. *She said she would be late.*
Les verbes les plus courants pour introduire le style indirect sont les suivants:

Verb + *that*	Verb + *name of person* + *that*	*Verb used with both structures*
answer	*tell*	*say (to so) that*
believe	*remind*	*admit (to so) that*
claim	*persuade*	*suggest (to so) that*
deny	*convince*	*mention (to so) that*

hope	*explain (to so) that*
knew	*point out (to so) that*
expect	*promise (so) that*
think	*show (so) that*
regret	*confess (to so) that*
	shout (to so) that
	whisper (to so) that

Pour rapporter des questions : *ask/wonder if/whether/where/how/when/what…*
Si le verbe qui introduit le style indirect est au passé, un certain nombre de changements seront nécessaires dans le reste de la phrase. P. 250

■ **Style indirect libre**

Le narrateur rapporte mots ou pensées au style indirect mais peut parfois omettre le verbe qui les introduit, si bien que le lecteur a l'impression d'entendre les mots directement. Mais la forme reste celle du style indirect.

Ex. *She promised to come back. She said she would write soon.* = style indirect
It had been such a wonderful week, so peaceful and happy. = style indirect libre
= *(She thought/said) it had been…*

■ **Narration**

Les mots sont résumés et non donnés exactement.
Ex. *He seemed happy and kept joking all evening.*

What is the effect of the technique used? Note that with narration the narrator is fully in control; with direct speech, he is almost forgotten. Indirect speech and free indirect speech are somewhere in between.

narrator most in control	– narration
	– indirect speech
	– free indirect speech
narrator almost forgotten	– direct speech

8 Tone

What is the narrator's tone?

calm	indignant	sarcastic
detached	ironic	sardonic
excited	joyful	satirical
flat	lyrical	serious
humble	mocking	solemn
humorous	playful	surprised
impersonal	resentful *(amer)*	

Be careful and do not confuse humour, irony and satire.

Humour: A type of writing which provokes smiles or laughter. It results from a comic perception of life. It is kind and sympathetic, not critical.
Irony: Saying the contrary of what you mean (e.g. "Nice day!" when it's raining heavily). Dramatic irony is the contrast between what a character says and what the reader knows (e.g. in Shakespeare's *Macbeth*, King Duncan admires the harmony of nature when he arrives at Macbeth's castle, but the reader knows he will be murdered there.)
Satire: The use of humour, wit (brilliant, clever language), absurdity or irony in order to criticise someone or something.

9 What stylistic effects can you notice?

– Are there any specific semantic fields? What images and metaphors are used? What is their effect?
– How can you characterize the style: are the sentences short and simple or complex, with many clauses?
– Are there parallel or contrasting structures, repetitions, echoes?
What is their effect?

exemple

Voici, à titre d'exemple, les grandes lignes d'un commentaire guidé à partir d'un texte de George Orwell.

The scene takes place on the Manor Farm. Word has gone round among the animals that old Major, a pig, has had a dream and wants to talk about it to the other animals. When Mr Jones, the farmer, has gone to bed, all the animals meet in the barn. This is a passage from Major's speech.

"Now, comrades, what is the nature of this life of ours? Let us face it: our lives are miserable, laborious, and short. We are born, we are given just so much food as will keep the breath in our bodies, and those of us who are capable of it are forced to work to the last atom of our strength; and the very instant that our usefulness has come to an end we are slaughtered with hideous cruelty. No animal in England knows the meaning of happiness or leisure after he is a year old. No animal in England is free. The life of an animal is misery and slavery: that is the plain truth.

"But is this simply part of the order of nature? Is it because this land of ours is so poor that it cannot afford a decent life to those who dwell upon it? No, comrades, a thousand times no! The soil of England is fertile, its climate is good, it is capable of affording food in abundance to an enormously greater number of animals than now inhabit it. This single farm of ours would support a dozen horses, twenty cows, hundreds of sheep – and all of them living in a comfort and a dignity that are now almost beyond our imagining. Why then do we continue in this miserable condition? Because nearly the whole of the produce of our labour is stolen from us by human beings. There, comrades, is the answer to all our problems. It is summed up in a single word – Man. Man is the only real enemy we have. Remove Man from the scene, and the root cause of hunger and overwork is abolished for ever.

"Man is the only creature that consumes without producing. He does not give milk, he does not lay eggs, he is too weak to pull the plough, he cannot run fast enough to catch rabbits. Yet he is lord of all the animals. He sets them to work, he gives back to them the bare minimum that will prevent them from starving, and the rest he keeps for himself. Our labour tills[1] the soil, our dung[2] fertilises it, and yet there is not one of us that owns more than his bare skin. You cows that I see before me, how many thousands of gallons of milk have you given during this last year? And what has happened to that milk which should have been breeding up sturdy calves? Every drop of it has gone down the throats of our enemies. And you hens, how many eggs have you laid in this last year, and how many of those eggs ever hatched into chickens? The rest have all gone to market to bring in money for Jones and his men. And you, Clover, where are those four foals you bore, who should have been the support and pleasure of your old age? Each was sold at a year old - you will never see one of them again. In return for your four confinements[3] and all your labour in the fields, what have you ever had except your bare rations and a stall?

"And even the miserable lives we lead are not allowed to reach their natural span[4]. For myself I do not grumble, for I am one of the lucky ones. I am twelve years old and have had over four hundred children. Such is the natural life of a pig. But no animal escapes the cruel knife in the end. You young porkers[5] who are sitting in front of me, every one of you will scream your lives out at the block within a year. To that horror we all must come – cows, pigs, hens, sheep, everyone. Even the horses and the dogs have no better fate. You, Boxer, the very day that those great muscles of yours lose their power, Jones will sell you to the knacker[6], who will cut your throat and boil you down for the foxhounds. As for the dogs, when they grow old and toothless, Jones ties a brick round their necks and drowns them in the nearest pond.

"Is it not crystal clear, then, comrades, that all the evils of this life of ours spring from the tyranny of human beings? Only get rid of Man, and the produce of our labour would be our own. Almost overnight we could become rich and free. What then must we do? Why, work night and day, body and soul, for the overthrow of the human race! That is my message to you, comrades: Rebellion! I do not know when that Rebellion will come, it might be in a week or in a hundred years, but I know, as surely as I see this straw beneath my feet, that sooner or later justice will be done. Fix your eyes on that, comrades, throughout the short remainder of your lives! And above all, pass on this message of mine to those who come after you, so that future generations shall carry on the struggle until it is victorious.

"And remember, comrades, your resolution must never falter. No argument must lead you astray. Never listen when they tell you that Man and the animals have a common interest, that the prosperity of the one is the prosperity of the others. It is all lies. Man serves the interests of no creature except himself. And among us animals let there be perfect unity, perfect comradeship in the struggle. All men are enemies. All animals are comrades."

1. **till:** *labourer.* 2. **dung:** *fumier.* 3. **confinement:** *accouchement.* 4. **span:** *durée.* 5. **porker:** *porc à l'engrais.* 6 **knacker:** *équarrisseur.*

The passage takes place at the very beginning of the novel. We have seen Mr Jones retiring and the animals making their way to the barn to listen to Major, the pig. Such a beginning is somewhat de-familiarizing for the reader. Are we going to read an animal story? A fable? Major's speech will help us answer the question.

1 What is the message Major wants to convey to the animals?

(summary of the main idea)

Major wished to gather the animals to explain to them that they are exploited by man. They work hard in miserable conditions ("work to the last atom of our strength"), they never benefit from the produce of their labour, which is taken by man (milk, for instance), their eggs or children are often sold, and they themselves are killed when they become useless. They are the victims of man, and the message is therefore the necessity of rebellion.

The structure of the text is clear and logical:

1. A description of the animals' lives and misery (paragraphs 1 to 4).
2. The logical conclusion: rebellion (paragraphs 5 and 6).

2 How are we to read the text?

At a first level, this is **an animal story**, which gives us a wonderful summary of the lives of farm animals. Most of the animals on a farm are mentioned and what is said about them is perfectly accurate. A wealth of details gives the speech verisimilitude (*vraisemblance*). For the reader, there is almost a shock of surprise at discovering how much of this is true, how exploited animals are. The speech can therefore be seen as self-sufficient, giving rise to both

– humour (the incongruousness of a pig pronouncing such a speech and calling other animals 'comrades')

– and pathos (with the allusion to the variety of cruel deaths the animals will suffer, at the end of the fourth paragraph: "cut your throat", "boil you down", "tie a brick round their necks", "drowns them"...)

The reader's pity is thus quickly aroused.

But a number of words and expressions are politically charged: comrades, slavery, enemy, consuming without producing, tyranny, overthrow, rebellion... It is therefore impossible not to read the text in a different way, not to see it as **an allegory**. Behind old Major we hear Lenin addressing the masses of oppressed people in a speech reminiscent of Marx's Communist Party Manifesto. Behind the labour of the animals we see the forced labour of the working class, behind the rebellion Major advocates we see a call for a proletarian revolution.

The beauty of Major's speech is that it can be read on these two levels. Alone, the first one would be mere fantasy, the second one too reductive. Its main interest lies in the double reading it lends itself to.

3 How successful is the speech?

As a negative to the world described in Major's speech we find a utopia, a world in which there would be "perfect unity" between the animals, in which problems would disappear once men had disappeared ("Only get rid of Man..."), in which all animals would live in "comfort" and "dignity". Indeed the setting is a pastoral one, not just because the action takes place on a farm, but because we have a description of a land of plenty at the beginning of the second paragraph, with words such as fertile, abundance, good climate. There is something highly optimistic about such a vision.

Yet it contains the seeds *(le germe)* of its own failure. When Major speaks of "the order of nature", he forgets about another aspect of nature, human or animal nature. It is animal nature which will make Major's dream impossible – indifferent cats, flighty mares, selfish pigs. Besides, the speech represents a simplistic vision of things (e.g. "Almost overnight we could become rich and free") and does not offer any solution beyond "rebellion". This is why it is warped *(perverti)* in spite of its appeal.

4 Is Orwell just satirizing political utopias?

Beyond the satire, Major's speech provides a good example of the way politicians make use of language. Orwell was fascinated by the use and misuse of language, and believed that it was at the root of all dishonesty, hypocrisy and tyranny.

Indeed, Major's use of language reveals his manipulative art.

To begin with, his rhetoric is based upon questions and answers. His questions are rhetorical, never allowing the animals any time for thought, replies or discussion. (At the end of the second paragraph for example, see the quick succession of question and answer: Why then...? Because...) At the same time, Major directly addresses the animals individually or as groups ("You cows... you, Clover... You, Boxer...") to involve them, to give them the impression that he is concerned about them. He appears to set up free choices when he is in fact in full control.

To be more striking, Major also relies on anaphora and repetition.

Anaphora: No animal in England.../You cows... You hens... You Clover...

Repetition: a number of key words are repeated throughout the speech (comrades/man/work/enemy/life) with an almost hypnotic effect.

This language of propaganda results in oversimplification. Things are either "the plain truth" (§1) or "lies" (last §); there is nothing but "enemies" or "comrades", life is either "slavery" or "comfort". Time too loses its qualities: things happen "overnight" and are "for ever."

This leads to a world in which thought is limited (and then banned, later on), something ominously announced by expressions such as "No argument must lead you astray"... "Never listen when they tell you..." In the end, language will be reduced to mottoes *(devises)* which simplify, reduce and are ideal to anaesthetize people's

minds. That this is the direction events are taking is clear from the two mottoes which end the speech: "All men are enemies. All animals are comrades."
The speech, which we can read at first almost as belonging to a fairy tale, turns out to be a political allegory but also a chilling reminder of the way totalitarianism can use language to control people's minds.

Ces points illustrent la structure d'un commentaire, qui devrait suivre la progression suivante :

1. Situer le passage dans l'oeuvre et présenter la problématique dont découlera le plan. = Introduction
2. Présenter la structure du texte (ses différentes parties ou mouvements).
3. Organiser les idées en deux ou trois parties, en gardant pour la première partie ce qui est le plus évident, et pour la dernière, le sens caché, mais le plus important, du texte.
4. Résumer les points principaux du commentaire, puis élargir la perspective. = Conclusion

exercices

1 Les passages qui suivent sont tous des débuts de romans. À quelles catégories du tableau ci-dessous appartiennent-ils ? Justifiez votre réponse.

	Point of view of a character	Outside point of view
First-person narrative		
Third-person narrative		

(1) I was out of work. But any day I expected to hear from up north. I lay on the sofa and listened to the rain. Now and then I'd lift up and look through the curtain for the mailman. (Raymond Carver, Collectors, in *Short Cuts*, Harvill 1993, c. Tess Gallagher)

(2) In understanding Darcy was the superior. Bingley was by no means deficient, but Darcy was clever. He was at the same time haughty, reserved, and fastidious, and his manners, though well bred, were not inviting. In that respect his friend had greatly the advantage. Bingley was sure of being liked wherever he appeared, Darcy was continually giving offence. (Jane Austen, *Pride and Prejudice*, Chapter 4)

(3) As Al saw it, there was only one solution. He had to get rid of the dog without Betty or the kids finding out about it. At night. It would have to be done at night. He would simply drive Suzy – well, someplace, later he'd decide where – open the door, push her out, drive away.

▲ Raymond Carver, Jerry and Molly and Sam, in *Short Cuts*, Harvill 1993, c. Tess Gallagher.

(4) My mother did not tell me they were coming. Afterwards she said she did not want me to appear nervous. I was surprised, for I thought she knew me well. Strangers would think I was calm. I did not cry as a baby. Only my mother would note the tightness along my jaw, the widening of my already wide eyes.

▲ Tracy Chevalier, *Girl with a Pearl Earring*, Harper Collins.

2 Associez les passages et la technique utilisée.

a. Derek phoned last night and said to tell you that he'd sent the parcel and no one asked any questions. I don't know what it means but he wanted you to get that message.

b. "But if you were so late, why didn't you take a taxi?" said Gary.
"I tried to ring them but the number was constantly engaged," Dora said.

c. Mrs Allen had been interviewed again. At first she claimed that she knew nothing about any bag. But when she was told it was a case of murder, she started talking with apparent frankness.
She had been about to leave the shopping mall when she had noticed the bag on the floor, pushed behind a litter bin. It looked almost new and she'd thought it must be broken to have been left there. She'd picked it up and immediately seen the purse inside. There was no one around, thank God, so she'd put the purse in her pocket…

d. Joan arrived out of breath and apologized for being late, explaining the train had been delayed.

(1) narration

(2) direct speech

(3) indirect (reported) speech

(4) free indirect speech

5. Analyser un poème

Quelques mots essentiels :
un vers = a line/verse = *des vers* : This speech is in verse. (= not in prose)
A stanza = *une strophe*

1 – Questions et repérage

Voici quelques-unes des questions que vous devez vous poser lorsque vous analysez un poème.

I What kind of poem?

Is the poem in free verse *(vers libre)* or is it a traditional form of poetry: a sonnet, a ballad, an ode…?

Here are some common forms in poetry:

The main poetic genres

Ballad: A poem which tells a story and was originally meant to be sung. A ballad is made up of quatrains (stanzas of four lines) rhyming abcb.
Elegy: A poem of lament for the death of someone or of something. It has no particular form.
Epic/heroic poem: A long narrative poem which relates the heroic actions of someone. It involves battles, superhuman actions, and the tone is elevated.
Free Verse: Poetry which has no regular metrical form, but which has a cadence of its own.
Nursery rhyme: Poetry for young children. It is often nonsensical (absurd) and is characterized by strong rhythm.
Ode: A lyric poem celebrating someone or something.
Pastoral: A poem which celebrates the joys of simple life among nature by describing the idyllic life of shepherds (*bergers*).
Sonnet: A 14-line lyric poem made up of
– two quatrains (= the octave) + two tercets (three line stanzas) = the sestet.
– or three quatrains + a couplet
The octave usually presents a situation; the sestet comments upon it and brings a resolution to the problem.
Visual poem: A poem in which the lines form a shape, often related to the subject of the poem.

2 Who and what?
Who speaks in the poem? An impersonal voice? Someone who speaks in the first/third person?
What is the structure (the different movements) of the poem? Does it correspond to the different stanzas?
What is the main idea expressed in the poem?

3 How?
What semantic fields prevail? (to prevail: *dominer*) Underline all the images and metaphors. P. 114 What is their effect?

4 The music of the poem
Study the following devices (*procédés*) and explain what their effect is and how they relate to the meaning of the poem.

A few poetic devices

the caesura: the pause in the middle of a line
an enjambment or run-on line: a line in which the syntax and meaning carry on to the next line

alliteration: the repetition of consonants at the beginning of words: burning bright
assonance: the repetition of vocalic sounds (= vowel sounds): The cat sat on the mat.
onomatopoeia: words with a sound similar to what they mean: hiss *(siffler)*
rhyme: the repetition of the final vowel + consonant: bright/light
off-rhyme: an imperfect rhyme, in which, for example, the vowel is different: pat/pet
eye-rhyme: a false rhyme, for the eye, not for the ear: move/love
the rhyme pattern *(l'agencement des rimes dans une strophe ou un poème)*
couplet rhymes: aabbccdd...
alternate rhymes: abab cdcd...
enclosing rhymes: abba cddc...

exemple

Voici un commentaire guidé de ce poème écrit par W.H. Auden en 1937.

Funeral Blues

Stop all the clocks, cut off the telephone,
Prevent the dog from barking with a juicy bone,
Silence the pianos and with muffled drum
Bring out the coffin, let the mourners come.

Let aeroplanes circle moaning overhead
Scribbling on the sky the message He Is Dead,
Put crepe bows round the white necks of the public doves,
Let the traffic policemen wear black cotton gloves.

He was my North, my South, my East and West,
My working week and my Sunday rest,
My noon, my midnight, my talk, my song;
I thought that love would last for ever; I was wrong.

The stars are not wanted now: put out every one;
Pack up the moon and dismantle the sun;
Pour away the ocean and sweep up the wood,
For nothing now can ever come to any good.

W. H. Auden

This is a poem of mourning *(lamentation)* for the death of a friend. Yet much of the imagery (for example the reference to a 'juicy bone'or to 'aeroplanes') is surprising in such a poem. Are we to take it seriously then?

1 What is the structure of the poem?

The poem is made up of four stanzas, which show a progression from home (stanza 1) to the surroundings (2) to the earth (3) and finally to the universe (4). It is as if there was a gradual contamination of the whole universe because of the poet's sorrow.
Another way of looking at the structure is to see that the first two stanzas reflect the imagery of the modern world (telephones, aeroplanes, policemen) whereas the last two contain more references to nature.

2 What genre does the poem belong to?

As in old **ballads** we have a speaker lamenting over his fate. Although this is not a ballad, we find the regular rhythm (mainly iambic) and four-line stanzas of the ballad, but rhyming differently from the ballad, in couplets here (aa, bb, cc...).
The title points to "**blues**", which are characterised by three-line stanzas, a melancholy tone, frequent repetitions and the voice of one person. As in blues, we have a lament here, the "I" of the speaker, but also flat, everyday language. Indeed the blues idiom (language) is often trite (banal) and ordinary. There is no attempt at elevating the language of the ordinary speakers. As in blues, the rhythm is also slow and dragging. Look for instance at the third line of the second stanza in which most of the words are monosyllables, forcing the voice to linger over the line.

3 What is the nature of the imagery and what is its effect?

Although there are elements of the ballad and the blues in the poem, it differs from both genres by its extravagant images and hyperboles: the aeroplanes circle in the sky, the doves wear black bows, the sun is dismantled... In fact the poem gradually moves from absurd, unexpected homely actions (for example, the mention of a "juicy bone") to impossible cosmic ones ("put out" the stars). It moves from incongruity in the first stanza, to unexpectedness, hyperboles and impossibility in the last one (for instance, "pour away the ocean").
Why use such extravagant imagery? It is as if all the ceremonial linked to death was exaggerated: the silence surrounding the coffin (stanza 1), the announcement of death and the clothes linked to mourning (stanza 2). Is this a parody of a poem of mourning? A criticism of sentimental moods and overstated (*exageré*) emotions? Although there are such elements in the poem, it is essentially a genuine cry of despair.

4 How is despair conveyed in the poem?

The third stanza differs from the others and is more personal. The previous orders are replaced by metaphors describing the loved one ("He was my North...") and end in a very direct line, the only one in which the "I" of the speaker is mentioned: "I thought that love would last forever: I was wrong". This is a very moving line

because of its abrupt end after the long first part, a contrast underlined by the fluid sonorities (l, r) of the first part opposed to the abruptness of the word "wrong". Another element which contributes to the intensity of the emotion is the use of imperatives, a rhetorical device which brings the poem closer to the dramatic immediacy of dialogue.
In fact the very excess which brings us close to parody also takes us beyond it into the world of despair. It is as if Auden was telling us that you cannot be excessive enough when it comes to the death of a loved one. The loved one is the only fixed spot in our world, the standard by which we judge everything. The loved one becomes the world: he is defined by the points of the compass, he gives time its meaning (lines 10 and 11), and when he goes the world disintegrates (see the strength of verbs such as "pour away", "dismantle", "pack up", which show the lover's need to do something physically, to destroy the world which has now become meaningless.)
The intensity of emotion explains the paradox we find in the poem:
– in stanzas 1 and 4, the world can stop or disappear
– in stanza 2, the world should be there to assert, to repeat the lover's death.
The world only matters if it speaks of the lover.

The poem which starts almost as parody turns into a very moving cry of despair.

2 – Rythme et métrique

En anglais parlé, le rythme est surtout lié à la succession de syllabes accentuées et de syllabes non accentuées. P. 268
La plupart des poèmes classiques ont aussi un rythme basé sur une telle alternance.
Le rythme iambique *(iambic rhythm)* – succession de pieds composés d'une syllabe non accentuée suivie d'une syllabe accentuée : ˘ ′ – est le rythme de base de la poésie classique anglaise.
Jusqu'au XVIIIe siècle, il a souvent été associé à des vers de cinq pieds (pentamètres) qui s'appelaient ainsi pentamètres iambiques *(iambic pentameters)*.
Dans les vers qui suivent par exemple, une description de l'homme entre deux extrêmes, les syllabes accentuées sont marquées ′, les syllabes non accentuées ˘.

˘ ′ ˘ ′ ˘ ′ ˘ ′ ˘ ′

He hangs between; in doubt to act, or rest,

˘ ′ ˘ ′ ˘ ′ ˘ ′ ˘ ′

In doubt to deem himself a god, or beast;

˘ ′ ˘ ′ ˘ ′ ˘ ′ ˘ ′

In doubt his mind or body to prefer… (Alexander Pope)

Notez que l'accent tombe pratiquement toujours sur la syllabe normalement accentuée du mot, et que les mots grammaticaux (articles, prépositions) sont rarement accentués. Le mot *between*, par exemple, ne pourra être accentué que sur la 2e syllabe. On appelle scansion une telle analyse métrique d'un vers. Tous les vers ne peuvent se scander de cette façon. Le vers libre, par exemple, obéit à d'autres règles, les vers pouvant correspondre à des unités de souffle ou de sens.

Les mesures les plus souvent utilisées	**Effet produit**
– **the iamb:** ˘ ´ (pied de deux syllabes) ˘ ´ ˘ ´ ˘ ´ ˘ ´ ˘ ´ The frost performs its secret ministry	regularity, monotony
– **the trochee:** ´ ˘ (pied de deux syllabes) ´ ˘ ´ ˘ ´ ˘ ´ Tyger, tyger, burning bright	heavy, hammering (*martelant*) rhythm
– **the anapest:** ˘ ˘ ´ (pied de trois syllabes) ˘ ˘ ´ ˘ ˘ ´ ˘ ˘ ´ ˘ ˘ ´ For the sky and the sea, and the sea and the sky	rapidity, lightness

Le rythme d'un vers ou d'un poème n'est pas toujours entièrement régulier. Par exemple, on trouvera souvent dans un rythme iambique des *trochees* en début de vers pour rompre la monotonie et souligner le sens. Dans le même poème de Pope cité plus haut, on trouve ainsi le vers suivant, qui commence par un *trochee* (ce qui accentue le poids du mot *chaos*) et se termine plus régulièrement par un rythme iambique. Les différents pieds ont été séparés par des barres obliques :

´ ˘ /˘ ´ / ˘ ´ /˘ ´ / ˘ ´
Chaos of thought and passion, all confused

exercices

1 Quelle est la forme de ces poèmes ou de ces extraits de poèmes ?

1.

A Chrismas tree

Star,
If you are
A love compassionate,
You will walk with us this year.
We face a glacial distance, who are here
Huddl'd[1]
At your feet.

▲ W. Burford, From *Man Now*, c. 1954, Southern Methodist University Press.

1. **huddl'd:** huddled: crowded together.

2. No longer mourn for me when I am dead
Than you shall hear the surly[1] sullen[2] bell
Give warning to the world that I am fled
From this vile world, with vilest worms[3] to dwell[4]:
Nay[5], if you read this line, remember not
The hand that writ[6] it, for I love you so
That I in your sweet thoughts would be forgot,
If thinking on me then should make you woe[7].
O if (I say) you look upon this verse,
When I, perhaps, compounded[8] am with clay[9],
Do not so much as my poor name rehearse[10],
But let your love even with my life decay[11];
Lest the wise world should look into your moan,
And mock you with me after I am gone. (W. Shakespeare)

1. **surly:** unfriendly. 2. **sullen:** *morose.* 3. **worms:** *vers de terre.* 4. **dwell:** live. 5. **Nay:** no. 6. **writ:** wrote. 7. **woe:** sadness, grief. 8. **compounded:** combined. 9. **clay:** *argile.* 10. **rehearse:** repeat. 11. **decay:** die.

3. Hickory dickory dock
The mouse ran up the clock
The clock struck one
The mouse ran down
Hickory dickory dock.

▲ Nursery rhyme.

4. As I walked out one evening,
Walking down Bristol Street,
The crowds upon the pavement
Were fields of harvest wheat.

And down by the brimming[1] river
I heard a lover sing
Under an arch of the railway:
"Love has no ending.

I'll love you, dear, I'll love you
Till China and Africa meet,
And the river jumps over the mountain
And the salmon sing in the street. [...]

▲ W.H. Auden, *As I Walked Out One Evening*, 1995, Faber & Faber/LNA.

1. **brimming:** full.

2 **Lorsqu'on parle du son des mots, il faut bien sûr penser à leur sonorité et ne pas se laisser toujours influencer par leur orthographe. Deux syllabes qui s'écrivent de la même façon se prononceront souvent différemment. Trouvez le ou les mots de la colonne 2 qui rime(nt) avec le mot de la colonne 1.**

love	move, above, wove
rough	tough, plough, bough
fine	feminine, mine, pine
woe	know, paw, no, now
face	pass, press, pace

3 **Comment pouvez-vous décrire les procédés utilisés dans les lettres, syllabes ou mots soulignés des vers qui suivent ?**

A. And the smooth stream in smoother numbers flow (A. Pope): . . .

B. Ah, Sunflower, weary of time,
Who countest[1] the steps of the sun;
Seeking after that sweet golden clime[2]
Where the traveller's journey is done; (W. Blake)

1. **countest:** archaic for 'count'. 2. **clime:** region.

C. Champagne is too fizzy[1] for me.

1. **fizzy:** making a hissing sound because of its bubbles.

D. True ease in writing comes from art, not chance,
As those move easiest who have learned to dance.
T'is[1] not enough no harshness gives offence,
The sound must seem an echo to the sense. (A. Pope)

1. **T'is:** it is.

E. Break, break, break,
On thy cold grey stones, O Sea! (Tennyson)

F. There was an Old Man who said "Hush!"
I perceive a young bird in this bush! (E. Lear)

4 **Il existe en anglais de nombreuses expressions constituées de deux mots qui sont synonymes ou, au contraire, antonymes. De plus, ces expressions contiennent souvent des répétitions de sons. Soulignez les consonnes ou voyelles répétées dans les exemples qui suivent (le sens des expressions vous est donné entre parenthèses.)**

hale and hearty (strong and healthy)
wear and tear (damage because of too much use)
kith and kin (friends and family)

first and foremost (first of all)
sink or swim (succeed or fail)
safe and sound (not hurt)
spick and span (clean and tidy)

5 Lequel de ces vers est un pentamètre iambique ?

(a) Here in the long unlovely street (Housman)
(b) Thy beauty shall no more be found (A. Marvell)
(c) No longer mourn for me when I am dead (W. Shakespeare)

6 Les comptines *(nursery rhymes)* sont souvent les premiers poèmes que les enfants entendent et répètent. Elles sont la plupart du temps dénuées de sens mais ont un rythme très marqué.
Scandez les deux comptines qui suivent.

(a) Jack and Jill
Went up the hill,
To fetch a pail of water;
Jack fell down
And broke his crown,
And Jill came tumbling after.

(b) Hickory dickory dock
The mouse went up the clock.
The clock struck one,
The mouse went down
Hickory dickory dock.

6. Analyser un passage de théâtre

Quelques mots essentiels :
an act, a scene
stage directions *(indications scéniques)*
the character's lines *(ses/sa réplique(s))*
a speech, a monologue
to play a part
the playwright *(le dramaturge)*, the stage director *(le metteur en scène)*, the actors
the setting *(le décor)*
the props *(les accessoires)*
a cue (the last words of a speech signalling the beginning of the next actor's words)
a performance *(une représentation)*

QUESTIONS ET REPÉRAGE

Vous ne pouvez analyser un extrait de théâtre comme s'il s'agissait de fiction ou de poésie. Il faut tout d'abord imaginer ce qui se passe sur scène. Voici quelques-uns des mots dont vous aurez besoin pour ce faire.

The theatre:

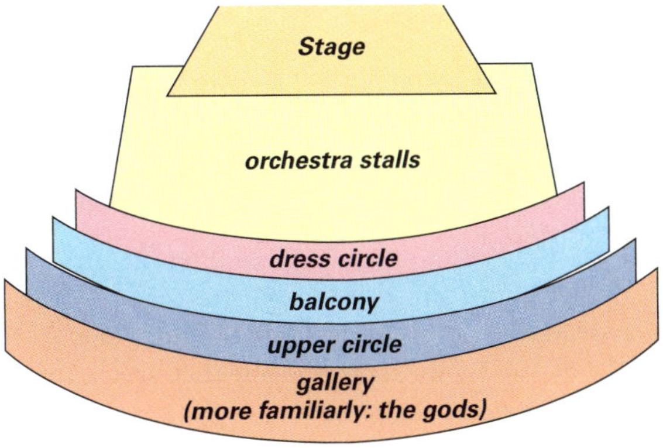

The stage:

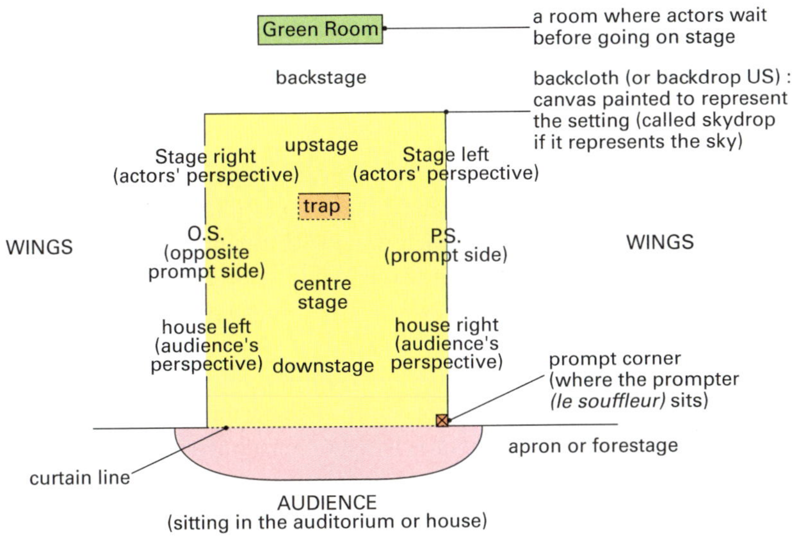

Voici les questions principales que vous devez vous poser lorsque vous étudiez un extrait de théâtre.

1 What kind of scene?

Is it a monologue or a dialogue between two or more characters?
Is the scene mainly comic, tragic, satirical...? Is there suspense?

2 Where?
Where does the scene take place?
Do you know anything about the setting? Is it important?

3 Who?
Who are the main characters?
What is the relationship between them? If necessary, draw a simple diagram to explain this relationship (family relationship, love, hatred, anger, etc.) Who speaks most?
Describe each of them: age, social class, language, ideas, personality...
Are they flat or round characters? (flat characters represent one single idea; round characters are more complex and capable of development).
How would you characterize their speech? Is it formal? standard? colloquial? Do they use slang *(argot)*? dialect?

4 What?
Look at the stage directions: what information do they give about the setting *(le décor)*, the movements of the characters on stage, the way they speak, their emotions?
Can you sum up what happens in the scene?
What are the main parts or movements in the scene?
What is the main effect of the scene? What is its message and significance? Is there any social satire? Is there humour?

5 What kind of play?
Is the passage part of a well-known dramatic form? Here are some common types:

The main theatrical genres

Theatre of the absurd: A type of theatre which reflects an existential view of life as absurd and of people as lost in a world they cannot understand rationally.
Comedy of manners: A comedy which deals with the manners of refined and fashionable society, as in the plays of Oscar Wilde. It often satirizes snobs, hypocrites, jealous husbands and foolish wives. The dialogue is often witty *(spirituel)* and brilliant.
Comedy of situation: A comedy based on complex plots, mistaken identities, confusing situations, more than on the study of character.
Farce: Comedy in which the humour is based on misunderstandings, boisterous (noisy) behaviour, absurd situations and humorously indecent behaviour.
Melodrama: A play which combines a romantic and thrilling plot and an appeal to emotions such as pity, horror or joy.
Problem play: A play of ideas, in which the characters are faced with social or moral issues. A solution to these problems is often suggested.
Tragedy: A serious play relating the events in the life of a person and leading to a catastrophe (tragic denouement).
Tragi-comedy: A play which combines elements of tragedy and comedy.

5 How?

How is the message conveyed? Is there realism, symbolism… in the way the characters are portrayed? Are there significant images and stylistic features?
How would you stage this scene if you were a stage-director?

exemple

Voici les grandes lignes d'un commentaire guidé à partir du tout début de *Hamlet*, de William Shakespeare.

1.1 *Enter* BARNARDO *and* FRANCISCO, *two sentinels*

BARNARDO Who's there?

FRANCISCO Nay[1] answer me. Stand and unfold yourself[2].

BARNARDO Long live the king!

FRANCISCO Barnardo?

BARNARDO He.

FRANCISCO You come most carefully upon your hour.

BARNARDO 'Tis[3] now struck twelve, get thee[4] to bed Francisco.

FRANCISCO For this relief[5] much thanks, 'tis bitter cold
And I am sick at heart.

BARNARDO Have you had quiet guard?

FRANCISCO Not a mouse stirring.

BARNARDO Well, good night.
If you do meet Horatio and Marcellus,
The rivals[6] of my watch, bid them[7] make haste.

FRANCISCO I think I hear them.

Enter HORATIO *and* MARCELLUS

Stand ho! Who is there?

HORATIO Friends to this ground[8].

MARCELLUS And liegemen[9] to the Dane[10].

FRANCISCO Give you good night.

MARCELLUS Oh farewell honest soldier,
Who hath[11] relieved you?

FRANCISCO Barnardo hath my place.
Give you good night. *Exit Francisco*

MARCELLUS Holla, Barnardo!

BARNARDO Say,
What, is Horatio there?

HORATIO A piece of him[12].

BARNARDO Welcome Horatio, welcome good Marcellus.

MARCELLUS What, has this thing appeared again tonight?

BARNARDO I have seen nothing.

MARCELLUS Horatio says 'tis but our fantasy[13],
And will not let belief take hold of him[14]
Touching[15] this dreaded[16] sight, twice seen of us
Therefore I have entreated him along
With us to watch the minutes of this night,
That if again this apparition come
He may approve our eyes[17], and speak to it.

HORATIO Tush, tush, 'twill not appear.

BARNARDO Sit down awhile,
And let us once again assail[18] your ears,
That are so fortified against our story,
What[19] we two nights have seen.

HORATIO Well, sit we down,
And let us hear Barnardo speak of this.

BARNARDO Last night of all,
When yond same star[20] that's westward from the pole[21]
Had made his course t'illume[22] that part of heaven
Where now it burns, Marcellus and myself,
The bell then beating[23] one -

Enter GHOST

MARCELLUS Peace, break thee off[24]. Look where it comes again.

BARNARDO In the same figure[25], like the king that's dead.

MARCELLUS Thou art[26] a scholar[27], speak to it Horatio.

BARNARDO Looks a not[28] like the king? Mark it Horatio.

HORATIO Most like. It harrows[29] me with fear and wonder.

BARNARDO It would be spoke[30] to.

MARCELLUS Question it Horatio.

HORATIO What art thou that usurp'st[31] this time of night,
Together with that fair and warlike form
In which the majesty of buried Denmark[32]
Did sometimes march? By heaven I charge thee speak.

MARCELLUS It is offended.

BARNARDO See, it stalks[33] away.

HORATIO Stay! Speak, speak, I charge thee speak!

Exit Ghost

1. **Nay:** no. 2. **Unfold yourself:** reveal who you are. 3. **'Tis:** it is. 4. **get thee:** go (thee is the now archaic second person singular). 5. **relief:** *relève (de la garde)*. 6. **rivals:** partners. 7. **bid them:** ask them to. 8. **ground:** here means country. 9. **liegemen to:** followers of. 10. **the Dane:** the Danish King. 11. **hath:** archaic for has. 12. **a piece of him:** Horatio is so cold that he is only a piece of himself. 13. **fantasy:** imagination. 14. **let belief take hold of him:** will not believe it. 15. **Touching:** about. 16. **dreaded:** terrible. 17. **approve our eyes:** confirm what we saw. 18. **assail:** attack. 19. **What:** with what. 20. **yond same star:** the very star over there. 21. **the pole:** the pole star. 22. **t'illume:** to illuminate. 23. **beating:** striking. 24. **break thee off:** stop. 25. **figure:** shape. 26. **thou art:** you are. 27. **a scholar:** *un érudit*. 28. **Looks a not:** does it not look. 29. **harrows:** disturbs. 30. **spoke:** spoken. 31. **usurpest:** take over something you have no right to. 32. **buried Denmark:** the buried king of Denmark (synecdoche). 33. **stalks:** walk haughtily *(hautainement)*

I Understanding what happens in the scene

Where does the scene take place? How many characters are they? What is the relationship between them? How many movements are there in the scene?

The play is set in Denmark, since Horatio and Marcellus call themselves "liegemen to the Dane" (15). This opening scene must be taking place in a castle or a fortified place, possibly on its battlements *(remparts)* since it is cold, the stage directions mention 'sentinels', and one sentinel is being replaced by another.

Four characters appear in this scene, besides the ghost. Three of them, Francisco, Barnardo and Marcellus are sentinels, or officers of the watch. The fourth character is Horatio, a friend of them, but also someone of a higher rank since he is described as a "scholar" (42).

There are three main movements in the scene, corresponding to the exits and entrances:

(1) lines 1 to 17: we witness the change of the guard: Francisco leaves and is replaced by Barnardo. Horatio and Marcellus soon join him.

(2) lines 18 to 39: the three men discuss something that has appeared to them already.

(3) The ghost of the dead king of Denmark appears. Horatio addresses him but the ghost disappears.

This structure is important because it creates an effect of suspense and mystery. We only gradually hear about the ghost. He is not mentioned in the first part, but only at line 21, when it is described as "this thing". Then it becomes "this dreaded sight" (25), then "this apparition" (28), and at last "a figure", "like the king". We are not directly told it is a ghost, which creates an impression of fear and mystery.

2 What is the main **atmosphere** conveyed by the scene? How does the syntax contribute to this?

The scene is full of questions. It starts with one, which is not answered, or rather which is answered by another question. The rest of the scene contains some ten questions, most of which never get an appropriate answer. Besides, there are very many short sentences in the first part of the text, giving it a staccato rhythm *(un rythme saccadé)*. All this creates an atmosphere of anxiety and fear, of threat and uneasiness. This is underlined by the fact that the soldiers seem perturbed. Francisco is "sick at heart", but we never know why.

So everything points to lack of understanding and mystery (Who is the ghost? Why does he come?). This is all the more striking as it is the first scene of the play: the curtain has gone up and the audience expects clarification, not mystery. We can note that the scene symbolically takes place at a time of transition: twelve o'clock (line 7).

This sense of uneasiness is political as well. The words "Friends to this ground" and "liegemen to the Dane" (15) evoke a country at war. The ghost appears "warlike" (47). The lexical field of war is also to be found in Barnardo's lines, as he prepares to tell his story and uses the words "assail" and "fortified" (31-32).

3 The **lexical field of vision and of the senses** is very rich in this scene. Analyse it and explain its significance.

Horatio is at first a sceptic who thinks the ghost is "fantasy" (23), whereas Marcellus and Barnardo insist on what they saw. Horatio too is convinced by what he sees at the end of the scene. This points to the importance of vision: the words see, watch, sight recur, and the guards are even called the "watch" (12).

In fact, all the senses become involved when it comes to understanding the apparition and interpreting the darkness. The men saw the ghost, then tell about him; others hear the tale; then all see the ghost again. Seeing is linked to telling and repeating the tale.

Besides, the scene highlights the problematic nature of appearances: can we really trust our eyes? The fact that all three characters see the ghost seems to point to its reality. Yet it does not speak, so that the audience feel as doubtful as the characters about its reality. It is speaking which confirms reality, something Horatio seems to feel when three times he asks the ghost to speak.

The power of language is also illustrated by the three types of style we find here: the colloquial dialogue at the beginning, Marcellus'slower speech and the flowery style of Bernardo's story. Indeed Barnardo's story is interrupted by the apparition of the ghost, as if his speech had conjured him up.

In the face of appearances which are difficult to interpret, only language remains stable. In this scene it is used both to question (to convey doubt and mystery) and to tell (and therefore to impose order on chaos).

4 How would you **stage this scene** if you were a stage director?

Since it is night, we could have a dark stage, with the short questions shouted in the dark, which would increase the feeling of mystery and fear described earlier.

2 Documents iconographiques

I. Conseils pour décrire et analyser un document iconographique

1 – Décrire

Quel que soit le type de document que vous avez à analyser (photo, peinture, publicité, dessin humoristique...), vous aurez dans un premier temps à le décrire. Voici un certain nombre d'expressions qui pourront vous aider dans votre description.

1 The dynamics of the picture:

Does the eye move from left to right, from top to bottom, diagonally...?

The scene can be represented on a large scale/on a small scale *(sur une grande échelle/sur une petite échelle)*.

What dominates is curves *(courbes)*/straight lines/geometrical forms.

The composition can be balanced/well-proportioned/symmetrical.

There is a strong sense of perspective.

There are several receding planes. *(plans qui s'éloignent)*

2 The layout *(la disposition, l'agencement)*

(in) the top left-hand corner	In the background/on the horizon/in the distance In the upper half/in the top part of the picture at the top	(in) the top right-hand corner
on the left/ left-hand side	in the middle (background) /middle distance	on the right/ right-hand side
the lower/bottom left-hand corner	In the foreground/In the lower part/half In the bottom part/at the bottom	the lower/bottom right-hand corner
	near the edge of the painting (the left/right/front/back edge...)	

P. 50 (DESCRIPTION SPATIALE)

3 The colours

The dominant colour(s) is/are...
A hue *(une teinte)*
a touch of blue, green...
The colours/shades can be bright/rich/vivid or restrained/delicate/soft
intense/strong/bright or subdued *(douces)*/soft/delicate
light or dark
warm or cool
A colour can fade into another one *(se fondre dans)*.
There can be a contrast of light and shade.
A bright colour can stand out against a dark background.
A dramatic lighting/a luminous atmosphere/a hard or soft light/deep shadows.
The light falls on... It brings.... into relief.
The lines can be firm or blurred *(floues)*.

4 The components *(les différents éléments)*

Are there any figures? *(personnages)*
What is the setting *(décor, surtout intérieur)* or the scenery *(paysage)* like?

5 A few useful expressions

It shows/represents/illustrates/symbolizes...
We can distinguish...
It reminds me of.../is reminiscent of.../makes me think of...
It conveys an impression of...
It creates an effect of...
The characters look sad, surprised, terrified....
They seem to...
If we now take a closer look at...
The setting is...

> He/It looks + adjective (he looks tired, surprised...) *(Il a l'air...)*
> He/It looks like + noun (He looks like a businessman) *(Il ressemble à...)*
> He/It looks as if/as though + preterit (He looks as though he had seen a ghost.) *(On dirait...)*

2 – COMMENTER

Votre commentaire doit toujours aller de l'explicite à l'implicite, de la description du document à l'étude du pourquoi (pourquoi a-t-il été créé, dans quel but, pour quel public, dans le cadre de quel mouvement artistique ?). Ce n'est qu'ensuite que vous pourrez donner votre opinion sur sa valeur commerciale, idéologique ou artistique.

Voici les différentes étapes possibles d'un commentaire :

1 What kind of visual document?

A cartoon (GB) or comic (US) *(un dessin humoristique)*
A comic strip (GB) or strip cartoon (US) *(une bande dessinée)*
A poster *(une affiche)*
A book/magazine cover
An ad(vertisement)
A photograph
A picture from a film/a still
A graph, a chart, a diagram
A collage
A painting (a landscape, a still-life *(une nature morte)*, a portrait)
A drawing

2 Where and when was it published/painted/drawn...?

3 Describe the document...

See above.

4 Beyond the description *(Au-delà de la description)*

If your picture is not self-evident, you may need to imagine the broader picture: what do you think happened just before? What will happen afterwards?
What is the purpose of the photograph/painting? Did the painter/photograph try to make a point? Is there a social/moral message?

5 Your own view or opinion.

exercices

1 Regardez le tableau de William Hogarth page 144 et complétez la description qui suit (en utilisant les mots donnés dans le désordre) afin de montrer le rapport spatial entre les différents éléments du tableau.

at – behind – below – between – foreground – in front – on the left – on the right – opposite – (the) background – the bottom left-hand – the left – the middle – the right – to the left – underneath (certains mots peuvent être utilisés plusieurs fois)

This is the first painting in a series of six which tell the story of a married couple. Its aim is to denounce the ill effects of a marriage based on financial and social interests rather than on love. The picture shows the last stages of the negotiations of the marriage contract.

▲ William Hogarth, *Marriage à la Mode*, 1745, The National Gallery, London I: *The Marriage Contract*.

The eye is first drawn to the two fathers, sitting at the table, in the … … is an Earl *(un Comte)*, sitting in a large chair which resembles a throne. He has gout (see his foot), a nobleman's disease, and is pointing to his family tree (… his right hand), which he is clearly proud of. … him sits the young woman's father, an alderman *(conseiller municipal)* of the City of London. He is carefully examining the marriage documents. It is clear that the alderman is paying a large amount of money so that his daughter may marry into the nobility, while the Earl only accepts such a marriage because he badly needs money. … the two of them, in the …, an open window reveals the large house which the earl is having built. Both the scaffolding *(l'échafaudage)*, which shows that the house is not finished, and the workmen doing nothing in front of it, point to the fact that there is not enough money to finish the construction. In the fourth picture in the series, we learn that the earl's name is Squanderfield (to squander is to spend money carelessly).

… the two fathers and the window, two other characters are to be seen: the earl's lawyer (notaire), standing … his master, … of the window, looking out, and the alderman's agent, … of him, handing out some papers to the earl.

The marriage is therefore to the advantage of the two fathers, but the young people do not seem to appreciate it. On … of the picture, sits the bride, … her future husband, on … and a lawyer, on … She looks sad and is pouting *(bouder)*.

Note that she is playing with her wedding-ring, the symbol of a marriage she does not want. The lawyer seems to be whispering to her, already announcing the future relationship between them. In the last picture in the series, we learn that his name is Silvertongue. ..., the bridegroom *(le jeune marié)* turns his back to his bride, showing his indifference to the marriage. He looks resigned. A mirror immediately ... the bridegroom shows the reflection of the young lawyer paying his court to the bride, but the bridegroom is too blind to see it. In the ... corner, ... the bridegroom, two dogs are chained, a symbol of the marriage which is being arranged.
On the walls, in ..., several pictures mostly represent scenes of catastrophe or martyrdom. Note in particular David killing Goliath (... the top, to the left of the large portrait), and ... it, on the left, St Sebastian. In ... of the four paintings on the left is a picture of Medusa.

2 En 1943, l'illustrateur américain Norman Rockwell conçut la couverture suivante pour le *Saturday Evening Post* à l'occasion du 1er avril. Il dit avoir glissé 45 erreurs dans son tableau.

▲ Reproduced in *Norman Rockwell Illustrator*, by Arthur Guptill, first published in 1946, Watson-Guptill Publications, a division of Billboard Publications, Inc.

Un certain nombre de ces erreurs portent sur les objets mentionnés ci-dessous. Faites pour chacun d'entre eux une phrase complète pour expliquer à quel endroit précis du tableau est l'erreur et en quoi elle consiste.

1. a spanner (*une clef à molette*)
2. skating shoes (*chaussures de patinage*)
3. a bottle and a glass
4. a piece of string
5. the clock
6. a bowtie (*un nœud papillon*)
7. a fish
8. a milk bottle
9. a raccoon (*un raton*)
10. a chessboard (*un échiquier*)
11. a blackbird (*un merle*)
12. scissors
13. ducks (*des canards*)
14. a zebra
15. a tap (*un robinet*)

2. Analyser une peinture ou une photographie

Voici quelques conseils généraux pour analyser une peinture ou une photographie.

1 – Peintures

Before you start:

– Do you know who the painter is? Is he/she part of an artistic movement? Is the painting abstract, realistic, surrealistic?
– Look at the title of the painting. Does it help you understand the painting?
– If you know when it was painted, is the date important?
– Is the painting a portrait/a landscape/a seascape (*une marine*)/a still life (*une nature morte*)?

Your commentary:

1 Describe what you see in the painting, then comment on the technique used.
It can be an oil painting (*une huile*), a watercolour (*une aquarelle*), a print (*une gravure*).
You can look at the picture from bottom to top/from top to bottom/from left to right…
The eye is led from… to…/is drawn towards…
The focus of attention is… (*le regard se porte sur*)
Is there a backcloth (*une toile de fond*) or a background (*un arrière-plan*)? Is there a sense of perspective?
Where does the light come from?

2 Is there symbolism in the painting? Does it convey a message? Does it reflect any particular artistic or cultural movement? Is the social or historical context relevant? (*pertinent*)

3 What is your personal reaction to it?

2 – Photographies

1 Is the photograph part of an advertisement, is it a still from a film, is it an art photograph, a portrait, a fashion photograph, a sports photograph, a news photograph, a feature shot *(une photo de reportage)*, an amateur photograph?

2 Describe the photograph, using some of the following vocabulary to talk about the technique used:
A photograph/a snapshot *(un instantané)*
A picture can be in colour or in black and white.
It has a particular framing *(cadrage)*.
It can be a long shot, a medium shot, a close shot or a close-up shot *(plan large, plan moyen, plan rapproché, gros plan)*
It can be a high-angle shot (= a downward view) *(plan en plongée)*, which usually reduces the subject, or a low-angle shot (= an upward view) *(plan en contre plongée)*, which often makes the subject look big and threatening.
A photograph can be blurred or out of focus *(floue)* or in focus. It can be overexposed *(surexposée)* or underexposed *(sous-exposée)*
The focus of the photograph is a person, a building, etc.
The person is seen facing the camera, in profile or with his/her back to the camera.

3 Comment on the technique and effect
– Has the photograph any artistic merit? Why?
– Who do you think took the photograph? Why?
– What idea or message do you think the photographer wants to convey?

4 Your opinion
What do you think of the picture? Do you like it? Why or why not?

3 – Photos ou séquences de films

1 What kind of film? a documentary? a silent movie *(film muet)*, a western? a thriller? a comedy? a horror movie? a sit com *(comédie de situation)*?

2 Describe the sequence
What happens in this sequence? Who are the characters? Is there a lot of action? Can you imagine what took place before? And what will take place afterwards?

3 Describe the technique
Describe the technique used, with the help of the following vocabulary:

1 **Range of view:** the distance between the camera and the scene:
– **Long shots** are taken from a distance.
– **Full shots** show the subject filling the frame.
– **Close ups** are close shots of persons, objects or details.
– **Zoom shots** are shots in which there is a rapid move closer to or away from the object or scene which is viewed.

2 The angle of view depends on the elevation and horizontality of the camera:
– a **BIRD'S EYE VIEW** is a shot taken from very high up; it dwarfs *(rapetisser, écraser)* the subject, creating an effect of omniscience, contempt, or superiority.
– a **HIGH ANGLE SHOT** is taken from above *(plongée)*: it makes the subject smaller and more vulnerable.
– a **LOW ANGLE SHOT** is taken from below *(contre-plongée)*, so that the viewer is dwarfed and the subject looks enormous or threatening.
– a **WIDE ANGLE SHOT**

3 Movement
– a **MOVING SHOT** is taken with the camera moving away from a scene or closer to it.
– a **PAN** is a shot in which the camera rotates horizontally.

4 Focus. An image, a detail, a scene… may be: **IN FOCUS** (sharp) or **OUT OF FOCUS** (blurred, fuzzy).

5 Cuts are abrupt transitions from one shot to another.

6 Transitions between two scenes or shots.
A common way of **BRIDGING** two shots is by using a **DISSOLVE**, that is to say by superimposing a second image over the first one, which gradually fades away. For a very short time, the two images are linked and united. This often brings out similarity or contrast in the two shots.

7 Montage: Montage can refer to the editing of a film.
FLASHBACKS show us past events
FLASHFORWARDS show us future events.

– How effective is this technique? How does it contribute to the atmosphere?
– What is the overall effect of the sequence? Is it frightening, moving, amusing…? Is there social satire? Is there any music which contributes to this?
– Do you find it effective? Do you like it?

Words you may also need:
the credits: *le générique*
dubbed: *doublé*
extras: *figurants*
the sound-track: *la bande son*
sound effects: *bruitage*
stunts: *cascades*
subtitles: *sous-titres*
a still: a single shot from a film
a scene filmed on location: *en décor naturel*
the screenplay: *le scénario*
the cast: *la distribution*

exemple 1

Voici un commentaire possible du tableau de Holbein *The Ambassadors* (1533), qui se trouve à la *National Gallery* à Londres. Il y a bien sûr dans ce commentaire des informations que vous ne pouvez pas déduire du tableau lui-même, mais c'est la démarche qui compte ici.

I Before you start

■ **The painter**

The German painter Holbein lived in London from 1532 to 1543, where he became official painter at the English court.

■ **The date**, 1533, is highly significant.

The English king Henry VIII was then married to Catherine of Aragon, but wanted the Pope *(le Pape)* to annul his marriage so that he could get married to Anne Boleyn

instead. The Pope refused, but by then Henry had already secretly married Anne Boleyn, who was pregnant (*enceinte*). A French ambassador was sent to London to arrange things with the Pope but he had no success: Henry VIII broke with the church of Rome and declared himself "Supreme Head of the English Church and Clergy". This was the starting point of the Reformation. So the painting of the French ambassador in 1533 (actually Jean de Dinteville) is quite meaningful.

2 Description

■ The composition

This is a double portrait. Two men are set at the edges of the painting, separated by shelves (*étagères*) showing books and instruments. It is unusual to find the figures shown apart from each other in a double painting, and we have to ask ourselves why Holbein chose such a composition. They are seen from a rather low point of view, which makes the two men even more imposing. They are seen against a green backcloth. We must also notice strong vertical and horizontal lines, with only a few diagonals in the middle part of the painting.

■ A description of the painting

– The eye is first drawn to the difference between the two men. On the left hand side, the man wears a short robe, typical of an ambassador's. The other man, on the contrary, wears a long robe: he is a clergyman.
Everything about the ambassador shows the authority and self-confidence of the man of the world: the prestigious order of St Michael around his neck, his rich clothes, his wide shoulders, his open coat, his legs firmly set wide apart. The figures on his dagger (*poignard*) tell us he is 29, and we know he was Jean de Dinteville, the French ambassador to London at the time.
The clergyman, a bishop (*évêque*) in fact and a friend of the ambassador, is seen as more introspective: he seems to look inward with his falling eyelids, and he keeps his long robe from showing his body. The figures on his Bible (under his right elbow) tell us he is 25. He was Georges de Selve, bishop of Lavaur.
The light shirt and fur worn by the ambassador also contrast with the dark robe of the bishop.
The painting thus records the meeting in London of the two friends from France.

– Between them, the shelves show instruments linked to applied mathematics: a celestial globe, a sundial (*cadran solaire*), a compass, a lute (music was then seen as a mathematical art). All this points to learning and magnificence. But we should note that the top shelf points to the heavenly and the celestial (a celestial sphere, a Bible), whereas the bottom shelf points to the terrestrial (the lute, a textbook on calculation). Is Holbein telling us that the two men are both similar (they have the same attitude, symmetrically placed in the painting, and share an interest in the sciences) but different (the worldly and the spiritual)?

– The scene, however, is also full of symbols of death: one of the strings of the lute is broken and the oblong figure in the foreground between the two men turns out to be a skull *(crâne)* when you stand on the side of the picture. Such visual tricks distorting images were called anamorphoses and were quite common at the time.

3 An interpretation

The double portrait reflects doubleness at other levels:

- Between the Middle Ages and the Renaissance. 1533 can be said to mark the beginning of the Renaissance. The painting still looks back to the Middle Ages, with its religious interpretations of the world (symbolised here by the Bible and the skull). But by including mathematical instruments, the painting also reflects the new values of the Renaissance and its desire to explain the world thanks to the study of natural sciences.

- The painting is also poised *(en équilibre)* between power (an ambassador, a bishop) and vanitas, that is to say the idea that everything, including power, is mortal and ends in the grave *(la tombe)*. It may be an allusion to the Dinteville family's motto *(devise)*: memento mori ("Remember that you are mortal.") This accounts for the balance between the strong vertical and horizontal lines and the realism of the picture on the one hand, and the diagonals and anamorphosis on the other hand.

The painting celebrates a new world of astronomy and music, while at the same time hinting *(laisser entendre)* that they may help us reach deeper meanings within the universe.

VOIR AUSSI LE COMMENTAIRE DU TABLEAU DE GRANT WOOD, P. 345.

exemple 2

Voici un court commentaire d'une photographie de Tony Ray-Jones: *Glyndebourne* (1967).

What first looks like an idyllic and ordinary country scene – a picnic in a field – soon strikes us as quite strange: why is the couple in evening dress? The answer is to be found in the title of the photograph. Glyndebourne, in Sussex, is an open air theatre where an annual opera festival takes place in the summer. Among its traditions is the custom of wearing evening dress and of holding elaborate picnics in the garden during the interval.

This photograph is based on contrast. The human beings in the foreground appear as both similar to and different from the cows in the background, the two groups being separated by the horizontal line of the grass ditch *(fossé)*. Although both human beings and cattle are eating, although both present marked black and white contrasts, the highly organized picnic (note the table and chairs, the plates, glasses, wine and baskets, all brought for the occasion) and the apparent self-absorption of the two characters

are opposed to the freer world of the cows and sheep. What we have here is the meeting of nature and culture or sophistication. The result is both humorous and ironic.
But the photograph is also a picture of British insularity and eccentricity, of the extraordinary lengths to which people will go to maintain traditions. As Ray-Jones wrote in 1968: "For me there is something very special and rather humorous about the English way of life and I wish to record it from my particular point of view before it becomes more Americanized."

↗ exercice

Voici un tableau et un commentaire de ce tableau.
Dans quel ordre les points suivants sont-ils mentionnés dans le commentaire ? Numérotez-les de 1 à 8

a. A general description of the subject
b. An explanation of the title
c. The artist
d. The light
e. The main effect
f. The perspective
g. The point of view
h. The type of painting

This oil painting by the American artist Edward Hopper, was painted in 1942. It is a figurative painting, which represents a late-night diner (a café), in which

▲ Edward Hopper (1882-1967), *Nighthawks*, 1942, Art Institute of Chicago.

three customers are sitting at the counter. A waiter in white bends down to prepare a drink. Outside, the street is deserted. There are several realistic details – the saltcellar *(salière)* and peppershaker *(poivrier)*, the cups, the box for napkins, the hot water containers... – and the architecture of the brownish building in the background clearly situates the scene in an American city. But although the subject matter is quite ordinary, the painting has an extraordinarily powerful effect. Why?

One of the reasons is the theatrical contrast in colours and lighting. The interior of the diner is brightly illuminated and contrasts with the eerie *(étrange)*, greenish darkness outside. It is as if the light fell upon a stage in a darkened theatre. This is emphasized by the fact that the characters are seen from the outside, through the window, framed *(encadrés)* by dark walls. It is as if the spectator were looking into an aquarium, separated from the characters by a glass pane. And the perspective is strange too, making the diner seem enormous. (Hopper was fascinated by the movies and his composition here may reflect the influence of cinematic techniques.)

The effect is to separate the characters from the viewer and to accentuate their isolation and their loneliness. Indeed, each seems lost in his or her thoughts, they are not talking to each other, even though two of them are standing next to each other and might be friends, lovers, or husband and wife. The impression given is that there is no plot which links them, no relationship, that what we see is a mere setting, characters in a glass cage.

This is a painting about urban isolation. Hopper said about it: "unconsciously, probably, I was painting the loneliness of a large city." But the characters also look small, dwarfed *(écrasés, rapetissés)* and vulnerable so that the painting also conveys a sense of threat and suspense, as if something was about to happen. All this explains the title of the painting, *Nighthawks*. A nighthawk is a nocturnal bird (a hawk: *un faucon*) or a nocturnal prowler *(rôdeur)*. Indeed, two French translations have been given for this painting: *Oiseaux de nuit* and *Les Rôdeurs de nuit*.

3. Analyser une publicité

Les différentes étapes d'un commentaire

1 Contexte

– Where did the ad appear? In a magazine? On a hoarding (GB) or billboard (US)? *(un panneau publicitaire)* Is it part of a TV commercial?
– When do you think the advertisement appeared?
– What is the ad(vertisement) for? A product? A cause?

2 Description

– Describe the advertisement, which can contain:

– a picture
– a catch phrase *(une accroche)*: Surf here
– a logo
– copy (the text which explains why you should buy that particular 'brand' *(marque)* or make)

Here the copy ("With wireless broadband through Wanadoo's Livebox you can have the Internet on tap anywhere in your home. For more information visit www.wanadoo.co.uk.") contains a pun *(un jeu de mot)*. "On tap" means available *(disponible)*; but a tap is also what you turn to get water *(un robinet)*.

3 Commentaire

– Who is the advertisement targeted at (a target: *une cible*)/aimed at/directed to (wards)? Who are the potential buyers? Teenagers? Pensioners (*retraités*)? Parents? Businessmen?... How do you know? Are the type of people represented on the advertisement significant?
– Is it based on stereotypes?
– What means are used? humour, persuasion, irony, technical information...?

4 Votre opinion

– Do you find the advertisement convincing and successful? Why or why not?

exemple

This is a fairly old advertisement, which appeared on posters in Britain in 1982. Its aim was to promote black Levi Strauss jeans.
What strikes us first is that the picture is very simple: it shows a huge flock of white sheep moving towards the left of the picture. On the right hand side, however, there is a single black sheep heading (*se dirigeant*) in the other direction. The use of the black sheep to symbolise the originality and the difference represented by black jeans is echoed by the words BLACK LEVI'S at the bottom of the advert. The Levi logo suitably appears in white letters on a black background. There is no copy (*texte*) to accompany the picture, perhaps because there is no need to explain or justify what most people were familiar with in a different colour, but there is a catch phrase: WHEN THE WORLD ZIGS, ZAG. There is, of course, no verb 'to zig'and no verb 'to zag', but the sentence plays on the word 'zigzag', once again conveying the idea that black jeans are different, not for ordinary people, that they are a mark of originality.

Everything about this advertisement shows it is aimed at a fashionable, sophisticated audience: Both the picture and the catch-phrase are subtle rather than forceful. The method is indirect since the jeans are not shown, so that the viewer has to think and draw his own conclusions. The targeted audience is clearly streetwise *(futé)* young people, and the advertisement used is bound to flatter them: they are different from the masses and more sophisticated, therefore black Levis are for them.
Behind what may appear at first like a rather boring picture (showing nothing but sheep), there is in fact a very powerful message.

exercice

Regardez cette publicité et choisissez les réponses qui conviennent. Il peut y en avoir plus d'une par question.

What is this advertisement for?
- clothes
- a bike
- an airline

What sort of public is targeted here?
- people who love animals
- people who love going fast
- people who love adventure
- people who love comfort

What means does this advertisement use to create an impact on the viewer?
- humour
- shock tactics
- persuasion
- irony
- an original idea
- a stereotype
- the viewer's curiosity
- the viewer's disapproval

4. Analyser un dessin humoristique

Les différentes étapes d'un commentaire

- Describe what the cartoon represents. Where did it appear?
- Is there a caption? (une légende) Is there a pun (un jeu de mots) in the caption?
- What is the aim of the cartoon? Just to amuse? To comment on a political or social event or tendency? If so, which one?
- In a cartoon, there are often many details which relate to the main themes. For instance, cartoons often make use of symbols. Comment on these details.
- Do you find the cartoon amusing? persuasive? irritating?

Describing a cartoon: words and expressions

the cartoonist: *le dessinateur*
a caricature
a frame (one of the drawings in a strip cartoon)
a caption: *une légende*
a bubble or a speech balloon: *une bulle*
to draw
to attack; to criticize; to expose: *dénoncer*
to lampoon: *tourner en dérision*
to ridicule, to make fun of
funny, humorous, amusing
grim humour: *humour noir*
absurd, nonsensical
irony, satire

exemple

Two men, in a relaxed pose, are having a discussion as they might have in a pub (the one on the left seems to be holding a glass of beer). They are standing on a globe of the earth, over Europe. Their heads are not visible, hidden as they are behind billowing *(qui monte en volutes)* smoke which comes belching out of tall chimneys on both sides. The smoke rises from factories in the United States to the west, and in India and China to the east. So thick and black is the smoke that the two men must clearly be choking *(étouffer)*.
Part of the humour of the cartoon springs from the fact that the men are talking normally, as if the smoke had not reached them. Besides, they are discussing the Kyoto Protocol, which is an attempt to reduce greenhouse gas emissions. Their concern with global warming *(le réchauffement de la planète)* (which might affect their lives in decades to come) seems almost irrelevant compared to the black smoke which already engulfs

them. But the cartoon also relies on a linguistic pun. The answer of the man on the right is "Don't hold your breath", an expression which means that the event is unlikely to take place (you therefore should not hold your breath – that is to say stop breathing – while you are waiting for it to take place): he thus proves quite lucid in his belief that global warming is not going to be stopped so easily. Yet the literal meaning of his words is "Keep breathing!", which is quite funny considering the smoke which they are inhaling.

But beyond this humorous exchange, a very serious situation is hinted at. We must first note that the cartoon was published in *The Economist* on February 19th 2005, three days exactly after the Kyoto Protocol came into force *(entré en vigueur)*. The European Union ratified the Kyoto Treaty, and introduced quotas in the industrial emission of carbon dioxide. Yet the United States did not ratify the treaty; nor did China. As for India, it is exempted from the framework of the treaty. Hence the mention of these three countries, which seem to be threatening Europe with their toxic fumes, the tall chimneys of their factories also being reminiscent of smoking guns.

This cartoon therefore first captures the attention of the reader because of its amusing drawing and its pun, but soon leads him or her to consider the alarming consequences of some of the most powerful countries in the world not ratifying the Kyoto treaty. Everyone should be concerned, even Europeans, who should not keep their heads in the sand, as these two men seem to be doing.

exercices

1 Associez ces symboles, que l'on trouve souvent dans les dessins politiques, et ce qu'ils représentent

A. John Bull
B. the bear
C. the cock
D. the donkey *(l'âne)*
E. the eagle
F. the elephant
G. the leek *(le poireau)*
H. the rose
I. the shamrock *(le trèfle)*
J. the thistle *(le chardon)*
K. Uncle Sam

1. America
2. Britain
3. England
4. France
5. Ireland
6. Russia
7. Scotland
8. The Democratic Party (US)
9. The Republican Party (US)
10. Wales

2 Regardez ces deux dessins et choisissez la phrase qui résume le mieux leur signification. P. 292

▲ *The Economist*, June 5, 2004.

1. Religion is dominated by politics.
2. Religious issues are what separates Republicans and Democrats.
3. Republicans and Democrats are competing *(rivaliser)* to get religious votes.
4. The church cannot choose between the two main parties.

▲ *The Economist*, April 17, 2004.

A. Soldiers would like to leave Iraq but cannot.
B. America's involvement *(engagement)* in Iraq is going to be as long as the Vietnam one was.
C. Instead of fighting, soldiers have to deal with material problems in Iraq.
D. America regrets its presence in Iraq.

5. Analyser un tableau ou un graphique

1 – Quelques formes de tableaux et graphiques

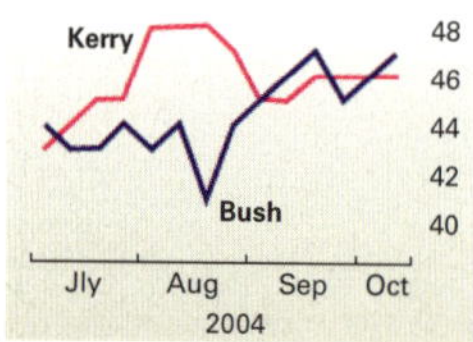

A graph

.... a dotted line

------ a broken line

—— a solid line

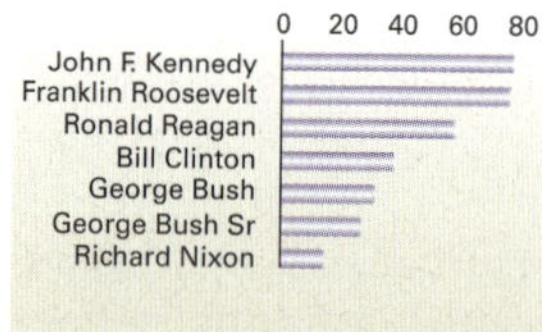

A bar chart

sections

Industrial production 1959-67			
	1959	1963	1967
Britain	105	119	133
W. Germany	107	137	158
France	112	166	212
USA	113	133	168
Japan	120	212	347

A table

columns & lines

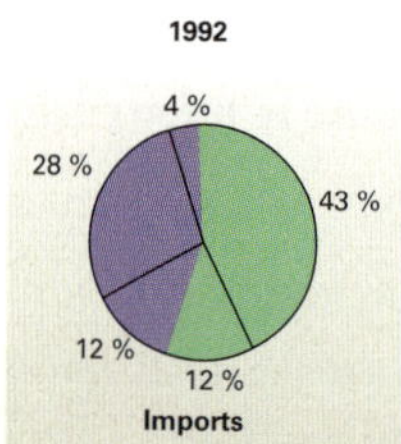

A pie chart

sections, slices, shares

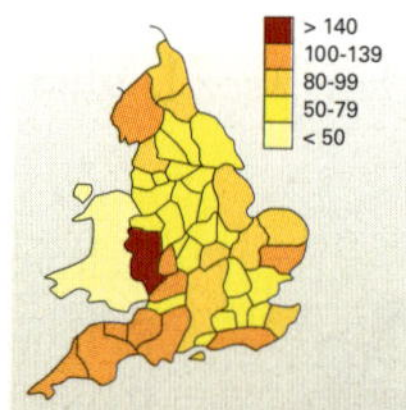

A map

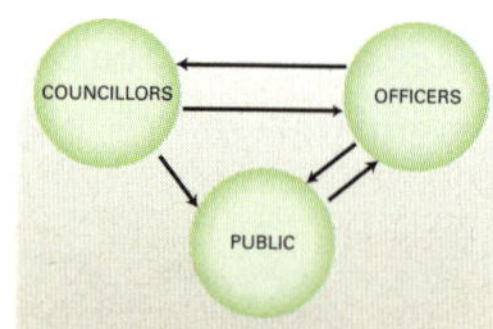

A diagram

arrows

2 – Les étapes d'un commentaire

1 Describe the document.

- Where did the graph or table appear? How reliable *(sérieux, fiable)* is this source?
- What period is considered? What indicators are considered?
- Describe the main point of the table and graph. What does it show?

P. 90

2 Comment on the results and show a critical mind.

- How can you explain the trend *(la tendance)* or result shown? Can any cultural, political… event account for it *(l'expliquer)*?
- Do you think the choice of indicators is neutral? Or do you think another result could have been reached by presenting the figures differently?

exemple

Voici, à titre d'exemple, le commentaire de deux documents parus dans *The Economist* le 1er mai 2004.

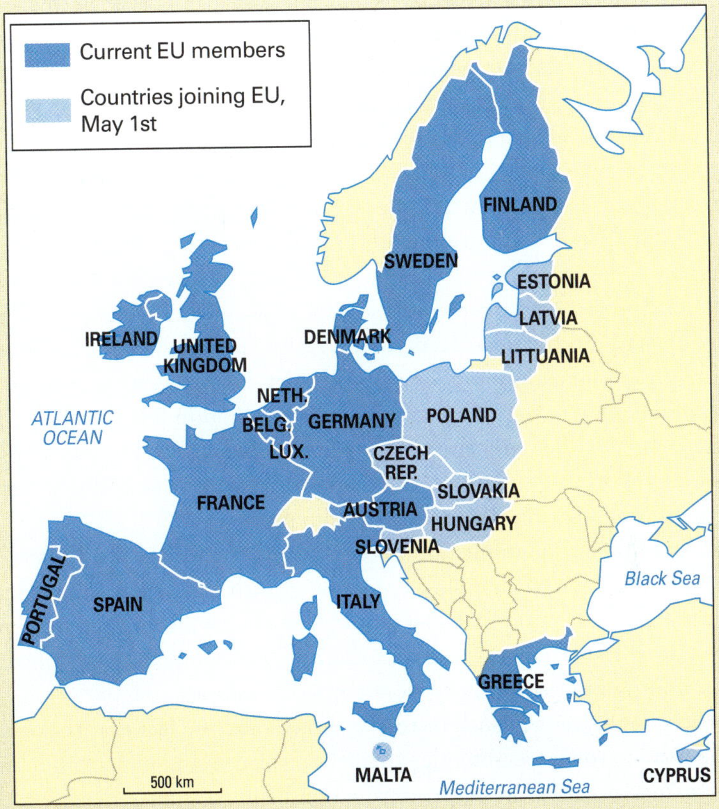

Growing pains?

Enlargement date	Countries joining	Population % addition	GDP (PPP) % addition	GDP per head, entrants as % of existing average
1973	Britain, Denmark, Ireland	33,4	31,9	95,5
1981	Greece	3,7	1,8	48,4
1986	Portugal, Spain	17,8	11,0	62,2
1995	Austria, Finland, Sweden	6,3	6,5	103,6
2004*	Cyprus, Czech Republic , Estonia, Hungary, Latvia, Lithuania, Malta, Poland, Slovakia, Slovenia	19,6	9,1	46,5

Sources: EIU; Eurostat; IMF; OECD.

*2003 data

Both the map and the table are about the enlargement of the European Union. They were published in *The Economist* on May 1st 2004, the very day when ten new countries became members of the European Union.
The map shows the current EU members and the countries which joined the EU on May 1st. These countries are mainly from central Europe, that is to say from ex-Communist countries, and form an enormous geographical bloc to the East of the European Union. This also means that the EU now stretches from Portugal to Poland. The only exceptions are Malta and Cyprus.
What the table adds to this is questions and doubts. Indeed, its title takes the form of a question: Growing pains? *(Difficultés de croissance?)* The expression refers to the temporary difficulties an organisation is faced with when it develops. Although the expression is qualified by a question mark, it still points to problems. What are they? The ten new members are impressive in size, adding almost 20 % to the population of the EU. Yet the 1973 enlargement was proportionately much larger and caused no problem. The main problem has to do with GDP (gross domestic product = *PIB*), as shown in the second and third columns: these new countries are significantly poorer than the other member states. The average GDP per head in less than half (46.5) the average GDP of the other countries. It is true that Greece's GDP was almost as low when it joined the EU in 1981, but it is easier to "absorb" one country representing 3.7 % of the EU population than to include ten more.
These figures explain why public opinion was mostly hostile to the EU enlargement in May 2004. Already worried by slow economic growth and high unemployment, existing EU members were afraid that they would have to contribute even more money to give to the poorer new members, and that their countries might be swamped *(submergés)* by new immigrants accepting to work for lower salaries.
The table, however, leaves out such factors as growth and the fact that the new member states have faster-growing economies than those of existing members. This should provide large markets for Europe's companies and thus revitalise European economy.

↗ exercices

Le texte qui suit décrit le tableau ci-contre. Complétez ce texte avec les adjectifs et participes donnés dans le désordre. Certains adjectifs sont employés plusieurs fois.

sharp – more – evenly – growing – pronounced – both – early – less – continuing – higher

The social composition of the Cabinet reveals a tendency towards the ❶ embourgeoisement of party leaderships as well as a ❷ contrast between the two party elites. Thus, since the ❸ part of the century, Conservative Cabinets have

become ❹ middle class and ❺ aristocratic, Labour Cabinets, ❻ middle class and ❼ working class.
But there are still ❽ contrasts. Whereas the public school/Oxbridge element has increased in ❾ Conservative and Labour Cabinets in the post-war period and also constitutes a ❿ proportion of them than it does of the respective parliamentary parties, it is much more ⓫ in Conservative Cabinets. Thus, Tory[1] Cabinets in the post-1945 era have been overwhelmingly composed of people of middle-class origins, but Labour Cabinets have been fairly ⓬ divided between ministers with working-class and those with middle-class backgrounds.

▲ *Contemporary British Politics*, Coxall & Robins, Macmillan 1994.

1. **Tory:** Conservative.

Education and class origins of Cabinet ministers, 1916-84

	Background of Cabinet Ministers (%)			
	1916-1955		1955-1984	
	Conservative	Labour	Conservative	Labour
All public schools	76.5	26.1	87.1	32.1
Eton, Harrow	45.9	7.6	36.3	3.5
Oxbridge	63.2	27.6	72.8	42.8
Elem/Sec	4.0	50.7	2.5	37.5
All Universities	71.4	44.6	81.6	62.5
Aristocrat	31.6	6.1	18.1	1.8
Middle Class	65.3	38.4	74.0	44.6
Working Class	3.0	55.3	2.6	41.0
No Data	-	-	4.0	12.6
Number	98	65	77	56

Source: Extracted from Burch and Moran (1985).

III Traduire

I Avant toute traduction...

1 – L'analyse du texte

Avant toute traduction, il est indispensable de lire le texte plusieurs fois, très attentivement, et d'en faire une analyse.

→ Que vous apprennent la source du texte (article de journal ? quel journal ? extrait de roman ? britannique ? américain ?....), le nom de l'auteur, la date de publication, le titre de l'extrait lui même ?

→ Quel est le sens global du texte ? Pouvez vous répondre à des questions du type *Who? Where? When? What? Why?*

→ Comment le texte est-il organisé ? De façon logique, chronologique ? Soulignez les mots de liaison qui vous permettent de vous repérer.

→ À quel temps le texte est-il écrit ? Ce temps est-il le même tout au long du texte, ou bien y a-t-il des retours en arrière, des visées dans le futur, des présents à valeur générale... ? Si le texte n'est pas uniformément au même temps, utilisez des crayons de couleurs différentes pour bien faire ressortir sa structure temporelle.

→ Quel point de vue a-t-on dans le texte ? Celui d'un journaliste ? (objectif ou non ?) Celui d'un narrateur qui écrit à la première personne ? Celui d'un narrateur extérieur et omniscient ?

Notez l'utilisation des modaux.

→ Quel est le ton du texte ? Factuel, amusé, indigné... ?

→ Quel est son registre ? Langue familière, soutenue, argotique ?

→ Remarquez-vous des effets stylistiques, des jeux de mots, des échos, un champ sémantique particulièrement riche que vous devez garder dans la traduction... ?

2 – La compréhension du texte

Toujours avant de traduire, il faut passer de la compréhension globale à la compréhension de détail. Vous allez sans doute être arrêtés par des mots inconnus. Il est préférable, dans un premier temps, et afin d'acquérir une méthode, de chercher à inférer leur sens plutôt que de chercher celui-ci dans un dictionnaire.

→ Pouvez-vous comprendre le sens d'après la racine, ou la formation du mot ? (Mais attention aux faux-amis !)

She is always overrreacting (*overreacting* = *over* + *react* + *ing*). Le préfixe *over* indique le surplus ou l'excès. *To overreact,* c'est donc réagir de manière excessive. On pourrait donc traduire la phrase par : « Elle exagère toujours./Elle dramatise tout ».

→ Si ce n'est pas le cas, essayez d'inférer le sens en vous demandant ce qui pourrait logiquement apparaître à cet endroit dans la phrase.

Il suffit souvent d'imaginer que vous avez un blanc à la place du mot que vous ne comprenez pas.
Dans les quelques lignes qui suivent, imaginez que vous ne connaissiez pas le sens des deux mots soulignés.
Squatting at the edge of the pond [...] Raphael found himself staring at a small school of very small fish a few feet away. Very tiny fish! [...] Pickerel? (Joyce Carol Oates)
Vous connaissez bien sûr le mot *school* dans son sens d'école, mais un tel sens serait absurde ici. Raphael regarde un petit ... de petits poissons.
C'est un sens proche de « groupe » qui s'impose ici. En effet, *a school of fish*, c'est un banc de poissons.
Quant à *pickerel*, il s'agit d'un type de poisson. Vous avez deux éléments qui doivent vous permettre d'éliminer des non-sens : ces poissons sont des poissons d'étang *(the pond)* et ils sont minuscules *(tiny fish)*. *A pickerel* est en fait un petit brochet. Un jour d'examen, une traduction de bon sens telle que carpillon (petite carpe) serait à peine pénalisée, alors qu'une traduction telle que sole (poisson de mer) le serait beaucoup plus lourdement.
Toute inférence est un travail de bon sens.

Exemple de traduction automatique par ordinateur aboutissant à un non sens.

Pour effectuer une nouvelle traduction
Tapez ou collez, ci-dessous, le texte (jusqu'à 300 caractères) que vous désirez traduire :

Squatting at the edge of the pond (...) Raphael found himself staring at a small school of very small fish a few feet away. Very tiny fish! (...) Pickerel?

Voici la traduction de votre texte en français
S'accroupissant au bord de l'étang, (...) Raphaël s'est trouvé regarder fixement une petite école des poissons très petits quelques pieds de distance. Poissons très minuscules ! (...) Pickerel ?

Dans un second temps, on peut avoir recours au dictionnaire. Utilisez, si vous le pouvez, un dictionnaire unilingue (anglais-anglais), qui vous expliquera le sens du mot anglais. Ceci vous obligera à rechercher l'équivalent français le plus approprié. L'avantage est double : vous entraîner à la gymnastique mentale nécessaire pour chercher le mot juste (elle vous sera indispensable un jour d'examen, lorsque vous ne disposerez pas d'un dictionnaire), vous permettre de chercher le mot qui convient le mieux dans votre contexte (ce mot n'est pas nécessairement un de ceux mentionnés dans un dictionnaire bilingue.)

Vous pourrez enfin utiliser le dictionnaire bilingue (anglais-français), qui vous permettra de vérifier ou d'améliorer votre traduction.

P. 172 (UTILISATION DU DICTIONNAIRE)

Toujours à ce stade du travail, c'est-à-dire avant de traduire, arrêtez-vous sur chacune des phrases complexes du texte afin d'en bien comprendre la structure. Soulignez ou entourez le sujet et le verbe principal, utilisez d'autres couleurs pour les propositions relatives… jusqu'au moment ou la structure de la phrase vous semblera parfaitement claire.

3 – La traduction

Lorsque vous avez l'impression d'être allé aussi loin que possible dans votre compréhension du texte, vous pouvez commencer à traduire en faisant un premier brouillon. Les conseils des chapitres qui suivent vous seront alors utiles.

exercices

1 Faites l'analyse préalable du texte ci-dessous, comme si vous deviez le traduire ou en traduire une partie et remplissez la grille qui suit.

The path took us along to the side of the greenhouse and the butler opened a door for me and stood aside. It opened into a sort of vestibule that was about as warm as a slow oven. He came in after me, shut the outer door, opened an inner door and we went through that. Then it was really hot. The air was thick, wet, steamy and larded with the cloying smell of tropical orchids in bloom. The glass walls and roof were heavily misted and big drops of moisture splashed down on the plants. The light had an unreal greenish color, like light filtered through an aquarium tank. The plants filled the place, a forest of them, with nasty meaty leaves and stalks like the newly washed fingers of dead men. They smelled as overpowering as boiling alcohol under a blanket.

The butler did his best to get me through without being smacked in the face by the sodden leaves, and after a while we came to a clearing in the middle of the jungle, under the domed roof. Here, in a space of hexagonal flags, an old red Turkish rug was laid down and on the rug was a wheel chair, and in the wheel chair an old and obviously dying man watched us come with black eyes from which all fire had died long ago, but which still had the coal-black directness of the eyes in the portrait that hung above the mantel in the hall. The rest of his face was a leaden mask, with the bloodless lips and the sharp nose and the

sunken temples and the outward-turning earlobes of approaching dissolution. His long narrow body was wrapped – in that heat – in a traveling rug and a faded red bathrobe. His thin clawlike hands were folded loosely on the rug, purple-nailed. A few locks of dry white hair clung to his scalp, like wild flowers fighting for life on a bare rock.
The butler stood in front of him and said: "This is Mr. Marlowe, General."
The old man didn't move or speak, or even nod. He just looked at me lifelessly.
The butler pushed a damp wicker chair against the backs of my legs and I sat down. He took my hat with a deft scoop.
Then the old man dragged his voice up from the bottom of a well and said: "Brandy, Norris. How do you like your brandy, sir?"
"Any way at all," I said.

▲ Raymond Chandler, *The Big Sleep*, 1939.

Source, auteur, date…	
Who? Where? When? What? Why?	
Organisation du texte	Soulignez les mots de liaison ou expressions qui montrent la structure du texte.
Temps	
Point de vue/modaux	
Ton/registre	
Procédés stylistiques	

2 Inférez le sens des mots ci-dessous et choisissez l'équivalent qui vous semble le mieux convenir.

(1) larded with: 1 heavy with 2 provided with 3 compared with
(2) meaty: 1 green 2 thick, like flesh 3 lovely
(3) stalks: 1 buds *(bourgeons)* 2 stems *(tiges)* 3 blossoms *(fleurs)*
(4) smacked: 1 kissed 2 hit 3 surprised
(5) sodden: 1 saturated with water 2 rapid 3 luminous
(6) clearing: 1 a place where there is no light 2 a small hill 3 a place without any trees in a forest
(7) clawlike: 1 like the end of a bird's foot 2 like the end of a dog's foot 3 like the end of a horse's foot
(8) scoop: 1 laugh 2 thought 3 movement

II CONSEILS GÉNÉRAUX POUR LA TRADUCTION

Tout d'abord, une triple mise en garde:
– Ne faites pas d'omissions: elles sont très fortement pénalisées. Si vous ne connaissez pas le sens d'un mot, essayez de le déduire d'après le contexte. Relisez attentivement votre traduction au moins une fois pour vérifier que vous n'avez pas oublié de traduire un mot du texte.
– Ne proposez pas deux traductions: vous devez faire un choix.
– N'oubliez pas de traduire le titre de l'extrait, mais ne traduisez pas celui de l'œuvre dont est tiré le texte. On ne peut en effet traduire le titre de l'oeuvre que si l'on a lu l'oeuvre entière.

1 – QUE TRADUIRE ?

■ Il est préférable de ne pas traduire les **noms et prénoms**, même lorsqu'il existe un équivalent en français. Les personnes mentionnées ont des noms anglo-saxons: ne les francisez pas!

Exceptions: les noms de souverains: *King Edward* (le roi Edouard), *James I* (Jacques Ier); certains surnoms ou noms intentionnellement significatifs: *Mr Know-All* (Monsieur Je-Sais-Tout).

■ Pour la même raison, il est préférable de garder les **titres** anglais *(Mr, Mrs, Miss)*, ou français en thème, plutôt que de les traduire (Monsieur, Madame, Mademoiselle). On pourra cependant traduire les titres de noblesse.
The Duke of Edinburgh → Le Duc d'Édimbourg.

■ Pour les **termes géographiques, noms de lieux, termes historiques, titres de livres**, il faut respecter l'usage. Demandez-vous s'il existe une traduction française connue. *The Thames* se traduira bien sûr par la Tamise, alors qu'on ne traduira pas *National Gallery* (L'après-midi, nous avons visité la *National Gallery*.)
They now live in Clifton Terrace. → Ils habitent maintenant *Clifton Terrace.*
J'étais rue de l'Odéon. → *I was in the* rue de l'Odéon. (Notez que lorsqu'on traduit vers l'anglais le nom français de la rue est gardé mais la plupart du temps précédé de l'article défini.)

■ Convertissez les **mesures.** P. 86 Transformez donc les *miles* en kilomètres, les *Fahrenheit* en Celsius, les *pounds* en livres. N'oubliez pas de vous demander alors si vous devez faire une conversion précise ou bien donner simplement un ordre de grandeur.

Comparez la taille donnée:
– sur un passeport: *Height: 5 ft 10 inches (= five feet ten inches)* → 1m 76 (Ici une taille précise est nécessaire.)
– et une simple évaluation. *I've only seen her once, but she's quite tall, about 5ft 10 inches.* → plus d'un mètre soixante dix, peut-être un mètre soixante-quinze. (Ici une taille précise, par exemple un mètre soixante et onze, serait absurde)

■ On ne convertit pas l'argent étranger en francs ou en euros.
Évitez les « notes du traducteur » : elles alourdissent la traduction et ne sont qu'un constat d'échec.

2 – Le respect du texte de départ

Une bonne traduction doit éviter deux écueils, deux extrêmes, d'un côté le calque, de l'autre une traduction trop ornée ou qui se situe trop loin du texte de départ.
Considérez par exemple cette phrase et les trois traductions qui suivent.
For years he did battle for a change in the law.
1 Pendant des années il fit une bataille pour un changement dans la loi.
2 Pendant des années il se battit contre vents et marées pour que la loi soit révoquée.
3 Pendant des années il se battit pour faire changer la loi.

1 Le calque
Dans la phrase 1 la traduction mot à mot aboutit à une phrase incompréhensible, à du charabia.

2 Le non-respect du texte
Dans la phrase 2, la traduction est claire et en bon français, mais elle ne respecte pas le texte de départ. elle le récrit. En anglais *to do battle for sthg*, c'est « lutter pour quelque chose ». L'ajout de « contre vents et marées » n'est pas nécessaire et transforme inutilement le texte. De même, si « révoquer une loi » est une bonne collocation, le texte de départ parle d'un changement et non d'une révocation.

3 La troisième traduction, plus neutre et plus simple, rend beaucoup mieux compte du texte de départ.

Respecter le texte, c'est aussi le respecter stylistiquement. Si le texte de départ contient des réseaux lexicaux ou des répétitions volontaires, vous devez garder ces effets dans le texte d'arrivée.
Vous devez également respecter le registre du texte, son niveau de langue.

3 – Enfin...

Relisez attentivement votre traduction, en prêtant tout particulièrement attention aux points suivants.

■ **L'orthographe et la ponctuation.** Attention tout particulièrement à la ponctuation grammaticale (accords, accent ou absence d'accent entraînant un changement de temps, « fut » au lieu de « fût » par exemple).

■ **La qualité du français.** Vérifiez que vos temps sont cohérents, vérifiez les accords, les règles de grammaire de base (par exemple l'utilisation du subjonctif après « bien que »), les formes du passé simple, souvent malmenées.

- **Les collocations.** Une collocation est une association courante de deux ou plusieurs termes. En anglais on dira *"He gave me a smile."* alors qu'en français on « fait » un sourire. « Donner un sourire » serait extrêmement maladroit. Attardez-vous donc quelques instants sur chacune des expressions que vous avez utilisées et demandez-vous si elle est effectivement correcte ou si vous n'avez pas été influencé par la langue de départ (calque). Mettez mentalement l'expression dans une autre phrase, ce qui vous permettra de vous détacher du texte que vous traduisez et d'être plus critique.
- Évitez **les omissions.**

exercices

1 Traduisez.

(1) King Edward VI reigned after Richard Lionheart.

(2) I had two pounds left, not enough for a taxi to drive me ten miles.

(3) I took *The Times* and *A Midsummer Night's Dream* to read in the train.

(4) In the Victoria and Albert Museum, there are several pictures by Sir Peter Lely.

(5) *Combien de temps faudra-t-il pour aller de Douvres à Édimbourg en voiture ?*

2 Dans les phrases qui suivent, le calque conduit à un contresens. Corrigez les traductions.

(1) *For him to have apologized was quite something !*
Pour lui, s'être excusé ce n'était pas rien.

(2) *They thought, he knew, he had the solution.*
Ils pensaient qu'il savait avoir la solution.

(3) *She is sure to come.*
Elle est sûre de venir.

(4) *The cat licked the plate clean.*
Le chat lécha l'assiette propre.

(5) *The athlete ran into the stadium.*
L'athlète courut dans le stade.

(6) *He went on to say that there was no immediate danger.*
Il continua à dire qu'il n'y avait pas de danger dans l'immédiat.

(7) *I do not think much of his new play.*
Je ne pense pas beaucoup/souvent à sa nouvelle pièce.

(8) *She already knew the book, which is excellent.*
Elle connaissait déjà le livre qui est excellent.

III UTILISER UN DICTIONNAIRE

Le dictionnaire est un instrument indispensable pour comprendre le sens de mots inconnus, mais aussi pour savoir comment ces mots se prononcent ou comment ils s'emploient. Cependant beaucoup d'erreurs de traduction viennent d'une mauvaise utilisation du dictionnaire.

Il est donc nécessaire de :

→ bien se familiariser avec les dictionnaires que l'on utilise. Il faut étudier l'organisation des entrées, les abréviations utilisées, la signification des symboles.

→ essayer de travailler avec un dictionnaire unilingue. En effet le sens du mot dont on a besoin, dans un contexte donné, n'est pas nécessairement l'un des sens mentionnés dans un dictionnaire bilingue. De plus, l'utilisation du dictionnaire unilingue force à faire l'effort mental de recherche du mot juste dont on a besoin.

→ ne pas se contenter de chercher un mot ; regarder aussi comment il se construit (ceci est particulièrement important en thème). Il faut donc un dictionnaire qui donne des phrases en contexte.

1 – LE DICTIONNAIRE UNILINGUE

Voici, à titre d'exemple, ce que l'on peut trouver au mot *grate* dans le *Cambridge International Dictionary of English* (1995), et comment on peut lire ces entrées.

grate FIRE /greɪt/ *n* [C] a metal structure which holds coal or wood in a fireplace • *There was a fire burning* **in** *the grate.* • PIC > **Fires and space heaters**

grate ANNOY /greɪt/ *v* [I] (esp. of an unpleasant noise) to annoy you • *After a while her voice really started to grate* **on** *me.* • *He's got one of those voices that really grates* **on** *your* **nerves!** • *I can tolerate her voice for a while but then it starts to grate.* • *It's the way she's always talking about herself – it just grates* **on** *me.*

grate *obj* COOKING /greɪt/ *v* [T] to rub (food) against a GRATER (= metal device with sharp holes in it), in order to cut into a lot of small pieces • *Could you grate the cheese for me?* • PIC > **Food preparation**

grat-ed /£'greɪ-tɪd, $-t̬ɪd/ *adj* [not gradable] • *grated cheese/carrots/ nutmeg*

grat-er /£'greɪ-tər, $-t̬ər/ *n* [C] • A grater is a metal device with holes surrounded by sharp edges used to cut food into small pieces: *a cheese grater* • PIC > **Kitchen**

grate RUB TOGETHER /greɪt/ *v* [I] (of two hard objects) to rub together, sometimes making a sharp unpleasant sound • *After a while the hard ends of the bones grate against each other instead of gliding smoothly over one another.* • *I can't bear the noise of the chair grating on the stone floor.*

grat-ing /£'greɪ-tɪŋ/ adj • *There was a horrible grating* **sound** *as she tried to move her leg.*

→ Chaque mot en retrait correspond à un sens différent (4 sens différents ici) ; le champ sémantique auquel appartient ce mot est encadré pour que l'on puisse rapidement distinguer les sens.

→ Les mots dérivés sont mentionnés dans chaque entrée (ex. : *grated*, *grater*)

→ prononciation

→ catégorie grammaticale : v (verbe), n (nom), adj (adjectif)…

→ Des informations grammaticales complémentaires :

I : (verbe) intransitif

T : (verbe) transitif

C : (nom) comptable (U serait pour un nom non comptable)

→ définition

→ en italique : des exemples

2 – LE DICTIONNAIRE BILINGUE

Voici l'exemple de l'entrée « racheter » dans le dictionnaire bilingue *Robert & Collins.*

racheter [raʃ(ə)te] [5] 1 **vt** a *objet que l'on possédait avant* to buy back, repurchase; *nouvel objet* to buy *ou* purchase another; *pain, lait*, to buy some more; *objet d'occasion* to buy, purchase; *usine en faillite*, to buy up *ou* out *ou* over. **je lui ai racheté son vieux transistor** I've bought his old transistor from *ou* off him; **il a racheté toutes les parts de son associé** he bought his partner out, he bought up all his partner's shares; **j'ai dû ~ du tissu** I had to buy more material.

b *(se libérer de) dette, rente* to redeem.

c *esclave, otage* to ransom, pay a ransom for; *(Rel) pécheur* to redeem. **il n'y en a pas un pour ~ l'autre*** they're both (just) as bad as each other.

d *(réparer) péché, crime* to atone for, expiate; *mauvaise conduite, faute* to make amends for, make up for; *imperfection* to make up *ou* compensate for (*par* by).

e *(Archit)* to modify.

2 **se racheter vpr** *(pécheur)* to redeem o.s.; *[criminel]* to make amends. **Essaie de te ~ en t'excusant** try and make up for it *ou* try to make amends by apologizing.

▲ Le Robert & Collins Senior, troisième édition, 1993.

→ deux emplois différents marqués par des numéros : le verbe transitif ; le verbe pronominal (se racheter)

→ des sous catégories indiquées par des lettres.

→ le signe ~ remplace le mot dans les exemples.

exercices

1 Dictionnaire unilingue : exemple du mot *grate* P. 172

(1) Combien de sens différents du mot *grate* sont-ils mentionnés ?

(2) En prononçant le mot *grater*, met-on l'accent sur la première ou la seconde syllabe ?

(3) Complétez avec la préposition qui convient : *He said he asked for a divorce because her sharp voice grated … him.*

(4) Cherchez le sens du mot *grate* ou son dérivé dans les phrases qui suivent, puis traduisez ces phrases.

The window grates when you open it.

There were some logs (bûches) *in the grate.*

I put grated celery in my salad.

Her affected voice grates on my nerves.

2 Dictionnaire unilingue : exemple du mot *tear*
Comment prononcer le mot *tear* dans les phrases qui suivent ?

(a) Don't tear the paper : we'll need it.

(b) There were tears of joy running down her cheeks.

(c) There's no need to tear the room apart.

tear CRY /£ tɪəʳ, $ tɪr/ *n* [C usually pl] a drop of salty liquid which flows from the eye, as a result of strong emotion, esp. unhappiness, or pain • *tears* **of** *remorse/regret/happiness/ joy/laughter* • *Did you notice the tears* **in** *his* **eyes** *when he talked about Diane?* • *We laughed until the tears* **ran/rolled down** *our cheeks.* • *I felt a tear* **trickle down** *my nose.* • *She* **burst into** *tears* (= suddenly started to cry). • *Her* **eyes filled with** *tears as she told me about her son.* • *Why do arguments with you always* **reduce** *me* **to** *tears* (= make me cry)*?* • *I won't* **shed (any)** *tears* (= I will note be unhappy) *when he goes, I can tell you!* • *I found him* **in tears** (= crying) *in his bedroom.* • **Tear gas** is a gas used by some police and armed forces to control crowds of people. It hurts the eyes and makes them produce tears. • *(infml)* A **tear jerker** is a book, film, play etc. which has a sad story that is intended to make people cry or be sad: *I'd recommend that you take a pile of tissues with you when you see that film – it's a* **real** *tear jerker!* • *"The Tears of a Clown"* (title of a song by Smokey Robinson, 1970) • See also TEARDROP.

tear-ful /£'tɪə-fᵊl, $'tɪr-/ *adj* • *Waving Peter off at the airport had made me feel a bit tearful* (= sad and wanting to cry). • *After a tearful farewell at the station, we went our separate ways.* • *Katy's always a bit tearful* (= She tends to cry) *when it's time to go back to school.*

tear-ful-ly /£'tɪə-fᵊl-i, $'tɪr-/ *adv* • *We said goodbye tearfully and then he went to board his plane.*

tear-ful-ness /£'tɪə-fᵊl-nəs, $'tɪr-/ *n* [U]

tear *(obj)* SEPARATE /£ teəʳ, $ ter/ *v past simple* **tore** /£ tɔːʳ, $ tɔːr/ *past part* **torn** /£tɔːn, $tɔːn/ to pull or be pulled apart, or to pull pieces off • *You have to be very careful with books this old because the paper tends to tear very easily.* [I] • *The pastry tore as I was putting it into the dish.* [I] • *I tore my skirt on the chair as I stood up.* [T] • *A couple of pages had been torn* **out of/from** *the book.* [T] • *He tore the letter* **up** (= tore it into small pieces). [M] • *(fig.) The employer just tore* **up** (= treated as totally unimportant) *the agreement with the union without consultation.* [M] • *She tore his cheque* **into shreds** (= small pieces) *and threw them in the bin.* [T] • *(fig. infml) The examiner just tore my thesis/me* **to shreds** (= severely criticized my work/me). [T] • *The dogs tore the rabbit* **apart/to pieces**. [T] • *(fig.) Our department was torn* **apart/to pieces** (= destroyed) *by silly quarrels.* [T] • *(fig.) She tore the room* **apart** (= moved everything, opened all drawers, cupboards, etc.) *looking for her ring.* [M] • *You've torn* **a hole** *in the knee of your trousers.* [T] • *She tore* **(off)** *a strip of material to make a bandage.* [T/M] • If you tear **off** your clothes you remove them quickly and carelessly: *I tore my sweaty clothes off and jumped into the shower.* [M] • *(Br and Aust)* If you **tear a strip off** someone/**tear** them **off a strip** you criticize them severely. • If you tear someone **away from** somewhere, you make them leave there: *They had to tear the little boy away from his dead cat.* [T] ◦ *I had to tear* **myself** *away from the party at 10 o'clock, but I didn't want to go.* [T] • *(esp. disapproving)* To tear **down** something, esp. a vertical structure, is to destroy it: *They tore down the most beautiful old buildings to put up those monstrosities.* [M] ◦ *My fence was torn down in the storm.* [M] • If you are **tearing** your **hair out over** a problem, you are feeling a lot of anxiety over it: *She's been tearing her hair out over the final chapter of her novel for the last month.* • *The pictures of hungry children* **tore at** *my* **heart/tore** *my* **heart out** (= made me very sad). • *Unfortunately, if he doesn't agree with you, he tends to* **tear into** *you* (= attack you with words).

tear /£ teəʳ, $ ter/ *n* [C] • *Have you seen you've got a tear in the sleeve of your shirt.*

▲ Cambridge International Dictionary of English (1995).

3 Complétez avec l'adjectif ou le participe passé qui convient :

(a) a … person (so who cries a lot)

(b) a … piece of paper (damaged)

(c) a … hurry (great hurry)

4 Cherchez le sens du mot tear ou son dérivé dans les phrases qui suivent, puis traduisez-les.

(a) There's a tear at the bottom of your trousers.

(b) She could not tear herself away from her friends.

(c) The play was a real tear jerker.

(d) They tore off to follow the taxi.

(e) He had to tell his mother, and she tore a strip off him.

(f) He's torn between his love and his duty.

(g) It did not take them long to tear his theory to shreds.

5 Dictionnaire bilingue : exemple du mot « racheter » P. 173
Complétez les phrases avec la préposition qui convient.

(a) He wants to make amends … all the pain he caused.

(b) I'm sorry I sold my bike and I'll try to buy it …

(c) He made up … his blunder … sending her flowers.

(d) If his car is for sale, I'll buy it … him.

IV Les procédés de traduction

Dans leur *Stylistique comparée du français et de l'anglais* (1958), J.-P. Vinay et J. Darbelnet proposent une classification des procédés de traduction dont voici les principales catégories :

Emprunt	Le mot étranger est utilisé. *He sent me an e-mail.* → Il m'a envoyé un **e-mail**.
Transposition	Changement de catégorie grammaticale lorsqu'on passe dans l'autre langue. *As prices keep rising…* → Avec la montée continue des prix… (le verbe *rising* devient un nom, « montée », tandis que le verbe *keep* est traduit par un adjectif « continue ».)

	Il faut noter tout particulièrement le chassé croisé, qui consiste en une double transposition et qui est surtout utilisé pour les verbes de mouvement suivis d'une particule adverbiale et pour les structures résultatives. *He tiptoed out of the room.* Il est sorti de la pièce sur la pointe des pieds. On peut également ajouter le procédé qui consiste à **étoffer**. L'étoffement est une forme de transposition, l'emploi de plusieurs mots pour traduire un mot dans la langue de départ : on a, par exemple, souvent recours à l'étoffement pour traduire certaines prépositions. *We're having air-conditioning installed against the predicted heat wave.* Nous faisons installer la climatisation **en prévision de** la vague de chaleur annoncée.
Modulation	Changement de point de vue. Par exemple passage de l'affirmatif au négatif. *She's rather plain* → Elle est sans charme. Elle n'a rien d'une beauté.
Équivalence	On cherche une équivalence au niveau du message tout entier. C'est le procédé auquel on a souvent recours lorsqu'on traduit les expressions idiomatiques, les proverbes, les expressions figées. *Don't count your chickens before they are hatched.* → Il ne faut pas vendre la peau de l'ours avant de l'avoir tué.

Si tous ces procédés sont importants, c'est qu'ils permettent d'éviter le **calque**, c'est à dire la traduction littérale, mot à mot qui peut mener soit à des contresens soit à des traductions extrêmement peu naturelles.

↗ exercices

1 Repérez les procédés utilisés dans les passages en gras des traductions qui suivent.

(1) *Strangely enough, he refused.* → **Chose curieuse**, il a refusé.

(2) *We met in a pub last year.* → On s'est rencontrés au **pub** l'année dernière.

(3) *There remains the question of who will be blamed.* → Il reste la question **de savoir** qui sera tenu pour responsable.

(4) Téléphone-moi à ton arrivée. → *Give me a ring when* ***you arrive****.*

2 Traduisez les phrases qui suivent en utilisant un chassé croisé.

(1) *The old man shuffled along behind her.*

(2) *The bullet hissed past him.*

(3) *My geranium pots have been blown away.*

(4) Il a traversé la Manche à la nage.

3 Traduisez les phrases qui suivent en étoffant les prépositions.

(1) *She was jealous and watched his apartment for other women.*

(2) *All trains to London will be delayed.*

(3) *He whistled for the dog.*

(4) *They are stocking wood against the winter.*

4 Traduisez les phrases qui suivent en utilisant des transpositions pour rendre les mots soulignés.

(1) *He* ***merely*** *nodded.*

(2) *She looked at me* ***with a smile****.*

(3) *As soon as the store* ***opened****, the crowd rushed in.*

(4) Elle **s'appelle** Lila.

5 Traduisez les phrases qui suivent en utilisant des équivalences.

(1) (En levant son verre) *Cheers!*

(2) *He was as pleased as Punch.*

(3) *Every cloud has a silver lining.* (proverbe)

(4) (Après qu'on vous a remercié) De rien.

V Quelques réflexes : version

1 – Les formes verbales

Attention à la traduction des formes verbales suivantes.

1 *Present perfect* = bilan

- présent : *We've been married for ten years now.* Voilà maintenant dix ans que nous sommes mariés. (On relie passé et présent)
- passé composé : *He's now left home.* Il a maintenant quitté la maison. (action terminée mais aucune référence temporelle)

2 *Prétérit*

- passé simple (langue + soutenue) ou passé composé (langue + familière ou journalistique) : actions passées s'inscrivant dans une suite.

→ *He braked, stopped and jumped out of the car.* Il freina, s'arrêta, et sauta de la voiture.

- Imparfait : descriptions, sentiments, vérités générales

→ *When I was a child, I was terrified of the neighbour's big dog.*
Lorsque j'étais enfant, le gros chien du voisin me terrifiait.

Attention à la traduction de ***would***. Ne confondez pas le *would* du conditionnel et le *would* qui indique une habitude dans le passé.

→ *If I asked him to help, he would come at once.*
Si je lui demandais de m'aider, il viendrait tout de suite.

→ *When I asked him to come, he would come at once.*
Lorsque je lui demandais de m'aider, il venait tout de suite.

2 – Les modaux

Ils sont la cause de nombreuses erreurs. Reportez-vous à la page 204 s'ils vous posent encore des problèmes.

3 – Les faux amis

Les faux amis sont des mots dont la forme est proche ou semblable à celle de mots français, mais dont le sens est différent.
Certains mots sont toujours faux amis (ex. : *grief* = peine, douleur) ; d'autres ne le sont que parfois (ex. : *dramatic* a souvent le sens de « spectaculaire », mais peut aussi signifier « dramatique »).

4 – Le passif

Le passif s'emploie beaucoup plus souvent en anglais qu'en français. En version, il faut toujours se demander si l'on peut calquer le passif ou s'il est préférable de traduire par « on », ou par une forme pronominale ou impersonnelle.

→ *She is said to be very depressed.* On la dit très déprimée.
→ *Tea can be drunk cold.* Le thé peut se boire froid. (forme pronominale)
→ *This will have to be done in winter.* Il faudra le faire en hiver. (forme impersonnelle)

5 – Les verbes à particules et les formes résultatives

Beaucoup de verbes anglais qui décrivent des mouvements sont suivis de particules adverbiales décrivant le résultat de ces mouvements. On les traduit alors très souvent en ayant recours à un chassé croisé. Il en va de même pour de nombreuses structures résultatives dans lesquelles le verbe décrit le moyen, la cause, et l'adjectif ou le syntagme prépositionnel qui suivent le résultat.

He ran out of the room.

Il sortit de la pièce en courant.

They threatened her into accepting.

Ils la firent accepter à force de menaces.

They groped their way out of the tunnel.

Ils sortirent du tunnel à tâtons.

6 – LES DÉTERMINANTS

Les articles définis et indéfinis ne s'emploient pas de la même façon en anglais et en français. Soyez vigilants et demandez-vous toujours si votre traduction n'est pas un calque maladroit en français. Voici quelques exemples de différences entre l'anglais et le français.

→ *My father is a doctor.* → Mon père est docteur.
→ *President Bush* → Le président Bush
→ *A Portrait of the Artist* (titre de livre ou tableau) → Portrait de l'artiste

> Attention également à l'emploi quasi automatique du possessif en anglais devant les parties du corps. En français, on préfère l'article défini.
> *I've sprained my ankle.* → Je me suis foulé la cheville.

7 – LES FORMES EN *-ING*

Le participe présent s'emploie beaucoup plus couramment en anglais qu'en français. Pensez à ne pas calquer.

→ *The very idea of Philip leaving her was absurd.*
L'idée même que Philip puisse la quitter était absurde.
→ *Taking a handkerchief out of his pocket, he mopped his brow.* → Il tira un mouchoir de sa poche et s'épongea le front. (Ce qui est moins lourd que : Tirant…).
→ *She heard the sound of footsteps approaching.*
Elle entendit le bruit de pas qui s'approchaient.

8 – LA TRADUCTION DES *TAGS*

> Attention à ne pas traduire systématiquement les tags par « n'est-ce-pas » et à ne pas calquer les reprises par auxiliaires. Demandez-vous à chaque fois ce que vous diriez naturellement dans le contexte ou la situation. Vous devrez faire particulièrement attention au registre.

- *She's nice, isn't she ?* → Elle est gentille, hein ?
- *You didn't think I was going to let them get away with it, did you ?* → Tu ne pensais tout de même pas que j'allais les laisser s'en tirer à si bon compte ?
- *She can't drive, but I can.* → Elle ne conduit pas, mais moi si.
- *"They've decided to stay another few days." "They have ?"* → « Ils ont décidé de rester quelques jours de plus. – Ah oui ? »

9 – Les mots composés

Attention, le premier élément qualifie le second, comme le ferait un adjectif. *A horse race*, c'est un type de course (une course de chevaux), alors que *a race horse* c'est un type de cheval (un cheval de course).

exercices

1 Les mots soulignés sont-ils faux amis ou non dans des phrases qui suivent ?

(1) I have total **confidence** in him.

(2) This is by far the best **period** in this painter's work.

(3) It is difficult to live with someone who is so **particular**.

(4) We can no longer **ignore** such behaviour.

(5) He is **susceptible** to colds.

(6) We know he is guilty, but how can we **prove** it ?

(7) The director **resigned** when the letter was published.

(8) She is too **sensible** to have given up such a good job.

(9) This **minute** telephone is only two inches long.

(10) I gave him the **benefit** of the doubt.

2 Traduisez les phrases qui suivent en évitant l'emploi du passif.

(1) She was said to be very firm.

(2) She was told to be very firm.

(3) They are expected to have left the country.

(4) Skirts are worn very long this winter.

(5) He called his secretary and was brought the latest report.

3 Traduisez les phrases qui suivent en utilisant un chassé croisé.

(1) He kicked the door open.

(2) He limped his way down the street.

(3) The water was streaming in.

(4) He talked himself hoarse.

4 Traduisez les phrases qui suivent en prêtant tout particulièrement attention à la traduction des participes présents.

(1) They followed several corridors, finally arriving in front of a locked door.

(2) She fell into the snow, damaging her skirt, which reminded her of childhood games.

(3) He said I was lucky, having inherited such a house.

(4) He heard someone calling him and recognized Dan's voice.

VI Quelques réflexes : thème

1 – Les formes verbales

Voici quelques formes verbales qui sont souvent source d'erreurs en thème.

1 Traduction du **présent** français

– *present:*

→ Le loir passe l'hiver à dormir. *A dormouse sleeps through the winter.* (vérité générale.)

– *present + ing :*

→ Ce mois-ci, j'apprends à conduire. *This month, I'm learning how to drive.*

– *present perfect :*

→ Je suis ce cours depuis 3 mois. *I have been attending this class for the past 3 months.* (bilan présent d'une action commencée dans le passé.)

> Mais attention, le présent de narration français se traduira le plus souvent par un prétérit en anglais. Le duc intrigua pendant des mois pour obtenir la couronne. En décembre il est roi. *For months, the Duke schemed to get the crown. In December, he succeeded to the throne.*

2 Traduction du **conditionnel** français

Notez bien les trois types de conditions.

– S'il arrive à l'heure, nous prendrons le train de 10 heures. (possibilité)

→ *If he arrives on time, we'll take the 10 o'clock train.*

– S'il arrivait à l'heure, nous prendrions le train de 10 heures. (beaucoup plus hypothétique)

→ *If he arrived on time, we would take the 10 o'clock train.*

– S'il était arrivé à l'heure, nous aurions pris le train de 10 heures. (possibilité dans le passé, qui ne s'est pas réalisée)

→ *If he had arrived on time, we would have taken the 10 o'clock train.*

> Mais attention !
> – Dans les subordonnées de temps (introduites par *when, as soon as, until, after, the moment…*) on emploie le prétérit en anglais au lieu du conditionnel français (de même que le présent au lieu du futur). Ces subordonnées fonctionnent comme des hypothétiques introduites par *if*.
> → Il m'a dit qu'il me téléphonerait dès qu'il recevrait la lettre.
> *He told me that he would phone me as soon as he received the letter.*
> – Certains conditionnels français sont utilisés pour décrire l'irréel. C'est le passif qu'on emploie en anglais.
> → L'avion se serait écrasé après le décollage.
> *The plane is said to have crashed after taking off.*

3 N'oubliez pas la différence fondamentale entre le *preterit* et le *present perfect*.
– *preterit* : actions passées, terminées et datées
– *present perfect* : bilan d'une activité commencée dans le passé et qui n'est pas terminée.

2 – L'ordre des mots dans la phrase

Il faut toujours chercher à respecter l'ordre Sujet-Verbe-Complément dans la phrase anglaise. Ceci signifie que :
– l'on trouve rarement en anglais des phrases aussi disloquées qu'en français.
→ Mais lui, de son fils, il n'avait toujours aucune nouvelle.
→ *But he still had no news from his son.*
– il faut essayer de ne pas séparer le verbe de son complément d'objet direct.
→ Je te donnerai à ce moment là le livre et le disque.
→ *I will then give you the book and the record.*
– les compléments adverbiaux se placeront plus volontiers en début ou en fin de phrase.
→ Il prenait très souvent l'été sa voiture. → *In the summer, he very often took his car.*

3 – Les modaux

Pensez à utiliser des modaux en anglais.
→ Il n'est peut-être pas rentré car il aurait dû téléphoner.
→ *He may not be back, for he should have phoned.*
→ Par temps clair, on voit la tour Eiffel. → *On a clear day, you can see the Eiffel Tower.*
Testez vos réflexes Modaux en faisant l'exercice p. 00.

4 – Les verbes à particules

Pensez à utiliser des verbes à particules et à effectuer un chassé croisé P. 176.

Il fit le tour de l'église en boitant.

He hobbled his way round the church.

5 – Les prépositions

Les prépositions sont plus chargées de sens en anglais qu'en français. **P. 56-58 ET 82-84 RELATIONS SPATIALES/RELATIONS TEMPORELLES.** Il faut donc bien réfléchir à leur valeur avant de les traduire et éviter tout automatisme du type « de = *of* ».
Voici, par exemple, quelques traductions possibles des prépositions.

■ « à »
- Il habite **à** Rouen. *He lives* ***in*** *Rouen.* (absence de mouvement)
- Il va **à** Rouen tous les mardi. *He goes* ***to*** *Rouen every Tuesday.* (mouvement vers)
- Je l'ai vu rentrer **à** la poste. *I saw him walk* ***into*** *the post office.* (entrée dans un lieu)
- **À** l'entracte, j'ai lu le programme.
  During *the interval, I read the programme.* (pendant une durée)
- Il lui jeta le gant **à** la figure. *He threw the glove* ***at*** *his face.* (agressivité)

■ « **de** »
- Le livre **de** John. *John****'s*** *book.*
- Il revient **de** Londres. *He's just back* ***from*** *London.*
- La plus jolie fille **du** village. *The prettiest girl* ***in*** *the village.*
- C'est un poème **de** William Blake. *It's a poem* ***by*** *William Blake.*
- Elle était malade **de** peur. *She was sick* ***with*** *fear.*

■ « **dans** »
- Il est tombé **dans** la mare. Heureusement, elle fait **dans les** 50 cm de profondeur seulement. *He fell* ***into*** *the pond which, fortunately, is only* ***about*** *one foot and a half deep.*
- J'ai cru voir un visage connu **dans** la foule.
  I thought I recognized a familiar face ***among*** *the crowd.*
- Peux-tu me donner une réponse **dans** les quinze jours ?
  Can you give me an answer ***within*** *a fortnight ?*
- C'est un vin qu'il faut boire **dans** des verres en cristal.
  This is a wine you should drink ***out of*** *crystal glasses.*
- Je pris un stylo **dans** le tiroir. *I took a pen* ***from*** *the drawer.*

6 – Les possessifs

L'anglais tend à utiliser un possessif pour décrire les parties du corps, là où l'article défini est employé en français.
- Il lui prit le bras. *He took her arm.*
- Les mains dans les poches, elle le regardait d'un air effronté.
  With her hands in her pockets, she looked at him brazenly.

7 – La préférence de l'anglais pour le concret

Là où en français on tend à préférer les notions abstraites, l'hypothétique et le virtuel (avec le mode subjonctif, par exemple), en anglais on préférera actualiser, c'est-à-dire envisager les mêmes faits par rapport à une situation concrète, par rapport à l'énonciateur à un moment donné.

Ainsi :

– on traduit souvent les substantifs abstraits français par des formes verbales en anglais.

➜ La construction du Panthéon…
  → *When the Pantheon was built…*

➜ L'accession à la propriété est le rêve de tous les Anglais.
  → *Acquiring a house is every Englishman's dream.*

– l'anglais préfère les formes conjuguées là où en français on trouve plus volontiers des formes non conjuguées (infinitif par exemple)

➜ Ce n'est pas le genre de personne à oublier un rendez-vous.
  → *He's not the sort of person who would forget an appointment.*

➜ Avant de conclure, je vais vous raconter…
  → *Before I conclude, let me…*

– l'anglais utilise plus souvent des formes modales (qui mettent en valeur le point de vue de l'énonciateur dans une situation précise).

➜ Ils sont probablement arrivés à l'heure qu'il est.
  → *They will have arrived by now.*

exercices

1 Traduire les phrases qui suivent en prêtant tout particulièrement attention à l'emploi des formes verbales.

(1) Après des semaines de préparation, tout était prêt, la veille au soir, pour le jour J. Le lendemain, il se lève à six heures…

(2) Il se lève à six heures depuis qu'il travaille à Nancy.

(3) Il se lève toujours à six heures du matin.

(4) J'ai lu beaucoup de livres : j'adore cela !

(5) J'ai lu beaucoup de livres quand j'étais à l'hôpital.

2 Complétez les phrases qui suivent avec la forme verbale qui convient.

(1) *I'll buy the CD when I … my first pay cheque.*
☐ *got* ☐ *will get* ☐ *get* ☐ *would get*

(2) *Even if he had locked the door, I … to escape.*
☐ *would have been able* ☐ *would be able* ☐ *will be able* ☐ *was able*

(3) *Nothing is certain at the moment, but the singer … have committed suicide.*
☐ *would* ☐ *will* ☐ *is believed to* ☐ *was believed to*

(4) *I know that if he felt lonely, he … give us a ring.*
☐ *will* ☐ *would* ☐ *did* ☐ *is expected to*

3 **Traduisez les phrases qui suivent, en prêtant tout particulièrement attention à l'ordre des mots.**

(1) Il avait oublié, en faisant ses bagages, la carte qu'on lui avait donnée.

(2) Il allait parfois au parc.

(3) Elle sortit, d'un placard, une bouteille de cognac.

(4) Il expliqua, avec force gestes, ce qui s'était passé.

4 **Choisissez le modal qui permet de compléter les traductions qui suivent.**

(1) Quand il n'y a pas de circulation dans la rue, on entend ce que disent les voisins.
When there is no traffic in the street, you … hear what the neighbours say.
☐ *may* ☐ *might* ☐ *can* ☐ *could*

(2) Il faut qu'il travaille plus s'il veut réussir son examen.
He … work more if he wants to pass his exam.
☐ *should* ☐ *must* ☐ *will* ☐ *ought to*

(3) Il y a de la lumière dans sa chambre : il doit travailler.
There's a light in his room : He …
☐ *must work* ☐ *must be working* ☐ *has to work* ☐ *might be working*

(4) On sonne, mais cela ne peut pas être Pierre ; il est trop tôt.
Someone's at the door, but it … be Pierre : it's too early.
☐ *may not* ☐ *could not* ☐ *must not* ☐ *can't*

(5) Si tu laisses ta bicyclette dans le hangar, tu devrais fermer la porte à clé.
If you leave your bicycle in the shed, you … lock the door.
☐ *must* ☐ *should* ☐ *have to* ☐ *might*

(6) Ne touche pas au chien. Il pourrait te mordre.
Don't touch the dog. It … bite you.
☐ *might* ☐ *can* ☐ *must* ☐ *will*

(7) Il n'est pas impossible qu'il pleuve cet après-midi.
It … rain this afternoon.
☐ *can* ☐ *cannot* ☐ *could not* ☐ *may*

(8) Votre billet n'est plus valable. Il vous faut en acheter un autre.
Your ticket is no longer valid. You … buy another one.
☐ *must* ☐ *should* ☐ *have to* ☐ *could*

5 **Choisissez la préposition qui convient parmi celles qui suivent :**
about – out of – at – into – through – in.

(1) Il prit l'enfant dans ses bras. He took the child … his arms.

(2) La table fait dans les deux mètres de long. The table is … two metres long.

(3) À 11 heures, il est toujours au bureau. At 11, he is always … the office.

(4) À 10 heures, il était dans son bureau. At 11, he was … his office.

(5) J'entends le vent souffler dans les arbres. I can hear the wind blowing … the trees.

(6) Je bois toujours mon thé dans une chope. I always drink tea … a mug.

6 Traduisez les phrases qui suivent à l'aide d'un chassé croisé et en combinant un verbe de la première colonne et une particule adverbiale de la seconde.

(1) Il a fait le tour de la ville en bicyclette.

(2) L'autobus est passé devant nous sans s'arrêter.

(3) Il réussit à entrer furtivement dans la maison.

(4) Il revint en courant pour aider l'enfant.

(5) Il partit en boitant.

cycle	back
drive	into
limp	off
run	past
sneak	round

IV S'EXPRIMER CORRECTEMENT

I À L'ÉCRIT

1. LES VERBES *BE*, *HAVE* ET *DO*

Ils peuvent être auxiliaires ou verbes simples.

1 – *Be*

Be peut être **auxiliaire**. Il n'est pas alors porteur de sens, mais sert à former :
– la forme *be* + V + *-ing* :
→ *I was running when I fell.* Je courais lorsque je suis tombé.
→ *They were not driving very fast.* Ils n'allaient pas très vite.
– le passif :
→ *My bag was stolen in the shop.* On m'a volé mon sac dans le magasin.
– la forme *be to*, que l'on utilise pour des plans, pour des actions prévues :
→ *The Queen is to leave for China next week.*
La reine doit se rendre en Chine la semaine prochaine.

Be peut aussi être un **simple verbe** qui sert à :
– décrire une situation (être, se situer, se trouver)
→ *My house is near a river.* Ma maison est près d'une rivière.
→ *They'll (= they will) be in London for Christmas.* Ils seront à Londres pour Noël.
– décrire une caractéristique du sujet :
→ *She is very clever.* Elle est très intelligente.
→ *He is in his mid-sixties.* Il a environ 65 ans.
→ *I'm still sleepy.* J'ai encore sommeil.
Notez qu'en français, c'est souvent le verbe avoir que l'on utilisera alors.

On utilise parfois ***be* à la forme *be* + V + *-ing*** pour parler de comportements ponctuels, souvent avec une touche d'irritation. P. 196
→ *You're being ridiculous!* Tu te comportes de façon ridicule!

Notez la structure ***there is/there are*** (il y a, dans un sens non temporel).
■ L'accord se fait avec le nom qui suit :
→ *There is a flat for sale.* Il y a un appartement à vendre.
→ *There are pencils in the drawer.* Il y a des crayons dans le tiroir.
Notez que, dans cette structure, on peut contracter *there is* (*there's*), mais pas *there are*.
■ Cette structure peut se rencontrer à tous les temps :
→ *Will there be snow tonight?* Est-ce qu'il y aura de la neige ce soir ?
→ *There were two robberies last week.* Il y a eu deux cambriolages la semaine dernière.
→ *If he was dismissed, there would be a strike.* S'il était renvoyé, il y aurait une grève.

■ Dans cette structure, *there* peut être suivi d'un modal ou de *used to*.

→ *There should be a better recording of the play.*
Il devrait y avoir un meilleur enregistrement de la pièce.

→ *There used to be a path here.* Autrefois, il y avait ici un chemin.

2 – *Have*

Have peut être **auxiliaire** et permet alors de former le *present perfect* et le *past perfect*, ainsi que de parler de faits passés avec les modaux. P. 182

→ *Have you read his letter?* Avez-vous lu sa lettre?

→ *I had already bought the book he gave me.* J'avais déjà acheté le livre qu'il m'a offert.

→ *He might have had an accident.* Il aurait pu avoir un accident.

Have peut également être un **verbe simple**. Il se conjugue alors avec *do* et les formes contractées (*'ve*) sont alors impossibles.

■ Sens de **posséder**

→ *I have a dog and two cats.* J'ai un chien et deux chats.

→ *What sort of computer do you have?* Quel type d'ordinateur as-tu ?

Au présent, et avec ce sens, le verbe *have* peut être remplacé par *have got*, qui se conjugue sans l'auxiliaire *do*, et peut avoir une forme contractée : *I've got a dog and two cats. What sort of computer have you got?*

Il ne peut pas prendre la forme V + *-ing*.

■ Sens de **prendre** (une boisson, un repas) ou de faire une activité.

→ *We had breakfast at 7.* Nous avons pris notre petit-déjeuner à 7 heures.

→ *Let's have a look at the map.* Regardons la carte.

Avec ce sens, *have* ne peut pas être remplacé par *have got*, mais la forme V + *-ing* est possible.

→ *I was having a nap when she rang.* Je faisais un petit somme quand elle a téléphoné.

■ Suivi de *to* et d'un verbe à l'infinitif, *have* exprime une **obligation**. Il se conjugue, là encore, avec *do*.

→ *Do we have to wear a dress?* Est-ce qu'il faut que nous mettions une robe ?

Have to peut être remplacé par *have got to*, qui se conjugue sans *do*.

→ *Have you got to go soon?* Est-ce qu'il faut que tu partes bientôt ?

3 – *Do*

Do peut être **auxiliaire** et permet de former

– les formes négatives et interrogatives du présent simple et du prétérit :

→ *I didn't say that!* Je n'ai pas dit ça !

– l'impératif à la forme négative :

→ *Don't play near the lake!* Ne joue pas près du lac !

Il permet aussi d'insister (*Do come!* Viens donc ! *But I do like it.* Mais si, j'aime cela.) et est utilisé pour les reprises. *John went to the cinema, but Fred didn't (= didn't go to the cinema). She runs faster that her sister does (= than her sister runs).*

En tant que **verbe simple**, *do* se comporte comme n'importe quel autre verbe et se conjugue donc avec l'auxiliaire *do*.

→ *Did you do your homework before watching TV?*
As-tu fait tes devoirs avant de regarder la télévision ?

Attention à ne pas confondre *do* et *make*, qui correspondent tous deux au français « faire ». Même si *do* est surtout employé pour une activité à laquelle on se livre (*to do the dishes*, faire la vaisselle), et *make* pour quelque chose que l'on crée, il y a beaucoup d'autres emplois et il est nécessaire de connaître autant d'expressions que possible. Mais c'est toujours *do* que l'on emploie dans l'expression *do + the/any/some + -ing*: *to do the shopping* (faire les courses) *I'll do the talking.* C'est moi qui parlerai. *Have you done any cycling lately?* As-tu fait de la bicyclette récemment ?

do the dishes: faire la vaisselle	*make a cake…:* faire un gâteau…
do one's hair: se coiffer	*make a mistake:* faire une erreur
do some work: travailler	*make a difference:* faire la différence
do 70 mph: faire 120 km/heure	*make one's bed:* faire son lit

exercices

1 Traduisez.

(1) Il pleut.
(2) Il est très âgé.
(3) Elle a peur.
(4) Elle a entre trente et quarante ans.
(5) Il est au bureau tous les matins.
(6) Je crois qu'ils ont raison.

2 Complétez les traductions qui suivent.

(1) Il y a trente étudiants dans la classe.
… *thirty students in the class.*

(2) Il y avait un porte-monnaie, un stylo et deux livres dans le sac qu'on m'a volé.
… *a purse, a fountain pen and two books in the bag which was stolen from me.*

(3) Autrefois, il y avait 2 000 habitants dans ce village.
… *2 000 inhabitants in this village.*

(4) Il devrait y avoir une loi contre de telles pratiques.
… *a law against such practices.*

(5) Il doit y avoir une erreur.
… *a mistake.*

3 **Récrivez les phrases qui suivent en utilisant *have got* lorsque cela est possible.**

(1) Did you have fun at the party?
(2) How much money do you have?
(3) Will you have a car in California?
(4) You have to spend less money.
(5) They don't have a swimming pool.
(6) I always have a bath when I get up.

4 **Faites correspondre les expressions et leur traduction.**

Do
1. do a favour
2. do a job
3. do a translation
4. do harm
5. do one's best
6. do one's duty
7. do one's homework
8. do the housework
9. do the washing up

a. faire de son mieux
b. faire du mal
c. faire la vaisselle
d. faire le ménage
e. faire ses devoirs
f. faire son devoir
g. faire un travail
h. faire une traduction
i. rendre un service

Make
1. make a call
2. make a fuss
3. make a lot of money
4. make a movement
5. make a profit
6. make an apology
7. make an attempt
8. make arrangements
9. make war

a. faire des histoires
b. faire la guerre
c. faire un bénéfice
d. faire un essai
e. faire un mouvement
f. gagner beaucoup d'argent
g. passer un coup de téléphone
h. prendre des dispositions
i. présenter ses excuses

2. PHRASES AFFIRMATIVES, NÉGATIVES, INTERROGATIVES, EXCLAMATIVES

Un auxiliaire (*have, be, do* ou un modal) est nécessaire pour former les phrases interrogatives, négatives et interro-négatives.

Affirmation	Négation	Interrogation	Interro-négation
John is in his room.	*John is not in his room.*	*Is John in his room?*	*Isn't John in his room? (= Is John not…)*
They lost their keys.	*They did not lose their keys.*	*Did they lose their keys?*	*Didn't they lose their keys? (= Did they not...)*
Mike has gone to Leeds.	*Mike has not gone to Leeds.*	*Has Mike gone to Leeds? Leeds?*	*Hasn't Mike gone to Leeds? (= Has Mike not)*
Mary should ring you.	*Mary should not ring you.*	*Should Mary ring you?*	*Shouldn't Mary ring you? (= Should Mary not…)*

Quand la phrase commence par un mot interrogatif (*Who/Whose/What/When/Where/Why/How*), on utilise l'auxiliaire et l'inversion, sauf quand le mot interrogatif est sujet du verbe :
– *When did they leave?* Quand sont-ils partis ?
– *Why have they lied?* Pourquoi ont-ils menti ?
– *Whose book did you take?* À qui appartient le livre que tu as pris ?
– *Which of the two books did you prefer?* Lequel des deux livres as-tu préféré ?
Mais : – *Who broke the glass?* Qui a cassé le verre ?
– *What caused the accident?* Qu'est-ce qui a causé l'accident ?

Les prépositions se placent à la fin de la question :
– *What were you waiting for?* Qu'attendais-tu ?

N'oubliez pas les mots interrogatifs commençant par *how* : *how much/many* (quelle quantité de), *how far* (à quelle distance), *how often* (à quelle fréquence), etc.

Phrases exclamatives

Les principales structures exclamatives sont :
– *How* + phrase affirmative : *How they panicked!* Comme ils se sont affolés !
– *How* + adjectif/adverbe : *How ridiculous she looked!* Comme elle avait l'air ridicule !
– *What* (+ *a*) + nom dénombrable : *What a film! What actors!* Quel film ! Quels acteurs !
– *What* + nom indénombrable : *What intelligence!* Quelle intelligence !

On trouve l'article *a* devant des indénombrables dans des expressions figées : *What a fuss!* (Que d'histoires !) ; *What a shame* (Quelle honte !) ; *What a pity!* (Quel dommage !).

Attention à ne pas confondre exclamations et questions, notamment en ce qui concerne l'ordre des mots :
How old is he? Quel âge a-t-il ? (Question, donc inversion sujet-verbe)
How old he is! Qu'il est âgé ! (Exclamation : pas d'inversion sujet-verbe)

VOIR AUSSI LES EXCLAMATIONS AVEC *SO* ET *SUCH*, P. 240.

exercice

Trouvez la question qui correspond aux mots soulignés.

(1) I bought it <u>three days ago</u>, in Dover.
(2) I'll come <u>by car</u>: my mother will lend me hers.
(3) I can't wait because <u>the deadline is tomorrow</u>.
(4) It was <u>their idea</u> to give this party.
(5) He gave me <u>three pounds</u> for helping him.
(6) He should have <u>retired</u> two years ago.

3. *Tags*, reprises, réponses brèves

1 – *Tags*

Ces fins de phrases avec reprise de l'auxiliaire sont très courantes en anglais parlé. Elles n'expriment pas une véritable question mais servent à demander la confirmation de quelque chose dont on est sûr. On les forme :

– avec un *tag* négatif si la phrase est affirmative, et un *tag* affirmatif si la phrase est négative

– en utilisant le pronom personnel qui correspond au sujet de la phrase

– en utilisant le même auxiliaire que dans la phrase, ou *do* si la phrase ne contient pas d'auxiliaire.

→ *You're tired, aren't you?* Tu es fatigué, n'est-ce pas ?

→ *John hasn't failed, has he?* John n'a pas échoué, hein/dis ?

→ *The government can't raise taxes again, can they?*
Le gouvernement ne peut pas à nouveau augmenter les impôts, n'est-ce pas ?

→ *But she earns $20 an hour doing this job, doesn't she?*
Mais elle gagne 20 dollars de l'heure à faire ce travail, non ?

L'impératif est repris :

– par *will* à la seconde personne : *Stop crying, will you?*

– par *shall* à la première personne : *Let's ring them, shall we?*

P. 270 (INTONATION)

Les pronoms *everyone*, *everybody*, *someone*, *anybody*, etc, sont repris par *they*.

→ *Someone could have lent me a pen, couldn't they?*
Quelqu'un aurait pu me prêter un stylo, non ?

2 – Reprises

***So* + auxiliaire + sujet** permet de traduire Moi /lui/elle/ eux… aussi

***Neither/Nor* + auxiliaire + sujet** permet de traduire Moi/lui/elle/eux… non plus.

→ *"I've forgotten my book." "And so have I."* « J'ai oublié mon livre. – Moi aussi. »

→ *The supermarket will be closed on Monday, and so will the baker's.*
Le supermarché sera fermé lundi, et le boulanger aussi.

→ *"She doesn't like leeks." "Neither do her children."*
« Elle n'aime pas les poireaux. – Ses enfants non plus. »

3 – Réponses brèves

■ **Réponse en utilisant l'auxiliaire seul, et sans répéter le verbe.**

En anglais, on répond rarement *Yes* ou *No* seuls. On préfère accompagner *yes* ou *no* d'une reprise du verbe par l'auxiliaire.

→ *"Did you like the film?" "Yes I did."/"No, I didn't."*
« As-tu aimé le film ? – Oui./Non. »

→ *"Will he go to Japan?" "Yes, he will."/"No, he won't."*
« Est-ce qu'il ira au Japon ? – Oui./ Non. »
→ *"Who can spell the word onomatopoeia?" "I can!"/"I can't."*
« Qui peut épeler le mot onomatopée ? – Moi (je sais) !/Pas moi ! »

Lorsqu'il n'y a pas d'auxiliaire dans la question, on utilise *do* dans la réponse.
→ *"Who came on Sunday?" " John and Marie did."*
« Qui est venu dimanche ? – John et Marie. »

■ **Réponse en utilisant Verbe + *so/to***
→ *"Is she angry?" "I believe so."* « Elle est en colère? – Je le crois. »
→ *"Did you see the Turner exhibition?" "I wanted to, but didn't."*
« As-tu vu l'exposition Turner ? – Je voulais la voir, mais je ne l'ai pas fait. »

– Quelques verbes pouvant être suivis de *so* (Sujet + V + *so*)
think – be afraid – believe – hope – suppose – guess – expect
Lorsqu'on répond en utilisant les verbes *seem/hear/understand*, on emploie *so* avant : *So* + Sujet + V :
→ *"He's resigned?" "So I understand."*
« Il a donné sa démission ? – C'est ce que j'ai compris. »

À la forme négative, les verbes *hope* et *be afraid* sont suivis de *not* :
→ *"Will he give a party?" "I hope not."/"I don't think so."*
« Est-ce qu'il va faire une fête ? – J'espère que non./Je ne pense pas. »

– Quelques verbes pouvant être suivis de *to* (S + V + *to*)
want – would love – would like – be obliged – be allowed – be asked
→ *"Will you go to the States with them?" "I'd love to, but I won't be asked to."*
« Irez-vous aux États-Unis avec eux ? – J'aimerais beaucoup (y aller), mais ils ne m'inviteront pas. »
Le verbe est sous-entendu (*I'd love to go/I won't be asked to go*).

exercices

1 Complétez les phrases qui suivent avec le *tag* qui convient.
(1) They should build more housing for the poor, …
(2) Last month, she won a camera in the lottery, …
(3) They hadn't yet met in those years, …
(4) They'd rather stay at home, …
(5) They'd better do something about poverty, …
(6) The children aren't in bed, …

2 Traduisez.

(1) « Le prix de l'essence ne cesse de monter. – Le prix du gaz aussi. »

(2) Elle pourrait avoir des problèmes, et son mari aussi.

(3) « Je ne peux pas supporter les gens hypocrites. – Moi non plus. »

(4) « Le Royaume-Uni prépare une nouvelle loi sur l'immigration. – La France aussi. »

(5) « Je ne suis jamais entré dans un pub quand j'étais en Angleterre ! – Ma sœur non plus, mais moi, si. »

3 Donnez une réponse brève, en utilisant le pronom et le verbe donnés entre parenthèses.

(1) "Are they back from Spain?" "Yes, ..." (I + think)

(2) "Is he badly injured?" "No, ..." (I + believe)

(3) "Would they like to come for a meal?" "Yes, ..." (they + would love)

(4) "The Prime Minister has been reelected?" " Yes, ..." (I + understand)

(5) "Do you think she would lend us money?" "No, ..." (I + be afraid)

(6) "They're always quarrelling." "..." (it + seem)

4. L'IMPÉRATIF

L'impératif, qui sert à donner des ordres, des instructions, des recommandations, se forme de la façon suivante :

	Forme affirmative	Forme négative	Insistance	Reprise par auxiliaire
2e personne	**Verbe simple** *Come over here!* Viens ici ! *Give me the book!* Donne-moi le livre !	***Don't* + Verbe** *Don't forget!* N'oublie pas ! *Don't laugh!* Ne riez pas !	***Do* + Verbe** *Do apologize!* Surtout, excuse-toi.	***Will you?*** *Do tell him, will you?* Tu lui dis bien, hein ?
1re personne pluriel	***Let us* (=*Let's*) + Verbe** *Let's sit down!* Asseyons-nous !	***Let's not* + V ou *Don't let us* + V** *Let's not quarrel.* Ne nous querellons pas.	***Do* + *let us* + V** *Do let us go!* Laissez-nous partir, je vous en prie !	***Shall we?*** *Let's go to the cinema, shall we?* Allons au cinéma, d'accord ?

exercice

Traduisez.

(1) Ne fume pas ici !

(2) Veux-tu bien rester tranquille !

(3) Allons nous promener dans le parc.

(4) Et si on achetait ce disque pour son anniversaire ?

(5) Ne soyons pas trop critiques.

5. Les temps et l'aspect

Les systèmes des temps sont très différents en anglais et en français. Il est donc préférable d'essayer de comprendre le système anglais sans avoir recours à une traduction du français. Il existe deux temps en anglais : le présent et le prétérit. Il existe également deux façons d'envisager l'action (aspects), qui peuvent se combiner à ces temps : la forme en *be* V + *-ing* et la forme en *have* + participe passé.

1 – Le présent

Le présent simple

Forme :
-*s* à la 3e personne du singulier (*wants*) On ajoute un *e* avant le *s* quand le verbe se termine en *o* (*go* → *goes*) ou en *ch, sh, s, x, z* (*push* → *pushes*). Une terminaison en consonne + *y* devient *ies* (*marry* → *marries*).
– Formes négatives et interrogatives formées avec *do* : *I do not want.../Does he want...*
– Formes contractées : *don't* (= do not) ; *doesn't* (= does not)

Il permet de :
– parler d'une vérité générale :
→ *It often rains in winter.* Il pleut souvent en hiver.
– parler d'un fait, d'une condition ou d'une action habituelle, à valeur générale, qui ne dépendent pas des circonstances particulières du moment.
→ *Sue lives in Birmingham.* Sue habite Birmingham.
→ *He doesn't like fish.* Il n'aime pas le poisson.
→ *I go skiing every Christmas.* Je fais du ski tous les ans à Noël.
– parler d'une action future, qu'on envisage de façon neutre, comme quelque chose sur laquelle l'énonciateur n'a pas de prise.
→ *The plane leaves at 5, so we'd better hurry.*
L'avion part à 5 heures, nous ferions mieux de nous dépêcher.

On peut parfois rencontrer le présent simple dans un récit :
– quand un reportage est fait en direct à la radio ou à la télévision :
→ *Davidson shoots! The ball goes right into the net!*
Davidson tire ! La balle va droit dans le filet !
– lorsqu'on raconte une histoire drôle :
→ *There's this woman who comes into the bus and says...*
C'est l'histoire d'une femme qui rentre dans l'autobus et dit...
– lorsqu'on décrit une série d'images formant un récit (bande dessinée par exemple).
→ *The man comes back home and opens the door.*
L'homme rentre chez lui et ouvre la porte.

■ Le présent avec la forme *be* V + *-ing*

Forme :
– *be* V + *-ing* → *They are going. Are we going?*
– V + *-ing* : orthographe
- verbe se terminant par un seul *e* → le *e* disparaît (*write* → *writing*)
- verbe d'une syllabe se terminant en consonne + voyelle + consonne : on double la consonne finale (*put* → *putting*)
- verbe de plus d'une syllabe se terminant comme ci-dessus : on double la consonne finale si l'accent est sur la dernière syllabe (*be'gin* → *beginning*, mais *'alter* → *altering*)
- verbe se terminant en *c* : on ajoute un *k* (*picnic* → *picnicking*)
– formes contractées : *I'm/They're/You're/He isn't/He's not/You aren't/You're not*

Il permet de :
– décrire un processus en cours de déroulement au moment où l'énonciateur parle.
→ *I'm trying to drive in this nail. Can you come and help?* J'essaie de planter ce clou. Peux-tu venir m'aider ? (Il s'agit ici d'une activité ponctuelle, qu'on peut contraster avec l'activité répétée de : *I always try to watch the news everyday.* J'essaie toujours de regarder les informations tous les jours à la télévision.)
→ *Prices are now rising very quickly.* Les prix montent maintenant très vite.
– parler d'actions futures prévues par l'énonciateur.
→ *We're dining out tonight.* Nous dînons en ville ce soir.

Attention !
Lorsque *always* précède la forme *be* + V-*ing*, l'énonciateur exprime son irritation devant une action qui se reproduit trop souvent. P. 187

Comparez :
→ *You always work on Saturday nights.* Tu travailles toujours le samedi soir.
(Constatation neutre d'une vérité, action répétée chaque samedi.)

→ *I know it's Saturday, but he's working.* Je sais qu'on est samedi, mais il travaille. (Phénomène temporaire, il travaille en ce moment.)
→ *We can't go out: John's working to-night.* Nous ne pouvons pas sortir : John travaille ce soir. (Action prévue, c'est ce qu'on dit le matin ou l'après-midi.)
→ *You're always working on Saturday nights!* Il faut toujours que tu travailles le samedi soir ! (Irritation devant une action répétée.)

Certains verbes exprimant un état ou un résultat sont **incompatibles avec la forme *be* V + *-ing*** puisqu'elle décrit un processus en cours de déroulement.
Il s'agit :
– des verbes de perception : *see* (voir), *hear* (entendre), *taste* (goûter), *smell* (sentir, odorat), *sound* (sembler, ce qu'on entend). Mais avec *look* ou *listen* la perception est volontaire et la forme en *be* V + *-ing* est donc possible.
→ *I'm listening to their new record. It sounds wonderful.*
J'écoute leur nouveau disque. Il a l'air fantastique.
– des verbes exprimant une activité intellectuelle ou des sentiments *(hate, love, like, think, believe, admire, mean, agree, want, understand, remember...)*
– des verbes exprimant l'apparence *(look, seem)* ou une caractéristique (*cost* – coûter, *belong* – appartenir, *own* – posséder...)

Mais attention, certains de ces verbes peuvent être employés, dans des sens différents avec ou sans la forme *be* V + *-ing* :

Forme simple	*Be* V + *-ing*
He thinks I'm wrong. Il pense que j'ai tort. = croire que	*I'm thinking of retiring.* J'envisage de prendre ma retraite. *I'm thinking about the consequences.* Je pense aux conséquences. = envisager ou réfléchir
Do you have a driving licence? As tu ton permis de conduire ? = posséder	*We're having lunch.* On est en train de déjeuner. = activités
I see you've changed your mind. Je vois que tu as changé d'avis. = perception visuelle ou intellectuelle	*She's seeing her boss this morning.* Elle voit son patron ce matin. *They've been seeing each other for two months.* Ils sortent ensemble depuis deux mois. = rendez-vous
We feel he's right. Nous pensons qu'il a raison. = penser, considérer que	*He's feeling better.* Il se sent mieux. = se sentir

2 – Le prétérit

■ Prétérit simple

Forme :
– V + *-ed* (*shout → shouted/did not shout/did they shout?*)
Mais attention aux formes des verbes irréguliers.
– orthographe
- verbe se terminant par un *e* : on ajoute seulement un *d* : *hate → hated*
- verbe se terminant en *y* : il devient *i* : *marry → married*
- pour le redoublement de la consonne finale on suit les mêmes règles que pour V + *-ing*

On utilise le prétérit pour décrire une action, un événement, un état appartenant à un passé maintenant révolu et daté. Cet emploi du prétérit inscrit l'action dans une chronologie.
→ *I gave him the letter yesterday.* Je lui ai donné la lettre hier.
→ *I saw him often when I lived in Bath.* Je le voyais souvent lorsque j'habitais à Bath.

C'est donc le temps que l'on utilise le plus souvent pour un récit.
→ *I had a dream last night. I was in a boat and I suddenly saw a giant fish with the head of a man.* J'ai fait un rêve la nuit dernière. J'étais en bateau et soudain j'ai vu un énorme poisson à tête d'homme.
Notez les indications temporelles dans les exemples ci-dessus (*yesterday, when I lived…, last night*) qui situent bien les faits dans le passé.

C'est aussi le prétérit simple (alors aussi appelé « prétérit modal ») que l'on utilise pour parler de l'irréel dans les structures suivantes :

wish *would ('d) rather* *It's time* *If only*	+ pronom/nom + prétérit

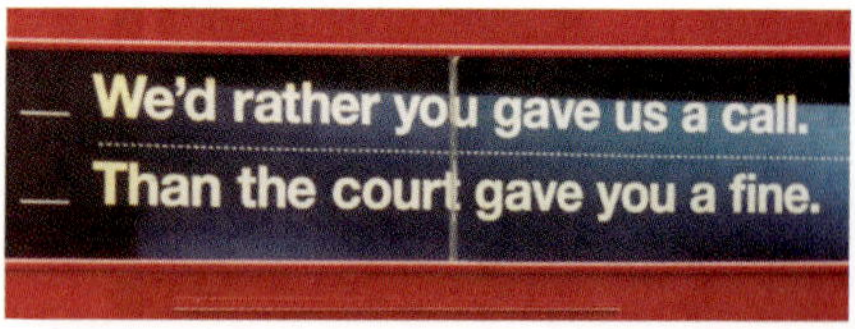

→ *I wish she were here.* J'aimerais qu'elle soit ici.
(On utilise alors *were* à toutes les personnes.)
→ *They wish their daughter earned more.* Ils regrettent que leur fille ne gagne pas plus.
→ *I would rather you told her yourself.* Je préférerais que ce soit toi qui lui dises.
(Avec cette structure le pronom doit être différent du sujet.)
→ *It's time you found a job.* Il est temps que tu trouves un travail.

VOIR AUSSI L'EMPLOI DE *USED TO* POUR PARLER DU PASSÉ RÉVOLU, P. 211.

■ Le prétérit avec la forme *Be* V + *-ing*

Avec cette forme l'énonciateur met l'accent sur le déroulement de l'action dans le passé.
→ *We were talking very loud and did not hear the telephone.*
Nous parlions très fort et n'avons pas entendu le téléphone.

Elle est particulièrement employée pour parler d'une action ponctuelle (prétérit simple) qui s'inscrit au milieu d'une action plus longue en cours (prétérit *be* V + *-ing*).

→ *They were watching television when the doorbell rang.*
Ils regardaient la télévision quand on a sonné.

3 – Le *present perfect*

Forme : *have* conjugué + participe passé

Il permet à l'énonciateur d'établir un lien entre le passé et le présent
– parce que la situation ou l'action a commencé dans le passé et est encore vraie.
→ *I've wanted to do that for years.* Voilà des années que je veux faire cela.
– parce qu'on fait un bilan d'une situation, de quelque chose fait dans un passé récent mais dont c'est le résultat qui nous intéresse.
→ *You've dyed your hair! It suits you.* Tu t'es teint les cheveux ! Cela te va bien.
→ *Have you finished your homework?* As-tu fini tes devoirs ?

On emploie donc souvent le *present perfect* avec un certain nombre d'adverbes et expressions qui décrivent la situation présente par rapport au passé : *just* (tout juste), *recently* (récemment), *already* (déjà), *never* (jamais), *not yet* (pas encore), *so far* (jusqu'ici), *it's the first/second/only time* (c'est la première/seconde/seule fois…), *ever* dans une phrase interrogative (jamais).
→ *I have not bought my ticket yet.* Je n'ai pas encore acheté mon billet.
→ *Have you ever been to Greece?* Es-tu jamais allé en Grèce?

■ Le *present perfect* avec la forme *Be* V + *-ing*

L'énonciateur donne alors sa réaction à l'activité du sujet.
Comparez :
→ *You've written the letter.* Tu as écrit la lettre.
On met l'accent sur le résultat, sur le fait que la lettre est terminée.
→ *You've been writing the letter.*
On met plus l'accent sur l'activité d'écriture ou sur la surprise de l'énonciateur.

On emploie souvent cette forme lorsqu'on peut encore voir les marques laissées par l'activité.
→ *You're all wet! You've been walking in the rain.*
Tu es trempé ! Tu as marché sous la pluie !
→ *Your hands are dirty. You've been playing in the mud again.*
Tes mains sont sales. Tu as encore joué dans la boue!
C'est la raison pour laquelle cette forme exprime fréquemment une irritation ou une accusation.
→ *You've been drinking again!*
Tu as encore bu! (sous entendu : cela se voit, ou se sent.)

4 – La traduction du français « depuis »

Lorsque depuis introduit une durée, on le traduit par *for*. Lorsqu'il introduit le point de départ (heure, date, événement...) d'une action ou d'un état, on le traduit par *since*. Puisqu'on décrit alors un lien entre le passé et le présent (une action qui a commencé dans le passé et continue), c'est le *present perfect* qu'on emploie dans la principale.

I've lived in London	– *since 1998.*
	– *since I was five.* (*since* + fait passé, donc au prétérit)
	– *since I got married.*
I've been waiting	– *since two o'clock.*
	– *since he phoned me.*
I've worked on my project	– *for two hours.*
	– *for the past three years.*

Notez que « depuis deux heures », par exemple, peut signifier une durée (pendant deux heures de suite → *for two hours*) ou un point de départ (depuis que l'horloge a sonné deux heures → *since two o'clock.*). Notez aussi qu'en français, c'est un présent que l'on trouve dans la principale : J'attends depuis deux heures. Je vis à Londres depuis 1998.

> *For* + durée peut être compatible avec un verbe au prétérit dans la principale, lorsque l'action décrite est terminée. *For* correspond alors au français « pendant ».
> → *I lived in London for 3 years, between 2000 and 2003.*
> J'ai habité Londres pendant 3 ans, entre 2000 et 2003.

Ces expressions avec « depuis » permettent aussi de traduire des phrases telles que : « Cela fait... que... » ou « Il y a... que... ».

→ Il y a cinq ans que je n'ai pas eu de ses nouvelles.
= Je n'ai pas eu de ses nouvelles depuis 5 ans. *I haven't heard from him for 5 years.*

→ Cela fait trois jours qu'il pleut.
= Il pleut depuis 3 jours. *It has been raining for 3 days.*

> Lorsque « il y a » indique un moment du passé et non une durée, on emploiera *ago* (juste après l'expression de durée) et un prétérit.
> → Je l'ai rencontré il y a trois jours. *I met him three days ago.*
> → Cela s'est passé il y a très longtemps. *It happened ages ago.*

5 – Le *past perfect*

Forme : *had* + participe passé

Il permet de faire le lien entre un moment du passé et un autre moment antérieur.

→ *I wanted to mow the lawn yesterday, but it had rained during the night and the grass was still wet.* Je voulais tondre la pelouse hier, mais il avait plu pendant la nuit et l'herbe était encore mouillée. *It had rained* est antérieur à *the grass was still wet...*

C'est pourquoi cette structure permet souvent de donner une explication de faits passés.

→ *I had forgotten my keys and had to wait in the garden.*
J'avais oublié mes clés et j'ai dû attendre dans le jardin.

■ ***Past perfect* avec la forme *Be* V + *-ing***

On insiste alors sur l'activité plutôt que sur le résultat.

→ *He had been walking all the way from the station and was exhausted.*
Il avait fait le trajet à pied depuis la gare et était épuisé.

Le *past perfect* s'emploie comme le *present perfect* avec *for* ou *since* pour établir un lien entre deux moments du passé.

→ *I met him in 1999. He had been married for ten years.*
Je l'ai rencontré en 1999. Il était marié depuis dix ans.

→ *When he rang last month, I hadn't heard from him since his accident.* Lorsqu'il a téléphoné le mois dernier, je n'avais pas eu de ses nouvelles depuis son accident.

→ *She'd been drinking in the pub since 7 o'clock and was in no state to drive.*
Elle buvait au pub depuis 7 heures et n'était pas en état de conduire.

exercices

Le présent

1 Pouvez-vous utiliser le présent simple en anglais pour traduire les phrases qui suivent ? Si oui, traduisez-les.

(1) J'arrive ! Je pars tout de suite !

(2) Nous jouons souvent au bridge ensemble.

(3) Le cèdre pousse très lentement.

(4) Nous nous lèverons de bonne heure demain matin pour aller au marché.

(5) Je ne me lève jamais avant 10 heures le dimanche !

2 Complétez les traductions qui suivent avec un présent simple ou en *be* V + *-ing*. Le verbe vous est donné entre parenthèses.

(1) Nous partons en vacances au Portugal. *We ... to Portugal for our holiday. (go)*

(2) Tu passes ton temps à regarder des matchs de football!
You ... football matches. (watch)

(3) Elle ne porte pas de rouge, elle n'aime que le noir.
She ... red; she only ... black. (wear, like)

(4) Pierre est dans le jardin, où il arrose la pelouse. Je trouve qu'il a l'air fatigué.
Pierre is in the garden, where he ... the lawn. I ... that he ... tired. (water, think, look)

(5) Est-ce que ce stylo appartient à quelqu'un ? *… to anyone? (belong)*

(6) « Pourquoi est-ce que tu cours ? – Parce que je cours toujours pour prendre mon train : c'est bon pour la santé ! » *"Why …?" "Because I … to catch my train: it's good for your health!" (run)*

(7) « Tu veux acheter ces chaussures ? – Je ne pense pas. Il faut que j'économise car j'envisage d'acheter une voiture. » *"… to buy these shoes?" "… so. I must save up for … of buying a car." (want – think – think)*

LE PRÉTÉRIT

3 Complétez les phrases avec le prétérit des verbes donnés dans le désordre.

shut – take – run – choose – jump – strike – push – try – leave – take – threaten

Pursued by the police, the man … over a fence and … across the road. Several passers-by … to stop him, but he … them aside and … to enter a café. There, he … a man hostage, … to kill him, and … himself up with him in the café. When the hostage tried to flee, he … him, … all the money from the till (la caisse), and … through the back door.

4 Traduisez.

(1) Ils préféreraient que vous arriviez de bonne heure.

(2) Martha pensait qu'il était temps que son fils quitte la maison.

(3) J'aimerais qu'il m'invite plus souvent.

(4) Qu'elle dommage que je ne sois pas aussi riche que ma cousine !

(5) Il préférerait que son amie lui dise la vérité.

5 Complétez les phrases avec les verbes donnés entre parenthèses au prétérit simple ou au prétérit *be* V + *-ing* :

(1) I … (wash) my car when I … (see) the accident.

(2) In those days, I always … (wash) my car when I … (return) from holidays.

(3) I … (catch) sight of you in town this morning. What … (you + do) there?

(4) Yesterday I … (read) a story about a man who … (wake up) while the doctors … (perform) an operation on him.

PRESENT PERFECT

6 Complétez les phrases qui suivent avec l'adverbe qui convient.

(1) Don't buy the record: I have … done so.

(2) The price of houses has … risen sharply.

(3) Have you … met a well-known actor?

(4) I've … rung your sister, and she says she's fine.

(5) The price of petrol has … reached £1 a litre, but may soon do so.

7 Les phrases qui suivent sont au passé composé français. Traduisez-les en faisant le choix du prétérit ou du *present perfect*.

(1) « Je n'ai jamais vu *La Guerre des étoiles*. – Moi je l'ai vu l'an dernier pendant les vacances d'été. »

(2) « J'ai fini mes révisions ! – Mais tu as dit cela la semaine dernière ! »

(3) La situation économique s'est améliorée après l'élection du nouveau président, mais elle s'est récemment détériorée.

(4) J'ai fait beaucoup de voile (= *to go sailing*) quand j'étais au lycée, mais c'est la première fois que je fais de la planche à voile (= *to windsurf*).

8 Complétez les phrases qui suivent avec les verbes donnés entre parenthèses au *present perfect* simple ou à la forme *be* V + *-ing* :

(1) You … (play) for two hours. It's time you stopped.

(2) Now that you … (play) the video game, you can take it back to the library.

(3) We … (come) to give you a hand with the cooking.

(4) Look at the carpet! Someone … (walk) here with muddy feet.

(5) I … (watch) the news to get the latest casualty figures.

(6) It's strange: I think someone … (watch) us all morning from the house opposite.

Depuis

9 Complétez les phrases qui suivent avec *for* ou *since*.

(1) I haven't seen her … Christmas.

(2) We haven't been to the concert … the holidays.

(3) Unemployment has been rising … two months.

(4) Things are quiet here; nothing has happened … a long time.

(5) She's had a new job … last Monday.

10 Traduisez.

(1) Je ne suis pas allé à la piscine depuis qu'elle a rouvert.

(2) J'aime les escargots depuis que j'en ai mangé chez vous.

(3) Leur maison est inondée (*to flood*) depuis une semaine.

(4) J'ai lu ce livre il y a trois mois.

(5) Il y a trois mois que je n'ai rien lu.

PAST PERFECT

11 Complétez les phrases qui suivent avec les verbes donnés entre parenthèses au *preterit*, *present perfect* ou au *past perfect* (forme simple ou forme *be* V + *-ing*).

(1) When the telephone call … (come) with the news that she had been awarded the prize for her first novel, Lorie … (paint) the dining-room walls and her hands … (be) full of yellow paint.

(2) "Can you make me a cup of tea, Joan? I … (drive) for hours and feel very thirsty. I … (have + not) anything to drink since I … (leave) home this morning."

(3) In September 2005, the price of petrol … (rise) for several months, and many people … (choose) to use public transportation instead of their cars.

(4) They … (invite) us to the restaurant twice before, but this was the first time we … (see + ever) their home.

(5) He is now 21, and although he … (be born) in London, and … (grow up) in London, he … (make up one's mind + now) to buy a flat in Glasgow.

6. Les modaux

Les modaux permettent à l'énonciateur de donner son point de vue, son jugement sur un événement. Ils permettent par exemple à l'énonciateur de dire si l'action ou l'état est possible, probable, nécessaire, obligatoire.
Comparez :
***He works hard.* Il travaille dur.**
→ simple assertion neutre. L'énonciateur exprime un fait sans le juger.
***He can work hard.* Il est capable de travailler dur.**
***He must work hard.* Il faut qu'il travaille dur.**
→ L'énonciateur émet un jugement.

■ Les formes présent, prétérit et contractées des modaux

Modal présent	Prétérit	Formes contractées
can	*could*	*cannot = can't; could not = couldn't*
may	*might*	
must	pas de prétérit	*must not = mustn't*
shall	*should*	*shall not = shan't; should not = shouldn't*
will	*would*	*will = 'll; will not = won't* *would = 'd; would not = wouldn't*

■ Les caractéristiques des modaux

– Ils ne sont pas précédés de *to*, ils ne se conjuguent pas avec *do*, ils ne prennent pas la marque s de la troisième personne du singulier.
– Ils sont suivis du verbe sans *to* (jamais de *that*, du verbe avec *to*, de la forme V + *-ing* ou d'un autre modal).
– Forme négative : Modal + *not* + verbe.
→ *He should not say that.* Il ne devrait pas dire cela.
– Forme interrogative : Modal + sujet + verbe.
→ *Can she swim?* Est-ce qu'elle sait nager ?

1 – La capacité : *can/be able to*

Can/could permettent d'exprimer la capacité, physique ou intellectuelle.
→ *I can't lift it: it's too heavy.* Je ne peux pas le soulever. C'est trop lourd.
→ *Can you tell me the time?* Pouvez-vous me dire l'heure ?
→ *I had a sore throat and could not speak.* J'avais mal à la gorge et ne pouvais pas parler.

Les verbes de perception s'emploient souvent précédés de *can*.
→ *They could hear steps approaching.* Ils entendaient des pas qui se rapprochaient.
→ *Can you see the house over there?* Vous voyez la maison là-bas ?
(Notez qu'en général on n'utilisera pas le verbe pouvoir dans la traduction française.)

Could peut aussi exprimer une capacité potentielle, hypothétique.
– au moment présent (il correspond alors à un conditionnel en français) :
→ *You could walk there if you wanted to.* Tu pourrais y aller à pied si tu voulais.
– au passé avec *could* + *have* + participe passé (il correspond alors à un conditionnel passé en français) :
→ *You could have written another essay.* Tu aurais pu écrire un autre essai.
(Comme en français, la phrase peut exprimer la possibilité ou l'irritation, le reproche.)

Lorsque *can/could* correspondent à « être capable de », ils peuvent être remplacés par *be able to* (à la forme négative : *not be able to* ou *be unable to*).
→ *She can swim two miles. She is able to swim two miles.*
Elle peut/est capable de faire trois kilomètres à la nage.

Au passé, *was/were able to* s'emploie surtout pour décrire la réalisation d'une capacité à un moment particulier :
→ *One day, when he was six, he was able to swim across the lake.*
Un jour, lorsqu'il avait six ans, il a réussi à traverser le lac à la nage.

Could s'emploiera plutôt pour une capacité plus générale.
→ *At six, he could already run more quickly than his friends.*
À six ans, il courait déjà plus vite que ses amis.

Be able to ne s'emploie généralement pas avec les verbes de perception.
Mais c'est cette forme qu'on utilisera dans des structures où *can* est impossible (après *will* ou un modal, après *to*...).

→ *I would love to be able to play the violin.* J'aimerais tellement savoir jouer du violon.

2 – La permission : *may/can*

May et *can* permettent d'exprimer la permission.

Demande de permission	Autorisation	Refus
On peut employer *can, could* et *may* (par ordre croissant de politesse) *Can I leave the table?* *Could I leave the table?* *May I leave the table?* Est-ce que je peux/Puis-je me lever de table ?	*Can* et *may* permettent de donner une autorisation. *You can/may go now.* Tu peux y aller maintenant.	*Cannot* (ou *can't*) et *may not* permettent de refuser une permission, d'interdire. *You cannot/may not go out before you've finished your homework.* Tu ne sortiras pas/Tu n'as pas le droit de sortir tant que tu n'auras pas fini tes devoirs.

On peut aussi utiliser *be allowed* to pour parler de permission.
On utilise cette forme :

– pour parler d'autorisation ou d'interdiction officielle, lorsque cela fait partie d'un règlement par exemple.

→ *You're not allowed to use fountain pens in this library.*
On n'a pas le droit d'utiliser un stylo à encre dans cette bibliothèque.

– dans les structures où *can* ou *may* sont impossibles (après *will, to*, etc.)

→ *When you are a boarder, you will not be allowed to go out after 10 p.m.*
Lorsque tu seras interne, tu n'auras pas le droit de sortir après 22 heures.

– au *present perfect* et *past perfect*, ainsi qu'au prétérit.

→ *In those days, girls were not allowed to wear mini-skirts to school.*
À cette époque les jeunes filles n'avaient pas le droit d'aller à l'école en mini-jupe.

3 – Du possible au certain : *may/can/should/ought to/must*

Les modaux ci-contre permettent à l'énonciateur de dire si l'action est probable ou quasiment certaine.
Might, could, may, should et *must* peuvent être suivis de la forme *be* V + *-ing* pour décrire un procès en cours de déroulement.

→ *He may be sitting for his exam right now.*
Il est peut-être en train de passer son examen à l'heure qu'il est.

DU MOINS PROBABLE ⟶ AU PLUS PROBABLE (QUASI CERTITUDE)

MIGHT	*COULD*	*MAY*	*SHOULD / OUGHT TO*	*WILL*	*MUST*
Il s'agit d'une simple éventualité (ce n'est pas impossible). *They might bring their daughter along.* Il se pourrait qu'ils viennent avec leur fille.	L'événement semble tout à fait possible. *They could already be in New York.* Peut-être sont-ils déjà à New York.	L'énonciateur est un peu plus sûr. *He may have phoned and left a message. We'll see.* Il a peut-être téléphoné et laissé un message. On verra.	L'énonciateur pense que l'événement est très probable. *They should arrive on Sunday.* Ils devraient arriver dimanche. *I ought to finish my essay tonight.* Je devrais terminer mon essai ce soir.	L'énonciateur parle d'une forte probabilité *It's a letter from America. It will be John.* C'est une lettre des États-Unis. Elle doit venir de John.	L'énonciateur est pratiquement sûr. Il fait une déduction logique. *I've heard he's back. You must be delighted.* On m'a dit qu'il était de retour. Vous devez être ravis.

Formes négatives

MIGHT NOT *He might not want to come.* Il se pourrait qu'il n'ait pas envie de venir.		*MAY NOT* *She may not be back.* Peut-être n'est-elle pas rentrée.			*CAN'T* *He can't be 18 already!* Il ne peut pas avoir déjà 18 ans!

Pour parler du passé

MIGHT HAVE + part. passé *You might have cut your finger.* Tu aurais pu te couper le doigt.	*COULD* + *HAVE* + part. passé (forme active seulement) *This could have caused a fire.* Cela aurait pu provoquer un feu.	*MAY* + *HAVE* + part. passé. *The driver may not have seen the other car.* Le conducteur n'a peut-être pas vu l'autre voiture.	*SHOULD* + *HAVE* + part. passé *It's ten o'clock: they should have landed.* Il est dix heures. Ils devraient avoir atterri.	*WILL* + *HAVE* + part. passé *He is not here yet. They will have kept him at the office.* Il n'est pas encore là. Ils ont dû le retenir au bureau.	*MUST* + *HAVE* + Part. passé *They must have sent the letter from London.* Ils ont dû envoyer la lettre de Londres. **Forme négative :** *They can't have sent...* Ils n'ont pas pu... *They couldn't have sent...* Il n'est pas possible qu'ils aient...

Attention, avec *must*, ne confondez pas :

– *Must* + verbe simple décrivant une activité, un processus = devoir, obligation.

→ *He must work more.* Il lui faut travailler plus.

– *Must* + même verbe à la forme + *be* V + *-ing* = forte probabilité.

→ *He must be working right now.*

Il doit travailler en ce moment. (= il est en train de travailler)

La probabilité peut aussi s'exprimer grâce aux expressions *be likely to* (probabilité), *be bound to* et *be sure to* (certitude). Mais attention aux structures possibles :

→ *He is likely to be promoted.* Il a de fortes chances d'être promu.
ou : *It is likely that he will be promoted.*

→ *They're bound to be disappointed.* (seule structure possible)
Ils seront déçus, c'est inévitable.

→ *They are sure to be invited.* Il est sûr qu'ils seront invités. (point de vue extérieur)
mais : *They are sure that they will be invited.* Ils sont sûrs qu'ils seront invités.

4 – L'OBLIGATION : *MUST*

■ ***Must*** (qui peut aussi exprimer la presque certitude, P. 206) est utilisé pour parler d'une obligation.

→ *We must try to help them.* Nous devons essayer de les aider.

→ *They think the university must be opened to all.*
Ils pensent que l'université doit être ouverte à tous.

■ ***Have to*** peut être utilisé à la place de *must*. Il se conjugue avec l'auxiliaire *do*.
– Au présent on l'emploie lorsque l'obligation est extérieure à l'énonciateur, ne dépend pas de lui.

→ *Do I have to change (trains) in Birmingham?*
Est-ce qu'il faut que je change de train à Birmingham ?

Lorsque la contrainte vient de l'énonciateur, c'est *must* qu'on utilise.

→ *I must try to be more patient.* Il faut que j'essaye d'être plus patient.

Comparez :

→ *All workers must wear helmets on this site.* Le port du casque est obligatoire sur le chantier. (C'est ce que dit la direction.)

→ *You have to wear a helmet, or they won't let you in.* Il faut que vous portiez un casque, sinon on ne vous laissera pas entrer. (C'est le règlement, je n'y suis pour rien.)

– On emploie également *have to* lorsque *must* est impossible (au prétérit, au *present perfect*, après *to*, *will* etc.)

→ *You will have to give him a reason.* Il te faudra lui donner une raison.

→ *They had to wait two hours in the rain.* Ils ont dû attendre deux heures sous la pluie.

■ **À la forme négative,** il faut distinguer :

– *mustn't* = une interdiction

→ *You mustn't play near the river.* Il ne faut pas aller jouer près de la rivière.

– not + have to = une absence d'obligation

→ *You don't have to carry your passport.*
Vous n'êtes pas obligés d'avoir votre passeport sur vous.

■ ***Need not*** peut également exprimer l'absence d'obligation. Il peut se construire comme un modal :

→ *You need not (= needn't) come.* Il n'est pas nécéssaire que tu viennes.

Mais peut aussi se construire comme un verbe normal :

→ *You don't need to give me a reason.* Tu n'as pas besoin de me donner une raison.

■ Pour donner un ordre ou interdire quelque chose, on peut également utiliser *be to*.

→ *You are to stay in your room.* Tu dois rester dans ta chambre.

→ *You are not to walk on the lawn.* Tu ne dois pas marcher sur la pelouse.

5 – Le conseil : *should/ought to*

Should s'emploie surtout lorsque l'énonciateur donne un conseil personnel.

→ *You should read his new novel.* Tu devrais lire son nouveau roman.

Ought to s'emploie de préférence lorsqu'on parle d'une règle de bon sens ou d'usage.

→ *You ought to wash this silk blouse by hand.*
Tu devrais laver ce corsage en soie à la main.

Au passé, on emploie *should/ought to* + *have* + part. passé :

→ *You shouldn't have cooked the meat so much.*
Tu n'aurais pas dû tant faire cuire la viande.

6 – Les conditions : *will/would*

Will et *would* sont utilisés après des propositions en *if*. Notez bien les trois formes possibles :

– ***If* + présent → *will*** : on parle d'une possibilité future

→ *If it doesn't rain, we'll (= we will) go sailing.*
S'il ne pleut pas nous ferons de la voile.

– ***If* + prétérit → *would*** : on parle de quelque chose d'hypothétique, de beaucoup moins probable

→ *If it rained, we would have to take the bus.*
S'il pleuvait, il nous faudrait prendre l'autobus.

– ***If* + *past perfect* → *would have* + part. passé :** on parle de quelque chose qui aurait pu mais ne s'est pas réalisé dans le passé.

→ *If it had rained, the road would have been even more slippery.*
S'il avait plu, la route aurait été encore plus glissante.

Notez la différence entre

– *If I was/she was/you were* : on parle d'une possibilité

→ *If she really was in the shop at the time, why wouldn't she say so?* Si elle était vraiment dans le magasin à cette heure-là, pourquoi ne le dirait-elle pas ?

– *If* + sujet + *were* à toutes les personnes : on parle de quelque chose d'irréel, de quasiment impossible.

→ *If I were the President of the United States…* Si j'étais président des États-Unis…

Notez aussi que, dans un style soutenu, on peut utiliser une inversion dans la proposition subordonnée :

→ *If I had met her…* = *Had I met her…* Si je l'avais rencontrée…

→ *If he phoned/If he should phone…* = *Should he phone…* Si jamais il téléphonait…

Notez que les subordonnées de temps (commençant par *when, as soon as, until…*) se comportent comme les propositions en *if* : on y utilise un présent (au lieu du futur français) et un prétérit (au lieu du conditionnel français).

→ *As soon as I know his name, I'll give it to you.*
Dès que je connaîtrai son nom, je te le donnerai.

→ *He said he would phone me when he had finished.*
Il m'a dit qu'il me téléphonerait quand il aurait terminé.

→ *He would have complained as soon as he had been told.*
Il se serait plaint dès qu'il aurait su.

7 – Autres emplois de *would*

Would sert à exprimer le conditionnel plus généralement.

→ *They promised that they would keep in touch.* Ils promirent qu'ils garderaient le contact.

→ *Would you like to sit down?* Voulez-vous (= voudriez-vous) vous asseoir ?

À la première personne du singulier et du pluriel, *should* est également possible :

→ *I should tell you if I knew.* Je te le dirais si je le savais.

Attention, ne confondez pas la forme contractée de *would*, *'d*, et la même forme contractée de *had*. Souvenez-vous que *would* est suivi du verbe sans *to*, *had* d'un participe passé.

→ *I'd accept* = *I would accept*

→ *I'd accepted* = *I had accepted*

Avec un verbe comme *read*, dont le participe passé est semblable à la forme verbale simple, seul le contexte peut vous aider :

→ *I'd read the book twice already.* (= *I had read*) J'avais déjà lu le livre deux fois.

→ *I'd read the book if I were you.* (= *I would read*) À ta place, je lirais le livre.

Would et *used to*

Would peut être utilisé pour décrire une habitude, des actions répétées ou une caractéristique du sujet dans le passé.

→ *We spent a week in the hotel. We would get up late and go for a swim before breakfast.* Nous sommes restés une semaine à l'hôtel. Nous nous levions tard et allions nager avant le petit-déjeuner.

> Attention, à la forme négative, *would not* prend le sens de refuser de (sauf dans les phrases conditionnelles).
> *She would not come with us.* Elle refusait de venir avec nous.

Will peut avoir le même sens au présent :

→ *She will take a little walk round the garden every morning.*
Elle fait (Il lui faut) son petit tour de jardin tous les matins.

Used to peut aussi exprimer un fait passé, mais on l'emploie lorsqu'on insiste sur le fait qu'il s'agit de quelque chose de révolu, qui n'est plus vrai maintenant.

→ *When I was a child, we used to skate on the pond.*
Nous faisions du patin sur l'étang quand j'étais petit.

On l'utilise aussi pour un état :

→ *There used to be fields here. Now there's a road.*
Autrefois il y avait ici des champs. Maintenant, il y a une route.

Used to se conjugue avec *do* : *Did you use to smoke the pipe?*

> Attention à ne pas confondre *used to* et *be* + *used to* + V + *-ing*/nom
> Cette dernière forme sert à décrire une habitude passée, présente ou future.
> → *I'm not used to going to bed so late.* Je n'ai pas l'habitude de me coucher si tard.
> → *I wasn't used to drinking alcohol.* Je n'avais pas l'habitude de boire de l'alcool.
> → *You will soon become/get used to working with her.*
> Tu t'habitueras vite à travailler avec elle.

8 – PARLER DU FUTUR : *WILL/SHALL*

Plusieurs modaux ou expressions permettent de parler du futur.

Will/shall

Le modal *will* s'emploie à toutes les personnes pour parler du futur, surtout lorsqu'il s'agit de parler d'une prédiction ou de la volonté de l'énonciateur de faire quelque chose.

→ *We'll probably spend a few days in Egypt.*
Nous passerons sans doute quelques jours en Égypte.

→ *They will never win the elections.* Ils ne gagneront jamais les élections.

Avec *will*, l'événement n'est pas ancré dans un futur précis.

À la première personne du singulier et du pluriel, on peut employer *shall* dans une langue soignée.

→ *We shall let them know.* Nous leur ferons savoir.

À la forme interrogative *shall* s'emploie à la première personne pour faire une offre ou demander un avis.

→ *Shall I help you?* Voulez-vous que je vous aide?

À la forme interrogative, et surtout à la forme négative, *will* peut prendre un sens de **volonté**.

→ *She just won't leave her room.* Elle refuse tout simplement de quitter sa chambre.

→ *Will you stay for a few days?* Est-ce que vous voulez rester quelques jours?

■ ***Be going to***

On l'utilise pour parler de quelque chose de décidé, d'arrangé à l'avance, ou pour prédire un fait qui semble inévitable étant donné les circonstances.

→ *You can have the car tonight: we're going to watch the football match on TV.*
Tu peux prendre la voiture ce soir, on va regarder le match de football à la télévision.

→ *Look at the sky! It's going to rain before long.*
Regarde le ciel ! Il va bientôt pleuvoir.

■ **Le présent en *be* V + *-ing***

Cette forme permet de parler de plans personnels.

→ *We're moving out next week.* Nous déménageons la semaine prochaine.

■ **Le présent simple**

Il permet de parler d'une action future, qu'on envisage de façon objective et sur laquelle l'énonciateur n'a pas de prise.

→ *The train stops at Birmingham and reaches Glasgow at 9.*
Le train s'arrête à Birmingham et arrive à Glasgow à 9 heures.

■ ***Be to***

Cette forme ne s'emploie qu'au présent et au prétérit pour parler d'un programme officiel ou d'un événement considéré avec le recul du temps.

→ *The Queen is to open the new museum tomorrow.*
La reine doit inaugurer le nouveau musée demain.

Et pour parler d'un programme non réalisé :

→ *The Queen was to have gone to Wales, but cancelled her visit.*
La reine devait aller au Pays de Galles mais a annulé sa visite.

→ *He was to die at twenty.* Il devait mourir à 20 ans. (fatalité)

→ *Her novel was to become a best-seller.* Son roman allait devenir un best-seller.

■ ***Be about to***

Avec *be about to*, on parle d'un futur immédiat.

→ *We were just about to start dinner when he arrived.*
Nous allions juste commencer à dîner lorsqu'il est arrivé.

8 – 'D RATHER (= WOULD RATHER)/'D BETTER (= HAD BETTER)

Had better + V = ferait/s/ent mieux de

→ *You'd better get your hair cut before the interview.*
Tu ferais mieux de te faire couper les cheveux avant l'entretien.

Autres formes : *You'd better not go... Hadn't you better go...*

Would rather + V = préférerais/t/ent

→ *They'd rather go to the cinema.* Ils préféreraient aller au cinéma.

Autres formes : *They'd rather not work... Would they rather work...?*

Lorsque la préférence concerne ce que fait une autre personne, on pourra employer la structure :

→ *They'd rather she lived close to the university.*
Ils préféreraient qu'elle habite près de l'université.

Pour parler d'une préférence non réalisée, on dira :

→ *I'd rather he hadn't told me.* J'aurais préféré qu'il ne m'en parle pas.

Enfin, il faut noter la structure suivante pour parler d'une comparaison :

→ *She'd rather drive than fly.* Elle préfère conduire plutôt que de voyager en avion.

exercices

CAPACITÉ

1 Complétez les phrases qui suivent avec *can* ou *be able to* au temps qui convient suivi du verbe donné entre parenthèses, à la forme qui convient.

(1) When I was a child, you ... (skate) on this pond, and we often did in winter.
(2) ... (walk + you) a little faster? We ... (get + perhaps) an earlier train.
(3) ... (hear + you) me? The line is bad, but I ... (speak + not) any louder.
(4) They were ill and ... (come + not), which I understand. But they ... (write) a few lines to apologize the next day.
(5) Our computer broke down because of a virus last night, but he ... (repair) it.
(6) The sky was so clear last week, that we ... (see) the Alps in the distance.

2 Traduisez.

(1) Vous auriez pu vous excuser !
(2) Tous les soirs, j'entends les voisins prendre leur douche.
(3) Comment pourrais-je améliorer mon travail ?
(4) Je n'ai pas pu fermer la fenêtre ce matin. Peux-tu m'aider ?
(5) Je ne sais pas si je pourrai venir la semaine prochaine.

PERMISSION

3 Traduisez.

(1) Est-ce que nous pourrions emprunter votre téléphone portable ?

(2) Il est interdit d'utiliser un téléphone portable dans le musée.

(3) Papa, j'peux prendre la voiture ce soir ?

(4) Il a le droit de sortir seul depuis son anniversaire.

(5) Vous pouvez prendre ces chaises ; j'en ai d'autres.

DU POSSIBLE AU CERTAIN

4 Récrivez les phrases qui suivent en utilisant un modal ou une expression équivalente, à la forme qui convient.

(1) Surely it is not eight o'clock yet.

(2) Perhaps he would have accepted if we had asked him.

(3) Surely they told her the truth.

(4) It is possible that he will resign.

(5) There's a vague possibility that they took refuge somewhere.

(6) We'll probably have a sunny day tomorrow.

(7) Who's at the door? It's got to be the pizza we ordered!

(8) She's going to succeed. I'm sure of it.

(9) She's going to succeed. She knows it.

5 Complétez les phrases qui suivent avec la forme correcte du modal et du verbe donné entre parenthèses.

(1) Think twice before you buy this flat or you ... (regret) it.

(2) I've lost my keys. I ... (leave) them in my car: I can't see any other possibility.

(3) There were floods last months, but they... ... (reach) our house as it is on a hill. And anyway, we were insured.

(4) We'll have to move as it ... (take) months to repair the damage caused by the fire.

(5) Betty's sitting for her exam tomorrow. I'm sure she ... (revise) her maths right now.

L'OBLIGATION

6 Complétez avec *must* ou *have to*, au temps qui convient et à la forme affirmative ou négative.

(1) I think he ... be feeling sorry for himself.

(2) Miriam was in a hurry because she ... be at the dentist's at 5.

(3) You ... be on time, or they won't let you on the plane.
(4) Someone had already paid for it, so I ... give them any money.
(5) Remember that you ... mention the present: you promised you wouldn't.
(6) The government ... lower taxes if they want to be re-elected.

7 Traduisez.

(1) J'ai eu un train direct (*a through train*), si bien que je n'ai pas eu à changer.
(2) Est-ce que nous aurons à faire la cuisine dans le chalet ?
(3) Le docteur dit que tu dois porter tes lunettes tout le temps.
(4) L'école reprend mardi, mais nous devons y aller lundi pour prendre nos livres.
(5) Mon ordinateur est tombé en panne hier, et j'ai dû rester au bureau pour attendre le réparateur.

LE CONSEIL

8 Complétez les phrases qui suivent avec *should* ou *ought to* et le verbe donné entre parenthèses à la forme qui convient.

(1) You ... (take off) these wet shoes: look at my carpet now!
(2) They ... (tell) him the truth: it'll be worse if he finds out by himself.
(3) The Conservatives say the government ... (lower) taxes to encourage spending.
(4) I think we ... (decide) to plant more trees when they had their last meeting.
(5) People ... (drive) more slowly along this dangerous stretch of road.

LES CONDITIONS

9 Complétez les phrases avec le verbe entre parenthèses au temps qui convient.

(1) If you ... (be) my son, I ... (be) very angry.
(2) Had they been more polite, I ... (ask) them to stay.
(3) She promised that she would give me his address as soon as he ... (send) it.
(4) When he ... (ring) the bell, we'll go and hide in the garden.
(5) If he ... (inherit + not) so much money, he would not have bought such a big house.
(6) Should they complain, the hotel ... (give) them their money back.

WOULD, USED TO, BE USED TO

10 Complétez les phrases qui suivent avec le verbe donné entre parenthèses, à la forme et au temps qui conviennent.

(1) Over the years, he got ... (live) in a cold house.
(2) In those days, people ... (have) candles instead of electricity.

(3) After a meal, Simon ... (smoke + always) a pipe.
(4) I'm exhausted! I'm ... (walk + not) so much!
(5) The discipline is very strict, but you'll get ... it.
(6) Mummy, ... (have + really) a parrot when you were a child?

Parler du futur

11 Complétez avec le modal ou l'expression qui convient.

(1) Hurry up! We ... (leave)!
(2) If I win in the lottery, I ... (buy) a car.
(3) An international conference on pollution ... (take place) in Tokyo in July.
(4) We ... (dine out) tonight and should be back around 11.
(5) We have run out of petrol and the car ... (stop) any minute now.
(6) The Prime Minister ... (fly) to India on an official visit the day after he was killed.
(7) Don't worry. I'm sure my parents ... (love) you.
(8) Who ... (lay) the table tonight? (= whose turn is it?)

Had better/would rather

12 Traduisez.

(1) Ne feriez-vous pas mieux d'aller voir un médecin dès que possible ?
(2) J'aurais préféré qu'il ne parte pas vivre à l'étranger.
(3) Je préférerais payer plus d'impôts plutôt que d'avoir de tels transports en commun.
(4) Ils préféreraient que vous leur envoyiez un e-mail.
(5) Tu ferais mieux de regarder la route au lieu de me regarder.

7. Verbe + préposition ou/et particule

Il ne faut pas confondre particules et prépositions, même si la plupart des particules sont aussi prépositions.

■ Une particule modifie le sens du verbe, et un complément n'est pas nécessaire (mais possible) après la particule. *Put* : mettre, poser ; *put on* : mettre, enfiler un vêtement ; *put off* : retarder, remettre à plus tard. *Make* : faire ; *make up* : inventer ; *make off* : se sauver

→ *I saw her put on her coat.* (complément) Je l'ai vue enfiler son manteau.

→ *He stole her bag before making off.* (pas de complément)
Il a volé son sac avant de s'enfuir.

Place du complément et de la particule

– Le complément se place avant la particule lorsqu'il s'agit d'un pronom.

→ *Look it up in the dictionary.* Vérifie-le dans le dictionnaire.

– Les autres compléments se placent avant ou après la particule mais un complément assez long se placera après.

→ *Turn it off!* (Éteins-le !)

→ *Turn off the light. Turn the light off.* Éteins la lumière.

→ *Can you turn off the heater which is in the bedroom?*
Peux-tu fermer le chauffage dans la chambre ?

■ Une préposition permet d'introduire un nom ou groupe nominal.
He stared at the girl. (*at* + nom)
He asked for a cup of tea. (*for* + nom)

Place du complément et de la préposition

Lorsqu'un verbe a deux compléments (complément d'objet direct et complément d'objet indirect), deux structures sont possibles :

→ ❶ *He lent Eric his record.* ou ❷ *He lent his record to Eric.* Il a prêté son disque à Eric.

→ ❶ *He found her a house.* ou ❷ *He found a house for her.* Il lui a trouvé une maison.

Si les deux compléments sont des pronoms, seule la deuxième structure est possible.

→ *He found it for her.* Il la lui a trouvée.

■ Un verbe à particule peut être suivi d'une préposition :

→ *I couldn't get through to John.* Je n'ai pas réussi à me faire comprendre de John.
(*through* = particule, *get through* = communiquer ; *to* = préposition)

1 – Quelques particules

Il est possible de deviner le sens global de certains verbes à particules si l'on se souvient que celles-ci sont souvent porteuses de sens. Voici quelques-uns des sens principaux.

■ ***About:*** idée de mouvement dans tous les sens.
→ *He was wandering about.* Il errait.

■ ***Across:*** traversée, passage d'un endroit à l'autre.
→ *Come across to our house tonight.* Venez chez nous ce soir.

■ ***Along:*** suivre, accompagner.
→ *We went to the movies and she came along.*
Nous sommes allés au cinéma et elle est venue avec nous.

■ ***Around*** (ou ***round***) : mouvement circulaire.
→ *It's not the road we want: turn round!* Ce n'est pas la bonne route : fais demi-tour !

■ ***Aside:*** mettre de côté, éloigner.
→ *He pushed all the papers aside and got up.* Il écarta tous les papiers et se leva.

■ ***Away:*** idée d'éloignement, parfois jusqu'à disparition.
→ *They've gone away together.* Ils se sont enfuis ensemble.

■ ***Back:*** retour, mouvement vers l'arrière (spatial ou temporel).
→ *Put it back where it belongs.* Remets-le à sa place.

■ ***Down:*** mouvement vers le bas, diminution.
→ *They will pull down these slums.* Ils vont démolir ces taudis.

■ ***In:*** mouvement vers l'intérieur.
→ *You can plug it in here.* Tu peux le brancher ici.

■ ***Off:*** éloignement (parfois jusqu'à séparation), arrêt.
→ *Do you think this stain will wash off?* Crois-tu que cette tache partira au lavage ?

■ ***On:*** continuité, mettre ou prendre quelque chose.
→ *He's put on weight.* Il a pris du poids.

■ ***Out:*** mouvement vers l'extérieur (sortir, produire quelque chose, extraire) ou idée d'achèvement ou d'usure.
→ *He pulled out a gun from his pocket.* Il tira un pistolet de sa poche.

■ ***Over:*** recouvrir, passer d'un endroit/état à un autre.
→ *He bent over to look at the child.* Il se pencha en avant pour regarder l'enfant.

■ ***Through:*** passer à travers.
→ *The table is too wide: it won't go through the door.*
La table est trop large : elle ne passera pas par la porte.

■ ***Up:*** mouvement vers le haut, idée de terminer quelque chose, d'augmenter quelque chose.
→ *Drink up your tea.* Finis de boire ton thé.

2 – Quelques verbes se construisant avec des prépositions

■ ***On:*** *comment on:* commenter ; *depend on:* dépendre de ; *rely on:* compter sur

■ ***At:*** *arrive at:* arriver à un endroit ; *look at:* regarder ; *stare at:* dévisager ; *gaze at:* contempler ; *glare at:* regarder avec colère ; *hint at:* insinuer

■ ***Against:*** *protest against:* protester contre ; *react against:* réagir contre ; *warn against:* prévenir de

■ ***About:*** *talk about:* parler de ; *worry about:* s'inquiéter au sujet de ; *joke about:* plaisanter à propos de

■ ***In:*** *believe in:* croire en ; *delight in:* prendre plaisir à ; *take part in:* participer à

■ ***From:*** *borrow sthg from sb:* emprunter qch à qq ; *discourage sb from:* décourager qq de ; *escape from:* s'échapper de ; *prevent sb from:* empêcher qq de ; *suffer from:* souffrir de

■ ***For:*** *apologize for:* s'excuser de ; *ask for:* demander qch ; *blame sb for sthg:* tenir qq responsable de ; *long for:* désirer ardemment ; *hope for:* espérer ; *pay for:* payer ; *wait for:* attendre

- ***Of:*** *accuse sb of:* accuser de ; *approve of:* approuver ; *remind sb of:* rappeler qch à qq ; *get rid of:* se débarrasser de ; *smell of:* sentir ; *taste of:* avoir le goût de ; *think of:* penser à
- ***To:*** *belong to:* appartenir à ; *listen to:* écouter ; *reply to sb:* répondre à ; *react to:* réagir à ; *yield to:* céder à VOIR AUSSI P. 255-256
- ***With:*** *agree with:* être d'accord avec ; *help sb with:* aider qq à faire qch ; *quarrel with:* se quereller avec ; *fight with/against:* se battre avec

exercice

Complétez les phrases avec la particule qui convient parmi celles qui suivent :
away – back – down – in – off – out – up

1. You must fill … the questionnaire and send it … .
2. Sorry! I take … what I said: it was stupid.
3. She let … a cry when she saw the policeman at the door.
4. They had people leave the room for fear the bomb might go … .
5. He has turned … the offer of a job, because it was not paid enough.
6. The play was put … until the following week because the main actress was ill.
7. She became raving mad and had to be put … in a mental institution.
8. The truth came … at last during the enquiry.

8. Le nom

1 – Le pluriel

Formation du pluriel

N'oubliez pas les **règles principales de formation du pluriel** :
– on ajoute un e aux mots se terminant par -s / -x /- z /- ch /-sh : *a church* → *several churches*
– on ajoute un e à certains mots se terminant en -o : *a potato* → *two potatoes* (mais *cellos, photos*)
– la plupart des noms se terminant en -f ou- fe, ont un pluriel en ves : *a leaf* → *leaves*
– lorsque le nom se termine en consonne + -y, le pluriel est en ies : *a party* → *several parties*
– la plupart des noms se terminant en -is ont un pluriel en es : *a basis* → *bases*
– les mots d'origine grecque en -on ont un pluriel en a : *a phenomenon* → *phenomena*

Certains noms ont un **pluriel irrégulier** :
man (homme) → *men* ; *woman* (femme) → *women* ; *tooth* (dent) → *teeth* ; *goose* (oie) → *geese* ; *foot* (pied) → *feet* ; *child* (enfant) → *children* ; *ox* (bœuf) → *oxen*

Certains noms sont **invariables** :
sheep, fish, fruit, trout (truite), *deer* (daim), *aircraft* (avion)
→ *a sheep* (un mouton) → *two sheep*
Fish et *fruit* peuvent se rencontrer au pluriel avec le sens de différents types de poissons ou de fruits.

Forme et accord

Forme	Exemples	Accord
Noms invariables se terminant par un -s et qui peuvent être singuliers ou pluriels	*crossroads* (carrefour), *works* (usine), *means* (moyen), *species* (espèce), *series* (série), *headquarters* (quartier général)	Verbe singulier ou pluriel ex. *Is there a better means of solving the problem?* Est-ce qu'il y a une meilleure façon de résoudre le problème ? *Several means of transportation are possible.* Plusieurs moyens de communication sont possibles.
Noms se terminant par un -s mais suivis d'un verbe au singulier : maladies, jeux	*news* (les informations), *billiards* (le billard), *mumps* (les oreillons)	*What is the news?* Quelles sont les nouvelles ?
Noms toujours pluriels	*goods* (des biens), *looks* (l'apparence), *wages* (le salaire), *stairs* (l'escalier), *customs* (la douane), *brains* (l'intelligence) mais *a brain* (un cerveau)	Verbe pluriel *Be careful, these stairs are very steep.* Attention, cet escalier est très raide.
Les noms d'objets doubles sont pluriels	*scissors* (ciseaux), *glasses/spectacles* (lunettes), et les noms de vêtements couvrant les jambes : *trousers* (pantalon(s), *jeans* (jean), *pyjamas* (pyjama), *shorts* (short), *tights* (collant), *panties/knickers* (culotte)...	Verbe au pluriel *Where are your pyjamas?* Où est ton pyjama ?

Noms de sciences en -ics	*Physics, mathematics, politics, economics*	Verbe singulier ou pluriel. *Linguistics is/are a recent science.* La linguistique est une science récente.
Les collectifs : mots singuliers décrivant un groupe de personnes	*Family, party* (groupe), *public, press, crowd, company, audience* (spectateurs), *crew* (équipage), *government, jury*…	Deux possibilités : – verbe au singulier si on considère l'unité qu'ils forment : *The audience was enthusiastic.* Les spectateurs étaient enthousiastes. – verbe au pluriel si on considère les personnes du groupe séparément : *The audience were divided.* Les spectateurs étaient partagés.
Collectifs à sens pluriel uniquement	*Police, people, clergy, cattle*	Verbe au pluriel *The police know who is responsible.* La police sait qui est responsable.

Attention !
En anglais on a tendance à utiliser le pluriel lorsqu'on décrit les caractéristiques de plusieurs personnes, là où on préfère souvent le singulier en français.
Comparez :
→ *The Smiths and the Davidsons are renovating their house.*
(une seule maison : Les deux familles habitent la même maison.)
→ *The Smiths and the Davidsons are renovating their houses.* (plusieurs maisons)
En français, on dirait « leur maison » dans les deux cas.
Notez dans cet exemple l'emploi du s en anglais à la fin du nom de famille pour parler de la famille tout entière. P. 226

2 – Dénombrables et indénombrables

■ Les indénombrables sont des noms que l'on ne peut pas compter, par exemple *water* ou *rugby*. Ces noms :
– ne peuvent être précédés de l'article a/an ou de chiffres.
→ On a une très bonne eau à la campagne. *We have very good water in the country.*
– ne peuvent pas prendre la marque du pluriel.
→ Les conseils qu'il m'a donnés… *The advice he gave me…*

Principaux indénombrables :
– les noms de matières : *wood, wine, brick…*
– les noms abstraits : *fear, love, literature, jealousy…*

– les noms de couleurs : *red, green, blue…*
– les noms de sports ou d'activités : *baseball, cricket, tennis, cycling, cooking…*
– les noms de langues : *Chinese, Portuguese, English…*
– les noms de maladies : *(the) flu* (la grippe), *cancer, measles* (la rougeole)…
– les noms renvoyant à un ensemble d'éléments : *furniture* (le mobilier), *luggage* (des bagages)

■ Certains mots peuvent être **dénombrables ou non, avec un sens différent**

– *work* : le travail, du travail	– *a work* : une œuvre
– *cloth* : du tissu	– *a cloth* : un chiffon
– *country* : la campagne	– *a country* : un pays
– *business* : les affaires	– *a business* : une entreprise
– *coffee* : du café	– *a coffee* : une tasse de café

→ *Business is slack in Britain now, but he has a flourishing business.* Les affaires vont mal en Grande Bretagne en ce moment, mais lui a une entreprise prospère.

■ Certains **noms d'animaux et de viandes** sont différents :

– *a pig* : un porc	– *pork* : du porc
– *a calf* : un veau	– *veal* : du veau
– *an ox*: un bœuf	– *beef* : du bœuf
– *a sheep*: un mouton	– *mutton* : du mouton

■ Pour beaucoup d'indénombrables, on utilisera
– soit un autre mot :

work: du travail	*a job*: un travail
travel : les voyages	*a trip, a journey* : un voyage.

– soit un mot comme *a piece of* (appelé dénombreur) qui permet de parler d'une ou plusieurs unités.

Quelques dénombreurs :
– *a piece of (news, luggage, advice, information, furniture…)*
– *an article of (clothing…)*
– *a cup of (coffee, tea…)*
– *a glass of (wine, beer, milk…)*
– *a slice of (cake, toast…)* : une tranche de
– *a loaf of (bread…)* : une miche de pain, un pain
– *a flash of (lightning)* : un éclair
– *a bar of (soap…)* : un savon
– *a pound of (butter, rice…)* : une livre de

On peut également utiliser *some, the,* ou encore ne pas utiliser d'article devant un indénombrable.

→ Il m'a donné de bons conseils. → *He gave me good pieces of advice. / He gave me good advice. / He gave me some good advice.*

exercices

Le pluriel

1 Traduisez.

1. Il y avait une curieuse espèce d'oiseau sur les toits et parmi les feuilles.
2. J'ai abîmé mon collant en descendant l'escalier.
3. La police a arrêté l'hôtesse de l'air et tout l'équipage est maintenant en grève.
4. Il a beaucoup de bétail et environ une douzaine de moutons.
5. Les deux hommes avaient la main cachée dans la poche de leur pantalon.

Dénombrables et indénombrables

2 Traduisez.

1. Les nouvelles ne sont pas bonnes : il y a de plus en plus de grippes dans le village.
2. Si tu vas au marché, peux-tu acheter du porc, des fruits et une demi-livre de beurre ?
3. J'ai fait un court voyage à Londres car j'espérais y trouver un travail.
4. Demain, nous déménagerons les bagages et les meubles.
5. Les renseignements qu'il m'a donnés m'ont aidé à trouver du travail.

9. Les articles

1 – L'article zéro

L'article zéro (∅), c'est-à-dire l'absence d'article, permet de parler de quelque chose de général, qui n'est pas déterminé.

On l'emploie – avec des dénombrables au pluriel et les indénombrables (singulier), lorsqu'on considère la catégorie. – avec *man* et *woman* lorsqu'on les considère comme une catégorie.	*Cats don't like dogs.* Les chats n'aiment pas les chiens. *I couldn't find pears at the market.* Je n'ai pas trouvé de poires au marché. *I don't like cricket.* Je n'aime pas le cricket. *Man shouldn't fight against nature.* L'homme ne devrait pas lutter contre la nature.
Noms de jours et de mois	*They'll come in October.* Ils viendront en octobre.

Certains noms décrivant des lieux (*church, hospital, school, jail, bed, work, market*) s'emploient : – sans l'article quand on considère la fonction – avec l'article lorsqu'on considère le lieu précis	Comparez : – *I don't go to school on Saturdays.* Je ne vais pas à l'école le samedi. (= fonction) – *I went to the school to see the headmaster.* Je suis allé à l'école pour voir le directeur. (= bâtiment) – *I'm going into hospital tomorrow.* Je rentre à l'hôpital demain. (= comme malade) – *Walk past the hospital and turn right.* Longez l'hôpital puis tournez à droite. (= le bâtiment) – *Will you go by train or by car?* Irez-vous en train ou en voiture? – *I was reading in the train when…* Je lisais dans le train lorsque…
Noms de repas – Sans article quand on considère le type de repas de façon générale – Article lorsqu'un repas précis est défini par un adjectif, une relative…	Comparez : – *Breakfast is my favourite meal.* Le petit-déjeuner est mon repas favori. – *The breakfast we had in the hotel was delicious.* Le petit-déjeuner dans cet hôtel était délicieux.
Quelques cas particuliers : – *Television* ne prend l'article que lorsque l'on parle du poste. – Mais on dit *listen to the radio, go to the cinema, the theatre, the opera.* Pour « jouer d'un instrument », on trouvera l'article en anglais britannique seulement.	Comparez : – *She spends hours watching television.* Elle passe des heures à regarder la télévision. – *He has a tiny television in his mobile.* Il a une minuscule télévision dans son portable. – *He plays the violin.* (GB) – *He plays violin.* (US)

On emploie aussi l'article zéro devant :
– les noms propres, même lorsqu'ils sont précédés d'un titre ou d'un adjectif : *President Bush* (le président Bush), *Queen Victoria* (la reine Victoria), *Professor Fields* (le professeur Fields); *poor Johnny* (le pauvre Johnny).
– de nombreux noms géographiques. Les noms de pays : Germany, China… (mais l'article est nécessaire devant les noms pluriels (*the USA, the Netherlands* – les Pays-Bas) ou les noms définis par *of: the Republic of China.*) ; les noms de lacs, montagnes, régions (*Lake Superior, Mount Everest, Devon*, mais on emploie *the* devant un nom au pluriel ou un nom défini par *of*: the *Lake of Geneva, the Alps.*) Les noms de rues, de lieux publics: *Oxford Street, Buckingham Palace, Hyde Park.* Attention ! Les noms de rivières sont d'ordinaire précédés de *the: the (river) Seine.*

2 – A(N)

■ *A* + son de consonne, *an* + son de voyelle. Mais attention :
– Certains h de début de mot ne se prononcent pas.
On dira donc *an hour/an honour/an honest man/an heir*
– Le u, le o ou le eu au début de certains mot se prononcent [ju].
On dira donc: *a union/a useful thing/a one-man show*

■ *A(n)* s'emploie pour parler d'une unité qui n'est pas définie.
She gave me a book for my birthday. Elle m'a donné un livre pour mon anniversaire.
A(n) s'emploie donc souvent pour généraliser :
A book would make a nice gift. Un livre ferait un joli cadeau. (= N'importe quel livre)

■ Au pluriel, on pourra employer :
– l'artiche zéro : *I am terrified of spiders.* J'ai peur des araignées.
– some : *They need to take some measures to tackle unemployment.* Il faut qu'ils prennent des mesures pour faire face au chômage.

■ Quelques emplois spécifiques (toujours devant des dénombrables) là où l'article indéfini ne s'emploie pas en français :

Devant les noms de métier	*He's a secretary.* Il est secrétaire.
Au début des appositions	*She fled to Switzerland, a neutral country.* Elle s'enfuit en Suisse, pays neutre.
Après *without*	*She left without an umbrella.* Elle est sortie sans parapluie.
Dans les exclamatives après *what/such*	*What a strange story!* Quelle étrange histoire !
Dans certaines expressions pour parler de prix, vitesse, fréquence	*I was doing 50 miles an hour.* Je faisais 80 kilomètres à l'heure. *We go there twice a week.* Nous y allons deux fois par semaine. *Apples are 30p a pound.* Les pommes sont à 30p la livre.

3 – THE

■ *The* se prononce **ðə** devant les sons de consonne (comme pour a), et **ði:** devant les sons de voyelle (comme pour *an*).

■ *The* s'emploie pour parler de quelque chose de connu, de déjà mentionné.
→ *Why didn't you tell the teacher?* Pourquoi ne l'as-tu pas dit au professeur ?
(Le professeur de l'élève, elle le connaît.)

On l'emploie aussi quand le nom est défini par un superlatif ou par ce qui suit, par une relative ou un complément introduit par *of* par exemple.

→ *This is the book that she gave me for my birthday.*
Voici le livre qu'elle m'a donné pour mon anniversaire.

- *The* est souvent assez proche du français ce/cette.

→ *There was a man near the car... Suddenly, the man turned round...* Il y avait un homme près de la voiture. Soudain, l'homme se retourna... (Il s'agit de l'homme dont on vient de parler.)

- *The* s'emploie aussi :

– devant un nom dénombrable singulier pour parler d'une catégorie :
→ *The elephant has an excellent memory.* L'éléphant a une excellente mémoire.
– devant un adjectif employé comme nom, pour parler d'une catégorie: *the blind* (les aveugles), *the young* (les jeunes), *the unemployed* (les sans-emploi), l'adjectif ne prenant bien sûr pas la marque du pluriel. P. 240
– devant les noms qui désignent des concepts ou des notions bien connus de tous. *the earth* (la terre), *the sun* (le soleil), *the moon* (la lune), *the past, the present and the future.*
– devant un nom de famille au pluriel pour parler de la famille entière.
→ *the Warings:* la famille Waring P. 221

Attention ! On emploie un adjectif possessif en anglais pour les parties du corps et les vêtements là où on emploie un article défini en français.
→ *He was striding along, with his hat on his head.*
Il avançait à grands pas, le chapeau sur la tête.

↗ exercices

1 Complétez les articles qui suivent avec *a(n)*, *the* ou l'article Ø.

1\. ... man survived ... 18-storey fall from ... Cape Town hotel room and was well enough to call out to rescuers. ... Nicholas du Plooy broke his arm, ... leg and injured his neck on ... Tuesday when he landed on ... roof of ... hotel's reception, his fall apparently broken by ... metal roofing sheets.

▲ *The Times*, April 23, 2004.

2\. ... television for ... parrots has been launched to help ... bored birds to pass the time. The World Parrot Trust, based in Hayle, Cornwall, has produced what is believed to be ... world's first DVD for ... birds. Polly Vision, 80 minutes of ... images of ... wild parrots preening, feeding and flying, has been released as part of World Parrot Day on May 31.

▲ *The Times*, June 22, 2004.

3. … £80,000 boat designed by … Malcolm Barnsley, … Southampton engineer, to be … world's fastest has been launched. Sailrocket will challenge … speed sailing record in … Weymouth. She can reach more than 50 knots (57.5 mph), nearly twice that of … competition yacht.

▲ *The Times*, April 24, 2004.

2 Traduisez.

1. Il est chirurgien (*surgeon*) et travaille à l'hôpital trois fois par semaine.
2. Il est resté au soleil sans chapeau et a mal à la tête. Quel dommage !
3. Est-ce que les fantômes des morts reviennent parfois voir les vivants ?
4. Jean Brun, ingénieur à Lille, affirme que le téléphone portable peut être dangereux.
5. Nous aurons l'occasion de parler au professeur Barton pendant le déjeuner.

10. Les quantifieurs

Ils permettent de parler d'une quantité. Le choix du quantifieur dépend du nom qui suit, tout particulièrement de s'il est dénombrable ou indénombrable. P. 221

1 – (Un) peu de

Dénombrables	Indénombrables
(A) FEW + nom dénombrable pluriel *a few* = un peu de (on insiste sur une petite quantité) *few* = peu de (on insiste sur l'insuffisance) *A few people complained, but few of them lodged a complaint.* Quelques personnes se sont plaintes, mais peu d'entre elles ont porté plainte.	*(A) LITTLE* *a little* = un peu de (on insiste sur une petite quantité) *little* = peu de (on insiste sur l'insuffisance) Comparez : *Fortunately, I had a little energy left.* Heureusement, il me restait un peu d'énergie. *Unfortunately, I had little energy left.* Malheureusement, il ne me restait que peu d'énergie.

■ *Little* et *few* peuvent être précédés de :
– *so*: *Why do we have so little time?* Pourquoi avons-nous si peu de temps ?
– *too, very*: *Very few people turned up.* Très peu de gens sont venus.

2 – Beaucoup de

Dénombrables	**Indénombrables**
MANY Surtout dans les phrases négatives et interrogatives *Did you see many kangaroos in Australia?* As-tu vu beaucoup de kangourous en Australie?	*MUCH* Surtout dans les phrases négatives et interrogatives *There isn't much butter left.* Il ne reste pas beaucoup de beurre.
A LOT OF / LOTS OF / PLENTY OF Surtout dans les phrases affirmatives *A lot of books arrived damaged.* Beaucoup de livres sont arrivés abîmés. *There's plenty of bread.* Il y a beaucoup de pain.	
A NUMBER OF *A number of students complained.* Plusieurs étudiants se sont plaints.	*A GREAT DEAL OF* *There was a great deal of noise.* Il y avait beaucoup de bruit.

■ Much et many peuvent être précédés de
– *so*
→ *I don't need so much sleep.* Je n'ai pas besoin de tant de sommeil.
– *(far) too, very*
→ *They've got far too many problems.* Ils ont beaucoup trop de problèmes.
– *how* (dans les questions)
→ *How much money did she give you?* Combien d'argent t'a-t-elle donné ?

■ *Much* peut être adverbe et porter sur un verbe (phrase négative). Dans une phrase affirmative on emploiera *very much*.
→ He never talks much. Il ne parle jamais beaucoup.
→ I miss you very much. Tu me manques beaucoup.

■ *Most* (superlatif de *many/much*) s'emploie pour traduire « la plupart de ». Attention à la différence entre :
→ *Most films are only shown for a few weeks.* La plupart des films ne passent que pendant quelques semaines. (les films en général)
→ *Most of the films I saw were sad.* La plupart des films que j'ai vus étaient tristes. (catégorie réduite des films que j'ai vus)

■ *A lot, much, many, a few, a little...* peuvent s'employer seuls, le nom étant sous-entendu.
→ *"Is there any milk left?" "A little."* « Est-ce qu'il reste du lait ? – Un peu. »
→ *"Did she give you books?" "Yes, many."* « Elle t'a donné des livres ? – Oui, beaucoup. »
→ *"How many people were there?" "Just a few. / Quite a few."*
« Combien étiez-vous ? – Un tout petit nombre. / Assez nombreux. (Pas mal). »

3 – SOME, ANY, NO

■ *Some* et *any* permettent de parler d'une certaine quantité, *no* d'une quantité nulle. Ils s'emploient avec un indénombrable singulier ou un dénombrable pluriel : *some butter/ some books*

Quantifieur	Valeur, emploi	Exemples
SOME + *someone* *somebody* *something* (= une quantité certaine de…)	Phrases affirmatives : *SOME*	*Go and buy some milk.* Va acheter du lait. *Let's find something he will like.* Cherchons quelque chose qu'il aimera.
	Phrases négatives : *ANY*	*I don't want any (cake).* Je n'en veux pas./ Je ne veux pas de gâteau.
	Phrases interrogatives : – *SOME* si l'on attend une réponse positive (donc souvent par politesse, lorsqu'on propose quelque chose que l'on a) – *ANY* quand la question est plus neutre	*Would you like some cake?* Voulez-vous du gâteau ? *Is there anything I can do?* Est-ce que je peux faire quelque chose ? *Have you had any answer yet?* Avez-vous déjà eu une réponse ?
ANY + *anyone* *anybody* *anything* (une quantité hypothétique de)	*ANY* peut aussi s'employer dans une phrase affirmative, avec le sens de « n'importe qui ».	*Anyone could see that he was ill.* N'importe qui pouvait voir qu'il était malade. *Any book will do.* N'importe quel livre fera l'affaire.
NO + *nobody* *nothing* *no one* + verbe à la forme affirmative	*No* est équivalent à *not any*. On emploie plutôt – *No* en début de phrase – *Not any* dans les autres cas	*No footprints were to be seen.* Aucune trace de pas n'était visible. *They did not hear any noise.* Ils n'entendirent aucun bruit. *Nobody came.* Personne ne vint. *I did not see anybody.* Je n'ai vu personne.

■ Notez ces autres usages de some :
– *Some* + nombre = environ
→ *Some fifteen years ago*… Il y a environ quinze ans…
– *Some* + nom singulier (souvent dans une exclamative) = admiration
→ *This is some car!* Ça c'est ce que j'appelle une voiture !

■ Notez également que l'on emploie le pronom *none* à la place de *not one (of)* + nom/ *not any (of)* + nom :
→ *"Did you have any problem?" "None at all."*
« As-tu eu des problèmes ? – Pas du tout. »
→ *None of them understood what he meant.*
Aucun d'entre eux n'a compris ce qu'il voulait dire.

■ *Any* et *no* peuvent être adverbes et modifier un comparatif.
→ *Can you walk any better with this stick?*
Est-ce que vous marchez un peu mieux avec cette canne ?
→ *He is no worse than yesterday.* Il ne va pas plus mal qu'hier.

4 – EACH, EVERY, ALL

Ils renvoient à l'ensemble des éléments.

Quantifieur	+ …………	Valeur	Exemples
EACH	+ nom dénombrable au singulier et verbe au singulier Reprise par un singulier ou un pluriel	S'emploie pour deux ou plus d'éléments : on considère chaque élément l'un après l'autre.	*I talked to each student in turn.* J'ai parlé à chacun des étudiants l'un après l'autre. *Each participant came with the story he/she/they had written.* Chacun des participants est venu avec l'histoire qu'il avait écrite.
EVERY (+ *Everyone* *Everybody* *Everything*)		S'emploie pour plus de deux éléments : on considère l'ensemble, la totalité.	*He goes jogging every morning.* Il fait du jogging tous les matins. *Everyone knows how to drive, don't they?* Tout le monde sait conduire, n'est-ce pas ?
ALL	*All (the)* + nom dénombrable au pluriel *All the* + nom indénombrable	On considère la totalité. Avec les dénombrables, attention à la différence entre : *All cats like milk.* (tous les chats en général) *All (of) the cats I've known hated milk.* (ceux d'un groupe bien précis).	*All flights have been cancelled.* Tous les vols ont été annulés. *All the flights from Boston have been cancelled.* Tous les vols depuis Boston ont été annulés. *All the love I had ever felt…* Tout l'amour que j'avais jamais ressenti…

- Each peut aussi s'employer seul ou après une mesure, un prix, une quantité.

→ *Their three sons are each married.* Leurs trois fils sont mariés.

→ *These T-shirts cost $10 each.* Ces T-shirts coûtent 10 dollars pièce.

- Ne pas confondre *all* et *whole*, qui est adjectif et signifie « en entier ».

→ *She's drunk the whole bottle of gin!* Elle a bu toute la bouteille de gin !

5 – Parler de deux éléments

Both

Both a le même sens que *the two*, mais permet d'insister sur la similitude.

→ *Both brothers love cricket.* Les deux frères aiment le cricket.
Mais : *The two brothers are very different.* Les deux frères sont très différents.

Structures possibles

– *Both of* + pronom

→ *Both of them phoned.* Ils ont tous les deux téléphoné.

– *Both* + nom pluriel

→ *Both plays are very funny.* Les deux pièces sont très drôles.

– *Both of* + *the/these/those*/possessif + nom

→ *Both of her dresses suit her.* Ses deux robes lui vont bien.

– *Both* + nom + *and* + nom

→ *Both John and Mary gave money.* John et Mary ont tous les deux donné de l'argent.

– *Both* + verbe + *and* + verbe

→ *I both love and hate him!* Je l'aime et je le hais à la fois.

– *Both* peut aussi remplacer un nom.

→ *Both came.* Ils sont venus tous les deux.

Either/Neither

Either permet d'exprimer une similitude ou un choix entre deux possibilités (ou… ou… / l'un ou l'autre). Il est suivi d'un verbe au singulier.
Neither permet d'exclure deux possibilités (ni… ni…). Il est suivi d'un verbe au singulier et à la forme affirmative.

Structures possibles

– *Either/Neither* + *of* + pronom.

→ *Neither of them has given his answer.* Ni l'un ni l'autre n'a répondu.

– *Either/Neither* + nom singulier

→ *Neither project is good enough.* Aucun de ces deux projets n'est assez bon.

– *Either* et *neither* peuvent remplacer un nom.

→ *Either will do.* L'un ou l'autre conviendra.

– *Either/neither of* + *the/these/those*/possessif + nom

→ *She could be in either of these hotels.*
Elle pourrait être dans l'un ou l'autre de ces hôtels.

Either… or / neither… nor…

either/neither et *nor* doivent être suivis d'un mot de même nature, nom ou verbe :

→ *You can either swim or sink.* Tu peux nager ou couler.

→ *Neither the neighbours nor the passers-by saw her.*
Ni les voisins ni les passants ne l'ont vue.

6 – PARLER DE PLUS DE DEUX ÉLÉMENTS : LES NOMBRES

■ *Dozen, hundred, thousand, million…* sont invariables lorsqu'ils ont valeur d'adjectif avant un nom.

→ *three dozen eggs, some ten million people, two hundred and ten miles.*

Mais ils peuvent être employés comme noms au pluriel (suivis de *of* + nom).

→ *Hundreds of people came.* Des centaines de gens sont venus.

■ Si le nombre est associé à un ordinal *(first, second, third…)* ou à *only/other/last/next*, le nombre se place après ces mots contrairement à ce qui se passe en français.

→ *The first three months are the most difficult.*
Les trois premiers mois sont les plus difficiles.

→ *I can give you the other two records.*
Je peux te donner les deux autres disques.

exercices

(UN) PEU DE / BEAUCOUP DE

1 Complétez les phrases qui suivent avec le mot qui convient : a little – little – a few – few – many – too many – how many – much – too much – how much – a lot – so many.

1. Ask them to come: we need as … people as possible, for there is … to be done.
2. I get … phone calls, that I can't work … .
3. I put on weight in Italy, eating … spaghetti and drinking … wine.
4. We had … idea that he was so miserable, or we would have done something about it.
5. … suggestions were stupid, but … of them turned out to be interesting.
6. … suggestions were stupid, and … of them turned out to be interesting.
7. "Were you bored?" "…, he gave … figures in his speech."
8. … rooms do you need, and … can you pay?

SOME, ANY, NO

2 Complétez les phrases qui suivent avec *some, any, no* et leurs composés.

1. Have you had … news? Yes, … from the hospital phoned to say she was better.
2. I'd love … cream with this crumble, but I'm not sure there's … left.
3. Not … can do this exercise without making … mistake.
4. "I bought … pears at the market." "How much were they?" "… 80p a kilo, I think."
5. You mean you can't remember … about it? You're … better than me!
6. We spent a very boring evening with the Jones: … of them has … sense of humour.
7. … could tell that he had … hearing problems.
8. It was scary: there was … light at all, and they couldn't hear … noise.

PARLER DE DEUX ÉLÉMENTS

3 Récrivez les phrases qui suivent en utilisant *both, either* ou *neither* :

1. I hate mustard and I hate vinegar.
2. John and Mary can drive, but they have never owned a car.
3. I can't cook and I can't sew!
4. His first school report was poor. His second one was poor as well.
5. How can you work and, at the same time, listen to music?

11. *THIS* ET *THAT*

■ *This* (pluriel : *these*) et *that* (pluriel : *those*) peuvent :
– déterminer un nom :
→ *Can you see that girl in the red dress?* Tu vois cette fille en robe rouge ?
– remplacer un nom :
→ *I prefer those.* Je préfère ceux-là.

Attention ! Pour traduire celui/celle/ceux/celles-ci/là, on dira *this one/that one* au singulier, mais *these/those* au pluriel.

■ *This* et *these* s'emploient pour parler de quelque chose de proche de l'énonciateur dans le temps, dans l'espace, et du point de vue affectif. *That* et *those* s'emploient pour quelque chose de plus lointain.

→ *I bought my flat in 1980: in those days housing was cheap. But this year, prices have rocketed.* J'ai acheté mon appartement en 1980 ; à cette époque-là, l'immobilier était peu cher. Mais cette année, les prix ont monté en flèche.

→ *This house is very pretty, but I prefer that one over there, on the hillside.* Cette maison est très jolie, mais je préfère celle qui est là-bas sur la colline.

■ *That/those* s'emploient donc souvent avec une nuance de mépris et de rejet.

→ *And you call that a paper!* Et c'est ça que vous appelez un devoir !

■ *That/those* s'utilisent donc aussi quand on parle de quelque chose de connu de tous mais que l'on n'a pas sous les yeux.

→ *He's one of those people who never admit they're wrong.* Il fait partie de ces gens qui ne veulent jamais reconnaître qu'ils ont tort.

■ Ceci explique l'emploi de *this* et *that* dans **les présentations**.

→ *This is Agnès, and this is Paul.* Voici /Je te présente Agnès et voici Paul.

→ au téléphone : *Hello. This is Jeanne. Is that Pierre? Allô. C'est Jeanne à l'appareil. C'est Pierre?* (C'est Jeanne qui parle, donc *this*. Pierre est à l'autre bout du fil, donc *that*.)

■ *This* et *that* permettent également de reprendre ou d'annoncer les mots d'un texte.

– Pour annoncer, on emploie *this*.

→ *I'll tell you this: I'm not going to give up.* Laisse-moi te dire que moi, je n'abandonnerai pas.

– Pour reprendre ce qui précède, on peut employer *this* ou *that*.

→ *She was cheating on him. This/That was why he broke up with her.* Elle le trompait. Voilà pourquoi il a rompu.

■ *This* et *that* peuvent s'employer devant un adjectif, pour en renforcer le sens.

→ *The painting is this large.* Le tableau est grand comme ça. (L'énonciateur montre avec ses mains). *She's not that tall.* Elle n'est pas si grande que cela.

↗ exercice

Complétez les phrases qui suivent avec *this, that, these* ou *those*.

1. The way I see it is ...: she lied to protect... useless son of hers.
2. Can you remember ... second-hand car we saw in the garage last week? It wasn't ... expensive after all.
3. ... Lila. Is ... Joanna? ... is just to tell you that I've bought ... lamp we saw last week as a present for Sheila.
4. "They aren't ... rich." "... 's strange, because I thought they owned ... big factory near Oldham."
5. The painter's coming ... Tuesday to redecorate the house.

12. Les pronoms

1 – Les pronoms personnels

Forme :
Pronoms sujets : *I/you/he - she - it/we/they*
Pronoms compléments: *me/you/him - her - it/us/them*
Pronoms possessifs: *mine/yours/his - hers/ours/theirs*

■ En anglais on peut utiliser les pronoms *he* et *she* pour parler d'un animal familier.
→ *That's Tigger.* She's a very old cat.
On peut également employer *she/her* pour une voiture, un bateau, une locomotive de même que pour un pays.
→ *Look at this liner! She's beautiful!* Regarde ce paquebot ! Il est superbe !

■ Dans certaines structures, demandez-vous bien si le pronom est sujet ou complément.
→ *My friend and I stopped for a drink.* (*I* est sujet de *stopped*)
→ *"Who rang last night?" "It was me."* (*me* est complément de *was*)
Mais : *"Who rang last night?" "I did."* « Qui a téléphoné hier soir ? – Moi. »

■ En français, on insiste souvent en utilisant deux pronoms (Moi, je pense... Eux, ils...). En anglais on préfère marquer l'insistance en soulignant le mot.
→ She *is unbearable.* Elle, elle est insupportable.

■ Pronoms possessifs
→ *"I can't find my pen." "Take mine."* (*mine = my pen*)
→ *My cake is burnt, but yours isn't.* Mon gâteau est brûlé, mais pas le tien.
On n'emploie pas de pronom possessif correspondant à *it*.

■ Notez aussi la structure : *a* + nom + *of* + pronom possessif :
→ *He was a teacher of mine.* C'était un de mes professeurs.
Précédée de *this* ou *that*, cette structure contient une nuance d'irritation ou de mépris.
→ *Can't you tidy that room of yours!* Tu pourrais tout de même ranger ta chambre !

2 – Les pronoms réfléchis

Forme
myself/yourself/himself/herself/itself/ourselves/themselves

Ils s'emploient :
– Lorsque le sujet et le complément représentent la même personne.
→ *He heard himself scream.* Il s'entendit hurler.
→ *Did you hurt yourself?* Est-ce que tu t'es fait mal ?

– Sauf après une préposition de lieu ou après certains verbes qui contiennent déjà l'idée : *wash, dress, wake up...*

→ *Don't look behind you!* Ne regarde pas derrière toi !

→ *He never washes.* Il ne se lave jamais.

– Lorsqu'on veut insister.

→ *He built the house himself.* Il a construit la maison lui-même.

3 – Les pronoms réciproques

■ Les pronoms *each other* et *one another* sont utilisés pour parler de réciprocité. On emploie plutôt *each other* pour deux personnes, pour un rapport étroit, et *one another* dans les autres cas. Ils se placent toujours après le verbe.

→ *They hate each other.* Ils se détestent.

Mais lorsque l'idée de réciprocité est déjà présente dans le verbe, on n'utilise pas de pronom réciproque. → *They met two years ago.* Ils se sont rencontrés il y a deux ans.

■ Ne confondez pas pronoms réfléchis et pronoms réciproques :

→ *They defended themselves.* (chacun se défend → Ils se sont défendus).

→ *They defended each other.* (chacun défend l'autre → Ils se sont défendus.)

↗ exercice

Traduisez.

1. Ils s'accusent mutuellement de mentir, et moi, je ne sais pas que faire pour les aider.
2. Mon plombier fait mal son métier, et il se dit professionnel !
3. Je viens de faire changer mes fenêtres, mais mes voisins ont gardé les leurs.
4. Il ne se lave pas, se lève à 3 heures du matin et parle tout seul.
5. Un de mes amis s'est blessé en descendant l'escalier.

13. La traduction du français « on »

Sa traduction dépend de son sens dans la phrase.

– L'énonciateur s'exclut → *They, people* (plus général)

→ *In Ireland, they sing in pubs.* En Irlande, on chante dans les pubs. (L'énonciateur n'est pas irlandais).

– L'énonciateur fait partie du groupe → *We*

→ *We are 27 in our class.* On est 27 dans notre classe. (L'énonciateur est élève de la classe.)

– « On » peut être n'importe quelle personne → *You, Anyone*

→ *You can't walk a lot with these shoes.*
On ne peut pas marcher beaucoup avec ces chaussures.

– Valeur proverbiale de « on » → *One, You*

→ *One likes to rest after a long day's work.*
On aime bien se reposer après une longue journée de travail.

– « On » correspond à une source, un agent inconnu → *They, someone*, passif ou forme impersonnelle

→ *The plane has been hijacked.* On a détourné l'avion.

exercice

Traduisez.

1. On a essayé d'entrer par la fenêtre. (c'est la police qui parle)
2. On a essayé d'entrer par la fenêtre. (ce sont les voleurs qui parlent)
3. Depuis qu'on a volé la statue, on ferme l'église l'après-midi. (c'est le prêtre qui parle)
4. On m'a dit de remplir ce formulaire.
5. Et si on allait au cinéma? On joue *Les Dents de la mer* à l'Odéon.
6. Dans la vie, on n'a pas toujours le choix.

14. Génitif, nom + *of* + nom, noms composés

Ces trois structures permettent de relier deux noms.

1 – Génitif

Forme

's	*'*
– nom au singulier : *the cat's whiskers* *his mistress's house* – noms ayant un pluriel irrégulier et ne se terminant pas par s : *the children's toys*	– noms ayant un pluriel régulier en -s : *the dogs'biscuits*
's* ou *s	
– noms propres se terminant en s, tout particulièrement les noms classiques : *Socrates'views; Keats'poems* ou *Keats's poems*	

■ Le génitif permet de décrire un rapport d'appartenance, de parenté ou un rapport étroit entre les deux noms. Il s'emploie surtout avec :
– les noms de personnes ou d'animaux
→ *John's coat; Mrs Stone's house*
– les noms d'institutions, de pays, de lieux
→ *New York's inhabitants; the government's decision*
– mots décrivant des mesures dans l'espace ou le temps
→ *a ten miles'walk* (une promenade de 16 kilomètres) *today's paper* (le journal d'aujourd'hui) *a two months'holiday* (des vacances de deux mois)

■ Le génitif peut désigner une sous-catégorie : on parle alors de génitif générique.
→ *women's shoes* : des chaussures de femme (mais *the woman's shoes* : les chaussures de la femme) ; *a surgeon's knife* : un scalpel de chirurgien

Attention !
– l'article ne peut précéder que le premier nom
– dans un génitif générique, l'adjectif modifie l'ensemble des deux noms et se place donc avant : *a new [surgeon's knife]*
– dans l'autre type de génitif, l'adjectif se place devant celui des deux noms qui est qualifié.
→ *the [new government]'s policy:* la politique du nouveau gouvernement
→ *the government's [new policy]:* la nouvelle politique du gouvernement

■ On peut supprimer le nom à droite du génitif :
– quand ce nom vient d'être mentionné
→ *"Are these your keys?" "No, they're Paul's."* (= *Paul's keys*)
« Est-ce que ce sont tes clés ? – Non, ce sont celles de Paul. »
– quand le nom désigne un lieu :
→ *We're having supper at the Watsons'tonight.* Nous dînons chez les Watson. *I bought it at Harrod's.* (= *Harrod's store*) ; *St Paul's* (= *St Paul's cathedral*) ; *St Thomas's* (= *St Thomas's church*)
– dans l'expression *of* + nom + *'s*
→ *He's a friend of my uncle's.* C'est un ami de mon oncle.

2 – Noms composés

■ Dans les noms composés (nom + nom), c'est le second nom qui est le plus important, le premier ayant une valeur d'adjectif. *A horse race* (une course de chevaux) est un type de course. En revanche *a race horse* (un cheval de course) est un type de cheval. Le premier nom, ayant valeur d'adjectif, ne prend pas la marque du pluriel, sauf lorsqu'il est toujours au pluriel : *a garden gate* (un portail de jardin), *different garden gates* ; mais : *a goods train* (un train de marchandises), *a savings account* (un compte épargne)

■ Le mot composé n'est possible que s'il s'agit d'un sous-groupe, d'une sous-catégorie bien connus. On parle par exemple de *childhood friend* (ami d'enfance – un type d'ami bien connu), mais pas de *sports friend*, car il ne s'agit pas d'une sous-catégorie assez connue pour former un type.

■ Le mot composé est fréquent lorsque le premier nom décrit :
– la fonction (un maillot de bain : *a bathing suit*),
– la matière (un banc de pierre : *a stone bench*),
– l'origine géographique (la cathédrale de Chartres : *the Chartres cathedral*)
– la caractéristique principale (une calculatrice de poche : *a pocket calculator*),
– la période de temps (les vacances d'été : *the summer holidays*)
– le tout par opposition à la partie (le rebord de la fenêtre : *the window sill*)

3 – Nom + *of* + nom

■ Cette structure est utilisée dans la plupart des autres cas et :
– si le second nom est suivi par une longue relative ou groupe adjectival.
→ la réponse du rédacteur en chef : *the editor's answer*
→ la réponse du rédacteur en chef qui vient d'être nommé à la place de John Rogers : *the answer of the chief editor who has just been appointed to replace John Rogers*
– lorsqu'on parle d'une quantité
→ *a herd of buffaloes* (un troupeau de buffles), *a slice of bread* (une tranche de pain)
– avec les adjectifs employés comme noms :
→ *the problems of the poor* (les problèmes des pauvres)
Il faudra parfois utiliser une préposition lorsqu'on traduit nom + de + nom
→ Un tableau de Raphael : *a painting by Raphael*
→ Le plus joli jardin du village : *the prettiest garden in the village*

■ Dans un énoncé, l'information principale, nouvelle, a toujours tendance a être mentionnée en dernier. C'est pourquoi on notera la différence suivante :
→ *I happened to meet Sandra's English pen-friend when I was in Birmingham.* (On connaît Sandra. *English pen-friend* est l'élément nouveau, intéressant.)
→ *I happened to meet the English pen-friend of our former boss when I was in Birmingham.* (L'élément intéressant, surprenant est *our former boss*).

↗ exercice

Traduisez.

1. les vêtements de Tess
2. sa robe de soie
3. le secrétaire du président
4. les lettres des chômeurs
5. le veto du Japon
6. les nouvelles d'hier
7. l'opéra de Paris
8. un amateur de musique
9. la vieille carte de crédit de Paul
10. la plus belle fille du monde

15. L'ADJECTIF

Les adjectifs sont invariables en anglais.

1 – PLACE DES ADJECTIFS

■ **Les adjectifs épithètes** se placent avant le nom:
→ *She is a very bright girl.* Elle est très intelligente.
Cependant, ils se placent après les dérivés de *some, any* et *no*.
→ *Is there anything new?* Est-ce qu'il y a du nouveau?

■ Les **adjectifs attributs** se placent après le verbe *(be, become, seem, look)*.
→ *He seemed angry.* Il semblait en colère.
Dans certains cas, le verbe peut être sous-entendu. C'est souvent le cas avant les adjectifs en *-ible* ou *-able*.
→ *I'm sorry, Sir, we have no room available tonight.* (= *no room which is available*)
Nous sommes désolés, Monsieur, nous n'avons pas de chambre de libre ce soir.

■ Les nombres qui servent à numéroter pages, lignes, chapitres... se place après le nom, et ce nom n'est pas précédé de l'article: chapter 6, line 31, Act IV...

> Attention à la place de l'adjectif dans les structures suivantes:
> → *He is so/too good a friend.* C'est un si/trop bon ami. (*so/too* + adjectif)
> Mais: → *He is such a good friend.* C'est un si bon ami. (*such* + nom)

2 – ORDRE DES ADJECTIFS

■ **Adjectifs épithètes**: S'il y a plusieurs adjectifs épithètes, on les place du plus subjectif au plus objectif, du moins permanent au plus permanent.
L'ordre le plus courant est:
Effet + taille + âge/température + forme + couleur + origine + matériau + fonction
(subjectif) (objectif)
→ *beautiful - large - ancient - square - dark - Italian - iron - drinking (cup)*
→ *horrid - heavy - modern - irregular - green - rustic - wooden - garden (bench)*
Lorsqu'il y a plusieurs adjectifs, on les sépare par une virgule.

■ **Adjectifs attributs**: Lorsqu'il y en a plusieurs, on met *and* devant le dernier.
→ *His speech was short, interesting and amusing.*
Son discours était court, intéressant et amusant.

3 – CAS PARTICULIERS

■ Certains adjectifs **ne peuvent être qu'épithètes, d'autres qu'attributs.**
– Attributs seulement
Voici les principaux d'entre eux avec, entre parenthèses, un adjectif de même sens qui peut être utilisé comme épithète.

ill (*sick*), *alive* (*living*), *alike* (*similar*), *ajar* (*half-open*), *alone* (*solitary*), *afraid* (*scared, frightened*), *drunk* (*drunken*), *ashamed* (*shameful*).

→ *The two flats are much alike in size.*
Les deux appartements se ressemblent en termes de taille.

→ *They live in very similar houses.* Ils habitent des maisons très semblables.

On peut aussi utiliser une relative : *The man who is ill...*

– Au contraire, certains adjectifs décrivant un degré ne peuvent être qu'épithètes : *mere* (simple), *bare* (strict), *sheer* (pur), *utter* (complet, absolu), *main* (principal), *other* (autre).

→ *He was an utter stranger.* Il m'était complètement inconnu.

→ *By sheer luck...* Par pure chance...

■ Adjectifs employés comme noms

Certains adjectifs désignant des ensembles d'êtres humains s'emploient comme noms. Ils restent invariables, sont précédés de l'article *the* et ont une valeur de pluriel.
the poor (les pauvres), *the blind* (les aveugles), *the young* (les jeunes), *the deaf* (les sourds)
(Mais on dit : *a rich man/woman, the rich people who were at the hotel*)
Les adjectifs *black* et *white* fonctionnent de la même façon mais prennent la marque du pluriel : *the blacks/black people* (les noirs) ; *a black woman* (une (femme) noire)
Certains adjectifs décrivant des notions abstraites peuvent aussi s'employer comme noms, précédés de *the* : *the fantastic, the beautiful, the sublime...*

■ Adjectifs de nationalité

Adjectifs	Un seul habitant	Plusieurs habitants	Tous les habitants
Les adjectifs ***French, English, Welsh, Irish, Dutch, British***	*A* + adjectif + *man/woman*: *an Irishman,* *a French woman* *three Irishmen*	*Several/many/a few...* + adjectif + *people* *many English people*	*the + adjectif* *the French* *the English* *the Welsh*
Adjectifs en ***-ese* + *Swiss*** *Japanese, Chinese, Lebanese, Swiss*	*A/ many / several / some...* + nom semblable à l'adjectif et invariable *a Chinese, a Swiss, a Lebanese, some Portuguese*		*the* + adjectif *The Chinese,* *the Japanese*
Adjectifs en -an + Greek *American, Italian, German, Australian*	*A/many/several/some...* + nom semblable à l'adjectif et prenant la marque du pluriel *An Italian, two Italians, some Americans, several Greeks*		*the* + nom au pluriel *the Americans,* *the Germans,* *the Africans*
Autres adjectifs *Scottish, Polish, Spanish, Swedish...*	Nom différent de l'adjectif et pouvant prendre la marque du pluriel *a Scot, a Pole, a Spaniard, a Swede, several Spaniards*		*the* + nom au pluriel *the Swedes* *the Poles*

Notez qu'en anglais, on utilise une majuscule pour les adjectifs aussi bien que pour les noms de nationalité.

■ Ne confondez pas **les adjectifs en *-ed* et les adjectifs en *-ing***
→ *frightened* (terrifié) – *frightening* (terrifiant) ; *amused* (amusé) – *amusing* (amusant)

■ Il existe également des **adjectifs composés**, formés de deux termes.
Voici quelques formations parmi les plus courantes :
– nom ou adverbe + participe passé
→ *a handwritten letter* : une lettre écrite à la main
– nom ou adverbe + V + *-ing*
→ *a fast-moving vehicle* : un véhicule rapide
– nom + adjectif
→ *an airtight bag* : un sac hermétique
– adjectif + nom
→ *a low-quality product* : un produit de qualité inférieure
– adjectif + participe passé
→ *a high spirited child* : un enfant plein d'entrain
– adjectif + nom + *-ed*
→ *a dark-haired woman* : une femme aux cheveux bruns
– adjectif + adjectif
→ *a pale blue dress* : une robe bleu pâle
– chiffre + nom
→ *a three-hour play* : une pièce de trois heures

■ Certains adjectifs sont suivis d'un complément, d'une préposition + nom ou V + *-ing* :
responsible for/different from/used to/keen on/ashamed of/interested in/involved in/similar to/worried about/clever at/good at
→ *She's responsible for the accident.* Elle est responsable de l'accident.
→ *He's ashamed of lying to her.* Il a honte de lui avoir menti.

4 – Le comparatif

Supériorité

Forme
– On ajoute *-er* aux adjectifs d'une seule syllabe : *big* > *bigger*
– On ajoute *-er* aux adjectifs de deux syllabes se terminant par *-y* (qui devient *-ier* : *pretty* > *prettier*), *-er* (*clever* > *cleverer*), -le (*gentle* > *gentler*). Pour les autres adjectifs de deux syllabes, on utilise *more* + adjectif : *more childish*
– Adjectifs de trois syllabes et plus : *more* + adjectif : *more interesting*
Than permet d'introduire le terme avec lequel on compare.
He is cleverer than his brother. Il est plus intelligent que son frère.

Formes irrégulières
bad > *worse; good/well* > *better; far* > *farther/further*
old > *older* (régulier) ou *elder* (épithète seulement)

→ *She's bought a smaller flat.* Elle a acheté un appartement plus petit.
→ *I'm much busier this week.* Je suis beaucoup plus occupé cette semaine.
→ *This book is far more interesting than the other one.*
Ce livre est beaucoup plus intéressant que l'autre.
→ *Is he feeling worse or better than yesterday?*
Est-ce qu'il se sent mieux ou plus mal qu'hier ?

Infériorité

Forme
Less + adjectif (court ou long) (+ *than*) : *less short, less dangerous*
→ *This possibility is less risky than the first one.*
Cette possibilité est moins risquée que la première.

Égalité

Forme
as + adjectif + *as* Forme négative : *not as/so* + adj. + *as*
→ *My essay is not as long as John's.* Mon essai n'est pas aussi long que celui de John.

■ On peut employer les comparatifs de supériorité et d'infériorité **avec des noms pour parler de quantités** :
more… than…/fewer… than…/as many… as + nom pluriel
more… than…/less… than…/as much... as + nom singulier
→ *We have more time but fewer things to do.*
Nous avons plus de temps mais moins de choses à faire.
→ *This library has (twice/three times/ten times…) as many books as our local library.* Cette bibliothèque a (deux fois/trois fois/dix fois) plus de livres que notre bibliothèque municipale.

On peut aussi employer ces comparatifs avec **un adverbe ou un verbe** :
→ *She dresses more simply than her sister.* Elle s'habille plus simplement que sa sœur.
→ *I walk more than you do.* Je marche plus que toi.

■ Quelques structures formées à l'aide de comparatifs :
– de plus en plus/ moins en moins :
→ *It's getting funnier and funnier.* C'est de plus en plus drôle.
→ *He's more and more annoyed.* Il est de plus en plus irrité.
– plus… plus…/plus… moins…/moins… moins… :
→ *The busier I am, the less productive I get.* Plus je suis occupé, moins je suis productif.

– d'autant plus/moins que… : *all the* + comparatif + *as/since/because…*
→ *He felt all the more upset as he had no money left.*
Il était d'autant plus contrarié qu'il n'avait plus d'argent.
On peut également employer ces formes avec des noms ou des verbes.
→ *The more time I spend on it, the less I understand.*

5 – Le superlatif

Forme
Même règle que pour le comparatif, mais terminaison en *-est* pour les adjectifs courts (*biggest*) et *most/least* + adjectif pour les adjectifs longs (*most interesting*).

Formes irrégulières
bad > *the worst; good/well* > *the best; far* > *the farthest / the furthest*
old > *the eldest* (le plus âgé des frères/sœurs)
→ *The quickest way is along the river.* Le chemin le plus court est le long de la rivière.
→ *I bought the least expensive bag.* J'ai acheté le sac le moins cher.

Lorsqu'on compare deux éléments, on utilise le comparatif au lieu du superlatif.
→ *There are two Chinese restaurants in town: the better one is very close to here.*
Il y a deux restaurants chinois en ville : le meilleur est tout près d'ici.
Après un superlatif, on trouve la préposition *in* devant un lieu ou un ensemble de personnes. → *the tallest tree in the village* (l'arbre le plus haut du village)
On peut employer le superlatif avec un verbe : on supprime alors souvent *the* devant le superlatif. → *It was Peter who complained most.* C'est Peter qui s'est plaint le plus.

exercices

1 Récrivez les phrases qui suivent en utilisant un adjectif composé.

1. My cat has long hair. I have a … cat.
2. His job is not paid very well. He has a … job.
3. With his job, he makes a lot of money. He has a … job.
4. I have often heard this sentence quoted. This is a … sentence.
5. Does this skirt fit me or is it too tight? Is this skirt too … ?

2 Complétez les phrases avec les dérivés en *-ed* ou *-ing* des mots entre parenthèses.

1. He's not … in the job, because he doesn't find it … enough. (interest)
2. I spent a … afternoon listening to a … speech. (frustrate – bore)
3. They're … about their daughter's … tendency to skip classes. (worry)
4. You may find the news … but I wasn't … (surprise)

3 Traduisez.

1. C'est une délicieuse confiture d'abricot maison, semblable à celle que faisait ma grand-mère.
2. Dans ce tableau de Breughel, les aveugles mènent les estropiés.
3. C'est une employée trop consciencieuse pour avoir fait une telle erreur.
4. Tu n'aimes pas les jeunes, mais les jeunes que je connais sont très bien élevés.
5. Le chapitre 3 commence par la description d'une femme ivre et mal habillée.
6. Les Écossais et les Anglais sont britanniques, mais les Anglais chez qui j'ai habité le mois dernier n'aimaient pas les Écossais.

COMPARATIF ET SUPERLATIF

4 Complétez les phrases qui suivent avec le comparatif ou le superlatif des adjectifs entre parenthèses.

1. ... way of doing it is often ... (simple - good)
2. She is ... than her sister; in fact ... I know her, the more unpleasant I find her. (polite - well)
3. They felt all ... at seeing him as they thought he was their ... neighbour. (surprised - friendly)
4. Simon is ... of the two brothers, and by far ... (old - handsome)
5. I had to work ... than ever and it was ... month in my life! (hard - bad)
6. ... you go in this direction, ... you are to find a pub. (far - likely)

16. LA DÉRIVATION

On peut former d'autres mots à partir d'un mot de base en ajoutant préfixes (avant) et suffixes (après). Voici quelques-unes des principales possibilités.

1 – PRÉFIXES

Préfixe	Sens	Exemples
de- *dis-* *un-* *in- im- ir- il-*	Le mot prend le sens opposé.	– *decolonize* (décoloniser), *de-ice* (dégivrer) – *disagree* (ne pas être d'accord), *disembark* (débarquer) – *unhappy* (triste), *untie* (dénouer) – *irregular* (irrégulier), *impossible* (impossible), *inevitable* (inévitable), *illogical* (illogique)

over- *under-*	excès insuffisance	– *over-tired* (trop fatigué), *oversleep* (dormir trop tard) – *under-populated* (sous peuplé)
re-	répétition	– *retell* (redire)
mis-	erreur, action mal faite	– *mislead* (induire en erreur), *misread* (mal lire)
out-	faire mieux que, dépasser	– *outlive* (vivre plus longtemps que), *outrun* (courir plus vite que)
fore-	avant, à l'avant	– *foresee* (prévoir), *foretaste* (avant-goût)
up-	mouvement vers le haut	– *uphold* (soutenir), *upstream* (en amont)

2 – Suffixes

■ Verbe + ...

Suffixe	Sens	Exemples
-al	→ nom : l'action de	*revive* → *revival* (reprise), *refuse* → *refusal* (refus)
-er	→ nom : personne qui fait l'action	*play* → *player* (joueur), *sleep* → *sleeper* (dormeur)
-ee	→ nom : personne qui subit l'action du verbe	*employ* → *employee* (employé = la personne qui est employée)
-ing	→ nom : l'activité ou le résultat de l'action	*swim* → *swimming* (la nage), *bind* → *binding* (reliure)
-ation *-ment*	→ nom abstrait	*generalize* → *generalization* (généralisation), *develop* → *development* (développement)
-able/-ible	→ adjectif : qui peut être...	*eat* → *eatable* (mangeable)

■ Adjectif + ...

Suffixe	Sens	Exemples
-ity	→ nom : état	*banal* → *banality* (banalité)
-ness	→ nom abstrait	*selfish* → *selfishness* (égoïsme)

-ist	→ nom : occupation, membre d'un groupe	*royal* → *royalist* (royaliste)
-dom	→ nom : condition	*free* → *freedom* (liberté)
-en	→ verbe : devenir	*wide* → *widen* (élargir)
-ize *-ify*	→ verbe : rendre, transformer en	*modern* → *modernize* (moderniser), *simple* → *simplify* (simplifier)

■ **Nom + ...**

Suffixe	Sens	Exemples
-ish	→ adjectif : nationalité, caractéristique, souvent péjoratif	*Sweden* → *Swedish* (suédois), *self* → *selfish* (égoïste)
-y	→ adjectif : ayant l'apparence, le goût, les caractéristiques de…	*milk* → *milky* (laiteux), *noise* → *noisy* (bruyant)
-like	→ adjectif : qui ressemble à	*child* → *childlike* (qui ressemble à un enfant)
-ful *-ly*	→ adjectif : ayant la qualité du nom	*fright* → *frightful* (terrifiant), *month* → *monthly* (mensuel)
-ful	→ nom : quantité	*spoon* → *spoonful* (cuillérée)
-less	→ adjectif : dénué de…	*power* → *powerless* (impuissant)
-ian *-ese*	→ adjectif : appartenant à un groupe, à un pays	*Darwin* → *Darwinian* (darwinien), *China* → *Chinese* (chinois)
-hood *-ship*	→ nom : statut ou condition	*widow* → *widowhood* (veuvage), *dictator* → *dictatorship* (dictature)
-ism	→ nom : doctrine	*Catholic* → *Catholicism* (Catholicisme)
-ess	→ nom : nom féminin	*prince* → *princess* (princesse)

La plupart des adverbes se forment avec le suffixe *-ly* ou *-ward(s)* : *quietly* (calmement), *strangely* (étrangement), *northwards* (vers le nord).
Mais attention, certains adjectifs se terminent en *-ly* et ne peuvent pas devenir adverbes (ex. : *friendly*).

exercice

Complétez les phrases qui suivent avec un dérivé du mot donné entre parenthèses.

(1) The pretty … was hoping to reach … (act – star)

(2) We go jogging together, but he is a professional … and always … me. (run)

(3) They should … French punctuation: I keep … words. (simple – spell)

(4) I arrived at the party … and felt … (dress – fool)

(5) She's a … … and one day she's going to have an accident. (care – drive)

(6) This … water is not …: it would be … (dirt – drink – harm)

(7) His … has … his father's heart. (self – sad)

(8) You should never … the … of your enemies. (estimate – possible)

17. Le passif

Forme

Be + participe passé :

→ *My bag has been stolen.* On m'a volé mon sac.

et à la forme en V + *-ing* :

→ *My hair was being washed when…* On me lavait les cheveux lorsque…

Le complément d'agent (sujet du verbe à la forme active) peut être mentionné, introduit par *by*.

Forme active : *Jane Austen wrote* Pride and Prejudice.

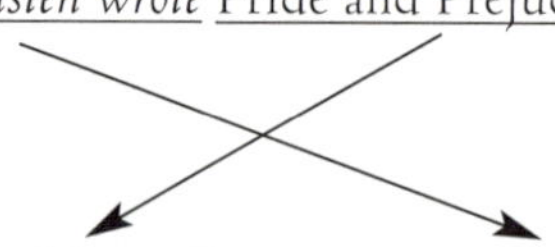

Forme passive : Pride and Prejudice *was written by Jane Austen.*

■ On emploie le passif en anglais :

– lorsqu'on ne connaît pas l'agent

→ *The plane was shot down.* L'avion a été abattu.

– ou lorsque l'agent est évident et n'a donc pas besoin d'être mentionné

→ *He was taken to jail.* On l'a emmené en prison.
(Il n'est pas nécessaire d'ajouter "*by the police*".)

– lorsqu'on veut garder l'information nouvelle (et principale) pour la fin de la phrase

→ *He was followed by another spy.* Il était suivi par un autre espion.

■ Le passif s'emploie avec la forme *be* V + *-ing* lorsqu'on met l'accent sur le déroulement de l'action.

→ *We had a secret meeting and exchanged our bags, without knowing that we were being watched.*
Nous eûmes un rendez-vous secret et échangeâmes nos sacs, sans savoir qu'on nous surveillait.

> **Attention !** En français le passif est beaucoup moins courant. Le passif anglais correspond donc très souvent à une forme française avec « on » pour sujet ou à une forme pronominale ou impersonnelle.
> → *Our house was broken into last week.*
> On s'est introduit dans notre maison la semaine dernière.
> → *Salmon can be eaten cold.*
> Le saumon peut se manger froid. (forme pronominale)

Certains verbes qui ont deux compléments ont deux formes passives possibles. Par exemple : *give, bring, sell, tell, write, send, lend, buy…*

I gave him the book. → *He was given the book.*

I gave him the book. → *The book was given to him.*

exercices

1 Récrivez les phrases qui suivent en utilisant le mot souligné comme sujet. Décidez si l'agent doit être mentionné ou non.

(1) They taught me that such behaviour is rude.
(2) They offered George the new job and he accepted it.
(3) Susie lent me the money I needed.
(4) Everyone calls him a liar.
(5) When I came back to the hotel, they were serving lunch.
(6) I think you should throw away these old trousers.

2 Traduisez en utilisant un passif.

(1) Ils ont été attaqués dans la rue.
(2) Je te téléphone pendant qu'on répare ma voiture.
(3) Le notaire *(lawyer)* leur a montré le contrat *(contract)*. (2 formes)
(4) La tarte aux pommes peut se servir avec de la glace.
(5) Sa demande *(request)* vient d'être refusée.

18. Le discours indirect

■ Le discours indirect permet de rapporter les paroles de quelqu'un en les intégrant à la narration.

Il est introduit par un certain nombre de verbes, par exemple :
say (*He said* (*to her*) *that…*)
tell (*He told her that…*: le pronom ou nom complément est obligatoire)
add (ajouter: *He added that…*), *mention* (mentionner: *He mentioned that…*), *state* (affirmer: *He stated that…*), *answer* (*He answered* (*her*) *that…*), *explain* (expliquer)

CHAPITRE : ÉCRIRE UN RÉCIT P. 19

Et pour rapporter une question :
ask (*He asked* (*her*) *if/whether/when/what…*)
wonder (*He wondered if/when/what/where…*)
want to know (*He wanted to know what/if/where/when…*)
"Don't go out, John", she said. → She told John not to go out.
"When will you be back?", she asked. → She asked when he would be back.

■ Le passage au discours indirect entraîne un certain nombre de changements lorsque le verbe d'introduction est au passé. (Il n'y a pas de changements lorsque ce verbe est au présent.)

DISCOURS DIRECT	DISCOURS INDIRECT
Syntaxe	
Question *"Are you alone?"* *"Where do you work?"* **Ordre ou conseil :** *"Don't leave her alone."*	Ordre des mots d'une phrase affirmative *He asked if I was alone.* *He asked where I worked.* *Warn/advise/forbid/order + noun + (not) to V* *He advised him/her not to leave her alone.*
Temps lorsque le verbe d'introduction est au passé	
Présent *"I want a cup of tea."* ***Present perfect*** *"They've never been keen on pets."* **Prétérit** *"Did you write to him?"* ***Will:*** **Expression du futur** *"We'll go to Japan."* **Impératif** *"Don't forget"*	**Prétérit** *She said she wanted a cup of tea.* ***Past perfect*** *He said they had never been keen on pets.* ***Past perfect*** *She asked if I had written to him.* ***Would*** *They said they would go to Japan.* ***Tell, order, ask… + noun + (not) to*** **+ Verbe** *She told me not to forget.*

Modaux	
Can, may *"He may still win."* ***Must, could, might, should, would, ought to*** *"You should try a little harder."*	***Could, might*** *She said he might still win.* ***Must, could, might, should, would, ought to*** *She said that I should try a little harder.*
Pronoms et possessifs	
Première personne: *I-we/me-us/my-our/mine-ours* *"I've lost my bag!"*	**Deuxième personne: *he-she-they/him-her-them/his-her-their/his-hers-theirs*** *She said that she had lost her bag.*
Espace et temps	
Here *"It's good to have you here".* *now* *today* *tomorrow* *next week* *yesterday* *last month* *two years ago* *"I saw him yesterday."*	*There* *She said it was good to have them there.* *then* *that day* *the next day* *the following week* *the day before* *the month before* *two years before* *She said that she had seen him the day before.*

exercice

Transposez au discours indirect.

(1) "When I am older, I will be a doctor", the boy told his mother.

(2) "There can't be a leak! I had the car repaired two months ago", she exclaimed.

(3) "Where did she hide the money?" he wondered.

(4) "I love it here," she declared, "and I'm going to stay until next month."

(5) "I'm just phoning to tell you I might be late, Mum, my car won't start," Joanna said.

(6) "Don't be late for your train," she advised him, "as it won't wait for you."

(7) "You should get yourself another suitcase: we can go and buy one tomorrow, if you wish," she told him.

(8) "Granny's always been fond of pets, so we must get her a dog," Peter said.

19. Les propositions relatives

■ Pour déterminer quel relatif utiliser, il faut d'abord décider si le pronom est sujet ou complément.

→ *I know the man who phoned.* (*who* est **sujet** de *phoned*)
Je connais l'homme qui a téléphoné.

→ *The man whom you met must be my uncle.* (*whom* est **complément** de *met*)
L'homme que tu as rencontré doit être mon oncle.

→ *That's the woman whose car was stolen.* (*whose* est **génitif**)

■ Il faut ensuite faire la différence entre les propositions déterminatives et les non-déterminatives.

– Une proposition relative déterminative donne une information nécessaire pour définir l'antécédent.

→ *The man who phoned at two didn't give his name.* On parle de l'homme qui a téléphoné à deux heures, et pas de celui qui a téléphoné à trois heures ou quatre heures.

– Une proposition relative non-déterminative ne fait qu'apporter une information de plus, comme si l'on avait une simple apposition. C'est pourquoi ce type de relative se trouve entre virgules.

→ *My sister, who is 18, has just entered university.*
Ma sœur, qui a 18 ans, vient tout juste d'entrer à l'université.

Comparez :

→ *My friend who is a painter lives in Kent.* (*"who is a painter"* permet de définir de quel ami il s'agit.)

→ *My friend John, who is a painter, lives in Kent.* (L'ami est déjà défini, c'est John, la relative ne fait qu'ajouter une précision sur lui.)

Type	Pronom sujet	Pronom complément
Déterminative	**Antécédent animé** *WHO* *THAT* (langue + courante) Ø impossible *The friend who speaks Russian will be here tonight.*	**Antécédent animé** *WHOM* (langue littéraire) *THAT* (plus courant) Ø" *He's a writer (that) I have never heard of.*
	Antécédent inanimé *WHICH* *THAT* Ø impossible *I'll buy the book which won the prize.*	**Antécédent inanimé** *WHICH* *THAT* (plus courant) Ø" *It's the sort of idea (that) you get when you can't sleep.*

Non déterminative	**Antécédent animé** *WHO* *That* impossible Ø impossible *My neighbour, who is 80, wants to get married again.*	**Antécédent animé** *WHOM* *That* impossible Ø impossible (*Who* dans une langue plus relâchée) *The last speaker, whom nobody knew, ended up leader of the party.*
	Antécédent inanimé *WHICH* *That* impossible Ø impossible *He's going to sell his garden, which is too big.*	**Antécédent inanimé** *WHICH* *That* impossible Ø impossible *The news, which he learnt on arriving, cheered him up.*

Lorsqu'il y a une **préposition** dans les relatives déterminatives complément, deux structures sont possibles :
– préposition à la fin de la relative :
→ *The firm (which/that) I was working for.* La société pour laquelle je travaillais.
C'est la structure la plus courante.
– préposition devant les relatifs *which* et *whom* (pas *that*) :
→ *The firm for which I was working.*

1 – La traduction de dont

- Antécédent humain ou avec lequel on peut employer un génitif : ***Whose***
→ The cat whose leg is broken is my neighbour's.
Le chat dont la patte est cassée est à mon voisin.

- Autres antécédents : **nom + *of which***
→ *The table the leg of which was broken has been repaired.*
La table dont le pied était cassé a été réparée.

On trouve cependant de plus en plus *whose* à la place de *of which*.

– Lorsque dont correspond à un complément d'adjectif ou de verbe, on le traduit par ***which***, ***that*** ou **Ø + préposition**.
→ Le pays dont je reviens. *The country (which, that) I come back from.*
→ L'enfant dont il est responsable… *The child (whom, that) he is responsible for.*
– Lorsque dont permet de parler d'une quantité on le traduira généralement par un quantifieur (***many, much, some, a few…***) + ***of*** + ***whom*** ou ***which***.
→ *The keys, some of which were rusty, lay on the floor.*
Les clés, dont certaines étaient rouillées, étaient par terre.

2 – Traduction de ce qui/ce que

– *What* signifie "*the thing that*" et permet d'annoncer ce qui suit.
→ *I'll tell you what I think.* Je vais te dire ce que je pense.
– Virgule + *which* permet de reprendre ce qui précède.
→ *He asked me to write a letter, which I did immediately.*
Il m'a demandé d'écrire une lettre, ce que j'ai fait tout de suite.

Attention ! Après *all*, on emploie *that* et non *what*.
All (that) he said was true. Tout ce qu'il a dit était vrai.

3 – *When, where, why*

Ils peuvent aussi reprendre un antécédent :
→ *He was born on the day when the armistice was signed.*
Il est né le jour où l'armistice a été signé.
→ *This is the bakery where I get my bread.* Voici la boulangerie où j'achète mon pain.
→ *He hasn't given me the reason why he wants to leave.*
Il ne m'a pas dit pourquoi il veut partir.

exercices

1 Complétez les phrases qui suivent avec le relatif qui convient, en ajoutant une préposition lorsque cela est nécessaire.

(1) The room … we slept was very cold.
(2) Their cottage, … is very old, needs restoring.
(3) The hikers, … had enormous rucksacks, looked very tired.
(4) I'm not going to vote for a party … policies I disapprove of.
(5) This is the play … he wrote about the first World War.
(6) He braked on an icy road, … is exactly what he shouldn't have done.
(7) All … I did was to tell him the subject … you were going to talk.
(8) I have ten students, three of … come from abroad.

2 Traduisez.

(1) Voilà le tableau dont je t'avais parlé.
(2) Ils ne fabriquent plus ce shampooing, dont les ventes avaient baissé.
(3) Ce livre, dont quelques pages sont abîmées, ne peut être vendu.
(4) Voici tout ce dont tu auras besoin.
(5) Le passant dont on avait volé le sac était furieux.

20. Les formes V + -*ing*/V + (*to*) + V

1 – Verbes suivis de V + -*ing*

Un certain nombre de verbes sont suivis de la forme V + *-ing*.
Voici les principaux :

Verbes décrivant le début, la fin, la continuation d'une action : *begin, start, stop, give up, finish, keep, continue, spend one's time*	*He gave up smoking when his son was born.* Il a cessé de fumer quand son fils est né.
Verbes décrivant l'appréciation ou non de quelque chose : *like, love, enjoy, appreciate, hate, dislike, detest, can't stand/ can't bear* (ne pas supporter), *miss* (qch qui vous manque), *tolerate*	*I can't bear walking in the snow.* Je déteste marcher dans la neige. *I miss hearing his voice.* Cela me manque de ne plus entendre sa voix.
Un certain nombre d'expressions : *It's no good/it's no use* (cela ne sert à rien de) *can't help* (ne pas pouvoir s'empêcher de), *it's (not) worth* (valoir – ou non – la peine de)	*It's no good asking me – there's nothing I can do.* Cela ne sert à rien de me le demander, je ne peux rien faire. *It's worth trying.* Cela vaut la peine d'essayer.
Autres verbes : *admit* (admettre), *acknowledge* (reconnaître), *consider* (envisager), *imagine, contemplate* (songer à), *suggest* (suggérer), *mind* (voir une objection à), *avoid* (éviter), *escape* (échapper à), *prevent* (empêcher), *risk* (risquer), *deny* (nier), *practise* (s'entraîner à)	*Do you mind lending me two pounds?* Est-ce que cela vous ennuierait de me prêter deux livres ? *You should avoid going out in such weather.* Vous devriez éviter de sortir par ce temps.

■ **On emploie la forme V + *-ing* après les prépositions.**

→ *He was accused of stealing some luggage.* On l'a accusé d'avoir volé des bagages.

→ *You can't start without fastening the seat-belt.*
Vous ne pouvez pas démarrer sans attacher la ceinture.

■ **Lorsque *to* est une préposition qui suit obligatoirement certains verbes**, elle est suivie de V + *-ing*. Les principaux verbes sont :
– *be used to/to be accustomed to* (être habitué à) : *I am not used to drinking wine.*
– *look forward to* (attendre avec impatience de) : *I look forward to meeting you.*
– *object to* (être contre) : *I object to helping him.*

– *take to* (se mettre à) : *He's taken to jogging every morning.*
– *get round to* (arriver à) : *I was busy and never got round to mowing the lawn.*
– *prefer doing sthg to doing sthg* (préférer… à…) : *I prefer swimming to cycling.*
– *amount to* (revenir à) : *It would amount to starting all over again.*
– *contribute to* (contribuer à) : *It contributed to raising salaries.*
– *devote… to…* (consacrer) : *He devotes his time to raising his children.*

■ **La forme V + *-ing* peut avoir pour sujet** un pronom complément ou un génitif.
→ *I don't like Phil/him coming back on his own so late.*
(Je n'aime pas que Phil/qu'il rentre tout seul si tard) Langue plus parlée
→ *I don't like Phil's/his coming back so late.* Langue plus écrite

■ **La forme V + *-ing* peut être sujet.**
→ *Staying in a four-star hotel is his idea of a holiday.*
Séjourner dans un hôtel quatre étoiles, voilà sa conception des vacances.
→ *Their sending the flowers was much appreciated.*
Le fait qu'ils aient envoyé des fleurs a été très apprécié.

2 – Verbes suivis de V + *-ing* ou du verbe avec ou sans *to*

■ **Les verbes de perception**
Hear (entendre), *listen* (écouter), *see* (voir), *watch* (regarder, suivre des yeux), *notice* (remarquer), *feel* (ressentir) peuvent être suivis de V + *-ing* ou d'un verbe simple, sans *to*.
– Avec V + *-ing*, on insiste sur le déroulement de l'action.
→ *I heard him tiptoeing up the stairs.*
Je l'ai entendu monter l'escalier sur la pointe des pieds.
– Avec le verbe sans *to*, on insiste sur l'ensemble de l'action.
→ *I watched him go up the steps and ring the bell.*
Je l'ai vu monter les marches et sonner.

Attention ! Au passif, *to* est nécessaire.
I saw him hit the other man. → *He was seen to hit the other man.*

Begin, start, intend
→ *He began to laugh.* ou *He began laughing.* Il se mit à rire.

Love, like, hate, prefer, forget, regret, remember
– avec V + *-ing*, on parle du passé ou d'une activité déjà connue, dont on a déjà fait l'expérience.
– avec *to* + verbe, on parle plutôt d'une activité à venir, envisagée.
→ *I remember writing to her.* Je me souviens lui avoir écrit.
→ *I must remember to write to him.* Il faut que je pense à lui écrire.

→ *I hate giving a talk.* Je déteste faire une conférence.
→ *I would hate to give a talk in front of such an audience.*
Je détesterais faire une conférence devant un tel auditoire.

Stop
Attention à la différence de sens :
→ *She stopped watching television.* Elle cessa de regarder la télévision.
→ *She stopped to watch television.*
Elle arrêta (ce qu'elle faisait) pour regarder la télévision.

Try
– *Try to* = essayer
→ *Try to lift it.* Essaie de le soulever. (C'est lourd et difficile à soulever)
– *Try* + V + *-ing* = faire un essai pour voir le résultat
→ *Try lifting it.* Essaie de le soulever. (Pour voir si cela permet de faire autre chose.)

Need
– Need to
→ *She needs to practise.* Elle a besoin de s'entraîner.
– Need + V + *-ing* : sens passif
→ *Your hair needs cutting.* Tes cheveux ont besoin d'être coupés.

3 – Verbes suivis de (complément) + (*to*) + verbe

Verbe	+ complément + Verbe	+ *to* + Verbe	+ complément + *to* + Verbe (Proposition infinitive)	Autres structures possibles
seem (sembler), *appear* (paraître), *decide* (décider), *agree* (être d'accord), *refuse* (refuser), *choose* (choisir), *manage* (parvenir à), *fail* (négliger de, ne pas arriver à), *hope* (espérer), *swear* (jurer)		*He refused to leave.* Il a refusé de partir.		
Ask (demander), *expect* (s'attendre à), *want* (vouloir), *wish* (souhaiter), *intend* (avoir l'intention		*He expected to win.* Il s'attendait à gagner.	*He expected his brother to win.* Il s'attendait à ce que son frère gagne.	

de), *ask* (demander), *offer* (proposer), *prefer* (préférer), *promise* (promettre), *propose* (proposer), *beg* (supplier)		*They want to buy a car.* Ils veulent acheter une voiture.	*She wants her father to buy her a car.* Elle veut que son père lui achète une voiture.	
Help (aider)	*She helped me clean the house.* Elle m'a aidé à nettoyer la maison.	*They helped to make the beds.* Ils ont aidé à faire les lits.	*She helped me to clean the house.*	
Let (laisser)	*She let him use her car.* Elle l'a laissé utiliser sa voiture.			
Wait (attendre)				*I waited <u>for</u> them to leave.* J'attendais qu'ils partent.
Allow (permettre), *force* (forcer), *order* (ordonner), *persuade* (persuader), *encourage* (encourager), *recommend* (recommander), *oblige* (obliger), *order* (ordonner), *advise* (conseiller), *invite* (inviter), *tell* (dire), *warn* (prévenir), *remind* (rappeler).			*They advised her not to spend so much.* Ils lui conseillèrent de ne pas dépenser tant.	

4 – *MAKE*, *HAVE* ET *GET* : TRADUCTION DE « FAIRE FAIRE »

Make* + nom + verbe sans *to : implique souvent une certaine contrainte.

→ *I made her give the money back.* Je l'ai obligée à rembourser l'argent.

Attention, *to* est nécessaire au passif.

→ *She was made to give the money back.* On l'obligea à rembourser l'argent.

Have* + nom + verbe sans *to : forme surtout utilisée en anglais américain. Il y a moins contrainte qu'avec *make*.

→ *I had her cancel the flight.* Je lui ai fait annuler le vol.

Get **+ nom +** ***to*** **+ verbe :** l'action implique une difficulté.

→ *It's difficult to get people to drive again after they've had an accident.*
Il est difficile de convaincre les gens de conduire à nouveau après qu'ils ont eu un accident.

Have/Get **+ nom + participe passé :** faire faire quelque chose par quelqu'un.

→ *We must have this fence repaired.*
Il faut que nous fassions réparer cette clôture.

Make **+ réfléchi + participe passé de verbes comme** ***understand, obey, hear*** **:**

→ *It took her a month to make herself obeyed.*
Il lui fallut un mois pour se faire respecter.

Mais attention, le français « faire faire » n'a pas toujours un sens causatif et se traduit souvent d'une autre façon.
Il a fait tomber le livre. *He dropped the book.*
Je n'arrive pas à faire démarrer la voiture. *I can't start the car.*
Essaie de ne pas les faire attendre. *Try not to keep them waiting.*
Fais-les entrer. *Show them in.*

exercices

VERBE + *-ING* OU VERBE + *TO* + VERBE

1 Complétez les phrases qui suivent avec le verbe et éventuellement le complément donnés entre parenthèses, à la forme qui convient.

(1) I suggested … the house, but she preferred … so. (sell – do + not)

(2) It's no use … a lot of money as he can't help … it immediately. You should wait …. (give + him – spend - grow up + him)

(3) I'd like … for a while, as I'm not used … so much. (stop – walk)

(4) I'm thinking of … a motorbike to avoid … in traffic jams during the rush-hours. (buy – be caught)

(5) I'll wait … before … as they promised … of the canary when I was away. (come back + them – leave – take care)

(6) This house needs … What you need … is find a good painter who can do the job during the Xmas holidays. (decorate – do)

(7) I stumbled and fell, and a passer-by stopped … … on my feet. (help + me – get back)

(8) The government is expected … new measures in order to prevent … the country. (take – enter + new immigrants)

(9) Do you mind … me a ring when you have finished … (give – work)
(10) I fail … why you need … a new pair of shoes. (see – buy)

***MAKE, HAVE* ET *GET* : TRADUCTION DE « FAIRE FAIRE »**

2 Traduisez.

(1) Je vais faire repeindre la chambre.
(2) La musique était si forte qu'il n'arrivait pas à se faire entendre.
(3) À l'armée on le fera obéir. (utiliser un passif)
(4) Ils font pousser des poireaux dans leur jardin.
(5) J'ai fait dire par ma secrétaire que je n'étais pas là.
(6) La ville vient de faire restaurer *(restore)* le château.

21. VERBE/ADJECTIF + *THAT*

■ Beaucoup de verbes peuvent être suivis d'une subordonnée introduite par *that*.
– *That* peut souvent être omis, par exemple avec les verbes qui suivent : *say* (dire), *think* (penser), *believe* (croire), *realize, understand* (se rendre compte), *admit* (admettre), *know* (savoir), *suppose* (supposer).
→ *I admit that I was wrong./I admit I was wrong.* J'admets que j'ai eu tort.

■ Avec d'autres verbes comme *answer, reply, accept*, on emploie presque toujours *that*.
→ *He answered that it was too late.* Il répondit qu'il était trop tard.

■ Après les verbes qui expriment une volonté comme *suggest* (suggérer), *recommend* (recommander), *insist* (insister), *order* (ordonner), *demand* (exiger)…
on peut employer :
– ou bien *should* :
→ *They insisted that he should apologize.* Ils ont insisté pour qu'il s'excuse.
– ou bien la forme verbale simple, sans *-s* :
→ *They insisted that he apologize.*

■ Après l'expression d'une opinion avec la structure *It is* + adjectif + *that (It is strange that, it is normal that, it is surprising that, it is a pity that, it is sad that…)*, on emploie :
– *should*
→ *It is strange that he should be behave so rudely.*
C'est étrange qu'il se comporte aussi grossièrement.
Et si l'on parle d'un fait passé : *It is strange that he should have behaved so rudely.*
– l'indicatif :
→ *It is strange that he behaves so rudely.*

exercice

Traduisez.

(1) Je suppose qu'il va démissionner maintenant.
(2) Ses amis avaient insisté pour qu'elle reste quelques jours.
(3) Ils exigèrent qu'on les rembourse.
(4) Il est dommage qu'ils ne se soient pas rencontrés plus tôt.
(5) Il est normal que vous soyez en colère.

22. Les adverbes

Un adverbe peut qualifier un adjectif *(very beautiful)*, un nom ou pronom *(only you)*, un verbe *(often heard)*, un autre adverbe *(hardly ever)*, ou une phrase tout entière *(Fortunately, he survived.)*
Il permet à l'énonciateur d'exprimer une opinion.

Il existe différents types d'adverbes :
– adverbes de fréquence : *often* (souvent), *rarely* (rarement), *sometimes* (parfois)
– adverbes de degré et de quantité : *almost* (presque), *completely* (complètement), *enough* (assez), *slightly* (un peu), *quite* (tout à fait), *hardly* (à peine)
– adverbes de lieu et de temps : *outside* (dehors), *underneath* (en dessous), *somewhere* (quelque part), *later* (plus tard), *tonight* (ce soir)
– adverbes de manière : *carefully* (attentivement), *slowly* (lentement), *strangely* (étrangement)
– adverbes servant à lier deux propositions : *besides* (de plus), *yet* (cependant)
– adverbes exprimant le point de vue de l'énonciateur : *perhaps* (peut-être), *probably* (probablement)

1 – Place des adverbes

Il faut tout d'abord prendre soin de ne pas séparer le verbe de son complément d'objet direct, comme on le fait souvent en français.
→ Il donne souvent des fêtes. *He often gives parties.*

L'adverbe peut être placé :

– En début de phrase, on trouvera plutôt les adverbes exprimant le point de vue de l'énonciateur, et les adverbes servant à lier deux propositions.
→ *Surely, you didn't agree.* Vous n'avez tout de même pas été d'accord.
→ *However, things got worse.* Cependant les choses empirèrent.

– En milieu de phrase, avant le verbe principal, mais après le premier auxiliaire ou modal, on trouve surtout les adverbes de degré, de fréquence, de manière. Si *be* est seul, l'adverbe se place après *be*. Si *do* ou le modal est seul, l'adverbe se place devant. Ces adverbes modifient directement le sens du verbe.

→ *I sometimes go to the cinema.* Je vais parfois au cinéma.

→ *He would certainly have won.* Il aurait sans doute gagné.

→ *She had almost given up.* Elle avait presque abandonné.

→ *She was terribly angry.* Elle était terriblement en colère.

→ *"Did you go to Stratford?" "I often did."*
« Tu allais à Stratford? – Oui, souvent. »

– Les adverbes de lieu, de temps et de manière qui modifient la phrase entière se placent plutôt en fin de phrase. L'adverbe de lieu précède d'ordinaire l'adverbe de temps.

→ *He came to the office yesterday.* Il est venu au bureau hier.

→ *He reacted quite well.* Il a très bien réagi.

– Lorsque les trois types d'adverbes sont présents, l'ordre le plus courant est :

manière – lieu – temps.

– Lorsque l'adverbe porte sur un adjectif, il se place généralement devant cet adjectif.

→ *You were quite right.* Vous aviez tout à fait raison.

2 – Quelques cas particuliers

■ Les adverbes à valeur négative ou restrictive *(hardly, scarcely, only)* peuvent se situer en début de phrase et sont alors suivis d'une inversion.

→ *Only then did she realize her mistake.*
Ce n'est qu'alors qu'elle se rendit compte de son erreur.

Notez aussi les deux structures suivantes :

→ *No sooner had she arrived than the phone rang.*

→ *Hardly had she arrived when the phone rang.*
À peine était-elle arrivée que le téléphone sonna.

■ *Enough* se place après l'adjectif mais avant le nom.

→ *Are you warm enough?* As-tu assez chaud ?

→ *Have you got enough blankets?* As-tu assez de couvertures ?

(C'est alors un déterminant.)

■ *No longer/no more*

On utilise *no longer* avant le verbe, *no more* en fin de phrase.

→ *I no longer use it.* Je ne l'utilise plus.

→ *I saw him no more.* Je ne le revis plus.

Any more et *any longer* s'utilisent dans des phrases affirmatives et négatives.

→ *I don't like it any more.* Je ne l'aime plus.

■ *Still* et *yet*

Ils correspondent au français « encore ». *Yet* s'emploie surtout dans des phrases négatives et interrogatives.

→ *He's not here yet.* Il n'est pas encore là.

→ *Has he come yet?* Est-il arrivé?

Still est utilisé pour une situation qui se prolonge.

→ *He is still at home.* Il vit toujours chez ses parents.

not yet : pas encore (on envisage l'avenir)

still not : toujours pas (une situation se perpétue)

■ *Never* et *ever*

Never = ne jamais :

→ *I have never read* Jane Eyre. Je n'ai jamais lu *Jane Eyre.*

Ever = jamais, à un moment donné :

→ *Have you ever eaten snake?* As-tu jamais mangé du serpent ?

exercices

1 Placez les adverbes entre parenthèses dans les phrases.

(1) They arrived. (in Norwich – late last night)
(2) They tried to lift the vase. (finally – carefully)
(3) She is tired; she is happy to be alive. (also – however – very – extremely)
(4) He could distinguish the tower although it was far away. (quite – almost)
(5) He jogs in the park. (seldom – these days)
(6) Have you seen such behaviour? (ever – honestly)
(7) He feels disappointed. (too – pretty)
(8) "Are you comfortable?" she asked me. (enough – often)

2 Traduisez.

1) Tu n'as pas encore 16 ans et tu ne peux pas voir ce film.
2) À peine avais-je ouvert la porte que j'entendis un bruit curieux.
3) Attendons, ce n'est pas encore assez chaud.
4) Es-tu jamais allé à Glasgow? Moi, je n'y vais plus en ce moment.

23. Verbes irréguliers

arise	arose	arisen	se lever
awake	awoke	awoken	(se) réveiller
be	was	been	être
bear	bore	borne	porter
beat	beat	beaten	battre
become	became	become	devenir
begin	began	begun	commencer
bend	bent	bent	courber
bet	bet	bet	parier
bind	bound	bound	lier
bite	bit	bitten	mordre
bleed	bled	bled	saigner
blow	blew	blown	souffler
break	broke	broken	casser
breed	bred	bred	élever
bring	brought	brought	apporter
broadcast	broadcast	broadcast	diffuser
build	built	built	construire
burn	burnt ®	burnt ®	brûler
burst	burst	burst	éclater
buy	bought	bought	acheter
cast	cast	cast	jeter, lancer
catch	caught	caught	attraper
choose	chose	chosen	choisir
cling	clung	clung	s'accrocher
come	came	come	venir
cost	cost	cost	coûter
creep	crept	crept	ramper
cut	cut	cut	couper
deal	dealt	dealt	distribuer
dig	dug	dug	creuser
do	did	done	faire
draw	drew	drawn	dessiner, tirer
dream	dreamt ®	dreamt ®	rêver
drink	drank	drunk	boire
drive	drove	driven	conduire
eat	ate	eaten	manger
fall	fell	fallen	tomber

feed	fed	fed	nourrir
feel	felt	felt	(res)sentir
fight	fought	fought	combattre
find	found	found	trouver
flee	fled	fled	fuir
fling	flung	flung	lancer
fly	flew	flown	voler
forbid	forbade	forbidden	interdire
forecast	forecast	forecast	prévoir
forget	forgot	forgotten	oublier
forgive	forgave	forgiven	pardonner
freeze	froze	frozen	geler
get	got	got/gotten (US)	obtenir
give	gave	given	donner
go	went	gone	aller
grind	ground	ground	moudre
grow	grew	grown	pousser
hang	hung	hung	pendre
have	had	had	avoir
hear	heard	heard	entendre
hide	hid	hidden	cacher
hit	hit	hit	frapper
hold	held	held	tenir
hurt	hurt	hurt	blesser
keep	kept	kept	garder
kneel	knelt ®	knelt ®	être à genoux
know	knew	known	savoir
lay	laid	laid	poser
lead	led	led	mener
lean	leant ®	leant ®	incliner
leap	leapt ®	leapt ®	sauter
learn	learnt ®	learnt ®	apprendre
leave	left	left	quitter
lend	lent	lent	prêter
let	let	let	laisser
lie	lay	lain	être allongé
light	lit ®	lit ®	allumer

® indique qu'il existe également une forme régulière.

lose	lost	lost	perdre
make	made	made	faire
mean	meant	meant	vouloir dire
meet	met	met	rencontrer
mow	mowed	mown ®	tondre
pay	paid	paid	payer
put	put	put	mettre
read	read	read	lire
ride	rode	ridden	être à vélo/ cheval
ring	rang	rung	sonner
rise	rose	risen	se lever
run	ran	run	courir
saw	sawed	sawn ®	scier
say	said	said	dire
see	saw	seen	voir
seek	sought	sought	chercher
sell	sold	sold	vendre
send	sent	sent	envoyer
set	set	set	placer
sew	sewed	sewn ®	coudre
shake	shook	shaken	secouer
shed	shed	shed	répandre, verser
shine	shone	shone	briller
shoot	shot	shot	tirer (fusil)
show	showed	shown ®	montrer
shrink	shrank	shrunk	rétrécir
shut	shut	shut	fermer
sing	sang	sung	chanter
sink	sank	sunk	sombrer, couler
sit	sat	sat	être assis
sleep	slept	slept	dormir
slide	slid	slid	glisser
smell	smelt ®	smelt ®	sentir
sow	sowed	sown ®	semer
speak	spoke	spoken	parler
spell	spelt ®	spelt ®	épeler
spend	spent	spent	dépenser
spill	spilt ®	spilt ®	répandre
spit	spat	spat	cracher
split	split	split	fendre
spoil	spoilt ®	spoilt ®	gâcher
spread	spread	spread	étaler
spring	sprang/ sprung	sprung	bondir
stand	stood	stood	être debout
steal	stole	stolen	dérober
stick	stuck	stuck	coller
sting	stung	stung	piquer
stink	stank/ stunk	stunk	sentir mauvais
stride	strode	stridden	marcher à grands pas
strike	struck	struck	frapper
swear	swore	sworn	jurer
sweep	swept	swept	balayer
swim	swam	swum	nager
swing	swung	swung	(se) balancer
take	took	taken	prendre
teach	taught	taught	enseigner
tear	tore	torn	déchirer
tell	told	told	dire
think	thought	thought	penser
throw	threw	thrown	lancer
tread	trod	trodden	fouler
understand	understood	understood	comprendre
wake	woke ®	woken ®	réveiller
wear	wore	worn	porter un vêtement
weave	wove	woven	tisser
weep	wept	wept	pleurer
win	won	won	gagner
wind	wound	wound	enrouler
wring	wrung	wrung	tordre
write	wrote	written	écrire

II À L'ORAL

1 – L'alphabet anglais

a	b	c	d	e	f	g	h	i	j	k	l	m
eɪ	biː	siː	diː	iː	ef	dʒiː	eɪtʃ	aɪ	dʒeɪ	keɪ	el	em

n	o	p	q	r	s	t	u	v	w	x	y	z
en	əʊ	piː	kjuː	ɑː	es	tiː	juː	viː	ˈdʌbəljuː	eks	waɪ	zed

2 – L'alphabet phonétique

italiques : signes graphiques correspondant aux sons
deux points après le signe phonétique : son long
deux signes : diphtongues

Vowels	Consonants
ɪ b*i*g, tr*i*p	p *p*et
e r*e*d, p*e*n	b *b*ack
æ f*a*t, r*a*t	t *t*en
ɒ h*o*t, r*o*t	d *d*ay
ʌ d*u*ck, c*u*p	k *k*ill
ʊ l*oo*k, b*oo*k	g *g*ive
ə *a*nnoy, work*er*	tʃ *ch*in
ɜː f*ir*st, g*ir*l	dʒ *j*am
uː p*oo*l, t*oo*	f *f*ive
ɔː c*au*ght, b*a*ll	v *v*isit
iː b*ee*f, dr*ea*m	θ *th*ing
ɑː f*ar*, f*a*st	ð *th*at
aɪ tr*y*, t*i*me	s *s*oon
aʊ n*ow*, br*ow*n	z *z*one
əʊ *o*ld, b*oa*t	ʃ *s*ure
ɪə d*ea*r, f*ea*r	ʒ trea*s*ure
eɪ gr*ea*t, f*a*te	h *h*at
eə p*ai*r, h*ai*r	m *m*oney
ɔɪ b*oy*, c*oi*n	n *n*ine
ʊə p*oo*r, t*ou*r	ŋ bri*ng*
	l *l*ove
	r *r*ead
	j *y*et
	w *w*et

3 – Quelques règles de prononciation

■ **Prononciation de la terminaison en *-ed*** (prétérit et participe passé)

→ Elle se prononce /ɪd/ après *t* ou *d* : *wanted* /'wɒntɪd/, *provided* /prə'vaɪdɪd/

→ Elle se prononce /t/ après /f/, /k/, /s/, /ʃ/, /p/, /θ/ (consonnes sourdes) : *baked* /beɪkt/, *laughed* /lɑːft/

→ Elle se prononce /d/ après les voyelles et les consonnes sonores (/b/, /d/, /g/, /m/, /n/, /ŋ/, /l/, /r/, /v/) : *prayed* /preɪd/, *conceived* /kən'siːvd/

■ **Prononciation de la terminaison en *-s*** (pluriel, génitif, troisième personne du singulier)

→ Elle se prononce /s/ après les consonnes sourdes (/p/, /t/, /k/, /f/, /θ/): *takes* /teɪks/, *pets* /pets/

→ Elle se prononce /z/ après les voyelles et les consonnes sonores (/b/, /d/, /g/, /m/, /n/, /ŋ/, /l/, /r/, /v/) : *games* /geɪmz/, *guys* /gaɪz/

→ Elle se prononce /ɪz/ après /s/, /z/, /ʃ/, /ʒ/: *damages* /'dæmɪdʒɪz/, *bushes* /bʊʃɪz/

■ **Voyelle + consonne finale** ⎤
Voyelle + deux consonnes ⎦ → **voyelle brève**
Voyelle + une seule consonne + voyelle → voyelle longue ou diphtongue

→ *kit* /kɪt/ *kitten* /kɪtn/ *kite* /kaɪt/
mat /mæt/ *matter* /mætə/ *mate* /meɪt/

Ceci explique pourquoi on redouble ou non la consonne finale des verbes lorsqu'on ajoute *-ed* ou *-ing* :
cut → *cutting* (pour garder le son ʌ)
hide → *hiding* (pour garder le son aɪ)

Pour la règle de redoublement ou non de la consonne finale, P. 196

Il y a cependant de nombreuses exceptions à cette règle de prononciation parmi des mots courants: *to live* /lɪv/ *prison* /'prɪzn/ *manage* /'mænɪdʒ/

> Attention à certaines lettres qui ne se prononcent pas:
> – k, lorsqu'il est suivi d'un n : *(k)night*, *(k)nee*, *(k)nock*
> – p, lorsqu'il est suivi d'un s en début de mot : *(p)sychology*, *(p)salm*
> – le n final après m : *autum(n)*
> – le b final après un m : *bom(b)*, ou le b avant un t: *dou(b)t*
> – et dans certains mots :
> • le d : *han(d)kerchief*, *gran(d)ma*
> • le t : *lis(t)en*, *Chris(t)mas*
> • le l devant certaines consonnes : *wou(l)d*, *ta(l)k*
> • le w : *(w)hom*, *(w)rite*

■ **Le h est toujours aspiré en début de mot**, avec quatre exceptions (*hour, honest, heir, honour*) *house* /haʊz/ (h aspiré) mais *hour* /aʊə/ (h non aspiré)

4 – L'ACCENT DE MOT

Dès qu'un mot anglais a plus d'une syllabe, l'une de ces syllabes est plus accentuée que les autres. En phonétique on la marque à l'aide d'un accent placé devant cette syllabe. Le mot *airplane*, par exemple, sera transcrit phonétiquement comme suit : /'eəpleɪn/
On trouve parfois un deuxième accent lorsque le mot est long. Il est indiqué par un accent avant la syllabe, en bas. *justification* : /ˌdʒʌstɪfɪ'keɪʃn/
Cet accent de mot est essentiel pour se faire comprendre car il entraîne le plus souvent une transformation du son des voyelles des syllabes non accentuées. Ces syllabes non accentuées sont souvent réduites, tendant vers le son /ə/ ou le son /ɪ/.
Comparez, par exemple, les différences dans les sons vocaliques du verbe et du nom écrits de même façon mais accentués de façon différente (le nom sur la première syllabe, le verbe sur la seconde) :
to record (l'accent est sur la deuxième syllabe) : /rɪ'kɔːd/
a record (l'accent est sur la première syllabe) : /'rekɔːd/
to accept : /ək'sept/
acceptation : /ˌæksep'teɪʃn/
to desert : /dɪ'zɜːt/
a desert : /'dezət/

Lorsqu'on apprend du vocabulaire, il est donc essentiel d'apprendre en même temps la prononciation des mots et la place des accents.
Il existe quelques règles qui permettent de savoir quelles syllabes sont accentuées ou non.

■ D'une façon générale, **les préfixes et les suffixes** ne sont pas accentués :
***dis**order* : /dɪs'ɔːdə/
dis**astr**ous : /dɪ'zɑːstrəs/
***un**rest* : /ʌn'est/
*lone**liness*** : /'ləʊnlinəs/
***mis**understand* : /ˌmɪsʌndə'stænd/

> **Exception :** les suffixes en *-ese, -ee, -eer, -ette, -oon, -oo, -teen, -esque, -aire*, qui eux prennent l'accent :
> *referee* : /ˌrefə'riː/
> *Chinese* : /ˌtʃaɪ'niːz/
> *majorette* : /ˌmeɪdʒə'ret/
> *seventeen* : /ˌsevn'tiːn/

■ **Le *a* que l'on trouve au début de nombreux verbes, prépositions ou adjectifs**, n'est pas accentué et se prononce /ə/
along : /ə'lɒŋ/ *awake* : /ə'weɪk/ *avoid* : /ə'vɔɪd/ *above* : /ə'bʌv/

■ L'accent tombe sur la **syllabe qui précède un suffixe en *-ity/-ion/-ious/-ient/-ial/-iar/-ic/-ical/-ican/-ify***
familiarity : /fəˌmɪlɪ'ærətɪ/
translation : /træns'leɪʃn/
institution : /ˌɪnstɪ'tjuːʃn/
political : /pə'lɪtɪkl/
regularity : /ˌregju'lærətɪ/
imagination : /ɪˌmædʒɪ'neɪʃn/
revision : /rɪ'vɪʒn/
economical : /ˌiːkə'nɒmɪkl/

Attention à ces exceptions : *'politics, 'Catholic, 'Arabic*

■ L'accent tombe **sur la syllabe qui précède les suffixes *-logy/-graphy/-sophy/-omy***
psychology : /saɪ'kɒlədʒɪ/ *geography* : /dʒi'ɒgrəfɪ/

■ L'accent tombe **deux syllabes avant les suffixes *-ate/-ize/-fy/-ism***
alternate : /'ɔːltəneɪt/
S'il n'y a qu'une syllabe avant *-ate*, l'accent tombe sur *-ate* dans les verbes seulement :
rotate : /rəʊ'teɪt/ *climate* : /'klaɪmət/

■ L'accent secondaire tombe deux syllabes avant l'accent principal (syllabes accentuées et non accentuées alternant ainsi) : *constitutional* : /ˌkɒnstɪ'tjuːʃnl/

■ Dans un nom composé, c'est d'ordinaire le premier mot uniquement qui se trouve accentué :
'bathing-suit 'phone box 'milk bottle
Mais le second mot porte l'accent principal
– lorsque le premier mot le qualifie comme le ferait une proposition relative :
→ *a travelling 'salesman* (= *a salesman who travels*)
– lorsque le premier mot décrit la matière dont le second est fait:
→ *silk 'shirt*

■ Lorsqu'un adjectif précède un nom, c'est d'ordinaire le second terme, le nom, qui porte l'accent principal. Comparez :
→ *a 'darkroom; a dark'room*

5 – L'ACCENT DE PHRASE

À l'intérieur d'une phrase, certains mots peuvent être moins accentués que d'autres. Il s'agit :
– de la plupart des auxiliaires, articles, pronoms et déterminants
→ *Did you go to the theatre?*
/ðə/
– des prépositions (sauf en début et en fin de phrase) :
→ *She wanted to pay. Whom did you give it to?*
/tə/ /tuː/
→ *"Where did you take it from?" "I took it from the drawer."*
/frɒm/ /frəm/
Mais les particules adverbiales restent accentuées. Comparez :
→ *Put on your coat.* (On accentue *on*.) *The book you put on the table.* (*on* n'est pas accentué.)
– des modaux, sauf à la forme négative, en fin ou en tête de phrase ou lorsqu'il y a insistance.
→ *I can you lend me one pound, if you like, of course, I can.*
/kən/ /kæn/

– *That* relatif n'est pas accentué. Mais le pronom démonstratif l'est.

→ *That wasn't the man that I saw!*
/ðæt/ /ðət/

L'accent de phrase tombe donc sur les mots les plus importants, c'est-à-dire ceux qui apportent le plus d'information.

→ *He ˈlocked the ˈdoor and ˈleft.*

→ *Have you ˈgot that comˈputer ˈgame?*

Lorsqu'on parle, la voix tend donc à sauter de syllabe accentuée en syllabe accentuée, passant rapidement sur les autres syllabes.

→ *ˈTell the ˈteacher that the ˈroom is ˈclosed.*

Quelques formes fortes et faibles des mêmes mots

	forme forte	forme faible		forme forte	forme faible
am	æm	əm	but	bʌt	bət
be	biː	bɪ	of	ɒv	əv
been	biːn	bɪn	to	tuː	tə
can	kæn	kən	as	æz	əz
have	hæv	həv	for	fɔː	fə
does	dʌz	dəz	me	miː	mɪ
was	wɒz	wəz	them	ðem	ðəm
could	kʊd	kəd	she	ʃiː	ʃɪ
must	mʌst	məst	some	sʌm	səm
should	ʃʊd	ʃəd	than	ðæn	ðən

6 – L'INTONATION

■ On utilise une intonation descendante :

– dans les phrases affirmatives, négatives et dans les ordres.

→ *I love this kind of weather.* ↘

– dans les questions commençant par *WH* :

→ *What shall we do afterwards?* ↘

– dans les tags, lorsqu'il n'y a pas vraiment question :

→ *You'll come, won't you?* ↘

– dans les exclamations :

→ *How tired you look!* ↘

– dans les impératifs :

→ *Come at once!* ↘

■ On utilise une intonation montante :

– Dans les questions qui demandent une réponse *Yes* ou *No* :

→ *Did you take your passport?* ↗

– Dans les tags, lorsqu'il s'agit d'une véritable question.
→ *He didn't apologize, did he?* ↗
– Dans les questions qui expriment l'incrédulité, le doute, la demande de répétition :
→ *Did you say she was drunk?* ↗

↗ exercices

1 Mettez l'accent dans les mots qui suivent.

a suspect	to suspect	an insult	to insult	balloon
biology	biological	philosophy	opinion	constitution
precious	industry	industrial	mathematics	republican
demonstrate	discriminate	career	a democrat	democratic
a rebel	to rebel	comedy	comedian	democratisation

2 Dans les phrases qui suivent, décidez si les mots en italiques ont une forme forte ou réduite. Soulignez ceux qui ont une forme forte.

I *could* never have done it. *Could* you?
"We'll come *for* lunch then." "No, not *for* lunch, after lunch."
"I've lost my keys. Do you know where they *are*?" "Yes, they*'re* in the kitchen."
That's not what I said. I said *that* he should have called before he came.

V Découvrir la culture

I English as a world language

English as a native language *(langue maternelle)*, or as a second language, is spoken by some 400 million people, which makes it the world's second language, Chinese being spoken by between two and three times as many people. But English is also the official language of a number of other countries (for example, it is one of the two official languages throughout India, it is an official language in some African countries such as Nigeria or Ghana) – a legacy *(héritage)* from Britain's colonial empire. Most of all, English is quickly turning into an international language used all over the world for commerce and business. The widespread use *(large utilisation)* of the internet, where some 90 % of the sites use English, can only speed up this process *(accélérer ce processus)*.

The countries in which English is a native, official or second language:

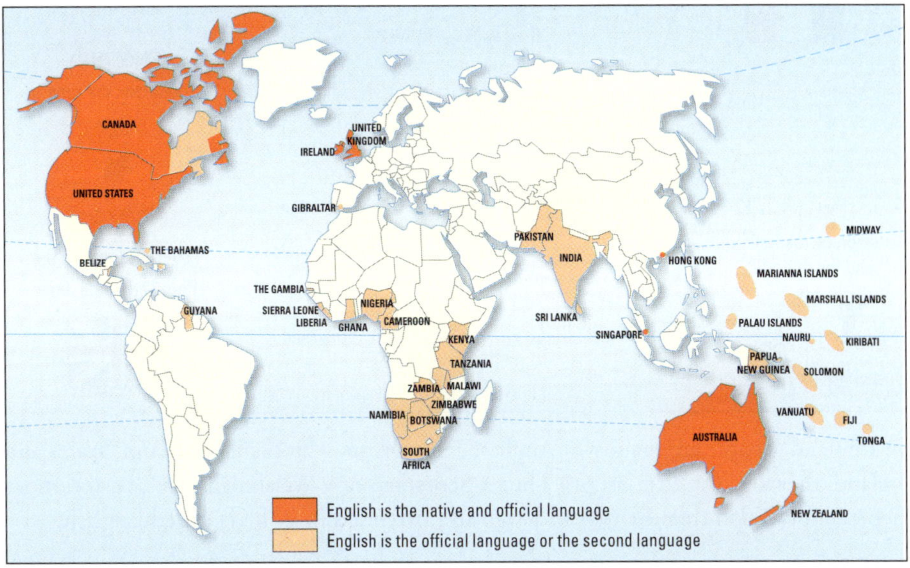

II The United Kingdom and the Republic of Ireland

1. A few geographical and political distinctions

- **the British Isles** = 2 islands: Great Britain + the whole of Ireland
  = A + B + C + D + E
- **Great Britain:** the larger of the two islands
  = A (England) + B (Wales) + C (Scotland)

- **The United Kingdom is the political country:**
  Great Britain + Northern Ireland (or Ulster) (A, B, C and D)
- **The Republic of Ireland** (E) is another political entity.
- **Poetic names:**

Albion: England (from albus, white in Latin, because of England's white cliffs (*falaises*))
Caledonia: Scotland
Cambria: Wales

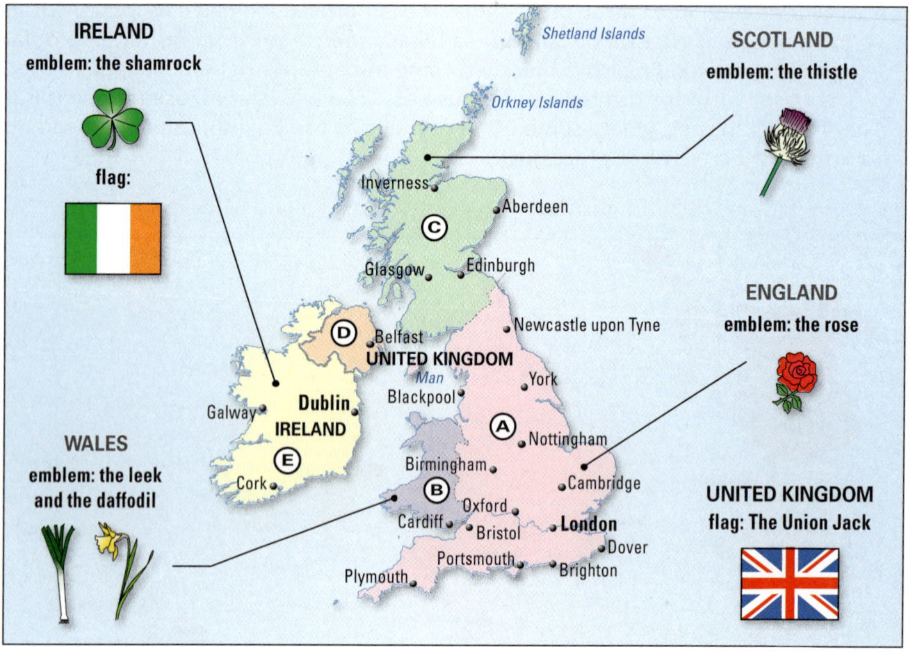

In England, people are mainly of Anglo-Saxon origin, whereas in Scotland, Wales and Ireland, they are of Celtic origin. Thus a Scotsman or a Welshman may well feel more Scottish or Welsh than British and even feel offended if (s)he is called English.

2. Emblems, patron saints and flags

	Emblems	Patron saints	Flags	
England	– The rose because it has always been linked to England. – The bulldog is another English emblem.	St George	The large red cross of St George on a white background	

Wales	– The leek *(le poireau)* because it was worn in caps *(porté sur le chapeau)* as a sign of identi-fication in battles, – The daffodil *(la jonquille)*, – The dragon.	St David		
Scotland	– The thistle *(le chardon)*, because it it said to have helped the Scots in battle.	St Andrew	The white diagonal cross of St Andrew on a blue background	All united in the Union Jack (a jack is a flag)
Ireland	– The shamrock (le trèfle), because St Patrick is said to have used it to explain the mystery of the Trinity. – The harp is another emblem.	St Patrick	The narrow diagonal red cross of St Patrick on a white background	

- The **flag of the Irish Republic** is green, white and orange:

– green for Irish Catholics
– orange for Northern Irish Protestants
– white as a symbol of peace between them

3. Royal anthem

There is no official national anthem *(hymne national)* in the United Kingdom, but the first stanza *(strophe)* of the royal anthem GOD SAVE THE QUEEN/KING is sung on official occasions. It is an anonymous patriotic song, first sung in 1745, when King George II defeated "Bonnie Prince Charlie", the pretender *(prétendant)* to the throne.

God save our gracious Queen
Long live our noble Queen,
God save the Queen!
Send her victorious,
Happy and glorious,
Long to reign over us:
God save the Queen!

Rule Britannia is a sort of unofficial national anthem. Written in 1740 by James Thomson and set to music by Arne, it is a hymn to the British empire and its ships, which ruled the ocean. Here are the first two stanzas:

Rule Britannia

When Britain first at Heav'n[1]'s command
Arose from out the azure main[2];
This was the charter[3] of the land,
And guardian angels sang this strain[4];
Rule, Britannia! Britannia, rule the waves:
Britons never will be slaves.

The nations not so blest[5] as thee,
Shall in their turns to tyrants fall;
While thou shalt[6] flourish[7] great and free,
The dread[8] and envy of them all.
Rule, Britannia! Britannia, rule the waves...

1. **Heav'n:** Heaven *(le ciel)*. 2. **main:** ocean. 3. **charter:** *charte*. 4. **strain:** *accords, accents (musicaux)*. 5. **blest:** blessed *(béni)*. 6. **thou shalt:** you will. 7. **flourish:** *prospérer*. 8. **dread:** terror.

4. Geography

■ **The counties** *(comtés)* **of the United Kingdom:**

The Home Counties: the counties around London (Kent, Surrey, Berkshire, Buckinghamshire, Hertfordshire, Middlesex, Essex).

The Shires: the counties of the Midlands whose names end in "shire", and which are famous for hunting *(la chasse)* (e.g. Leicestershire, Northamptonshire).

The British economy went through a radical reconversion after World War II. The traditional industries based on coal and iron (in The Midlands, South Wales, Lancashire) have gradually given way to service industries (*secteur tertiaire*) and to industries linked to the exploitation of the North Sea Oil (*pétrole de la Mer du Nord*). This has led to an increased North-South divide.

5. MAJOR DATES IN BRITISH HISTORY

■ The Romans

55-54 BC Julius Caesar invades England, which was then inhabited by a number of Celtic groups. The Roman occupation lasts for some 400 years, during which many roads and cities such as London (then called Londinium) are built. In 122, Hadrian (the Roman emperor) has a 185-kilometre wall built from coast to coast in the north of England to mark the northern boundary (= frontier) of the Roman empire and as a protection against tribes *(tribus)* from the north (the Picts in particular).

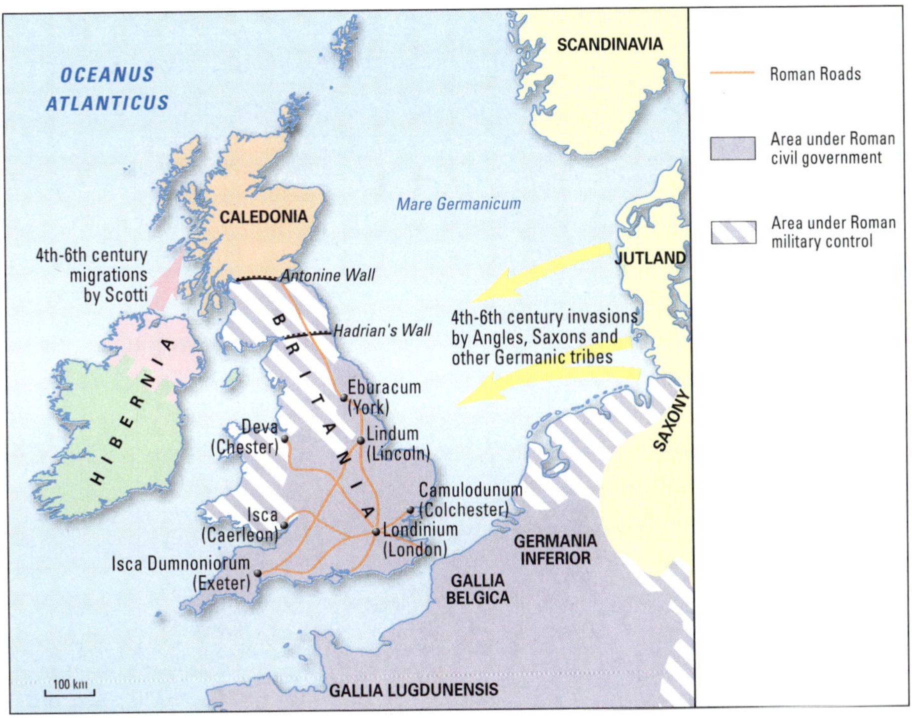

■ The Saxons

450-550 The Saxon Conquest. It follows the invasion of northern England by Picts and Scots, and the gradual withdrawal *(retrait)* from England of the Romans, who needed to defend Gaul. The new English settlers *(colons)* come from Germany (the Jutes and the Saxons) and from Denmark (the Angles). They establish the English language.

597 St Augustine begins converting the English to Christianity.

865 Danish Vikings invade the north of England.

871 Alfred the Great becomes king of Wessex (the southern part of England). He creates laws, sheriffs, a navy *(marine)*, encourages the conversion to Christianity and fights back the Vikings. The kingdom is divided into shires *(comtés)*. He also encourages the development of education.

1042 Edward the Confessor becomes king of England.

The Normans

1066 William the Conqueror (Duke of Normandy) defeats *(bat)* King Harold at the Battle of Hastings and becomes King of England. This is followed by the gradual invasion of England by the Normans.

1086 The Domesday Book lists all property *(propriétés)* and land in England. William I gradually establishes a feudal hierarchical structure *(structure hiérarchique féodale)* by giving land to barons, who themselves grant (give) some to knights *(chevaliers)*. The official language becomes French.

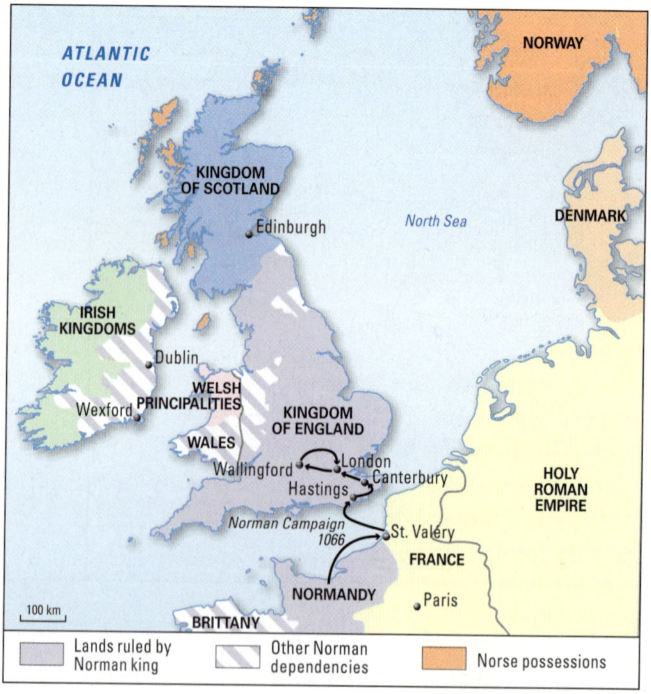

1100 Henry I becomes king. He unites the Saxons and the Normans, and rules over a kingdom which stretches *(s'étend)* from France (Normandy) to the north of England. Henry II rules over an even larger kingdom which also includes Anjou, Maine and Touraine. He reforms the system of laws, creating "Common Law", which bases decisions on customs *(coutumes)* rather than on a set of written laws.

1203-1204 Loss of Normandy and of most French land

1215 John Lackland *(Jean sans Terre)* is forced to sign the Magna Carta *(La Grande Charte)*, which establishes the protection of individuals against arbitrary imprisonment and the power of the king. All individuals now have a right to a "fair trial" *(un jugement équitable)*.

1284 Wales becomes part of the kingdom.

1295 Edward I summons his "Model Parliament", which a few decades later will separate into two chambers: the nobility and the clergy will form the House of Lords, whereas the House of Commons will be for representatives of towns and counties.

1305 Scottish revolt led by Robert Bruce: Scotland becomes independent.

1332 First meeting of Parliament, created by Edward I.

A Hundred and fifty years of war

1337-1453 The Hundred Years'War, a long conflict for the domination of France. England first holds large territories in France (1420: Treaty of Troyes), but France has gradually gained back its land (except for Calais) by the end of the war, in 1453.

1455-1485 The War of the Roses. It sets the House of York (whose emblem is the white rose) against the House of Lancaster (the red rose), rivals for the throne of England. In 1485, Henry Tudor (a Lancaster) marries Elizabeth of York, thus bringing unity again to England.

The Tudors and the Stuarts

1534 Act of Supremacy: King Henry VIII breaks with Rome in order to divorce his first wife (Catherine of Aragon) and marry Anne Boleyn, his mistress: he declares himself "Supreme Head of the English Church and Clergy". This is the starting point of the Reformation. Protestantism replaces the Catholic religion (the official religion before), the monasteries are closed and their land taken.

1558-1603 Reign of Elizabeth I. Anglicanism (a via media between Catholicism and Protestantism) becomes the established religion. Although Catholicism is still banned *(interdit)*, there is relative stability after a period of religious extremism (Edward VI's persecutions against the Catholics, then Mary I's persecutions against the Protestants.) Only Scotland remains outside the Anglican compromise, the radical John Knox being at the origin of the Scottish Presbyterian church (election of priests, belief in predestination), whose puritan

members were to oppose the Anglican church and the absolute power of the monarch. These dissidents were persecuted and many fled *(s'enfuirent)* abroad. Elizabeth's reign is a long one marked by the fear of an invasion to put a Catholic sovereign onto the throne.
In 1587, Mary Stuart (Queen of Scots) is executed for treason, and in 1588 the Spanish Armada, ships sent to invade Britain by the Catholic king of Spain, is defeated. The reign of Elizabeth is also a period of cultural development (music, poetry, the theatre – Shakespeare) and of maritime power.

1603 James VI of Scotland becomes James I of England. He believes in the Divine Right of Kings and his reign is marked by a growing conflict with Parliament.

1605 The Gunpowder plot *(la conspiration des poudres)* is a conspiracy by a few Catholics to blow up *(faire sauter)* the Houses of Parliament while the king and the whole government are inside. The plot is betrayed *(trahi, révélé)* and the conspirators executed. The discovery of the plot is still celebrated today on Guy Fawkes Day (November 5th) when bonfires *(feux de joie)* are lit and effigies of Guy Fawkes, the leader of the plot, burnt.

1611 Publication of the Authorized Version of the Bible (or King James's Bible.)

■ Two revolutions

1625-1649 Charles I succeeds James I. He increasingly tries to rule without Parliament, but in 1628 has to sign the Petition of Right (no taxes can be raised without the consent of Parliament).

1642-1648 The Civil War pits the supporters of Parliament (Puritans or Roundheads, led by Oliver Cromwell, and helped by the Scots) against the supporters of King Charles I (Cavaliers). The latter *(ces derniers)* are finally defeated.

1649 Charles I is executed and the monarchy is abolished.

1653-1658 The Commonwealth (a republic) is established, led by Cromwell, who has the title of Lord Protector of England, Scotland and Ireland, then by his son.

1660 Parliament calls Charles II (who was in exile in France) back to the throne. He increasingly tries to rule without Parliament, which was too hostile to royal power.

1665 The Great Plague *(peste)* in London

1666 The Great Fire of London

1679 Habeas Corpus Act (no imprisonment without trial)

1685 James II, a converted Catholic succeeds to the throne.

1688 The Glorious Revolution: the crown is taken from the Catholic James II and given to William III. The principle of Constitutional monarchy is established.

1689 The Bill of Rights *(Déclaration des droits)* establishes a parliamentary democracy by restraining *(en restreignant)* the power of the monarch.

1701 The Act of Settlement makes it impossible for a Catholic king to come onto the throne.

1707 Union between England and Scotland

The eighteenth century

1714 Beginning of the Hanoverian Dynasty *(Dynastie de Hanovre)*. Since Queen Anne, the last Stuart monarch, has no descendants, George I, belonging to the dynasty of the Electors of Hanover and a descendant of James I, comes to the throne. He is succeeded by his son, George II, and by the latter's grandson, George III. The principles of constitutional monarchy mean that the executive is in the hands of the king and his Cabinet, whose powers are restrained by Parliament, itself also responsible for voting laws. Two main parties appear at the beginning of the century: the Tories (more conservative) and the Whigs (more liberal).

1745 Jacobite rebellion defeated (the Jacobites were the supporters of James II's descendants).

1764 Invention of the Spinning Jenny *(machine à filer le coton)*. The industrial revolution begins to change the face of the country. The invention of the steam engine *(la machine à vapeur)* by Watt in1785 leads to the rapid development of railways. Canals are built.

1776 The American colonies become independent.

1801 Act of Union creating the United Kingdom of Great Britain and Ireland

1815 England (with the Duke of Wellington) defeats Napoleon at Waterloo.

1829 Catholics obtain freedom of worship (liberté religieuse).

1832 The first Reform Act extends the right to vote to the middle class.

The Victorian age

1837-1901 Reign of Queen Victoria. It is marked by the expansion of the empire and by Puritanism (strictness and austerity in social and religious matters).

1851 The Great Exhibition shows displays from countries all over the world, but is mainly a presentation of the latest technological achievements of British engineering.

1854-1856 Crimean War

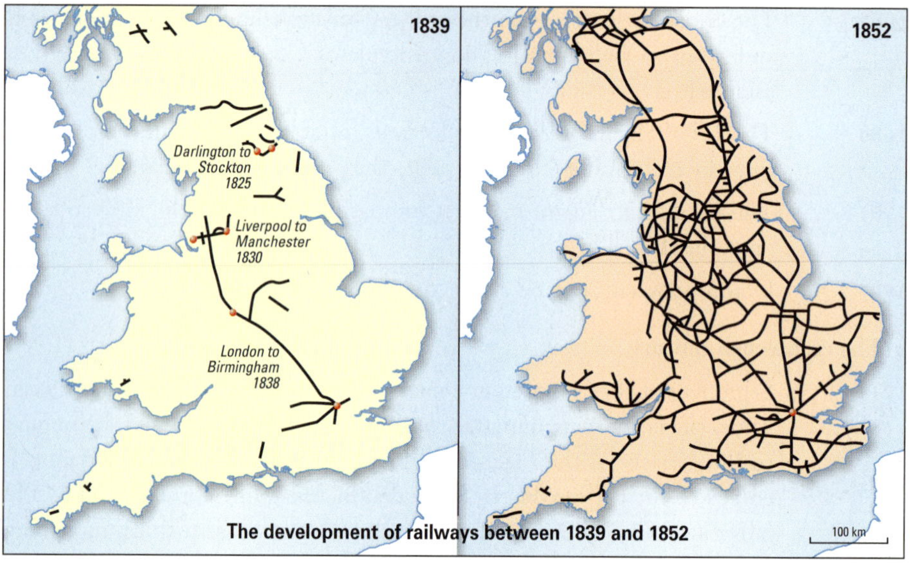

The development of railways between 1839 and 1852

1868	Creation of the Trade Union Congress *(fédération des syndicats britanniques)*
1870	Education Act (primary education becomes free for all)
1872	Ballot Act (voting becomes secret)
1876	Queen Victoria becomes Empress of India.
1899-1902	Boer War (in South Africa)

The twentieth century

1911	Parliament Act (The Lords lose their power of veto.)
1914	Britain enters World War I.
1916	Easter Rising in Dublin (P. 297-298)
1919	Women obtain the right to vote, after much campaigning on the part of the suffragettes.
1921	Ireland is divided into two. (P. 297-298)
1926	General strike *(grève générale)*, the result of a period of industrial crisis and unemployment *(chômage)*.
1928	Representation of the People Act: the vote is given to all men and women above 21.
1929	Beginning of the Great Depression: bankruptcies *(faillites)* and unemployment
1936	Edward VIII becomes king, but abdicates the same year to marry an American divorcee.
1939	Britain declares war on Germany. Led by Winston Churchill (P. 303), Britain shows courage and determination in the war against Nazi Germany.

1940 The Battle of Britain (air battles, Germany bombing strategic positions in Britain to prepare for an invasion); the Blitz (air raids on London). The war effort (rationing *(rationnement)*, women working in industry) helps to create a spirit of solidarity.

1944 D-Day (Allied forces land in France)

1945 End of World War II. The Labour government creates the Welfare State *(l'État-providence)*, which institutes the National Health Service *(Sécurité Sociale)*, welfare payments *(prestations sociales)*, unemployment benefits *(allocations de chômage)*, education for all.

1947-1949 Many former colonies (such as India, Pakistan, Kenya) reach independence.

1949 The UK becomes a member of NATO *(OTAN)*.

1951-1964 Conservative governments (Churchill, Eden, Macmillan, Home)

1964-1970 Labour government (Wilson): the death penalty is abolished, the Abortion Act legalizes termination of pregnancy and the Divorce Act liberalizes Divorce laws.

1969 Beginning of "The Troubles" in Northern Ireland (**P. 298**)

1973 Britain and Ireland enter the Common Market.

1979 During the "winter of discontent", many strikes *(grèves)* paralyze Britain.

1979-1990 The first woman Prime Minister, Margaret Thatcher (nicknamed "The Iron Lady"), introduces liberal policies: reduction of public spending, strict law and order policies *(mesures strictes d'ordre public)*, many privatizations, curbing the unions'power *(réduction du pouvoir des syndicats)*.

1982 Falklands War *(Guerre des Malouines)*, a conflict between Argentina and Britain after the Argentinians invaded the Falkland Islands. The war is short and won by Britain.

1994 The Channel Tunnel links Britain and France.

1997 Tony Blair becomes Prime Minister. Breaking with the traditional Labour doctrines, Tony Blair calls his party New Labour. It is often described as a "Third Way" between left and right, between social democracy and neo-liberalism: it is based on pragmatism and defends family values and social justice within a competitive market.

1999 Beginning of the reform of the House of Lords: hereditary peers (pairs héréditaires) can no longer sit in the House of Lords, which will consist mainly of appointed members. A Scottish Parliament and a Welsh Assembly are created, giving more direct power of decision to the people of these regions.

2003-2004 Britain sends troops to Iraq.

2005 Tony Blair is re-elected for a third term. Terrorist attacks cause huge explosions in London.

6. The government and the monarchy

The United Kingdom is a constitutional monarchy, which means that the powers of the sovereign are limited by those of Parliament.

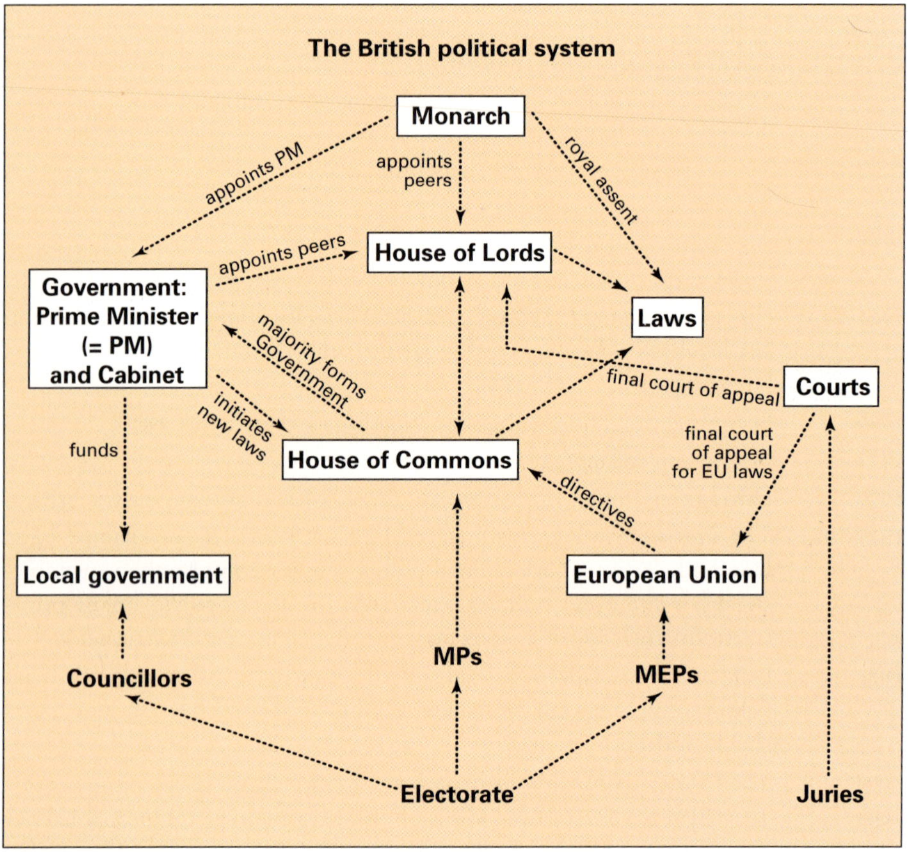

■ The Monarch

The sovereign is the Head of State, the Head of the Church of England and the Head of the Commonwealth. The British monarchy is hereditary, with male heirs *(héritiers)* having precedence over female heirs.

The functions of the sovereign are in fact limited and mainly symbolic since he or she must be politically impartial:

– appointing *(nommer)* the Prime Minister (but (s)he must be the leader of the party which won the general elections)

– creating new peers, appointing senior civil servants *(hauts fonctionnaires)* and granting honour *(octroyer des distinctions honorifiques)* (although mostly the result of recommendations)

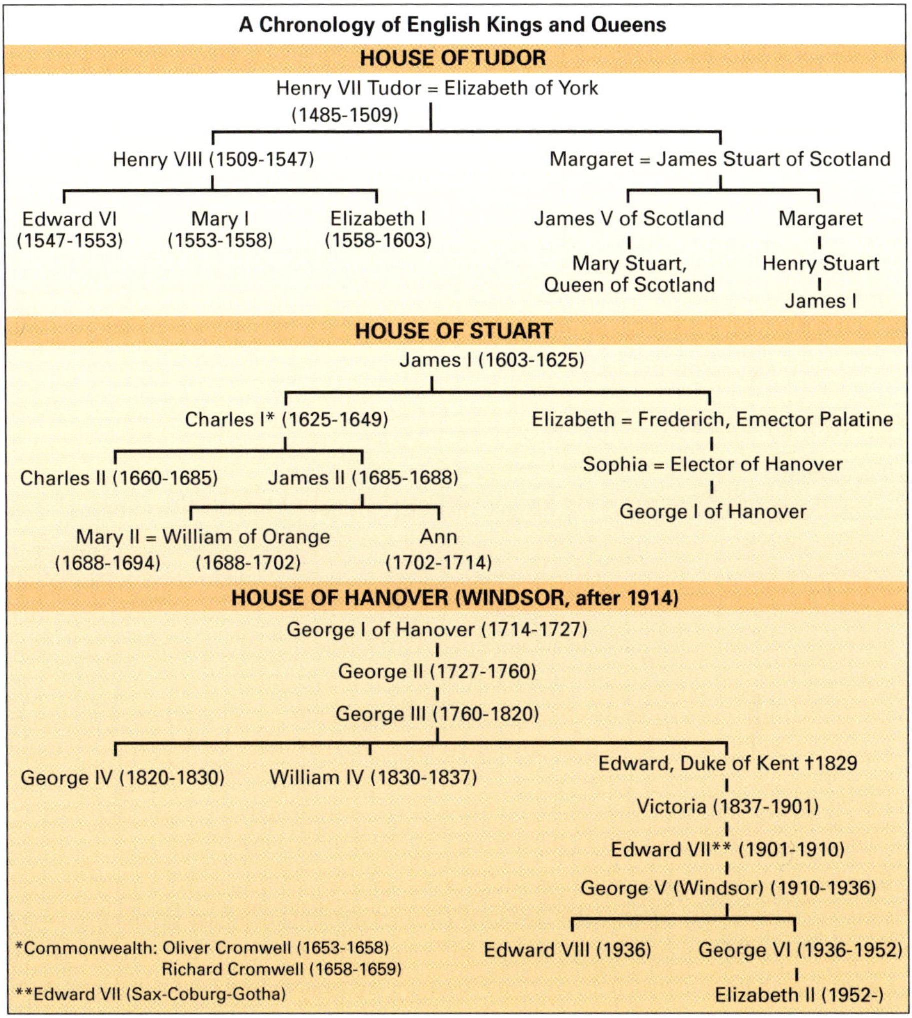

– opening Parliament (but her/his speech is written by the Prime Minister) – the time when the sovereign delivers the formal Speech from the Throne is the only time when (s)he is allowed to enter Parliament.
– signing the acts *(lois)* voted in Parliament
– declaring war & concluding international treaties – but only ratifying what the government decided.

The monarch mainly has a symbolic function as Head of the Commonwealth and representative of the nation, creating cohesion because of her/his popularity. The sovereign is a figurehead *(figure de proue)* who stands above party politics. Royal ceremonies with a great deal of pageantry *(pompe)* such as the State Opening of Parliament or royal visits are hugely popular. The royal family is also very active in a large number of charities.

The Monarchy has often been in crisis recently because of the behaviour of some members of the royal family (marital scandals *(scandales matrimoniaux)*, Prince Charles's divorce, then second marriage), because it is seen as too distant from the people, and because of its cost *(coût)*. However, it has also proved capable of change, for instance when the Queen cut her Civil List *(somme allouée à la famille royale)* in 1993 as a result of public criticism or when she agreed to pay taxes.

■ Britain has no written constitution, but a number of successive acts and laws provide what can be called an **unwritten constitution**: The Act of Supremacy (1534), the Petition of Right (1628), the Habeas Corpus Act (1679), the Bill of Rights (1689), the Act of Settlement (1701), the Act of Union (1707), the Parliament Act (1911). Look at the above chronology for more details.

THE LEGISLATIVE POWER

■ Parliament

It is made up of two houses: the House of Lords and the House of Commons, each providing checks on the other.

– The House of Lords (or Upper House – *Chambre haute*) is made up of non-elected members, called peers *(pairs du royaume)*: hereditary peers, peers appointed for life *(nommés à vie)*, high judicial officers, such as the Lord Chancellor *(ministre de la Justice/Garde des Sceaux)*, archbishops and bishops *(archevêques et évêques)*. But it is in the process of being reformed, with the gradual disappearance of hereditary peers (only 92 now remain in a phase of transition), so as to make it more democratic. Its main functions are to revise bills *(projets de loi)* from the House of Commons, to initiate new legislation and to debate (discuss) current issues *(questions, problèmes d'actualité)*. It is also a final Court of Appeal.

– The House of Commons is elected for a maximum of 5 years. After the General elections *(élections législatives)*, the leader of the party with the largest number of votes becomes Prime Minister. MPs (Members of Parliament) represent the interests of the members of their constituencies *(circonscriptions)*, discuss and vote on new legislation and control the executive (the ministers). A Speaker is elected, to chair *(présider)* all debates. Each party uses Whips to ensure party discipline (for example, making sure that MPs take part in important votes.) The majority party and the opposition sit facing each other.

Members in the House of Commons (30 June 2006)

Labour Party	353	Plaid Cymru	3
Conservative Party	196	Sinn Féin	5
Liberal Democrats	63	Social Democratic and Labour Party	3
Democratic Unionist Party	9	Respect	1
Scottish National Party	6	Independent	2
Ulster Unionist Party	1	+ Speaker and deputies	**Total = 646**

A front-bencher: a member of parliament who is part of the government (or of the shadow cabinet) and sits on the front benches *(banc des ministres)*.
A backbencher: a simple member of parliament.

the PM = the Prime Minister
an MP = a Member of Parliament
an MEP = a Member of the European Parliament

The passing of a bill

The different steps in the passing of a bill (called a bill *(projet de loi)* before it becomes an Act of Parliament *(loi)*):
– First Reading (the text of the bill is given to all members of Parliament to read).
– Second Reading: the bill is discussed, with arguments for and against presented.
– The bill and its implications is studied by a committee of MPs
– Third Reading: the bill is once again discussed in the House of Commons, with some amendments proposed by the committee.
– If approved the bill goes to the House of Lords, where the same steps take place.
– If the House of Lords accepts the bill, it becomes an Act of Parliament and receives "royal assent" *(assentiment royal)*.

EXECUTIVE POWER

The Prime Minister and the Cabinet

Most of the decision-making is in the hands of the Prime Minister and of the Cabinet he or she presides over.
The cabinet consists of the Prime Minister and of some 20 senior ministers. They meet every week and decide on government policy. Here are the names of some important members of the Cabinet:
The Lord Chancellor *(Le ministre de la Justice/Le Garde des Sceaux)*
The Chancellor of the Exchequer *(Le ministre des Finances)*
The Foreign Secretary *(Le ministre des Affaires Étrangères)*
The Home Secretary *(Le ministre de l'Intérieur)*
The Health Secretary *(Le ministre de la Santé)*

Prime Ministers since 1945

Clement Attlee (L) 1945-51
Winston Churchill (C) 1951-55
Anthony Eden (C) 1955-57
Harold Macmillan (C) 1957-63
Sir Alec Douglas-Home (C) 1963-64
Harold Wilson (L) 1964-70
Edward Heath (C) 1970-74
Harold Wilson (L) 1974-76
James Callaghan (L) 1976-79
Margaret Thatcher (C) 1979-90
John Major (C) 1990-97
Tony Blair (L) 1997-

■ **Parties**

There are two main parties which alternate in government:
– the Conservative Party *(Les Conservateurs)*, which traditionally defends right-wing liberal policies (low taxation, free economy, freedom of choice in education),
– the Labour Party *(Les Travaillistes)*, traditionally the party of the working class, defending public ownership and high public spending on social services and education. With his "third way", however, Tony Blair has placed his party, which he calls "New Labour", at the centre of the political spectrum *(éventail politique)*.
– A third party, the Liberal Democratic Party, which is more liberal, has recently played an important part too.

■ **General elections** *(élections législatives)* take place every five years, but the Prime Minister can call for new elections any time before the end of the five years. The age of voting is 18. The voting system used is the simple majority system (also called First-past-the-post System): the candidate who obtains the largest number of votes is elected (which disadvantages small parties and partly explains why only two main parties dominate British politics). The leader of the party which obtains a majority of seats in the House of Commons becomes Prime Minister.
The opposition party forms a Shadow Cabinet *(Cabinet fantôme)*.

7. Population

There are over 60 million inhabitants in Britain. The tendency is for the population to become older, for families to grow smaller, with an increasing number of one-parent families.

■ **Classes**

Class differences are still strongly marked in Britain, appearing mainly through education and accent. Regional speech characteristics practically disappear among the higher classes, who speak RP (Received Pronunciation). Localized accents and dialects become stronger and stronger as one moves down the class scale *(l'échelle des classes)*.
Traditional class distinctions are:
– the upper class (birth, inherited money)
– the middle class (money coming from one's profession)
– the lower middle class,
– the skilled working class *(ouvriers qualifiés)*,
– the unskilled working class.
– the underclass (unemployed, dependent & homeless *(sans abri)* people).
The children of the upper and middle classes remain the most likely to reach a position of power, in government or in business.

■ **Wealth and income** *(richesse et revenus)*

There is a very important gap between the highest incomes and the lowest ones. Among the latter, one finds a high proportion of:

– people from ethnic minorities (as opposed to white people)
– people from the North of England (as opposed to people from the South): one speaks of a North-South divide
– women as opposed to men.

Ethnic minorities

The British population is far more ethnically mixed than it used to be. Ethnic minority groups make up about 7,9 % of the British population.

Population Size (7.9% from a minority ethnic group)

	Total population		Minority ethnic population
	Count	%	%
White	54153898	92.1	n/a
Mixed	677117	1.2	14.6
Asian or Asian British			
Indian	1053411	1.8	22.7
Pakistani	747285	1.3	16.1
Bangladeshi	283063	0.5	6.1
Other Asian	247664	0.4	5.3
Black or Black British			
Black Caribbean	565876	1.0	12.2
Black African	485277	0.8	10.5
Black Other	97585	0.2	2.1
Chinese	247403	0.4	5.3
Other	230615	0.4	5.0
All minority ethnic population	4635296	7.9	100,0
All population	58789194	100,0	n/a

▲ The UK population: by ethnic group, April 2001, British National Statistics (www.statistics.gov.uk)

The Commission for Racial Equality investigates cases of racial discrimination, while the government encourages equal opportunities (*égalité des chances*) in all areas (*domaines*) of work.

8. Religion

The Church of England (or Anglican Church) is the established church in England (*religion officielle d'État*). In Scotland, the established Church is the Church of Scotland.

The sovereign is Head of both the Church of England and the Church of Scotland and appoints *(nomme)* the most senior clergy *(le haut clergé)* of the Church of England, on recommendation of the Prime Minister (twenty-six Church of England bishops sit in the House of Lords).
The fact that the church is a state church means that there are prayers *(prières)* in Parliament, at state ceremonies and at school.
There are no established churches in Wales and Ireland.

The Anglican Church is a compromise between the Catholic Church and the Protestant Churches.
– As in the Catholic Church, it is hierarchical, ruled by bishops *(évêques)*, and above them by two archbishops *(archevêques)*, the archbishop of York and the archbishop of Canterbury, the latter *(ce dernier)* being "Primate of all England".
– Its doctrines are closer to those of the Protestant Churches: they emphasize the importance of the Bible, and reject the Immaculate Conception and the cult of the Saints.
Anglican priests can marry and, since 1981, a number of women priest have been ordained.

There are several tendencies within the Anglican Church:
– High Church is closer to the Catholic Church, and stresses *(insiste sur)* the importance of rituals, sacraments and ceremonies.
– Low Church is closer to the Protestant Churches: it emphasizes *(insiste sur)* the importance of the Bible and prefers simple services and few ornaments.
– Broad Church believes in tolerance and liberalism.

The Church of Scotland is Presbyterian. It is ruled democratically by elected assemblies.

But Britain is also a multi-faith *(multireligieuse)* society, with many other Christian Churches:

Protestant churches	**Other denominations** *(confessions)*	**Catholic Church**	**Others**
– United Reformed – Church (Presbyterians and Congregationalists) – Baptist Church – Methodist Church	– Quakers – Unitarians – Seventh-Day Adventists – Pentecostal Church – Salvation Army – Jehovah's Witnesses – Christian Scientists	– Catholic Church	– Judaism

Britain has also many Muslims *(musulmans)*, Hindus, Sikhs and Buddhists.

9. THE MEDIA

Fleet Street (the street in the City where most newspapers used to be printed) is still used metonymically for the press, even though newspapers have now moved outside central London.

The British traditionally read many papers. A difference is made between the quality press (the more serious newspapers) and the popular press, which devotes most of their pages to sensational news (*nouvelles à sensation*). The difference used to be one of size (*taille*) too, the quality press consisting of broad-sheet newspapers (*journaux grand format*) and the popular press of tabloids (half the size of broadsheets), but this distinction is disappearing as most newspapers are now moving to the smaller size. Often attacked for intruding on the private lives of people (*s'ingérer dans la vie privée des gens*), the press has adopted a code of practice in order to try and self-regulate itself.

Papers	Political leaning, July 2006	Circulation (*tirage*)
Quality dailies		
The Times	Centre/Centre Right	656,862
The Guardian	Centre Left	380,211
The Daily Telegraph	Conservative	900,158
The Independent	Centre/Centre Left	241,660
The Financial Times	Libertarian	425,000
Quality Sunday papers		
The Observer	Left-wing	470,762
The Sunday Times	Centre/Centre Right	1,314,090
The Sunday Telegraph	Conservative	645,431
The Independent on Sunday	Centre/Centre Left	210,207
Popular dailies		
The Daily Mail	Right-wing	2,340,255
The Daily Express	Right-wing	844,729
The Sun	Right-wing/populist but has supported New Labour since 1997	3,148,700
The Daily Star	Right-wing	803,475
The Daily Mirror	Left-wing	1,635,843
The Evening Standard	Centre/Centre Right	309,908
Popular Sunday papers		
News of the World	Right-wing	3,471,415
The People	Populist	821,116
Sunday Express	Right-wing	830,006
Sunday Mirror	Left-wing	1,416,703
The Mail on Sunday	Right-wing	2,316,138
The Daily Star Sunday	Right-wing	406,241

The daily paper *Metro*, distributed free, has over one million daily readers.

A few magazines:
– *The Economist* (Independent/Liberal): political, financial and social topics.
– *The New Statesman* (Labour): political, social and cultural topics.
– *The Spectator* (Conservative): political, social and cultural topics.

The BBC (the British Broadcasting Corporation) is a publicly-funded corporation *(compagnie financée par des fonds publics)*, which broadcasts *(diffuse)* "in the public interest". It has five radio stations (Radio 1, 2, 3, 4 & 5) and two television channels (BBC1 (more popular) & BBC2 (more cultural)) BBC 3 and 4, BBC Parliament and BBC News 24 are for digital reception. It also broadcasts all over the world with the BBC world service. The BBC is politically impartial and does not broadcast any advertising. It is financed by a licence fee *(une redevance)*. There is also a commercial sector (financed by advertising), with ITV (Independent Television) Channels 4 and 5, as well as satellite and cable television.
Sky TV is available with satellite dishes.

10. Education

Education is compulsory *(obligatoire)* until the age of 16.

▪ Schools

• State schools are free and have to follow a National Curriculum (programme obligatoire), with obligatory and optional subjects.
– Comprehensive schools are co-educational (boys and girls together) and open to pupils of all abilities, who are often streamed *(répartis par niveaux)* depending on their level.
– Grammar schools are often more academically-oriented.

• Independent schools are private and often have very good academic records *(résultats scolaires)*. They include public schools, which are expensive, selective, mainly taking their pupils from the upper middle-class – but grants *(bourses)* are given to very bright children whose parents could not afford *(ne pourraient payer)* the tuition fees *(frais de scolarité)*. Preparatory schools prepare pupils for an entrance exam to enter public schools at the age of 13.
The "sacred nine", the nine best-known public schools are: Eton, Harrow, Rugby, Winchester, Westminster, Charterhouse, Shrewsbury, Merchant Taylor's, St Paul's.

Traditionally, British schools lay the stress on *(insistent sur)* sports, team spirit *(l'esprit d'équipe)*, loyalty and the development of character as much as on intellectual abilities. Morning assemblies (when the whole school meet for prayers and information concerning the day ahead), the practise of sports, school uniforms encourage a community spirit. Pupils later often wear their "old school tie" (a tie in the colours of their public school or university) to show their pride in their "alma mater" (the school or university they attended), and become part of an "old boy network" *(réseau)* of pupils or students who attended (went to) the same public school or university and who later keep in touch and help one another professionally.

Types of schools according to age of pupils		
State-funded		
Preschool	Nursery School/ Kindergarten	3 → 5
Primary schools	Primary school	5 → 11
	Infant school	5 → 7
	Junior school	7 → 11
Secondary schools	• Standard secondary school	11 → 18
	• Middle school	9 → 12/14
	Senior comprehensive school	12/14 → 18
	• Secondary school	11 → 16
	Sixth-form college	16 → 18
Independent		
	Preparatory school	
	Boys	7 → 13
	Girls	7 → 10
	Public school	10/13 → 18

Types of schools according to studies	
Comprehensive schools	Open to pupils of all abilities. A wide range of subjects taught.
Grammar schools	Academic studies
Secondary modern schools	Less academic studies
Independent schools	Often very academic

Classes in secondary schools		
Age	**Form**	**Year**
11	First form	6
12	Second form	7
13	Third form	8
14	Fourth form	9
15	Fifth form	10
16	Lower Sixth form	11
17	Upper Sixth form	12

In 1988, a National Curriculum (*programme*) was introduced: 30 % to 40 % of the time is devoted to three core subjects (*disciplines de base*): English, maths and sciences. Students choose among other disciplines for the rest of their studies.

■ Examinations

– GCSEs: you take your GCSEs (General Certificate of Secondary Education) at 16 (at the end of the 5th form), taking exams individually in different subjects. Students usually take from 5 to 8 subjects, which are graded (*notés*) from A down to G.
– A Levels (General Certificate of Education, Advanced levels) are taken at 18, at the end of secondary education. They are usually taken in 3 subjects. The results are important to get into the university of your choice, which might, for instance, require 3 Bs.

■ Universities

They are independent and select their students according to their A-level results. There are four types of universities:
– The old universities: Oxford, Cambridge (England), St Andrews, Glasgow, Aberdeen, Edinburgh (Scotland)
– The redbrick universities (late 19th century): ex: Leeds
– The new universities (built after WWII): ex: the University of Sussex at Brighton
– The former polytechnics (specialized in professional and technical education), which became universities in 1992

The Open University mainly provides correspondence courses for adults.
Most students choose to go to universities away from their homes, and live on campus. Teaching consists of both lectures (for large groups of students) and tutorial (when students meet in very small groups and read their essays to their tutors). Tuition fees *(frais de scolarité)* have recently been introduced and many students have to borrow money *(emprunter de l'argent)* in order to pay for their studies and lodgings. But student grants *(bourses)* are also given to students coming from poorer backgrounds.

Diplomas:
– BA = Bachelor of Arts *(équivalent de la licence littéraire)*
– BSc = Bachelor of Science *(équivalent de la licence scientifique)*
– MA = Master of Arts *(équivalent du Mastère)*
– MSc = Master of Science
– PhD = Doctor of Philosophy *(doctorat)*

11. Ireland

MAJOR DATES IN THE HISTORY OF IRELAND:

Conquests

432 Saint Patrick brings Christianity to Ireland, previously (= before) a Celtic country.

795 Viking invasions

12th century The Anglo Normans conquer Ireland. Henry II, the British king, becomes Lord of Ireland. A parliament is established in Dublin.

Under English domination

1541 Henry VIII brings the reformation to Ireland and is confirmed as King of Ireland by the Irish Parliament. English Protestants are sent to Ireland and colonise it. But the country remains essentially catholic.

1594-1603 Catholic Irish rebellion led by the Earl of Tyrone

17th century The best land is given to English settlers *(colons)*, thus ensuring *(garantir)* that the country remains in British hands.

1649 Cromwell crushes *(réprime)* an Irish rebellion, with massacres and further confiscation of land.

1690 The Catholic James II, having lost his throne after the Glorious Revolution, tries to recover it (= get it back) with the help of France and Ireland. He is defeated *(battu)* by William of Orange at the Battle of the Boyne.

18th century Further laws restrict the rights *(restreignent les droits)* of Catholics. Most of the land is owned by British landlords *(propriétaires britanniques)*, called "absentee landlords" because they live in Britain and employ poor Irish tenants *(métayers)* to work the land.

1795 The Orange Order is created, with the aim of maintaining Protestant domination over Ireland.

1800 Act of Union: Great Britain and Ireland become the United Kingdom. The Irish Parliament is abolished; Ireland ceases to be a 'colony' and sends MPs to Westminster.

1829 Roman Catholic Emancipation Act: Catholics are given the same rights as Protestants. But they represent a much poorer part of the population.

1845-1849 The Great Famine (due to a potato disease) leads to the death of over a million Irishmen and to massive emigration, mainly to the United States. In the second half of the century, poverty leads to the creation of several organizations to defend tenants'rights and nationalism.

Towards independence

1873 Home Rule League (Home Rule: *l'autonomie*) created by Parnell to try and gain self-government. Until 1916, there is rising tension between the nationalists, who want to get Home Rule, and the Protestants, who want to remain within the United Kingdom.

1916 Easter Rising: a rebellion by Irish Republicans is put down *(réprimer)* by the British army.

1918 The nationalist Party (Sinn Féin), led by de Valera, wins the majority of Irish seats at the election. They proclaim a Republic, with de Valera as President.

1919 Creation of the Irish Republican Army (IRA)

1921 Division of Ireland into Ulster (mainly Protestant) remaining part of the United Kingdom and the Irish Free State, a British dominion.

1937 The Irish Free State becomes a sovereign state, Eire.

1947 Eire becomes the Republic of Ireland. It leaves the Commonwealth in 1949. The Republic of Ireland has become increasingly prosperous since it joined the EEC, then entered the euro zone.

■ Northern Ireland

1968 Beginning of "The Troubles", years of tension and riots *(émeutes)* between the Protestant and Catholic communities in Ulster. The Protestants want to remain in the UK, the Catholics want Ulster to be reunited to the Republic of Ireland. Each community develops paramilitary organisations (the IRA – Irish Republican Army – for the Catholics, the UVF – Ulster Volunteer Force – for the Protestants) which commit acts of terrorism.

> **Nationalists** = the Catholics who want Northern Ireland reunited with the Republic of Ireland.
> **Loyalists** (also called **Orangemen**) = the Protestants who want Northern Ireland to remain part of the United Kingdom.

1972 The British government suspends the Irish parliament and applies *(applique)* far more repressive policies.

1985 Anglo-Irish agreement *(entente)* between the British and Irish governments: it marks the beginning of closer cooperation *(coopération plus étroite)*.

1998 Peace agreements (Good Friday Agreement): a democratic assembly is created to govern Northern Ireland.
Since then the Peace Process has been through ups and downs *(est passé par des hauts et des bas)*, and the assembly has been dissolved *(dissoute)* at times when the two main sides could not agree on issues such as the decommissioning (decommission: *retirer de la circulation*) of arms.

12. Britain and Ireland: a few keywords

Archers, The: A very popular radio serial *(feuilleton radiophonique)*, which has been running since 1951 and relates the life of a family of farmers.

Bank holidays: The official public holidays. In England, they are: Christmas Day, Boxing Day (December 26th), New Year's Day, Good Friday *(Vendredi saint)*, Easter Monday *(lundi de Pâques)*, May Day (the first Monday in May), late spring bank holiday (the last Monday in May), August bank holiday (the last Monday in August). If a bank holiday falls on a Saturday or a Sunday, the holiday is on the following Monday. In Scotland, Easter Monday is not a bank holiday but January 2nd is.

Blue-collar worker: An industrial worker (who wears blue overalls *(bleus de travail)* at work).

Capital punishment: It was abolished in Britain in 1965.

Channel Islands: Jersey and Guernsey are not part of the United Kingdom and have their own government. But they are Crown dependencies, with a Lieutenant-Governor representing the sovereign.

City: The financial district in London, where the Bank of England and the Stock Exchange *(la Bourse)* can be found. It is also called the Square Mile.

Cockney: a Cockney is a working-class person from the east end of London; the word also refers to the way they speak (a Cockney accent).

Common law: Unwritten law which derives from custom *(coutumes)* and the past decisions of judges. It plays an important part in the courts'decisions.

Cool Britannia: A pun on Rule Britannia, the National Anthem, it refers to London as the capital of fashion, the arts and the media. (from the word "cool").

Cricket: A typically English game, played between two teams of eleven on a grass pitch *(terrain)*, with a wicket *(guichet)* at each end. The wickets consist of cross pieces of wood *(bails)* resting on three vertical stumps *(piquets)*. In one of the teams, a bowler *(celui qui lance la balle)* tries to hit the bails defended by the opposite team's batsman *(batteur)*, or to cause the batsman to hit the ball back in such a way that it can be caught before it reaches the ground. The bowler's team is called the fielders; the batsmen's the batsmen. The latter's aim is to score runs, that is to say to run as many times as possible between the wickets (22 metres apart) before the ball is caught. One of the best-known pitches is Lord's in North London. The game is very popular in Britain, where there are matches between counties, as well as all over the Commonwealth with test matches setting Britain against Commonwealth countries.

Downing Street: the street in London where the Prime Minister and the Chancellor of the Exchequer live, at numbers 10 and 11 respectively.

Entente Cordiale: The Franco-British agreement signed in 1904.

Establishment: The word refers to the ruling class: the Queen and her family, the aristocracy, the Cabinet and the members of Parliament as well as the leading figures in the world of finance, diplomacy and in the church.

Gaelic: The word refers to two Celtic languages still spoken in the West of Scotland and in Northern Ireland.

Glass ceiling: The invisible barrier which, in spite of equal opportunities legislation *(lois sur l'égalité des chances)* prevents many women from reaching the same high responsibility jobs as men.

GMT: Greenwich Mean Time: the time of the 0° longitude meridian which passes through the Royal Observatory at Greenwich.

Guy Fawkes Night: On November 5, people celebrate the discovery of the Gunpowder Plot (a conspiracy to blow up the House of Lords and all the government to put a Catholic sovereign on the throne) by burning effigies of Guy Fawkes, the leader of the plot. There are bonfires, fireworks and children collect money, asking for a "penny for the guy".

Hogmanay: the Scottish word for New Year's Eve, which is widely celebrated in Scotland. Auld Lang Syne is sung at midnight.

Should auld acquaintance be forgot[1],
And never brought to mind[2] ?
Should auld acquaintance be forgot,
And days of auld lang syne[3] ?

1. Should old acquaintances (friends) be forgotten.
2. **brought to mind:** remembered.
3. **auld lang syne:** old long ago.

Hunting: Fox-hunting *(chasse au renard)*, a sport where the animal is chased after and killed by hounds *(chiens de meute)*, was an old, popular sport among the aristocracy and landowners *(propriétaires terriens)*. It was banned in 2005.

Jingoism: extreme nationalism, often linked with anti-Europeanism.

Meals and food: The main traditional British meals are:
– Early morning tea: tea drunk before breakfast, often in bed
– Breakfast: a full English breakfast can include porridge, bacon and eggs, sausages, black pudding *(boudin noir)*, mushrooms, tomatoes, sometimes even kippers *(hareng fumé)* or haddock and toast
– Elevenses: coffee or tea with biscuits around 11 a.m.
– Lunch: a sandwich or a meal
– Afternoon tea: tea, cakes and pastries
– Dinner: a full meal, usually including "meat and two veg" *(une viande et deux légumes)*

– In the north of England and Scotland, High Tea sometimes replaces the evening meal. It is taken early (around six p.m.) and consists of a cooked dish or of sandwiches and cakes accompanied by tea.
British food is increasingly being influenced by a large variety of international ethnic food.

NHS (National Health Service): the system of free medical care *(soins médicaux gratuits)* for the entire population, part of the Welfare State instituted by Labour after World War II. Treatment is available to all through local doctors (called GPs, General Practitioners). Although the quality of treatment provided by the NHS is excellent, it has been much criticised recently for long waiting lists (waiting to see a specialist or to undergo an operation) and shortage *(manque)* of beds.

National Lottery: Created in 1994, the National Lottery is hugely popular. It gives money to charities and cultural projects.

National Trust: an independent organisation to protect and preserve historic sites (castles, country houses, gardens...).

Nobility: There are five ranks of nobility (all sitting in the House of Lords): Duke, Marquess, Earl or Countess, Viscount, Baron or Baroness. Very few hereditary titles are now created.

Non-U: Abbreviation of "non upper-class". The term is used for an accent (or behaviour) which is not distinguished.

North-South Divide: A term used to refer to the difference between the north of England (which has suffered from the decline of traditional industries based on coal, iron, ship-building and textile) and the south (London and the City, new service *(tertiaire)* and high-tech industries).

Oxbridge: the universities of Oxford and Cambridge.

Poet Laureate: The official royal poet. He or she is appointed for life and writes verse for official occasions.

Poppy Day: Remembrance Day, in November, when people wear poppies *(coquelicots)* in their lapels *(revers de veste)* (reminiscent of the fields of northern France) in memory of those who died in the two World Wars.

Pubs: Most pubs have a public bar, where darts *(jeu de fléchettes:* a popular game played in pubs: small arrows *(fléchettes)* are thrown onto a round board divided in segments with different scores) and bar billiards are played. There is also a more refined lounge or saloon bar.

R.P.: Received Pronunciation: the standard way of pronouncing English for middle-class speakers in southern England.

Scottish Parliament: Since 2000, Scotland has had its own parliament, elected by proportional representation. It has limited tax-raising powers and decides how to spend the Scottish Office budget (health, education, law and order, justice, transport and local government).

Soap operas: Popular television serials *(feuilletons)* about a group of people in a particular community. Coronation Street, for example, is set among working-class people in a Manchester street, while East-Enders takes place in the East End of London.

Welsh assembly: Since 2000, Wales has had an elected assembly. It cannot raise taxes, but decides how to spend the Welsh Office budget.

Westminster: The London borough *(arrondissement)* where the Houses of Parliament are to be found. The word is therefore used metonymically for Parliament.

White-collar worker: Someone who works in an office or has a professional job. See blue-collar worker.

Whitehall: A street in London where many government departments and ministries are located. The word is therefore used metonymically for the civil service *(la fonction publique)*.

Yob: Back slang for boy: a young person who behaves in a violent and offensive way.

Yuppie: Young, upwardly mobile professional *(membre des professions libérales)*. A young, ambitious professional, with a good income *(revenus)*.

13. A few emblematic figures in British culture

Andy Capp: A character in a *Daily Mirror* comic strip. With his cloth cap *(casquette)* and cigarette, he is a crude caricature of the typical British working-class man, drinking as much as he can and working as little as he can.

Boadicea (or Boudicca): A Queen of a Celtic tribe who, in 60 AD, rebelled against the Romans, and led her tribe to destroy Roman settlements. She is one of the first British heroines.

Bond, James: The secret agent who is the hero of Ian Fleming's novels. His name is associated with sophistication, luxury, seductive women and exotic locations. A number of films (in which he is played by actors like Sean Connery and Roger Moore) made the character especially famous.

Bonnie Prince Charlie: The grandson of James II, and the last Stuart to claim the throne *(revendiquer le trône)* in 1745. Thanks to Walter Scott's historical novel *Waverley*, Charles Edward Stuart is seen as a romantic and courageous figure leading a rebellion.

Britannia: the personification of Britain, a woman with a helmet *(casque)*, trident and shield *(bouclier)*.

Bull, John: a personification of the typical Englishman: a plain, fat, kind Englishman resembling a bull dog.

Churchill, Sir Winston: British Prime Minister who led the war effort during World War II. His talent as an orator helped to galvanize the nation, with such statements as that he made in the House of Commons at the beginning of the war, explaining that he had "nothing to offer but blood, toil, tears and sweat." He stands for courage and determination in the face of adversity.

Diana, Princess of Wales: Prince Charles's first wife and the mother of William and Harry. Her youth and beauty, her criticism of some of the rituals of the monarchy, and her work with charities, against anti personal mines in particular, made her "the People's Princess", one of the best-loved members of the royal family.

***Frankenstein*:** A Gothic novel (1818) by Mary Shelley. Frankenstein is a scientist who succeeds in creating a monstrous human being, who eventually turns against his creator because he is denied (refused) affection. The name evokes the potential dangers of science.

King Arthur: A legendary King who, with the Knights of the Round Table, looked for the Holy Grail *(le Saint Graal)*, the cup used by Christ at the Last Supper. He is the archetype of the mythical king capable of heroic deeds *(actions)* and representing the hopes of a race. Many refuse to accept his death and believe he will reappear when the English nation needs him.

Nelson, Lord: An Admiral whose heroic feats *(exploits)* and victories, including that of Trafalgar where he died, make him the perfect hero. His life is made more tragic and romantic by his wounds (he lost the sight of an eye in battle, then lost an arm) and by his love affair with Lady Hamilton.

Robin Hood: A legendary outlaw *(hors-la-loi)*, whose exploits as he fought the Sheriff of Nottingham were sung in a number of ballads. He was popular for robbing from the rich (the Norman lords) to give to the poor (the Saxons).

Thatcher, Margaret: The first British woman prime minister, a post she held between 1979 and 1990. Her aggressive liberal politics, her dismantling of trade-unions *(démantèlement des syndicats)* and her firm handling *(la fermeté avec laquelle elle a conduit)* of the Falklands war gave her a reputation for toughness *(dureté, acharnement)* and intransigence and led to her nickname "The Iron Lady".

MAJOR TRENDS IN ENGLISH & IRISH LITERATURE

MEDIEVAL LITERATURE — RENAISSANCE LITERATURE

MAJOR DATES IN HISTORY
- 1337-1453 Hundred Years' War
- 1455-1485 Wars of the Roses
- 1509 Accession of Henry VIII
- 1534 Break with Rome

POETRY
- 1386-1400 CHAUCER *The Canterbury Tales* (stories told by pilgrims and ironically reflecting character and society)

FICTION & PROSE
- 1516 MORE *Utopia* Description of an ideal system of government

THE THEATRE
- 1508 *Everyman* A Morality play: Christian allegorical plays about the fight between good & evil)

SHAKESPEARE

Tragedies

1595	*Romeo and Juliet*
1599:	*Julius Caesar*
1600-1601	*Hamlet*
1603-1604	*Othello*
1605-1606	*King Lear*
1606:	*Macbeth*
1606:	*Antony and Cleopatra*
1608:	*Coriolanus*

History plays

1591-1592	*Henry VI*
1592-1593	*Richard III*
1595	*Richard II*
1596-1598	*Henry IV*
1598-1599	*Henry V*

PAINTING Portraits (HOLBEIN) & allegories — Miniatures (HILLIARD) — Portraits (VAN DYCK)

MUSIC Madrigals (W. BYRD) and Ayres (J. DOWLAND, T. CAMPION)

1558	1588	1603	1605	1625	1629
Accession of Elizabeth I	Spanish Armada defeated	Accession of James I	Gunpowder Plot	Accession of Charles I	Parliament abolished

1590-1596	1591	1609	1633
SPENSER *The Faerie Queene*	SIDNEY *Astrophel & Stella*	SHAKESPEARE *Sonnets*	DONNE *Poems* (metaphysical poetry: religious & love poetry developing paradoxes & unexpected images)

1590-1596 / 1591: Pastoral & allegorical poems; imitation & renewal of Petrarchan sonnets

1611	1625
Authorized Version of the Bible	BACON *Essays*

1588	1590	1606	1612
MARLOWE *Doctor Faustus*	SHAKESPEARE first plays	JONSON *Volpone*	SHAKESPEARE last plays

1590–1612: The Golden age of drama

Comedies

1590-1591 *Two Gentlemen of Verona*
The Taming of the Shrew
1594-1595 *Love Labour's Lost*
1595 *A Midsummer Night's Dream*
1596-1597 *The Merchant of Venice*
1597-1598 *The Merry Wives of Windsor*
1598 *Much Ado About Nothing*
1599-1600 *As You Like It*
1601 *Twelfth Night*
1604-1605 *All's Well that Ends Well*

Romances

1607 *Pericles*
1609 *The Winter's Tale*
1610 *Cymbeline*
1611 *The Tempest*

MAJOR DATES IN HISTORY

1642-1648	1649	1649-1660	1660	1665-1666
Civil War	Execution of Charles I	Commonwealth (Cromwell)	Restoration of Charles II	Great Plague and Great Fire of London

POETRY

1667	1681
MILTON, ***Paradise Lost*** A defence of Puritanism A didactic epic about the creation of the world & the fall of man)	**MARVELL** ***Poems*** **DRYDEN** ***Absalom & Achitophel***

FICTION & PROSE

1644	1651	1660-1669	1678
MILTON ***Areopagitica*** An attack against censorship	**HOBBES** ***Leviathan*** A justification of absolute governments	**PEPYS** ***Diary*** A day-to-day account of life during the Restoration)	**BUNYAN** ***The Pilgrim's Progress*** An allegory of a Christian's progress through life

Political and religious works

THE THEATRE

PAINTING Portraits (KNELLER, LELY)

THE RESTORATION AND THE EIGHTEENTH CENTURY

1688	1714	1745	1776	1789
The Glorious Revolution	**Accession of George I**	**Jacobite rebellion**	**American Declaration of Independence** **Steam engine invented**	**French Revolution**

1730	1734	1742	1757
THOMSON *The Seasons*	**POPE** *Essay on Man*	**YOUNG** *Night Thoughts*	**GRAY** *Odes*

Poetry of melancholy

1719	1726	1747-1749	1760-1767
DEFOE *Robinson Crusoe* A realistic description of survival through hard work	**SWIFT** *Gulliver's Travels* A political satire of Britain through the description of imaginary worlds	**RICHARDSON** *Clarissa* (epistolary) **FIELDING** *Tom Jones* (picaresque)	**STERNE** *Tristram Shandy* A digressive and sentimental novel

THE RISE OF THE NOVEL

1700	1707	1773	1777
CONGREVE *The Way of the World*	**FARQUHAR** *The Beaux' Stratagem*	**GOLDSMITH** *She Stoops to Conquer*	**SHERIDAN** *The School for Scandal*

RESTORATION COMEDY
humorous satire of the manners of the time

Witty comedy of manners

PAINTING **Social satire (HOGARTH)**
Conversation pieces (family portraits)
Portraits (REYNOLDS) Portraits + landscape (GAINSBOROUGH)

MUSIC **Church & instrumental music, operas (PURCELL, HANDEL)**

THE ROMANTIC AGE

MAJOR DATES IN HISTORY

1793	1805	1813	1825	1832
The Terror in France France & Britain at war	Trafalgar	Napoleon defeated at Waterloo	First railway	Reform Act (extends the right to vote)

POETRY

1789	1798	1805	1812	1816	1819-24	1820
BLAKE *Songs of Innocence*	WORDSWORTH & COLERIDGE, *The Lyrical Ballads*	WORDSWORTH *The Prelude*	BYRON, *Childe Harold's Pilgrimage*	COLERIDGE *Kubla Khan; Christabel*	BYRON *Don Juan*	KEATS *Odes* SHELLEY *Prometheus Unbound*

PRE-ROMANTICISM (1789)

FIRST GENERATION OF ROMANTIC POETS (1798–1805)

SECOND GENERATION OF ROMANTIC POETS (1819-24–1820)

FICTION & PROSE

1794	1813	1814	1816	1818
RADCLIFFE *The Mysteries of Udolpho*	AUSTEN, *Pride & Prejudice*	SCOTT *Waverley*	AUSTEN *Emma*	WOLLSTONECRAFT SHELLEY *Frankenstein*

Historical novels (1814)

Austen: lucid & ironic novels of manners (1813, 1816)

Gothic novels: a study of the effect of terror on sensitive minds (1794, 1818)

THE THEATRE

PAINTING

Visionary & Gothic (BLAKE, FUSELI)
Landscape painting (CONSTABLE, TURNER)

THE VICTORIAN AGE

1837	1838	1851	1854	1876	1880	1901
Accession of Queen Victoria	Beginning of the Chartist movement	Great Exhibition	Crimean War	Queen Victoria Empress of India	First Boer War	Accession of Edward VII

1832	1855
TENNYSON *Poems*	**BROWNING** *Men and Women*

VICTORIAN POETRY
(questionings and anxiety about man's place in the universe)

1847	1848	1850	1861	1865	1872	1886	1894	1896	1900
BRONTE E., *Wuthering Heights* **BRONTE C.,** *Jane Eyre*	**THACKERAY** *Vanity Fair*	**DICKENS** *David Copperfield*	**DICKENS** *Great Expectations*	**CARROLL** *Alice's Adventures in Wonderland*	**ELIOT** *Middlemarch*	**STEVENSON** *Dr Jekyll & Mr Hyde*	**KIPLING** *The Jungle Book*	**HARDY** *Jude the Obscure*	**CONRAD** *Lord Jim*

Bronte E., Bronte C.: Imaginative tales of passionate love

Thackeray, Dickens, Eliot: Realism + social and moral study of society

Stevenson, Kipling: Novels of adventure & action

Hardy: Determinism: tragic view of man as the victim of circumstance)

1894	1895
SHAW *Arms and the Man* (social concerns)	**WILDE** *The Importance of Being Ernest* (witty comedies)

A criticism of conventional morality

The Pre-Raphaelites (MILLAIS, ROSSETTI, BURNE-JONES)
Art Nouveau (MORRIS, BEARDSLEY)
Aestheticism (WHISTLER)

MAJOR DATES IN HISTORY

1901	1910	1914-1918	1916	1917	1921
Accession of Edward VII	Accession of George V	First World War	Irish Easter Rising	Treaty of Versailles	Partition of Ireland

POETRY

1914-1920	1922
First World War Poets: OWEN, BROOKE, SASSOON, THOMAS	ELIOT *The Waste Land*

Modernist poetry (collage, different voices, striking images to convey the chaos of modern society)

FICTION & PROSE

1907	1913	1922	1924
CONRAD *The Secret Agent*	LAWRENCE *Sons & Lovers*	JOYCE *Ulysses*	FORSTER *A Passage to India*

Experimentations with stream of consciousness (Woolf, Joyce), narrative technique (Conrad), and a study of relationships (Lawrence, Forster)

THE THEATRE

1907	1912	1924
SYNGE *The Playboy of the Western World*	SHAW *Pygmalion* (social concerns)	O'CASEY *Juno and the Paycock*

The Irish Renaissance (an attempt to reawaken Irish consciousness)

PAINTING

Post-impressionism (S. GORE, A. JOHN)
The Bloomsbury Group (FRY, GRANT, BELL)
Visionary paintings (STANLEY SPENCER)
Vorticism (NEVINSON)
Surrealism (NASH)
Abstraction (BEN NICHOLSON)

MUSIC

E. Elgar, V. Williams, B. Britten

UNTIL WORLD WAR II

1929	1933	1936	1936-1939	1939-1945	1940	1941	1944
New York Stock Exchange Crash	Hitler takes power in Germany	Accession of George VI	Spanish Civil War	Second World War	Battle of Britain Churchill Prime Minister	Pearl Harbour	D-Day

1928	1930	1933
YEATS *The Tower*	**AUDEN** *Poems*	**SPENDER** *Poems*
The poet of the Irish Renaissance	The Thirties' Poets political & social concerns	

1927	1932	1940
WOOLF *To the Lighthouse*	**HUXLEY** *Brave New World* Satire of society A warning of the dangers of science	**GREENE** *The Power & the Glory* Moral concerns with good & evil, guilt & salvation

1935
ELIOT *Murder in the Cathedral*

THE MODERN AGE:

MAJOR DATES IN HISTORY

1945-1951	1949	1951	1952	1956	1961
Labour government Nationalizations National Health Service	NATO created India independent	Churchill Prime Minister	Accession of Elizabeth II	Suez	South Africa becomes a Republic

POETRY

1952	1955	1958
THOMAS (D.) *Collected Poems*	LARKIN *The Less Deceived*	Betjeman, *Collected Poems*
Lyrical oneness with nature	detached, ironic, but compassionate view of life	

FICTION & PROSE

1945	1949	1952-1969	1954	1957	1957-1960	1959
WAUGH *Brideshead Revisited*	ORWELL *1984*	LESSING *The Children of Violence*	GOLDING *Lord of the Flies*	MURDOCH *The Sandcastle*	DURRELL *The Alexandria Quartet*	SILLITOE *The Loneliness of the Long Distance Runner*

THE THEATRE

1953	1956	1958
BECKETT *Waiting for Godot*	OSBORNE *Look Back in Anger*	ARDEN *Live Like Pigs* WESKER *Chicken Soup With Barley*

Angry Young Men (working class setting & concerns)

THE THEATRE OF THE ABSURD

PAINTING

Industrial scenes (LOWRY)
Pop Art (P. BLAKE, R. HAMILTON, D. HOCKNEY)
Op Art (B. RILEY)
Expressionism (F. BACON, H. HODGKIN)

AFTER WORLD WAR II

1964-1970	1973	1979-1990	1982	1985	1997	2003-2004
Wilson's Labour government	Britain joins the EEC	Mrs Thatcher's Conservative government	Falklands War	Anglo-Irish agreement	Tony Blair's New Labour wins the election	War on Iraq

1966	1970	1994
HEANEY *Death of a Naturalist*	**HUGHES** *Crow*	**HILL** *Collected Poems*

the violence & mystery of the natural world

1962	1966	1969	1981	1984	1989	1990	1992
BURGESS *A Clockwork Orange*	**RHYS** *Wide Sargasso Sea*	**FOWLES** *The French Lieutenant's Woman*	**RUSHDIE** *Midnight's Children*	**SWIFT** *Waterland*	**ISHIGURO** *The Remains of the Day*	**BYATT** *Possession*	**MC EWAN** *Black Dogs*

1960	1966	1971	1990	1994	1998
PINTER *The Dumb Waiter* *The Caretaker*	**STOPPARD** *Rosencrantz and Guildenstern are Dead* "Philosophical Farces"	**BOND** *Lear* Violence to reflect the brutality of society	**FRIEL** *Dancing at Lughnasa*	**BARKER** *Wounds to the Face*	**KANE** *Crave*

III The Commonwealth

■ The Empire

From the 16th to the 19th century the British colonies kept expanding all over the world. They often provided raw materials *(fournissaient des matières premières)*, which were manufactured in Britain. The American colonies seceded *(firent sécession)* in 1776, and Canada became a dominion in 1867. At the beginning of the 20th century, more and more colonies asked for their independence. Several countries gained their independence early in the century (Australia, New Zealand, South Africa). Others, mainly from Africa, Asia and the Caribbean, gained it in the years that followed World War II. Most of them chose to join the Commonwealth.

■ Towards the Commonwealth

In 1931, the Statute of Westminster defined the Commonwealth as a free association of independent states which had formerly (before) been part of the British Empire. All of them (republics, countries, like Canada, in which the Queen is Head of State, sultanates, etc) recognize the British sovereign as Head of the Commonwealth. There is no Commonwealth constitution but shared principles *(des principes partagés)* for peace, equality and prosperity. The association is mainly a cultural, educational, sporting and economic one. They also share the use of the English language.

■ The Commonwealth today

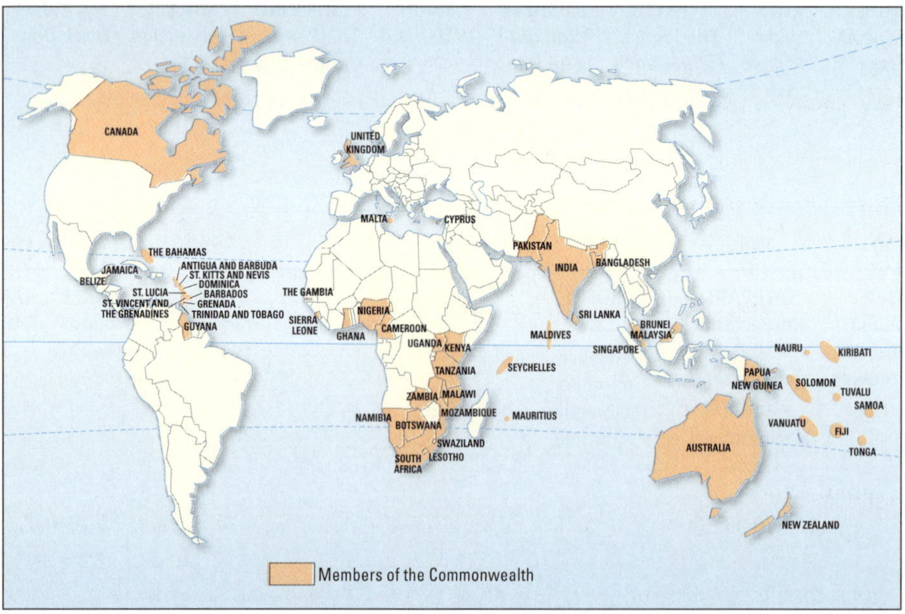

Here is some information about the largest Commonwealth countries.

AUSTRALIA

History

1770	Cook reaches the east coast of Australia and takes possession of Sydney for Britain. The land is inhabited by Aborigines.
1787	Britain starts using Australia as a penal colony *(colonie pour ses bagnards)*.
19th century	Important voluntary immigration from Britain. Convicts *(bagnards)* stop being sent to Australia around 1840.
1851	The Gold Rush brings waves of immigrants.
1901	Australia becomes independent.
1927	Canberra becomes the capital.
1967	The Aboriginal Australians are given full citizenship.
	Since WWII, there has been much immigration, particularly from Southeast Asia.
	One problem is that of the status of the Aboriginal people, long segregated against, and still living in greater poverty.
2001	In a referendum Australia decides to retain the monarchy.

Capital: Canberra
Type of government: a parliamentary democracy, with a Prime Minister, as in Britain. But it recognizes the English sovereign as Head of State. However, there is an increasingly strong movement in favour of transforming Australia into a republic.
A few major writers: Judith Wright (poetry) ; Patrick White, David Malouf, Robert Drewe, Peter Carey (novels).

NEW ZEALAND

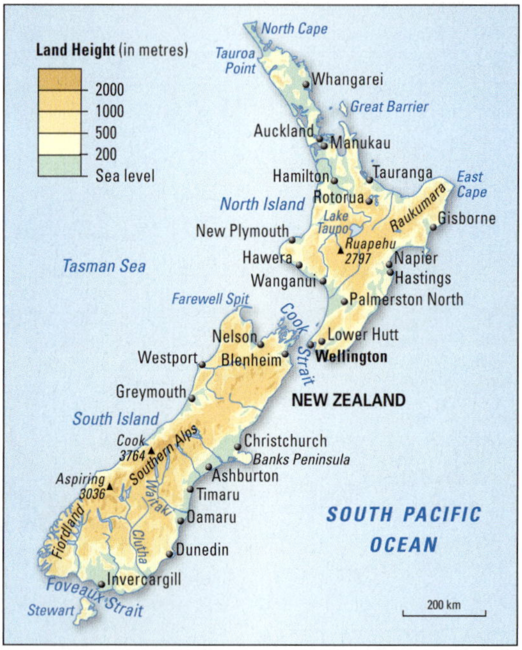

History

1769 Cook reaches New Zealand and claims it for Britain. The land is inhabited by Maoris.
British convicts *(bagnards)* are sent there.

1840 Treaty of Waitangi: New Zealand becomes a British colony and the Maori chiefs recognize the British sovereignty over the island. Several conflicts with the aboriginal Maoris occur until the end of the century.

1907 New Zealand becomes a dominion.

1947 New Zealand becomes independent within the Commonwealth.

Capital: Wellington.
Official languages: English and Maori
Type of government: Constitutional monarchy, with the British sovereign as Head of state.
A few major writers: Katherine Mansfield (short stories) ; Janet Frame (novels and stories).

CANADA

History

1534 Jacques Cartier establishes a French settlement *(colonie)*. At the end of the century, the country is inhabited by Eskimos, Indians, and a few white settlers and traders *(marchands)*.

17th century Beginning of the French colonization, chiefly along the St Lawrence River. Quebec and Montreal are established. But there is British colonization as well, with the Hudson Bay Company, trading in fish and fur *(fourrure)*, which leads to rivalry and conflict between the two countries.

1763 Treaty of Paris: France sells Quebec to the British.

1846 The boundary between The United States and Canada is established along the 49th parallel, all the way to the Pacific coast.

1867 British North America Act: the British colonies become a dominion. It consists of Quebec, Ontario, Nova Scotia and New Brunswick.

1869 Britain cedes the Hudson's Bay Company territories to Canada. They will form the remaining Canadian provinces.

1931 Canada becomes a member of the Commonwealth.

1982 Constitution Act: Canada remains within the Commonwealth but ceases to be a colony.

Capital: Ottawa

Canada is bilingual, English and French being the official languages.

Type of government: Parliamentary monarchy, with the British sovereign as Head of state. Although, theoretically, it is the Governor General (representing the British sovereign) who has executive power, it is in fact the Prime Minister who takes all deci-

sions. He/She is the leader of the party which has the majority of votes. Parliament consists of two houses: the House of Commons and the Senate.
A few major writers: Margaret Laurence, Mordecai Richler, (novels), Alice Munro (short stories), Margaret Atwood (poetry, novels and short stories).

SOUTH AFRICA

History

1650-1700	The country is settled by the Dutch, the French Huguenots and the Germans.
1881	First Boer War, won by the Boers (Dutch settlers).
1899-1902	Second Boer War, between Britain & the Afrikaners (Afrikaners = descendants of the Dutch colonists), won by Britain.
1910	South African Act: The different states become the Union of South Africa, which enters the Commonwealth.
1934	Creation of the National Party, for the political domination of the Afrikaners, who were in favour of separating the black and white communities.
1948	The National Party is elected.
1960	The Union of South Africa becomes a republic and leaves the Commonwealth. An apartheid policy is introduced. The white population is seen

as superior to and separated from the Blacks, the Coloureds (= half-castes), and the Asians. Under this "white rule", all places (schools, government buildings, buses...) are segregated. Black people live in townships within "homelands". Opposition parties, like the ANC (African National Congress), are banned *(interdits)* and their leaders imprisoned.

1961 Riots *(émeutes)* against apartheid in the black township of Soweto.

1989 De Klerk becomes president. Mandela (imprisoned for his role in the ANC) is released from prison and apartheid laws are abolished.

1993 Nelson Mandela and President De Klerk are awarded the Nobel Peace Prize.

1994 Nelson Mandela becomes President.

1996 New democratic constitution

1999 Thabo Mbeki becomes President. Programs of redistribution are established to help with the huge remaining disparities between the economic situations of the Whites and the Blacks.

Three capitals: Cape Town (legislative), Pretoria (executive), Blœmfontein (judicial).
11 official languages
Population: 76% Blacks; 13% Whites; 8.5 % Coloureds; 2.5% Asians
55% of the white population speak Afrikaans; 40% speak English.
Type of government: Republic
A few major novelists: Alan Paton, Nadine Gordimer, André Brink, J.M. Coetzee.

INDIA

History

15th-16th centuries East India Companies start trading *(faire du commerce)* with India.

1763 Treaty of Paris: British supremacy is declared over India

1876 Queen Victoria becomes Empress of India.

1919 Gandhi starts non-violent anti-British resistance. He advocates (recommends) civil disobedience *(résistance passive :* boycotts, refusal to pay taxes, refusal to vote) to gain Indian independence.

1947 India gains independence. It is partitioned (divided) between India (Hindus) and Pakistan (Muslims).

1948 Gandhi is assassinated. Nehru becomes Prime Minister.

1971 Eastern Pakistan wins its independence from Western Pakistan and becomes Bangladesh.

Capital: New Dehli
Type of government: Republic
Castes: because of the influence of Hinduism, society is divided into castes: there are 4 of them (the highest being the Brahmins, the lowest the Untouchables). Castes determine your way of life, your habits and rituals, whom you associate with.

Official languages: Hindi and English + 14 other national languages. English is also used by the different communities to communicate. **Religion:** Hinduism (83%); Islam (13%); Christianity (2.3%), Buddhism, Sikhism (2%).
A few major novelists: R.K. Narayan, Anita Desai, Vikram Seth, Hari Kunzru, Rohinton Mistry, Arundhati Roy.

NIGERIA

History

1885	Nigeria becomes a British protectorate.
1960	Nigeria gains its independence and remains in the Commonwealth.

Capital: Abuja.
Type of government: Republic
A few major writers: Chinua Achebe (novels), Ben Okri (novels), Wole Soyinka (plays).

THE CARIBBEAN

Caribbean countries within the Commonwealth: Antigua & Barbuda, Bahamas, Barbados, Belize, Dominica, Grenada, Guyana, Jamaica, St Kitts and Nevis, St Lucia, St Vincent and the Grenadines, Trinidad & Tobago. **A few major writers:** Jean Rhys (novels), V.S. Naipaul (novels); Derek Walcott (poetry).

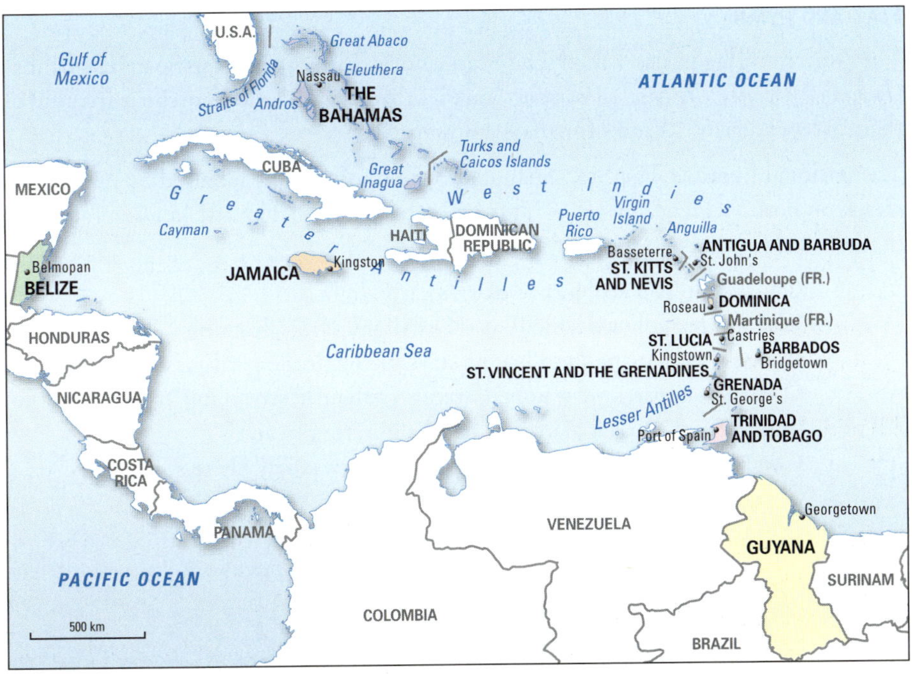

IV THE UNITED STATES

The United States is made up of 50 states, the federal capital being Washington D.C. (District of Columbia).

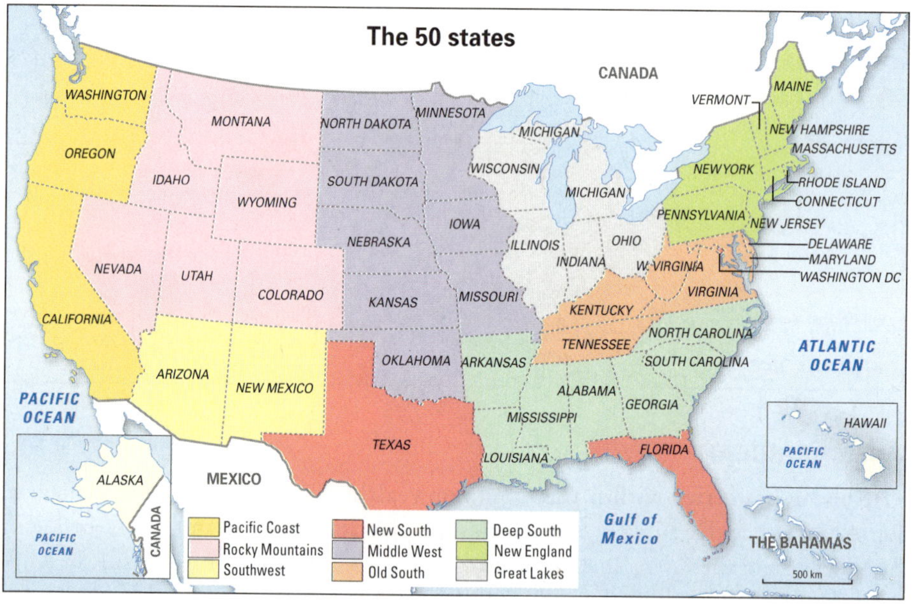

FLAG AND HYMN

The American **flag** is also called The Stars and Stripes or the Star-Spangled Banner *(la bannière étoilée)*. It has: 13 stripes (rayures) for the 13 colonies which fought for their independence; 50 stars for the 50 present states.

The **national hymn** is The Star-Spangled Banner, which was inspired by the British attack on Fort McHenry in 1814. This is the first stanza. The last line is a refrain in the following stanzas.

Oh, say can you see, by the dawn's early light,
What so proudly we hailed[1] at the twilight's last gleaming[2]?
Whose broad stripes and bright stars, through the perilous fight,
O'er the ramparts we watched, were so gallantly streaming[3]?
And the rockets' red glare, the bombs bursting in air,
Gave proof through the night that our flag was still there.
O say, does that star-spangled banner yet wave
O'er the land of the free and the home of the brave?

▲ Francis Scott Key (September 20, 1814)

1. **hailed:** greet with enthusiasm.
2. **gleaming:** faint light.
3. **streaming:** waving in the wind.

GEOGRAPHY

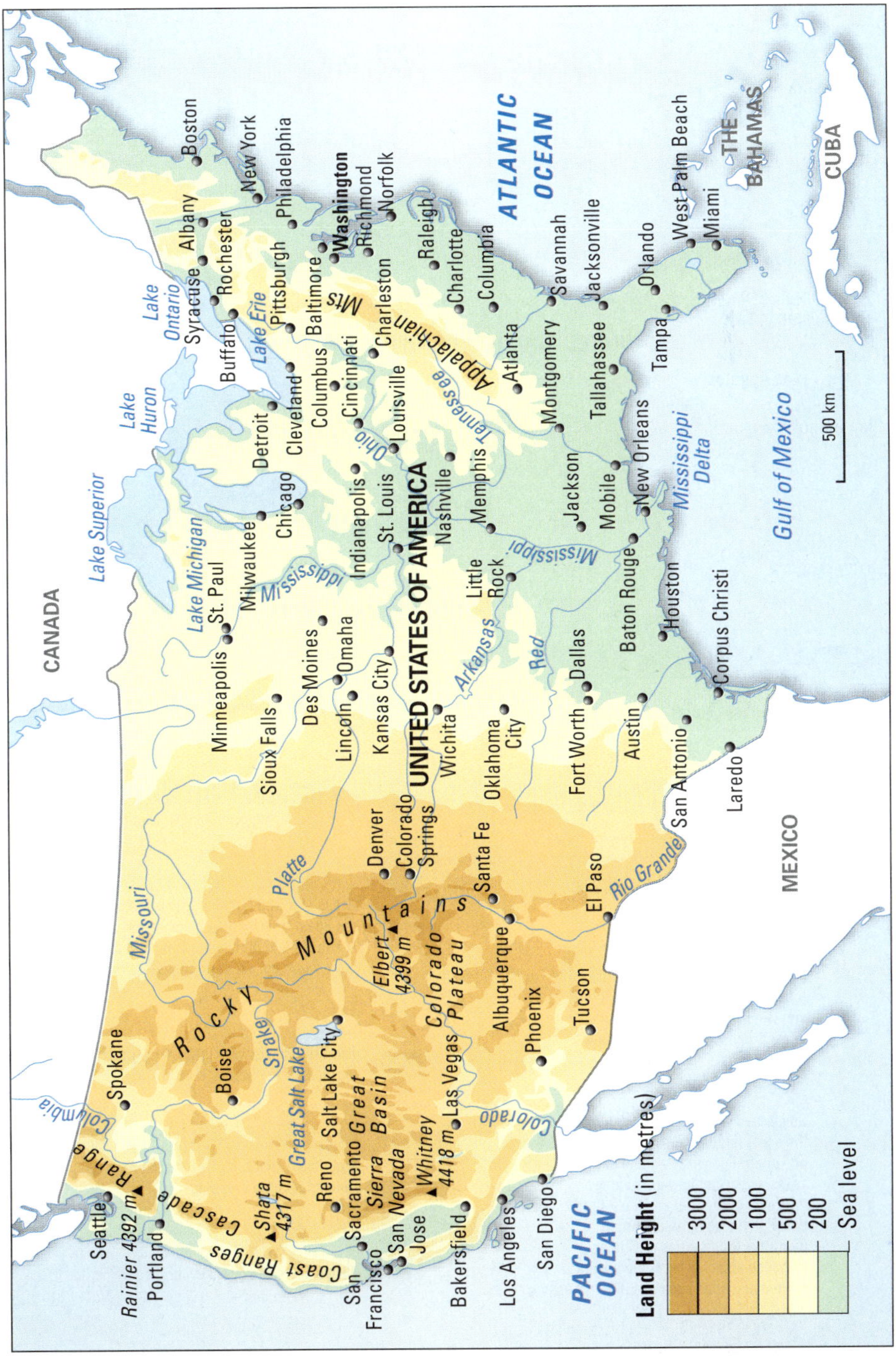
CANADA
UNITED STATES OF AMERICA
MEXICO
CUBA
THE BAHAMAS
ATLANTIC OCEAN
PACIFIC OCEAN
Gulf of Mexico
Mississippi Delta
Lake Superior
Lake Michigan
Lake Huron
Lake Erie
Lake Ontario
Great Salt Lake
Rocky Mountains
Appalachian Mts
Cascade Range
Coast Ranges
Sierra Nevada
Great Basin
Colorado Plateau
Rainier 4392 m
Shata 4317 m
Whitney 4418 m
Elbert 4399 m
Mississippi
Missouri
Ohio
Tennessee
Arkansas
Red
Platte
Snake
Columbia
Colorado
Rio Grande
Seattle
Portland
Spokane
Boise
San Francisco
San Jose
Sacramento
Reno
Salt Lake City
Bakersfield
Los Angeles
San Diego
Las Vegas
Phoenix
Tucson
Albuquerque
Santa Fe
El Paso
Denver
Colorado Springs
Minneapolis
St. Paul
Sioux Falls
Des Moines
Omaha
Lincoln
Kansas City
Wichita
Oklahoma City
Fort Worth
Dallas
Austin
San Antonio
Laredo
Corpus Christi
Houston
Baton Rouge
New Orleans
Mobile
Jackson
Little Rock
Memphis
Nashville
St. Louis
Indianapolis
Chicago
Milwaukee
Detroit
Cleveland
Columbus
Cincinnati
Louisville
Pittsburgh
Buffalo
Rochester
Syracuse
Albany
Boston
New York
Philadelphia
Baltimore
Washington
Richmond
Norfolk
Charleston
Raleigh
Charlotte
Columbia
Atlanta
Montgomery
Savannah
Jacksonville
Tallahassee
Orlando
Tampa
West Palm Beach
Miami
500 km
Land Height (in metres)
3000
2000
1000
500
200
Sea level

The main economic aeras of the US

- Large urban centres
- Atlantic coast megalopolis: many services (insurance, banking, administrative activities).
- Manufacturing Belt: old textile and manufacturing industries.
- Traditional manufacturing centres (coal industries in the Appalachians, steel and automobiles in Detroit...) in the process of adapting to new technologies.
- Sun Belt: a very active zone along the coast (industries linked to oil and natural gas in Louisiana and Texas, important harbours along the coast of the Gulf and the Pacific coast), but also agribusiness in California (huge farms relying on irrigation and high technology) and related activities such as food-processing.
- Most dynamic Sun Belt areas around large cities (LA, Houston, Seattle...).
- High tech businesses and parks (computers, bio-technology, "clean industries"...).
- Areas of mixed farming: fruit (citrus fruit along the coast from Florida to Louisiana), poultry in Arkansas and Alabama, peanuts in Georgia, soya, tobacco, corn and wheat).
- The Great plains with intensive agriculture (agribusiness): wheat, corn, soya
- Mountains, plateaux, forests: mainly ranching (cattle breeding)
- Active ports and intense maritime traffic

MAJORS DATES IN US HISTORY

The first colonies

1492 Christopher Columbus discovers America.

1607 The British Virginia Company is founded. In 1619, the first African slaves arrive to work on the tobacco plantations.

1620 Persecuted in Europe because of their religion, the Pilgrim Fathers (Puritans) reach America on the Mayflower and found the colony of Plymouth.

1681 Pennsylvania is founded by William Penn.
More emigrants will settle in America over the years, forming 13 colonies in the early 18th century. Most of them are drawn to America in order to flee from *(fuir)* tyranny or religious persecution.

1763 Treaty of Paris, which marks the end of French colonization.

Towards independence

1765 First revolts of the colonies against the imposition of taxes by the British

1773 The Boston Tea Party (The colonists refuse to pay taxes to Britain since they are not politically represented. When the British government try to impose a tax on tea, the colonists board *(montent à l'abordage)* the ships in Boston and throw the tea they carry into the sea.)

1774 The thirteen colonies suspend trade *(le commerce)* with Britain.

1775 Blockade of Boston harbor; beginning of the war for independence, between the colonies (backed *(soutenues)* by France) and Britain

1776 (July 4th) Declaration of Independence. The colonies separate from Britain.

IN CONGRESS, July 4, 1776.

The unanimous Declaration of the thirteen united States of America,

When in the Course of human events, it becomes necessary for one people to dissolve the political bands[1] which have connected them with another, and to assume among the powers of the earth, the separate and equal station[2] to which the Laws of Nature and of Nature's God entitle[3] them, a decent respect to the opinions of mankind requires that they should declare the causes which impel[4] them to the separation.
We hold these truths to be self-evident, that all men are created equal, that they are endowed[5] by their Creator with certain unalienable Rights, that among these are Life, Liberty and the pursuit of Happiness.

▲ The first paragraphs of the Declaration of Independence

1. **bands:** bonds *(contrats, liens)*. 2. **station:** position.
3. **entitle them:** give them a right to. 4. **impel:** force.
5. **endow:** *doter*.

1775-1783 War of Independence: The patriots (led by George Washington) against the Loyalists (those on the side of Britain). With the Treaty of Versailles (1783), Britain recognizes the independence of the United States of America.

1787 The American Constitution creates a federal government.

1789 George Washington becomes the first President of the United States.

1791 Bill of Rights: ten amendments are added to the Constitution in order to guarantee freedom of speech, freedom of press and freedom of worship.

Expansion

1803 Louisiana purchased (bought) from France. Beginning of the movement westward, to settle on virgin land (*terre vierge*). The 'frontier' (the limit between civilized and wild territories) will gradually move westward until 1890. This will be accompanied by many fights and treaties with the Indians who live on the land.

1808 Congress bans (prohibits) the importation of slaves.

1819 Florida purchased from Spain

1823 The Monroe doctrine: President Monroe opposes European colonization on the American continent.

1830 Indian Removal Act: In the decade which follows, American Indians are pushed further back in order to make way for the white settlers. In 1838, for example, the Cherokees who lived in Georgia are deported to Oklahoma. This is referred to as "The Trail of Tears" (*le sentier des larmes*).

1848 Texas, New Mexico and California are won after the war with Mexico.

1849	California Gold Rush: it encourages the movement westward.
1845-1855	First large wave of immigration, mainly from Ireland and central Europe

The Civil War

1860	Abraham Lincoln becomes President.
1861-1865	Civil War: 11 Southern states (the Confederate States) secede (leave the United States) to keep slavery, which they consider necessary to farm the extensive amount of land on their cotton, tobacco and rice plantations. They choose Jefferson Davis as their president. The northern states, on the contrary, are abolitionist (in favour of abolishing slavery). The north and the south also have different economic interests, the former wishing to protect their industrial production, the latter desiring free trade *(libre-échange)*. Lincoln is against secession and leads the war between the Union (the north) and the Confederacy (the South).
1863	Emancipation Proclamation: President Lincoln declares that all slaves are free. The British and the French side with the Union.
1865	The north wins the war and a 13th amendment is added to the Constitution, abolishing slavery. President Lincoln is assassinated by a supporter of the former Confederacy.
1865-1877	Reconstruction: The term applies to the rebuilding of the South, which has been ruined by the war. These are difficult years for the South because of the resentment *(ressentiment)* of the Southern whites and because many dishonest speculators try to take advantage of the situation. Although the 15th amendment gave black people voting rights in 1870, the South in fact enacts *(promulgue)* a series of laws, called Jim Crow Laws *(lois racistes)*, to encourage racial segregation: in schools, buses, public places... black people find themselves second-rate citizens. This is encouraged by secret societies like the Ku Klux Klan.

The Growth of the Nation

1867	The USA buys Alaska from Russia.
1869	First transcontinental railroad, which helps to bring cohesion between the states and which accelerates the movement westward
1870-1920	Second large wave of immigration, mainly from Southern, Central and Eastern Europe, and from China and Japan
1876	General Custer is defeated by the Sioux (led by Sitting Bull) at the Battle of Little Big Horn. This is just one event reflecting the growing resistance of the American Indians against their conditions of life. Indeed all through the 19th century, the American Indians are gradually forced into reservations, administered by the Bureau of Indian Affairs, where they are not allowed to develop their own culture.
1879	Edison invents the electric light bulb *(l'ampoule électrique)*.

1890 American Indians massacred at Wounded Knee. This marks the end of their resistance. 1890 is also the year when the frontier is officially closed.

1886 Creation of the American Federation of Labor, a union *(syndicat)* made necessary by the rapid growth of industry and of big business during the last two decades of the century.

1903 First flight of the Wright brothers

1908 Ford produces the Model T car.

1917 The USA enters WWI. It becomes a major power internationally.

Between two world wars

1920 Women get voting rights. Prohibition (making or selling alcohol is prohibited) leads to bootlegging (the illicit selling of alcohol).

1920-1929 The Jazz Age. This decade is a period of prosperity, during which consumerism reaches a climax: electrical appliances *(appareils électriques)*, cars, the radio, advertising become extremely popular. This is reflected in literature by the writings of the Lost Generation (Fitzgerald, Hemingway, Dos Passos) who expose *(dénoncent)* the concern with materialism. Corruption and bootlegging add to the decline of morals.

1924 Indian Citizenship Act (American Indians are given American citizenship).

1927 Lindbergh flies across the Atlantic Ocean.

1929 Increasing speculation leads to the Stock Exchange collapse *(effondrement de la bourse)* or Wall Street Crash (Black Thursday). Beginning of the depression years, when many banks and businesses go bankrupt *(font faillite)* and millions become unemployed.

1932 Roosevelt's New Deal to boost *(redonner du tonus à)* the economy, create jobs thanks to a program of public works, and help the poor and the unemployed. Roosevelt's reforms are also economic (The Agricultural Adjustment Act, to help farmers with subsidies *(subventions)*, the Tennessee Valley Authority, to use water for agriculture, the Banking Act, and social measures (the right of workers to belong to a union, social security). All these measures will be effective although unemployment will remain high until the United States enters the war against Germany.

World War II

1933 Many German Jewish refugees start arriving in America.

1941 The USA (which has so far maintained an isolationist policy) enters the war after the bombing of Pearl Harbor (a US navy base) by the Japanese.

1944 The allied forces land in Europe (on June 6, D-Day).

1945 The US drops atom bombs on Hiroshima and Nagasaki; Japan surrenders.

The Cold War

1947 The Marshall Plan brings financial and material help to countries which fight against communism. The relationship between the USA and the

USSR becomes increasingly tense *(tendue)*. This will lead to the Cold War in the 1950s.

1949 Creation of NATO (an alliance between the US and Western European countries in case of Soviet agression).

1950-1953 Korean War, between North Korea (communist and helped by the USSR) and South Korea (helped by the Americans).

1952 McCarthyism: Senator Mc Carthy leads a witch-hunt *(une chasse aux sorcières)* against communists in America. Many like Arthur Miller see a parallel with the trials for witchcraft *(procès pour sorcellerie)* in Puritan New England. (See his play *The Crucible*). An atmosphere of paranoia takes hold of America, with denunciations, trials and even executions, as in the case of Julius and Ethel Rosenberg, accused of spying for the USSR.

Civil Rights and the Vietnam War

1956 Montgomery bus boycott (black people protest against segregation on buses).

1960-1963 Kennedy becomes President. He starts a social policy called "the New Frontier": its aim is to put an end to segregation and to help the poorest in the country through welfare measures *(mesures d'aide sociale)*.

1961 Kennedy tries to invade Cuba and overthrow Castro, but fails. The following year, Soviet missiles are found in Cuba, which leads to a new crisis.

1963 Johnson becomes president after Kennedy is assassinated. He introduces extensive reforms to fight poverty, including Health insurance and aid to education.

1963 Martin Luther King leads a Civil Rights march on Washington to protest against segregation and inequality.

1964 The Civil Rights Act abolishes segregation.

1965 In spite of the Civil Rights Act, riots *(émeutes)* erupt in a number of larger cities.

With God On Our Side
(Bob Dylan)

Oh my name it is nothin'
My age it means less
The country I come from
Is called the Midwest
I's taught and brought up there
The laws to abide[1]
And that land that I live in
Has God on its side.

Oh the history books tell it
They tell it so well

The cavalries charged
The Indians fell
The cavalries charged
The Indians died
Oh the country was young
With God on its side.

I've learned to hate the Russians
All through my whole life
If another war starts
It's them we must fight
To hate them and fear them
To run and to hide
And accept it all bravely
With God on my side.

But now we got weapons
Of chemical dust
If fire them we're forced to
Then fire them we must
One push of the button
And a shot the world wide
And you never ask questions
When God's on your side.

▲ A few stanzas from a popular 1960s anti-war song by Bob Dylan.

1. **to abide by a law:** *respecter une loi.*

1964-1973 The Vietnam War, between the North (communist) and the South, helped by the Americans. Almost 60,000 American soldiers are killed and the United States finally has to retreat after growing dissatisfaction at home.

1968 Martin Luther King assassinated.

1969 First man on the moon.

1972 President Nixon signs the strategic Arms Limitation Treaty with the USSR.

1974 Nixon resigns (*démissionne*) after the Watergate scandal (He had ordered that the headquarters of the Democratic Party be broken into.)

Recent times

1980-1988 Presidency of Ronald Reagan, who introduces conservative and liberal policies.

1989 Fall of the Berlin Wall. End of the Cold War.

1991 Gulf War against Iraq. The United States forces Iraq to withdraw from Kuwait. It is the starting point of the New World Order, according to which the United States polices the world.

1992-2000 Presidency of Bill Clinton, who initiates social reforms and reduces the deficit

2001 Terrorist attacks against the USA: on September 11, the Twin Towers of the World Trade Center are destroyed, and the Pentagon is damaged. Almost three thousand people are killed.

2003 War against Iraq

2005 Although an Iraqi government is now in place, human rights abuses, continuing fighting and the death of US soldiers every day lead the public opinion to become more critical of the war.

The presidents of the United States

1789	George WASHINGTON	
1792	"	
1796	John ADAMS	
1800	Thomas JEFFERSON	
1804	"	
1808	James MADISON	
1812	"	
1816	James MONROE	
1820	"	
1824	John Quincy ADAMS	
1828	Andrew JACKSON	
1832	"	
1836	Martin VAN BUREN	
1840	William H. HARRISON	
1841	John TYLER	
1844	James K. POLK	
1848	Zachary TAYLOR	
1850	Millard FILLMORE	
1852	Franklin PIERCE	D
1856	James BUCHANAN	D
1860	Abraham LINCOLN	R
1864	"	
1865	Andrew JOHNSON	D
1868	Ulysses S. GRANT	R
1872	"	
1876	Rutherford B. HAYES	R
1880	James A. GARFIELD	R
1881	Chester A. ARTHUR	R
1884	Grover CLEVELAND	D
1888	Benjamin HARRISON	R
1892	Grover CLEVELAND	D
1896	William McKINLEY	R
1900	"	
1901	Theodore ROOSEVELT	R
1904	"	
1908	William H. TAFT	R
1912	Woodrow WILSON	D
1916	"	
1920	Warren G. HARDING	R
1923	Calvin COOLIDGE	R
1924	"	
1928	Herbert C. HOOVER	R
1932	Franklin D. ROOSEVELT	D
1936	"	
1940	"	
1944	"	
1945	Harry S. TRUMAN	D
1948	"	
1952	Dwight D. EISENHOWER	R
1956	"	
1960	John F. KENNEDY	D
1963	Lyndon B. JOHNSON	D
1964	"	
1968	Richard M. NIXON	R
1972	"	
1974	Gerald R. FORD	R
1976	James E. CARTER, Jr,	D
1980	Ronald W. REAGAN	R
1984	"	
1988	George H. BUSH	R
1992	William J. CLINTON	D
2001	George W. BUSH	R
2005	"	

D= Democratic R = Republican

The political system

The American Constitution is a written document dating from 1787, to which 27 amendments have been added. The first ten, which describe the rights of the people, constitute the Bill of Rights.
There is balance *(un équilibre)* between the power of the federal government and that of the state governments.

The constitution is also based on the separation of powers – legislative, executive, judiciary – each being able to limit the powers of the others. This is called a system of **checks and balances** *(équilibre des pouvoirs)*

Executive power
= the President & Vice-President
The president is the head of the executive and the commander-in-chief of armed forces. He suggests new legislation to Congress but may veto the bills *(projets de loi)* which were not voted by two-thirds of Representatives. He appoints *(nomme)* Supreme Court Judges.
The President and Vice-President are elected for four years on the same ticket *(liste électorale)*. If the President is ill or resigns *(démissionne)* before the end of his term *(mandat)*, the Vice-President takes over. The President can be re-elected once only.
The President appoints the Secretaries of State

Legislative power = Congress
Congress proposes laws and votes to pass them. It also controls the executive (controls the budget, can, with a two-thirds majority, override *(passer outre à)* the President's veto of a bill, can impeach *(mettre en accusation)* the President.)
Congress is made up of:
– The House of Representatives (with the number of representatives proportional to the population of each state.) It consists of 435 members, elected for 2 years. They represent the interests of individuals.
– The Senate: 100 elected senators (two Senators for each state). Elected for 6 years, with one third of Senate renewed every two years.) They represent the interests of the state.

The Judiciary
= The Supreme Court
The highest court of justice. It checks that the laws (both federal and state laws) are constitutional and it interprets acts of Congress.
The Supreme Court is made up of 9 members, appointed by the President for life, but their nomination must be approved by the Senate.

WHAT THE CONSTITUTION CREATED

The Constitution's Framers set out to design a government in which no person or branch of government could become all-powerful. Thus, they carefully divided the powers of government among lawmakers, judges, and a chief executive, and they made it possible for each group to balance and check each other's powers. What major powers does the Constitution assign to each branch of government? How can each branch check the powers of the other two branches? The charts on this page provide clear answers.

THREE GOVERNMENT BRANCHES, EACH WITH SEPARATE POWERS...

CHIEF POWERS OF THE LEGISLATIVE BRANCH (Congress)

1. Passes federal laws
2. Raises taxes
3. Regulates foreign and interstate commerce
4. Declares war
5. Raises and funds the military
6. May borrow money by issuing bonds for sale

CHIEF POWERS OF THE EXECUTIVE BRANCH (The President)

1. Commander-in-Chief of the military
2. Makes treaties with other countries
3. Appoints ambassadors, federal judges, Supreme Court Justices, thousands of other federal officials
4. Administers U.S. laws
5. Acts as head of state

CHIEF POWERS OF THE JUDICIAL BRANCH (Supreme Court)

1. Makes final review of lower federal court rulings and appeals from state courts when they involve federal law or Constitutional issues
2. Is first and final court to hear cases involving foreign ambassadors
3. Rules on disputes between states

CONGRESS'S CHECKING POWER

Over the President

- May override President's veto.
- May impeach the President.
- Senate must ratify treaties President makes.
- Senate must approve President's nominees for ambassador, other high level jobs.
- Controls spending; can reject President's budget requests, including military funds.
- May investigate, reorganize Executive Branch departments.

Over the Supreme Court

- May propose amendments to the Constitution to override a Supreme Court ruling.
- Senate must approve Court nominees.
- May impeach federal judges.
- Decides jurisdiction of courts.
- May change size of Supreme Court.
- May create new, shut down old federal courts below Supreme Court level.

PRESIDENT'S CHECKING POWER

Over the Supreme Court

- Nominates Supreme Court Justices and lower federal court judges.
- May grant pardons to persons convicted of violating federal laws.
- May refuse to enforce a federal court order.

Over the Congress

- May veto laws passed by Congress.
- May order special sessions of Congress.
- As leader of political party, may pressure members of the party to vote a certain way.*
- May appeal directly to citizens to pressure their representatives in Congress to vote a certain way.*

SUPREME COURT'S CHECKING POWER

Over the President

- May rule that the President, other members of Executive Branch have acted unconstitutionally, exceeded their authority under law.
- May interpret treaties signed by President.

Over the Congress

- May rule that laws passed by Congress and signed by the President are unconstitutional and therefore illegal.

...AND THE ABILITY TO CHECK EACH OTHER

*Though not defined by the Constitution, these powers evolved over time.

■ States v Federal government

The Federal government is responsible for foreign policy, the armed forces, the FBI. States are responsible for all other matters concerning them. Each state has, like the country as a whole, a constitution, a governor, a House of Representatives and a Senate and its own courts. Different states often have very different laws (the age when you can drive, the death penalty, the educational system), but any law voted by the federal government must be applied by each state.

The executive consists of thirteen departments headed by secretaries *(ministres)*.

Here are some of the main departments:

The State Department *(Ministère des Affaires Étrangères)*

The Treasury *(Ministère des Finances)*

The Interior Department *(Ministère de l'Intérieur)*

The Defence Department *(Ministère des Armées)*

The Justice Department *(Ministère de la Justice)* headed by the Attorney general *(ministre de la justice)*.

■ A two-party system

– The Republicans (= the GOP, Grand Old Party). Their emblem is the elephant. It is a more conservative party on the side of big business, in favour of economic liberalism and against too powerful a central government.

– The Democrats. Their emblem is the donkey *(l'âne)*. They are traditionally more in favour of state intervention and closer to the minorities.

■ The elections

The President is not elected directly but by an electoral college, itself elected by the people. In each state, it is the candidate with the largest number of votes who gets all the votes in the electoral college.

This system makes it difficult for a smaller party to be more than a pressure group *(groupe de pression)*.

Electing the US president

When does an election take place?

The President and Vice-President are elected every four years. The election takes place in November, on the Tuesday following the first Monday.

The President can be elected for a second term, but not for a third one.

Who can run for President?

The candidates must be native-born US citizens, have resided in the United States for at least 14 years, and be at least 35 years of age.

How are the candidates of each party chosen?

First each party selects delegates:

– either in "primary elections" held in the states by secret ballot *(vote à bulletin secret)* of party members

– or in "caucuses" in other states, with public voting instead of secret ballot. Some delegates can also be chosen because they are prominent party members. During the summer which precedes each November election, political parties hold conventions, which are very large meetings attended by the delegates. A majority of delegate votes is needed for a candidate to win the party's nomination. He/she becomes the party's "nominee". Usually, the delegates let the chosen presidential candidate select a vice-presidential candidate.

The "ticket"
The candidates for President and Vice-President (also called the President's "running mate") run together on a "ticket": they will win together or lose together, and Americans cannot vote for one of the two and not the other.

The electoral college
The American presidential election is not a direct one. In November, elections are held in each of the 50 states and in the District of Columbia, where the voters choose "electors" (grands électeurs) who promise to vote for one of the tickets. These electors form the "Electoral College".
Each state has the same number of electors as it has senators (two for each state) and representatives (the number is proportional to the population of the state.) The District of Columbia (Washington) has three electors.

The result of the vote
In most states the "winner-take-all" system prevails, which is to say that the ticket which receives the largest number of votes in the states gets all the electors of the state. (The exceptions are Maine and Nebraska, where the electors are chosen by district.) This means that it is possible for a President to be elected although he had fewer votes than his/her rival.

Voting for the President
The Electoral College then votes for the President and Vice-President, each elector being given one vote. Normally, one of the tickets receives a majority of votes, so that the President and Vice-President are elected. If there is no majority, it is the House of Representatives which then chooses the President from the three candidates who received the largest number of votes in the Electoral College. It is the Senate which would then choose the Vice-President.

The official inauguration of the President takes place in January.

Religion

Religion plays an important part in the United States, where 90% of the population say they believe in God. Although church and state are separated, religion is omnipresent in political and everyday life: the President has to swear *(prêter serment)* on the Bible when he takes up office.

The Puritan religion of the early settlers has been enormously influential in encouraging hard work and in promoting *(promouvoir)* the idea that wealth and material success are not shameful *(honteux)* but are a sign of salvation *(salut)* and of God's blessing *(grâce)*.

Main religions in the United States

Protestant 54%	Roman Catholic 25%	Eastern Orthodoxy 3%
Mormon 2%	Jewish 2.5%	Muslim 1.5%
Buddhist 0.4%	Hindu 0.4%	Unitarian Universalist 0.4%

■ **A few specifically American churches:**

– The QUAKERS: The Quakers (also called Society of Friends) were established in Pennsylvania by William Penn in the 17th century. They believe in the "inner light" of Jesus Christ in the soul and reject such things as ornaments and sacraments. Their social commitment *(engagement social)* is very strong: throughout history they have been active against slavery, violence and war and in favour of prison reform and social justice.

– The MORMONS: Also called The Church of Jesus Christ of Latter-Day Saints, it was founded by Joseph Smith in 1830. The Mormons believe that Jesus Christ was revealed to early immigrants and will found a new Jerusalem in the United States. Conversion comes through baptism and can be undergone vicariously *(indirectement)* for the dead. Mormons do not drink alcohol or coffee, do not smoke, respect sexual abstinence and give two years' free service to the church. Their earlier habits of polygamy have now been abandoned. Many of them live in Salt Lake City, Utah.

– The AMISH: The Amish are a religious community who settled in Pennsylvania in the 18th century. They reject all forms of industrialisation and modernity, refusing radios, televisions, cars and fridges, and dressing in very simple and strict clothes.

The EVANGELICAL 'BORN AGAIN' MOVEMENT (someone is 'born again' when he/she has recovered his/her faith after a spiritual experience) has been steadily growing, linked to moral crusades and fundamentalist beliefs in a literal interpretation of the Bible as the word of God. Many fundamentalists also believe in creationism, refusing the Darwinian theory of evolution and defending the creation of the universe as it is told in the Book of Genesis.

EDUCATION

The Constitution makes no mention of free and compulsory education and each state is therefore free to organise education as it wishes.

■ **Types of schools:**

Before the age of 5: nursery school or kindergarten

– Age 5 to age 11: Elementary School or Grade School: first to sixth grades

– Age 11 to age18: High School
  - 11-15: Junior High School (or Middle School): grade six to grade nine
  - 15-18: Senior High School: grade nine to grade twelve

Pupils need to have a certain number of credits to graduate *(obtenir leur diplôme)* from High School, but credits can be obtained in a wide variety of subjects including non-academic ones like Home economics, Photography...).

At the end of the 12th grade, students take their High School Diploma. They graduate from High School. *(équivalent de passer son baccalauréat.)*

Higher education

To enter, you have to sit for a Scholastic Aptitude Test (SAT). Students apply for *(posent leur candidature auprès de)* different universities and, depending on their results, are accepted or refused. There is a wide range of levels in the United States, from Junior colleges (also called Community Colleges), which have two-year programs specialised in professional needs to well-known and very expensive universities such as Harvard or Berkeley.
Although the tuition fees *(frais de scolarité)* are very high and can reach $35,000 a year, many students are awarded grants *(bourses)*.

> The Ivy League is a group of old and prestigious universities: Brown, Columbia, Cornell, Dartmouth, Harvard, Princeton, Yale, University of Pennsylvania.
> The Seven Sisters is a group of seven highly respected colleges for women: Vassar, Wellesley, Smith, Bryn Mawr, Barnard, Radcliffe, Mount Holyoke.

College: 2– or 4– year cycles
1st year = freshman year
2nd year = sophomore year
3rd year = junior year
4th year = senior year
= leading to a Bachelor's Degree.

University: like colleges they prepare for a Bachelor's Degree, but also offer post-graduate work *(troisième cycle universitaire)*, leading to a Master's Degree, then PHD.

THE MEDIA

The press is all-powerful in the United States, as was shown when The Washington Post revealed the Watergate scandal, which led to the impeachment *(mise en accusation)* of President Nixon.
There are a few national papers *(The New York Times, The Wall Street Journal, The Washington Post, The Los Angeles Times, The Boston Globe, The Chicago Tribune)*. They contain both local news and syndicated columns *(articles de journalistes d'agence)* which appear in different newspapers all over the country.
Magazines include *Time*, *Newsweek*, *US News and World Report* and *Fortune*.

There are hundreds of radio and TV stations, for example:
ABC (American Broadcasting Corporation)
CBS (Columbia Broadcasting System)
NBC (National Broadcasting Company)
CNN (Cable Network News)

Population

The United States population reached 300,000,000 inhabitants in October 2006.
The United States is a Nation of Immigrants. In the 19th century particularly, the population grew rapidly, with the arrival of two main waves of immigrants fleeing *(fuir)* religious persecution and/or poverty:
– in the early years of the century, many Irish, English, Germans, Austrians and Scandinavians.
– in the last decades of the century, many immigrants arrived from central and southern Europe (Italians, Greeks, Armenians, Jews, Poles...).
In the twentieth century, the new immigrants mainly came from Asia (China, Japan, the Philippines...) and from Cuba, Mexico and South America.

For most of these people, the United States represented a land of freedom and opportunity, the possibility of a new departure after severing (cutting) their links with the mother country. Between 1892 and 1954, the new immigrants arrived at Ellis Island in New York harbour *(le port de New York)*, where they were inspected and either refused or accepted. Recent laws have limited the number of immigrants according to quotas which depend on professional needs.
Originally, the newly arrived immigrants aimed at merging into *(se fondre dans)* the American culture. America would be a "melting pot" *(un creuset)*. Recently, however, the tendency has been to show pride in one's origins and to retain one's cultural differences. The new aim is no longer a melting pot but a "mosaic" or a "salad bowl" in which the different elements remain identifiable.
Although the United States remains a land of opportunity, there is still a great deal of poverty, which mainly affects Blacks, Hispanics and single-parent families. There is also a great deal of illegal immigrants, many of them crossing the 2000-mile long US-Mexican border.

The main ethnic minorities

The Native Americans (formerly called Indians) (0.7%)
The Indian tribes and clans which lived in America before the arrival of the settlers *(colons)* lived close to nature, depending on fishing and hunting for their survival and believing in supernatural forces and spirits. The movement westward in the 19th century was accompanied by massacres and brought about *(entraîna)* the destruction of most of these native cultures. A series of treaties allocated reduced amounts of land

to the tribes and confined them into reservations. Many still live there today, as American citizens (they were given American citizenship in 1924) but with a special status which allows them to regulate their own affairs. In the 20th century, unemployment, disease, violence and alcoholism have become rampant *(règnent)* in the Indian communities.

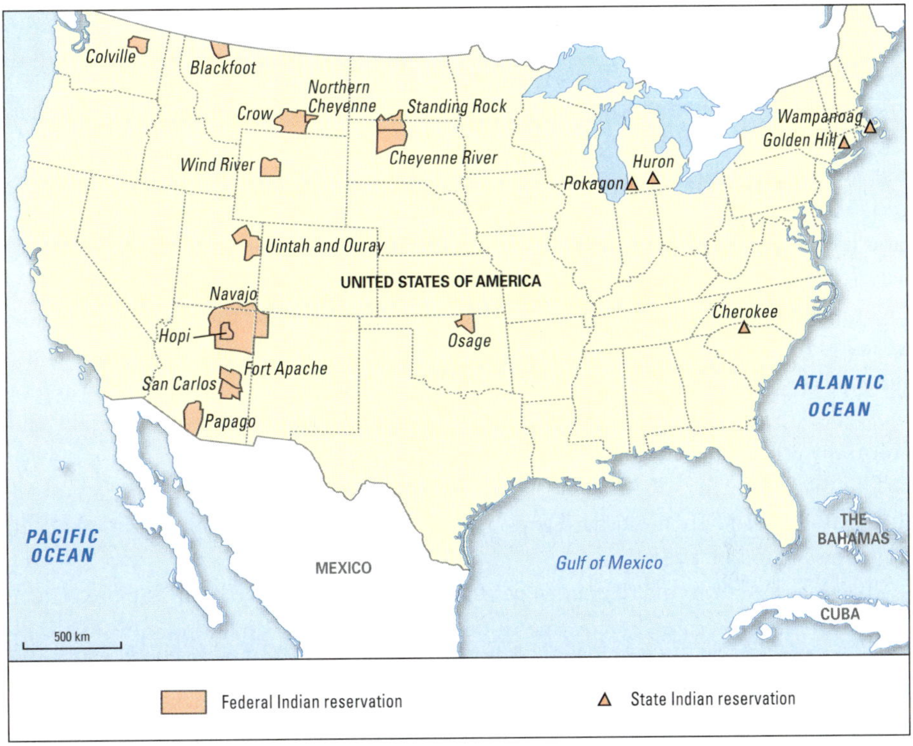

Black Americans (12.1%)

Until slavery was abolished, in 1865, some 15 million black people were brought from Africa to become slaves on the Southern plantations, a process known as the Black Ivory Trade *(le commerce de l'ivoire noir)*. On the plantations, they and their children became the property *(la propriété)* of the white owners, who made them work in the cotton, tobacco and rice fields. In the early 19th century, many northern states abolished slavery, and these became a destination for runaway slaves *(esclaves fugitifs)*, with many abolitionists organizing escape routes for them.

The Civil War pitted the industrial North, which was against slavery (which it did not need), against the agrarian South, which needed a lot of hands *(main-d'œuvre)* to work the land. After the victory of the north, all slaves were freed in 1865 (13th Amendment to the Constitution), became American citizens in 1868 (14th Amendment) and gained the right to vote in 1870.

In the Southern states, however, black people were often denied the right to vote and a policy of segregation ("separate but equal") or discrimination was gradually enforced *(appliquée)*, helped along by racist groups such as the Ku Klux Klan which maintained a climate of terror. By the end of the 19th century, segregation had become virtually legal in the South, with different schools for blacks and whites, different seats in restaurants, cinemas and buses.

Many black people migrated to northern cities, where they lived in ghettos. Several solutions to the problem were considered in the first half of the century, from separation (an independent black state?) to going back to Africa, or to fighting for civil rights through legal battles (the NAACP).

But mentalities gradually changed, particularly after World War II, when black soldiers fought alongside white ones. In 1954, the Supreme Court declared school segregation illegal. The next ten years were marked by the Civil Rights movement *(campagne pour les droits civils)*, led by Martin Luther King, to encourage non-violent protest in favour of equal civil rights for blacks and whites. This took the form of marches, boycotts or sit-ins. The 1964 Civil Rights Act finally put an end to discrimination.

But the law which brought political equality did not radically change the situation of most black people overnight *(du jour au lendemain)*. They were still economically and culturally at a disadvantage. Several movements appeared as a consequence:

– The Black Panthers, or the Black Muslims, who were in favour of more violent methods. (Indeed Martin Luther King, criticized by some for his non-violent approach, was assassinated in 1968).

– Affirmative Action *(discrimination positive)*, an attempt to take legal steps to reduce inequalities, for example by creating quotas of black workers in certain jobs or businesses (12% of the employees, the same percentage as that of black people in the whole US population) or by bussing (sending by bus) black children to white schools.

Nowadays, black people still live mainly in the south of the United States as well as in large cities. Although they are slowly becoming integrated, their average income *(revenus)* is still much lower than that of white people.

Black culture has been enormously popular and influential, particularly in the realm of music, with:

– **negro spirituals:** probably derived from Methodist hymns, they reflect humility, religious faith, the belief in a heavenly life to come, but also the misery of slavery.

– **blues:** secular songs of lament for solo voices

– **jazz:** mainly improvised music, which appeared at the beginning of the 20th century in the poor districts of New Orleans, it was influenced by ragtime (dance music with a syncopated rhythm) and the blues. It quickly spread north, where it took on a number of forms: swing, bebop, bop, etc.

Hispanic Americans (12.5%)

Most Hispanic-Americans immigrated to the United States in the 20th century, coming from Mexico, Cuba and Puerto Rico. Most of them have settled in the South

(California, Texas, Florida), although there is also a large Puerto Rican population in New York City. Another wave of immigrants later came from Nicaragua, the Dominican Republic and Colombia. This is why Spanish is so widely spoken in the United States.

Asian Americans

Coming from China, Japan, Vietnam and Korea, they have mostly settled on the west coast. Because they represent an educated minority, they have integrated more easily.

A FEW KEYWORDS IN AMERICAN CULTURE

Affirmative Action: Also called positive discrimination, it is a policy in favour of certain minority groups (women, black people). The policy helps to give preference to members of these under-represented groups, particularly when it comes to employment, scholarships *(bourses)* or financial aid. In many cases, quotas are set up for certain minorities. This, however, is sometimes criticized for leading to reverse discrimination *(racisme à l'envers)*.

American Dream, The: It is the dream of a promised land of liberty and equality which attracted so many immigrants to America. It is also the idea that, through courage, hard work and education, any American can go up the social ladder and succeed.

Baseball: Baseball is the national pastime in America. It is played by two teams of nine players on a large field, divided into four bases forming a diamond *(losange)*. Its outlines *(contour)* show the way a runner must run to score. A pitcher *(lanceur)* throws a ball towards the batter *(batteur)* in the opposite team. The latter tries to throw it back as far as possible to give him time to run a complete circuit around the bases. The game is played in nine innings *(manches)*.

Bible Belt, The: the Southeast of the United States, where there is a high proportion of Christians, and particularly of fundamentalists.

Bill of Rights: The name given to the first ten amendments to the Constitution.

1st Amendment: freedom of speech, freedom of religion, freedom of the press, freedom to hold public meetings.

2nd amendment: The right to keep and bear arms.

Broadway: a New York street which is famous for its theatres; the word symbolises the show business in New York. The shows they are mainly commercial so that smaller theatres in New York are said to be off-Broadway and more experimental productions are off-off Broadway.

Bussing: Taking children by bus to a school outside their district in order to encourage racial integration. Bussing was widely used in the 70s and 80s but is now more controversial.

Death Penalty, The: The death penalty is still legal in 37 American states, although several of them have stopped resorting to it *(ont cessé d'y avoir recours)* since 1976. A majority of Americans is still in favour of it, considering it as a deterrent *(une force de dissuasion)*. However, the death penalty remains controversial, especially after several death-row inmates *(prisonniers dans le couloir de la mort)* have been proved innocent.

Deep South, The: The Deep South is the name given to the southern states (for instance Alabama, Mississippi, Louisiana, South Carolina, Georgia) which formed the Confederacy defeated in the Civil War. They are deeply religious. See Bible Belt.
Dixie: A familiar word for the Southern states.
Ellis Island: From 1892 to 1943, Ellis Island (in New York harbour) was the place where the newly-arrived immigrants went through the necessary immigration procedures before entering the United States. There, their health was checked *(contrôlée)* and they were questioned about their destination and profession before being given a landing card *(carte de débarquement)*. Ellis Island is now a museum.
Four Freedoms, The: The four essential freedoms defined and promised by Roosevelt: freedom of speech, freedom of worship, freedom from want, freedom from fear.
Fourth Estate: The media, which is said to represent the fourth power after the government, the law and religion.
Frontier, The: The limit between the civilized, settled land and the "wilderness". The frontier gradually moved westward in the 19th century, encouraged by the 1848 California Gold Rush and by the Homestead Act (1862), which granted (= gave) 160 acres of land to any man ready to farm it. The movement westward can be summed up by Horace Greeley's well-known saying: "Go West, young man, and grow up with the country!" The spirit of the frontier has come to symbolise the American spirit: it is synonymous with individualism, courage, resilience *(ressort, élasticité)* and the search for opportunity.

Gated communities: Communities where the entry gates are locked to prevent the entrance of outsiders. Such communities have their own security systems and are often exclusive. They also contribute to a certain segregation since some are mainly for white people, others for black people, others for the elderly.

Halloween: The night of October 31, when it was believed that ghosts and witches could be seen. Children now celebrate Halloween by dressing up as witches, putting lights inside jack'o lanterns (hollowed pumpkins: *citrouilles vidées*), and going from door to door asking "Trick or treat?" (a treat, for instance candy, otherwise, they will play a trick on you *(jouer un tour)*.)
Hollywood: A district of Los Angeles, and the heart of the film industry, which was set up there in the early years of the 20th century. Over the past century, it was in Hollywood that such genres as the western, the musical, the slapstick comedy *(farce)* and the horror film were developed.
Hyphenated Americans: Americans who wish to assert their ethnic origins and call themselves Afro-Americans, Chinese-Americans or Hispano-Americans. (A hyphen: *un trait d'union*)
Independence Day: On July 4th, the Americans celebrate the anniversary of their declaration of Independence (July 4th 1776).
Inner cities: the central parts of cities, often more derelict *(abandonnés)* and with more social problems than the wealthier suburbs.
Land of Opportunity: The idea that the United States are a country where anyone can go up the social ladder and become rich through hard work.
Lobbies: pressure groups. Some of them are highly influential, for example:
– The National Rifle Association (which defends the free sale of firearms)
– The NAACP: National Association for the Advancement of Colored People, which defends the rights of black people
– NOW: National Organization of Women
Manifest Destiny: The idea, expressed by John L. O'Sullivan that the United States has a natural right to expand and "overspread the continent allotted by Providence for the development of our yearly multiplying millions" (1845). The expansion of America is thus seen as God's will.
Mason-Dixon Line: During the Civil War, this was the boundary (frontier) between the Southern States (the Confederacy) and the Northern States. The term is still used to refer to the division between the North and the South.
Medicare, Medicaid and Social Security are programs which provide medical help to the poor, the elderly the unemployed and the disabled *(les handicapés)*.
Melting Pot, The *(Le creuset)*: Millions of people immigrated to the United States in the 19th and 20th centuries, fleeing *(fuir)* poverty, political or religious persecution. The idea was originally that in the United States they would merge into a single race. But many people today want to keep their ethnic identities. They prefer speaking of a "salad bowl", a mosaic, a patchwork, or of ethnic pluralism.
Moral Majority, The: the religious, conservative, right-wing forces in American politics.
New Economy, The: A term which applies to the American economy of the 1990s and 2000s, an economy which is no longer based on heavy manufacturing, but which derives from information technology.

New World Order: The American foreign policy after the fall of the Berlin Wall and the Gulf War, according to which America sees itself as policeman to the world.
NRA: National Rifle Association. It is one of the most influential lobbies in the United States. They defend the right to keep and bear arms, a right enshrined *(inscrit)* in the Constitution (Second amendment). The idea that every citizen has a right to carry weapons derives from the Frontier spirit (individualism, self-reliance and the need to defend oneself), so that all attempts to control the use of guns has so far been limited. Between 60 and 70 million Americans possess firearms, leading to many accidents and homicides every year.
Pentagon: The huge building near Washington which is the headquarters of the US department of defence and which therefore symbolizes the US military power.
Pledge of Allegiance: a pledge *(gage, engagement, promesse)* of loyalty to the US flag: "I pledge allegiance to the flag of the United States of America and to the republic for which it stands, one nation, under God, indivisible, for liberty and justice for all." The pledge is still recited daily in many American schools.
Political correctness (PC): A rejection, in the wake of *(à la suite de)* the Civil Rights Movement of the 1960s, of a culture seen as dominated by dead white European males. PC took the form of curriculums *(programmes scolaires ou universitaires)* favouring the works of women and minorities; but it also attempted to reform language by avoiding words which might be considered as offensive by certain groups of people because of their gender, race or physical condition. It is thus better to say "a chairperson" rather than "a chairman", and a "native American" rather than an "American Indian".
Protestant Work Ethic: The idea that hard work is a way of serving God.
'Rags to Riches': An expression which sums up the possibility of climbing up the social ladder through hard work and will power *(Mot à mot: des haillons à la richesse)*.
Rust Belt: a number of states around the Great Lakes, where the decline of traditional heavy industry has led to economic problems (rust: *la rouille*).
Self-made man: If the American Dream is possible, then you can start from poverty and work your way up to wealth and/or a higher social position. You then become a self-made man, like J.D. Rockefeller. You can also say that you have gone "from rags to riches".
Self-reliance: The typically American idea that man should rely on himself *(compter sur lui-même)*, on his intellectual and physical abilities, to survive and prosper, just as America should rely on its own resources rather than perpetuate European traditions. The idea is developed in Emerson's essay *Self-Reliance* (1841) *(indépendance)*.
Silicon Valley: an area close to San Francisco specialized in high technology
Spanglish: a portmanteau word *(mot valise)* describing the mixture of Spanish and English spoken in some bilingual areas of the United States
Statue of Liberty: The statue which stands at the entrance of New York harbor, on Liberty Island. The work of the French sculptor Bartholdi, it symbolizes both liberty and all the immigrants who arrived in America to find that liberty.

A few lines from a poem by Emma Lazarus are written on its pedestal:

Give me your tired, your poor,
Your huddled[1] masses yearning[2] to be free,
The wretched[3] refuse[4] of your teeming[5] shore,
Send these, the homeless, tempest-tost[6], to me.
I lift my lamp beside the golden door!

1. **huddled:** *blotties*. 2. **yearning:** *aspirant à*. 3. **wretched:** *misérables*. 4. **refuse:** *détritus*.
5. **teeming:** *fourmillant*. 6. **tempest-tost = tempest-tossed:** *secoués par la tempête*.

Sun Belt, The: the name given to the Southern and Western States, with their hot climate.

Thanksgiving: On the 4th Thursday in November, people celebrate the arrival of the first pilgrims in America on the Mayflower. It is traditional to have a large family meal with turkey and cranberry jelly *(dinde et gelée aux airelles)*, sweet potatoes *(patates)* and pumpkin pie *(tarte à la citrouille)*.

Transcendentalism: A mid nineteenth century movement, best reflected in the works of Thoreau and Emerson. In a reaction against the Puritans' view of predestination, the Transcendentalists believed in a divine immanence within man and nature, thus making all men truly divine and equal.

Wall Street: The New York Street where the New York Stock Exchange *(la Bourse)* is situated.

WASP: The abbreviation of White Anglo-Saxon Protestant. Influential and wealthy white Americans, whose families have been in America for several generations.

World Trade Center: The twin towers of the World Trade Center were the highest buildings in the New York skyline until they were destroyed in the terrorist attacks of 9. 11. 2001.

Yuppies (Young urban professionals): Young professional people living in cities, with high incomes *(revenus)* and a fashionable lifestyle.

A FEW EMBLEMATIC FIGURES IN AMERICAN CULTURE

Al Capone: A well-known Chicago gangster who made his money with drugs, gambling *(jeux d'argent)* and the illicit sale of alcohol during the years of prohibition. Al Capone had a thousand gangsters working for him.

Babbit: The hero of a novel by Sinclair Lewis. He represents the narrow-mindedness *(étroitesse d'esprit)* and philistinism (materialism and indifference to culture) of middle-class America. He has given rise to the word "Babbittry".

Buffalo Bill: William Cody (1846-1917), who spread the myth of the frontier by his deeds *(exploits)* with the Pony Express (a service which carried mail from Kansas to California on horseback in ten days) and his killing of buffaloes to feed workers when the Kansas Pacific Railroad was built. In 1883, he created the "Wild West" show, which staged demonstrations of frontiersmen's skills and re-enactments *(reconstitu-*

tions) of historic events. It helped develop the myth of the frontier, with Buffalo Bill as its most emblematic figure.

Carnegie, Andrew: The typical self-made man who started as a poor immigrant boy and worked his way up, ending as the leading American steel manufacturer. He believed in the "Gospel of Wealth", a mixture of Protestant belief in hard work and of Darwinism, with the rich better at surviving and thus having a responsibility to help the poor. Carnegie's money was used for a large number of philanthropic activities.

Ford, Henry: An industrialist who, by introducing efficient assembly lines *(chaînes de montage)*, was the first to mass-produce cars in the United States. Many, like the Model T (also called Tin Lizzie), became extremely popular. Ford's name evokes mass production and low prices.

Gates, Bill: The founder of Microsoft, he symbolizes the power and dominance of a computer company.

Kennedy, John Fitzgerald: United States president between 1961 and 1963, when he was assassinated. He became a source of inspiration to many because of his youth, his energy, his culture and his vision of a New Frontier against poverty and segregation. His social commitment is summed up in one of the sentences he used when he took the oath of office *(prêter serment)*: "ask not what your country can do for you – ask what you can do for your country."

King, Martin Luther: One of the most influential leaders of the movement for racial equality. Influenced by Christianity and Gandhi's principles, King preached non-violent resistance to unfair laws *(lois injustes)*. He organised boycotts and sit-ins, which eventually led to the Civil Rights Act of 1964. He was assassinated in 1968.

Malcolm X: A highly influential black orator and member of the Black Muslims. He criticised the Civil Rights movement of Martin Luther King, refusing integration and calling instead for the establishment of a black nation within the United States. Malcolm X also refused non-violent means of protest. He had enormous influence among disillusioned black people. Malcolm X was assassinated in 1965.

Nader, Ralph: A lawyer who has devoted his life to the defence of consumers *(consommateurs)*. Nader has also led campaigns against pollution, nuclear energy and any threat to the environment. With his Public Citizen group, he is seen as a champion of citizen action in order to make business and government more accountable *(responsables)*.

Rockefeller, John D.: Rockefeller (1839-1937) entered the oil business at the end of the Civil War and consolidated the oil refineries by eliminating competitors. The richest man in America at the end of the 1890s, he was deeply religious, saying "God gave me the money", and devoted much of his money to various philanthropic activities.

Sitting Bull: The Sioux American Indian who led the war against US expansion westward in the nineteenth century. He helped defeat General Custer at the Battle of Little Big Horn (1876), but had to surrender *(se rendre)* in 1881. He later appeared in Buffalo Bill's Wild West Show.

Uncle Sam: The symbol of the United States. He was invented by cartoonists in the 19th century and usually resembles Abraham Lincoln, with a goatee (a small beard), and a star-spangled hat reminiscent of the American flag.
Uncle Tom: A kind and courageous black slave in Harriet Beecher Stowe's novel *Uncle Tom's Cabin* (1852). The name has become synonymous with humble cooperation with the whites and is used pejoratively to describe servile black Americans.
Washington, George: A national figure, who led the war of independence against Britain, helped draft (write) the Constitution and became the first American president.
Yankee: Originally a pejorative term used by Southerners to describe an American on the side of the Union during the Civil War. The word is still pejorative and refers to a typical American from New England.

It must be immediately clear to all that this painting is American. A man and a woman are seen posing in front of their house, a white house in the style known as American Gothic or Carpenter Gothic. They are dressed in the severe black and white clothes of late 19th century Midwestern farmers, the woman with her apron (*tablier*) and plain black dress, the man in a collarless shirt (*chemise sans col*) and overalls.
The dour and sour (*austère*) look of the two characters, their tight-lipped and stony faces (*air pincé et froid*), their stiff pose seem to illustrate the Puritan ethic and the virtues of hard work, symbolized by the pitchfork (*fourche*) which stands between them. Indeed, many details justify this interpretation. The top window of the house, with its medieval pointed arch, is reminiscent of a church and another church steeple appears over the tree tops, on the left hand side. The two characters look austere, resolute and sad: we imagine a life of rigid routines.
We also have the feeling that the painting reflects the parallelisms between man and his environment. The parallel lines of the three-pronged pitchfork (*fourche à trois dents*) are echoed in the pattern of the windows, in the lines in the man's face, in the seams (*coutures*) of his overalls and in the stripes (*rayures*) of his

Grant Wood, *American Gothic*.

►►► Continued on page 354

MAJOR TRENDS IN AMERICAN LITERATURE

FROM THE COLONIAL AGE

MAJOR DATES IN HISTORY

1607	1620	1775-1783	1776	1791	1803-1804
First English settlement at Jamestown	Mayflower Compact	War of Independence	Declaration of Independence	Bill of Rights	Louisiana Purchase Lewis & Clark expedition reaches the Pacific

POETRY

FICTION & PROSE

1771-1793	1776	1819-20
FRANKLIN *Autobiography*	PAINE *Common Sense* A defence of the Revolution	IRVING *The Sketch Book*

THE THEATRE

PAINTING Portraits (SMIBERT, FEKE)
Historical paintings (COPLEY, PEALE, STUART)

TO THE MID 19TH CENTURY

1848 — Gold Rush

1861-1865 — Civil War

1865 — Slavery abolished

1845 — POE *The Raven*

1847 — LONGFELLOW *Evangeline*
Moralistic poetry

1855 — WHITMAN *Leaves of Grass*
Prophetic poetry

1826 — COOPER *The Last of the Mohicans*

1840 — POE *Tales of the Grotesque and the Arabesque*

1841-1844 — EMERSON *Essays*

1850 — HAWTHORNE *The Scarlet Letter*

1851 — MELVILLE *Moby Dick*
STOWE *Uncle Tom's Cabin*
a denunciation of slavery

1854 — THOREAU *Walden*

Hawthorne, Poe, Melville: THE AMERICAN RENAISSANCE:
sombre, symbolic and imaginative works

TRANSCENDENTALISM
a celebration of the divinity of man
and his oneness with nature

Landscape painting (DURAND, COLE, CHURCH, KENSETT)
Genre painting (MOUNT, BINGHAM)

1865

MAJOR DATES IN HISTORY

- 1865-77 Reconstruction
- 1890 Frontier closed
- 1907 Peak immigration year
- 1917 US declares war on Germany

POETRY

- 1890-91 DICKINSON *Poems*
- 1916 SANDBURG *Chicago Poems*

FICTION & PROSE

- 1881 JAMES *The Portrait of a Lady*
- 1884 TWAIN *The Adventures of Huckleberry Finn* — a humorous novel of initiation & a satire on Southern society
- 1895 CRANE *The Red Badge of Courage*
- 1900 DREISER *Sister Carrie*
- 1903 LONDON *The Call of the Wild*
- 1905 WHARTON *The House of Mirth*

NATURALISM (1895–1903)

Psychological realism (1881–1905)

THE THEATRE

PAINTING Landscapes: the Luminists (HEADE, LANE); Aestheticism (WHISTLER); Portraits (SARGENT, CASSATT); Realism (HOMER, EAKINS);

1945

1919 — Prohibition

1929 — Wall Street crash leads to Depression years

1933 — Roosevelt President the New Deal

1941 — The U.S. enters WWII

1944 — Allied landing in Normandy

1945 — US bomb on Hiroshima Yalta

1922 — **ELIOT** *The Waste Land*
Modernism & Imagism (also influenced W.C. Williams, M. Moore & W. Stevens)

1926 — **HUGHES** *The Weary Blues*
The Harlem Renaissance (black cultural movement also reflected in the novels of Richard Wright: 1945, *Black Boy*)

1919 — **ANDERSON** *Winesburg, Ohio*

1922 — **LEWIS** *Babbitt*

A satire on the narrow-mindedness of small-town America

1925 — **FITZGERALD** *The Great Gatsby*

1929 — **FAULKNER** *The Sound and the Fury*
HEMINGWAY *A Farewell to Arms*

1936 — **DOS PASSOS** *USA*

1939 — **STEINBECK** *The Grapes of Wrath*

Social awareness

Fitzgerald, Hemingway, Dos Passos: THE LOST GENERATION Modernist techniques to reflect a sense of emptiness & loss

The Southern Renaissance (violent & grotesque characters reflecting guilt about and nostalgia for the Southern past)

1931 — **O'NEILL** *Mourning Becomes Electra*
(Plays which unite realism & symbolism)

The Ash Can School (HENRI, SLOAN); The Modernists (O'KEEFFE, STELLA, DAVIS); The precisionists (DEMUTH, SHEELER); The urban scene (HOPPER); The regionalists (BENTON, WOOD)

MUSIC **Negro spirituals, blues and ragtime, jazz (L. Armstrong, C. Basie, D. Ellington) operas, musical comedies, jazz (G. Gershwin)**

1945

MAJOR DATES IN HISTORY

1947	1950-1953	1953	1955-1956	1960	1963
Beginning of Cold War	Korean War	anti-communist crusade	Montgomery bus boycott	Kennedy president: New Frontier	Equal rights march on Washington Kennedy assassinated

POETRY

1946	1951	1956	1959	1965
BISHOP *North & South*	RICH *A Change of World*	GINSBERG *Howl*	LOWELL *Life Studies*	PLATH *Ariel*

The Beat poets: A reaction against mainstream values & culture

Confessional poets (lyrical & intimate expression of feelings)

FICTION & PROSE

1948	1952	1955	1957	1960	1961
MAILER *The Naked & the Dead*	ELLISON *Invisible Man*	NABOKOV *Lolita*	KEROUAC *On the Road* MALAMUD, *The Assistant*	UPDIKE *Rabbit, Run*	HELLER *Catch-22*

A few main trends in fiction:
The Beat Generation (religious ectasy and drugs as a way of rejecting conventions): Kerouac; **Southern literature** (Gothic trends: violence and grotesque characters to reflect the decadence of the South): Styron, McCullers, O'Connor, Capote, T. Williams; **Black voices** (suffering and estrangement): Ellison, Morrison; **Jewish voices** (the scars left by the Holocaust, the tensions between Jews and Gentiles, often related with distance & humour): Heller, Malamud, Bellow, Roth; **the use of farce, parody and absurdity to mock the convention of the novels:** Nabokov, Heller.

THE THEATRE

1947	1953	1962
WILLIAMS T. *A Streetcar Named Desire*	MILLER *The Crucible*	ALBEE *Who's Afraid of Virginia Woolf?* The theatre of the Absurd

Individuals crushed by materialism & conformity

PAINTING

Realism (WYETH)
Abstraction (POLLOCK, KLINE, DE KOONING, NEWMAN, ROTHKO)
Pop Art (JOHNS, RAUSCHENBERG, WARHOL, LICHTENSTEIN, ROSENQUIST)

2003

1964-1973	1969	1974	1981-1989	1993-2001	2001	2003
Vietnam War	First landing on the moon	Nixon impeached	Reagan president	Clinton president	terrorist attack against New York & Washington	War against Iraq

1999
RICH *Midnight Salvage*

1964	1965	1966	1978	1985	1987	1998	2001
BELLOW *Herzog*	O'CONNOR *Everything that Rises Must Converge*	CAPOTE *In Cold Blood* ROTH *Portnoy's Complaint* VONNEGUT *Slaughter-house-Five*	IRVING *The World According to Garp*	AUSTER *City of Glass*	MORRISSON *Beloved*	DELILLO *Under-world*	ROTH *The Human Stain*

1986	1994
SHEPARD *Fool for Love*	MAMET *American Buffalo*

MUSIC Classical music influenced by jazz (L. BERNSTEIN)

▸▸▸ Continued from page 347.

shirt. It is as if the harsh Midwestern environment, so hostile to the early pioneers, had seeped *(pénétré)* into their characters. Like the early pioneers, these two characters convey an impression of self-reliance, fortitude and individualism, as if they needed no one else. They seem to keep us out of their world rather than in it, forming a barrier between us and the house, itself another closed space with its blinds *(stores)* pulled down. Whether the two characters are husband and wife or father and daughter, the pitchfork held by the man seems to be protecting his wife or his daughter's chastity. But there are more homely touches as well: the potted plants on the porch (close to the woman, symbolizing domesticity), the cameo brooch she is wearing, the pitchfork which evokes haymaking.

No wonder this painting should have become a national icon.

But is Grant Wood's painting a realistic and meticulously detailed description of stern Midwestern characters, or is it a satire of such characters? Is the couple being mocked or praised? It is indeed difficult to decide between the serious and the parodic interpretations, even if Grant Wood denied any satirical intentions.

As a result, the painting has been endlessly parodied, thus proving that it is part of American popular culture. Modern parodies have reproduced the painting with the heads of well-known figures (presidents, stars) instead of the original couple, thus creating clashes or incongruousness. They become Mr and Mrs America, with added attributes and symbols.

V QUELQUES DIFFÉRENCES ENTRE L'ANGLAIS BRITANNIQUE ET AMÉRICAIN

LEXIQUE

GB	US	Français
autumn	fall	l'automne
a banknote	a bill	un billet de banque
the bill	the check	l'addition (au restaurant)
a biscuit	a cookie	un biscuit
the bonnet	the hood	le capot (d'une voiture)
the boot	the trunk	le coffre de voiture
braces	suspenders	des bretelles
a car	an automobile	une voiture
a car park	a parking lot	un parking
a caretaker	a janitor	un gardien d'immeuble
a chemist's	a drugstore	une pharmacie
chips	French fries	des frites
a cooker	a stove	une cuisinière
corn	wheat	du blé
crisps	chips	des pommes chips
a Curriculum Vitae (a CV)	a résumé	un Curriculum Vitae
dinner-jacket	a tuxedo	un smoking
the engine	the motor	le moteur
an estate agent	a realtor	un agent immobilier
a film	a movie	un film
the first floor	the second floor	le premier étage
a flat	an apartment	un appartement
football	soccer	le football
a form / a class	a grade	une classe (année d'étude)
the garden	the backyard	le jardin autour de la maison
a goods waggon	a freight car	un wagon de marchandises
the Blair government	the Bush administration	le gouvernement B...
the ground floor	the first floor	le rez de chaussée
a handbag	a purse	un sac à main
the high street	the main street	la grand rue
holidays	vacation	les vacances
ill	sick	malade
the lavatory / the toilet	the restroom	les toilettes
a lift	an elevator	un ascenseur
a lorry	a truck	un camion
a mark	a grade	une note (à un devoir)

a motorway	a highway	une autoroute
the pavement	the sidewalk	le trottoir
petrol	gas(oline)	l'essence
the police station	the precinct station	le commissariat de police
the post / to post	the mail / to mail	le courrier / poster
a pram	a baby carriage	un landau
a queue	a line	une file d'attente
the railway	the railroad	le chemin de fer
a rubber	an eraser	une gomme
rubbish	garbage	les ordures
a shop	a store	un magasin
a shopping centre	a shopping mall	un centre commercial
a sofa	a couch	un canapé
to stop	to quit	arrêter une occupation habituelle
sweets	candy	des bonbons
a tap	a faucet	un robinet
a taxi	a cab	un taxi
a time-table	a schedule	un horaire
a tin	a can	une boîte de conserve
the toilet(s)	the restroom	les toilettes
the town centre	downtown	le centre ville
a tram	a streetcar	un tramway
trousers	pants	un pantalon
a tyre	a tire	un pneu
the underground / tube	the subway	le métro
a vest	an undershirt	un maillot de corps
a waistcoat	a vest	un gilet
the windscreen	the windshield	le pare-brise

Différences orthographiques

GB → US

-our → -or	colour → color
-re → -er	centre → center
-ough → -ow	plough → plow
-ise → -ize	realise → realize
-ce → -se	offence → offense
-amme → -am	programme → program

Différences grammaticales

GB: Do you have the record?	US: Have you got the record?
GB: Have you phoned Simon?	US: Did you phone Simon?

got → gotten (We've gotten a new car.)

Différences de prononciation

a: France	GB: **frɑːns**	US: **fræns**
er: clerk	GB: **klaːk**	US: **klɜːk**
e/u: new	GB: **njuː**	US: **nuː**

prononciation du r

Dans un registre familier, l'anglais américain se rapproche souvent d'une écriture phonétique et simplifie l'orthographe:
thru (= through)
tonite (= tonight)
cheez = cheese
a donut = a doughnut

exercices

1 Récrivez les phrases qui suivent en anglais américain.

1. He left his lorry in the car park and took the lift to this friend's flat.
2. Do you have braces I can wear with this dinner-jacket?
3. I've never had a car, and can't tell the bonnet from the boot.

2 Récrivez les phrases qui suivent en anglais britannique.

1. He had his favorite meal of steak and French fries, asked for the check and left.
2. When she was in the restroom, she realized she had left her purse in the trunk.
3. We'll take a cab to go downtown.

I Communiquer

I 1. Écrire une lettre

1 England, Sunday 5th ......
Dear Papi,
It's very nice here. The weather is wonderful and the people are always kind and friendly, especially my landlady. She is a very good cook. She also helps me with my English. In fact, she is standing behind me now as I write this letter to look if there are any mistakes!
Wish you were here.
Hans
P.S. Please send more money soon.

2 Dear Mrs Smith/thank you for/it won't inconvenience you./Looking forward to meeting you/Yours Sincerely/Pierre Durand (signature)

3 Alan Green
22 Oakview Crescent
Basingstoke
The Librarian
Reading Public Library
Dear Sir,

I am writing in response to your advertisement of March 20th in *The Reading Gazette*. I would like to apply for the summer job of assistant in your library. My reason for applying is that I have always been interested in books and spend a lot of time in *libraries*. I enclose my CV, which will show you that I have indeed already worked a little in my school library. I would be happy to send you any other details you may require.

I hope you will consider my application and would be very pleased to come for an interview whenever it is convenient for you.

I look forward to hearing from you.

Yours faithfully,

4 (1) I would be grateful if you could send me your new catalogue. (2) We look forward to your reply. (3) With reference to your advertisement in *The Independent*, I would be grateful if you would send me further details. (4) Please find enclosed the list of prices tou asked for. (5) Lots of love to both of you. My regards to your father.

I 2. Écrire un courrier électronique

1 1. See you there. 2. tomorrow. 3. Great! 4. Do you want to? 5. See you before five. 6. Welcome back home! 7. before you go. 8. next week. 9. How are things with you? 10. What are you up to now? (Qu'est-ce que tu fais? Où en es-tu?)

2 1. F 2. J 3. H 4. O 5. G 6. M 7. B 8. E 9. K 10. C 11. I 12. N 13. A 14. L 15. D

I 3. Écrire une page de journal intime

1 a. Have decided to keep a diary. Will write in it everything that happens to me & J.
b. Tuesday. Was awoken at 6 by loud noise at (the) door. First thought it was the police after last night. Then realized it was Juliet.

2 I lay long in bed and then got up and was at the office... At noon I dined /... and then went to the office, where I was busy... I went home to supper ... heard ... had come... though it had... troubled... I went back to the office

I 5. Écrire un récit

1 The right order is: D - C - F - B - H - K - I - A - J - G - L - E

2 When Monsieur Jean opened his fridge <u>that morning</u>, he discovered that it was practically empty. He mentally made a list of all he needed to buy – coffee, sugar, pizza, camembert –, **wondered if there was anything else he had forgotten**, and left his flat. <u>As</u> he was going down the stairs, he met his concierge, Madame Colin, and **they greeted each other**.

"Go ahead! I'm such a slowpoke!", she said to him, motioning to him to pass her on the stairs, then commenting on the energy and youth of Monsieur Jean, who was already down the steps, whistling. A few minutes later, he was in the supermarket, filling his caddy with a variety of food. Meanwhile, just behind him, he heard a young woman was explaining to someone that she was doing a survey into the eating habits of people under 35 and wondering if she could ask them a few questions. Monsieur Jean turned round, looked at the pretty blonde, and immediatly fell in love.

I 6. Écrire un résumé

Meilleur résumé : 3.
Résumés rejetés: 1 (informations fausses/ information non essentielle) ; 2 (langue et style) ; 3 (résumé non objectif).

I 7. Écrire un essai

1 A: 2 – B: 3 – C: 1 – D: 5 – E: 4

2 A: 2 – B: 1 – C: 4

3 (1) D. The primary obstacle to wider adoption is the cost of handsets. (Topic sentence) – (2) F. In the rich world, these typically cost around $200 (though most pay less than this thanks to subsidies from network operators), or less than 1% of the average income per person. (Explanation of the word 'cost'. (I) in richer countries) – (3) E. In the developing world, in contrast, a $50 handset would account for 14% of the annual income of someone earning $1 a day. (Explanation of the word 'cost'. (II) in poorer countries.) – (4) A. So the first step in promoting the adoption of mobile phones, say operators in developing countries, is to reduce the cost of the handsets. (Logical solution to the problem.) – (5) C. Several such schemes are under way: in particular, several operators in developing countries have joined together to aggregate their buying power, and Motorola, the world's second-largest handset-maker, has agreed to supply up to 6m handsets for less than $40 each. (Examples of such experiments being carried out.) – (6) B. There is already talk of prices falling below $30 next year. (Consequence of these experiments.)

4 Voir le tableau ci-contre.

I 8. Communiquer par téléphone

1 1. M – 2. J – 3. I – 4. G – 5. H – 6. E – 7. C – 8. O – 9. L – 10. A – 11. D – 12. K – 13. F – 14. B – 15. N

2 1. voicemail – 2. hold on – 3. press – 4. tone – 5. mobile – 6. try

I 9. Ponctuer correctement

1 That is other people's money.
20% OFF ALL CDs
FOURTH FLOOR: CHILDREN'S TOYS
Il faut une virgule après "us", puisque Tony Blair n'appartient pas au parti Conservateur.

2 (1) All the people saw the film. /Some of the people only (those who saw the film) did. (2) The student was late, according to the teacher). /The teacher was late, according to the student. (3) Phil and Tom = the two brothers./Phil and Tom are other friends invited, not the two brothers. (4) Je demanderai à ceux qui n'ont pas encore décidé s'ils venaient ou non. /Je demanderai à ceux qui n'ont pas pris de décision de venir.

3 Charles the First walked and talked. Half an hour after, his head was cut off.

4 A 50-year-old school bus driver was arrested after driving so erratically that police were flooded with calls from motorists. Terrified children phoned their parents on their mobiles as they were driven home from school in Cirencester to Stroud, Gloucester, on Tuesday. (*The Times*, March 5, 2004)

Structure	Paragraph numbers	Link words & articulations
Introduction		
◆ The situation in Britain	§ 1	How far should...?
◆ The question it leads us to ask ourselves	§ 2	
Part I: Can the problem be solved politically?		
◆ The government has a duty to protect us, but it is not so obvious in the case of our diet.	§ 3-4	But / nevertheless
◆ → The journalist is neither for nor against government measures. The only thing which matters is what will work.	§ 5	Personally.../ but Moreover
Part II: The real problem = eating habits		
◆ Example of litter: we don't eat at home but on the streets	§ 6	Far deeper... and more... Why...
◆ A meal is no longer a social activity around the dining-room table	§ 7-9	Why...? In other words...
◆ → People do not need more information, but more of a family structure.	§ 10	If I am right... In fact...
◆ Asking children what they want to eat reduces variety	§ 11	Another problem This has the effect... The result is...
Conclusion		
◆ The resulting situation	§ 12	There is no doubt that...

❷ "Look here, it's no good!", said my Dad. We were in the car on the way back to London. My father had just collected me and my trunk from the posh girls' school that I attended. He had also just sat through Parents' Day, in the course of which I was presented with the Latin prize, the English Essay prize, and the prize for the girl who had done best in A-levels. (Adapted from M. Furlong)

II 1. Développement chronologique

❷ (1) until – (2) no sooner – (3) so far – (4) formerly – (5) soon – (6) meanwhile – (7) during – since – (8) as soon as – (9) yet – (10) for – still

❷ (a) during – (b) for – (c) for – (d) since – (e) since – (f) since

❷ (1) He must receive the book by the end of the month. (2) Last night, I worked until one o' clock in the morning. (3) Pierre has not given us his answer yet. (4) They have lived in London since they got married. (5) We'll go skiing while she is in New York. She will join us later. (6) No sooner had she stepped down from the train than (Hardly had she... when...) she realized that it was the wrong station.

❷ From – to No sooner – than – Soon – until – then – later – for - Two years later – for – later - as soon as – then – for – when / after – since – When - for

II 2. Développement logique

❷ 1. D – 2. E – 3. A – 4. B – 5. H – 6. K – 7. L – 8. G – 9. F – 10. J – 11. C – 12. I

❷ (1) provided that/so long as – (2) in case – (3) as though – (4) unlike – (5) neither – (6) though – (7) because of – (8) so that – (9) as a result – (10) in spite of – (11) although – (12) instead of

❷ (1) In spite of the rain, we had our picnic outside. (2) They'll let you in, provided you wear proper clothes. (3) Unlike her mother, Sarah is fair. (4) Having broken a leg, John missed school (/will miss school) for a week. (5) You can neither phone nor use your cell phone in this cinema. (6) John always made faces: hence his nickname Monkey. (7) I bought him a cell phone so that he might ring me at all times. (8) Instead of flying, take the train.

II 2. Description spatiale

1 1. ... is walking round the tree. 2. ... is walking along the hedge. 3. ... is sitting on the roof. 4. ... is walking away from the tree. 5. ... is walking across the road. 6. ... is jumping onto the mouse. 7. ... is walking through the hedge. 8. ... is sitting under the tree. 9. ... is jumping over the hedge. 10. ... is walking into the house. 11. ... is sitting behind the tree. 12. ... is walking to the tree.

2 1. He dived from the boat into the water. 2. Go along the public garden, past the bank and the chemist's and you'll find my house on the right. 3. Our hotel was opposite the opera, within a hundred yards of the station, but two kilometres (a mile and a half) from the museum. 4. She lives on the third floor, at number 3, rue du Lac. 5. The burglar went through the hedge and across the garden, ran round the house, then went down the steps which led to the cellar.

III 1. Socializing

1 heat up/take off/add /beat/mix/pour/ bake

2 King's School

3 1. I wonder if you could lend me the record. May I borrow the record? 2. Shall we have a drink before supper? Why don't you come and have a drink before supper? /Why not have a drink before supper? 3. I'd love to come to the wedding, but I can't. I regret not being able to come to the wedding.

4 1. "I'm terribly sorry: I forgot the book." " Don't worry."
2. "Let me introduce myself. I'm André." "Pleased to meet you."
3. "What about spending the weekend at our place in Normandy?"
"I'd love to. It's very kind of you."

III 2. Emotions

1 A. 1. e – 2. j – 3. f – 4. a – 5. i – 6. d – 7. c – 8. h – 9. g – 10. b
B. 1. c 2. g 3. e 4. d 5. a 6. b 7. h 8. Ff

2 1. This kind of jazz leaves me cold. 2. How incredible! 3. It is strange that he should not have called. 4. He's dying to tell you what happened. 5. I hate getting up early. 6. If I had known, I would have taken the train. 7. I would rather go to the theatre, if you don't mind. 8. He's won £500 in the lottery and is as pleased as Punch.

III 3. Mental activity

1 1. must – 2. do not have to – 3. are entitled to – 4. may not/may/can – 5. can/be careful not to – 6. must – 7. may/can

2 1. Is he qualified to be a taxi driver? 2. I fully share your views/opinion on this point. 3. It is difficult to say whether she is right or not. 4. I could not help feeling that there must be someone hiding in the house. 5. The child talked his/her mother into buying him/her the toy.

IV 1. Dates et références temporelles

1 1. at – 2. on - in – 3. at - during – 4. in - in – 5. at - in – 6. from - to - by – 7. for – 8. since – 9. on - at - in

2 1. mid-eighties – 2. Tuesday nights – 3. No sooner had he said the words than... – 4. 1999 – 5. The late nineties

3 eighteen seventy-one, eighteen thirty-four, nineteen thirteen, March the seven-

teenth, July the twelfth, two thousand and four/twenty o four, eleven
Dans le tableau: January the first, January the second, March the seventeenth, July the twelfth, December the twenty-fifth, December the twenty-sixth

IV 2. Mesures

Mélangez 225g de chocolat noir et 150 ml de crème fraîche.
Si vous mesurez 1m 52 et pesez 82 kg, alors vous avez des kilos en trop.
Demain les températures ne dépasseront guère les 10 degrés, mais pourraient atteindre 15 degrés en Cornouailles.
Continuez pendant environ trois kilomètres puis prenez le chemin à droite qui monte à l'église. Vous êtes à 400 mètres d'altitude et la vue est superbe.

IV 3. Chiffres

1 (1) In that country, some one million five hundred and eighty-one thousand people or eleven point two per cent of the population live on less than one dollar a day. (2) Our new postal code is seven five o o five and the telephone number o one four three double seven o two. (3) In maths, I got a fifteen out of twenty, a sixteen out of twenty and a six out of twenty, so that I was given twelve point thirty-three for the whole term. (4) Italy beat Spain three-two ... with a time of twenty-one point two seconds... (5) Seventy-two multiplied by thirteen is/equals nine hundred and thirty-five. (6) Nine thousand six hundred and eighty-two minus six hundred and fifty is/equals nine thousand and thirty-two. (7) Seven thousand and sixty-eight divided by forty-two is/equals one hundred and sixty-eight point twenty-eight. (8) Six hundred and fifty-one is an odd number; seventy-six is an even number.

2 A. 4 B. 5 C. 1 D. 8 E. 6 F. 7 G. 3 H. 2

3 twelve per cent/one hundred and seventy-six/up from seven per cent in sixty-one parliaments in nineteen fifty-five.
eleven out of one hundred and eighty
seventy million girls/sixty million boys
eight hundred and fifty million illiterate people
thirty per cent/sixty per cent/fifty-five per cent.
twenty/eleven out of thirty seven per cent

4 (1) twofold – (2) three times as high – (3) rose from.... to... – (4) by – (5) over

5 (1) Most Americans were affected by the depression in the 1930s. (2) It is free for the under-fourteens. (3) She must be in her mid-forties, but she does not look her age. (4) If he has a thirty-six-year-old mother, he can't be 35!

II Analyser

1. De la lecture à l'analyse

1 WHO? Jasvinder Sanghera. Age? Now: 39. Then: from 14 to 15
WHERE? In England. She now lives in Derby.
WHEN? Two different moments are described: - over 20 years ago/now
WHAT?/WHY? She ran away so as not to marry the man her parents wanted her to marry. She now works to help people in the Asian community in Britain.

2 seldom: rarely; cut him dead: pretended not to see him; propinquity: proximity; assuage: reduce; went down with: was ill with; worn: very tired; brooding: having dark thoughts; rebuke: reprimand; dwelling: living; dawn: appear

3 torn/attending/shortly/attack/south/middle/vicious/weather/injuries/centre/people/reported/staff/calls/unable/cancelled/filled/feet

4 1. A– 2. B– 3. B– 4. B– 5. C

2. Analyser un article de journal

HEADLINES

1 The longest marriage in the world.
Parents are to pay for their children's sins.
Ex-butler is jailed.
Brothers are held over the Bombay train blasts.

2 A poll shows that the Tories are at a 13-year high.
A thief who stole the medals of an Olympic gold medallist is jailed.
Greece is transfixed by the case of a murdered boy.
There are plans to fit numberplates to bicycles in order to catch lawless riders.
Tony Blair has plans to bring about a ceasefire in the conflict.

3 – To be driven to = to be led to, but the use of the verb 'drive' is also a direct allusion to the subject of the article, the car.
– Babel refers to the Bible (Genesis) and the building of a tower intended to reach heaven, but which God punished by making the builders' speech mutually unintelligible. It therefore conveys the idea of confusion leading nowhere.
– "Law and disorder" is a distortion of the expression "law and order (l'ordre public) and thus points to Britain's poor record in that field.

4 1. (c)– 2. (b) – 3. (b)

ORGANISATION

5 The occasion is the Queen's eightieth birthday.
The lead-in
The monarchy is compared with the Church of England.
The monarchy

6 **I. The strength of the monarchy**
1. The monarchy has often been unpopular. Yet Queen Elizabeth II is not.
2. The monarchy compared with the Church of England
The monarchy has not lost its popularity. Yet the Church of England is in decline.
II. The reasons for this strength
1. Many people are indifferent to the monarchy and therefore do not oppose it.
By contraste indifference to The Church works against it.
2. The Queen avoids controversy.
But there are controversial issues in the Church of England.
3. The decline of political ideology. There is practically no anti-monarchism in Britain.
But the fact that the Queen is non-partisan does not bring people to the Church of England.

BIAS

7 c and e are biased: c because of the word 'maniac', which is not objective, and because of the pun Harry/hurry; e because of the use of the modal 'must', which expresses the writer's opinion, and because of the verb 'quit', which is familiar.

8 1. The man in red is the logo of the *Daily Express* (look at the title of the newspaper). He is a crusader, someone who campaigns in favour of a cause. In fact, he is St George, the patron saint of England, since it is his emblem (a red cross on a white background) which you can see on his shield. And it is interesting to note that this newspaper was published on April 23, which is St George's saint's day.
At the end of his spear, you can see the head of Tony Blair, or rather of a caricature of Tony Blair, with a frown and large ears, which make him look horrible and rather devilish.
The newspaper is clearly crusading against Tony Blair, and this crude *("grossier, rudimentaire")* and oversimplified picture announces the newspaper's bias.
2. The lack of objectivity also appears through the enormous headline. As for the figure, it seems grossly exaggerated. It is difficult to believe it can be right, when the Labour Party had, at that date, an unheard of majority in the House of Commons.
3. have had enough of

WORKING ON AN ARTICLE

9 1. Both *The New York Times* and *Le Monde* are serious, intellectual newspapers. We therefore expect a serious, neutral article.
The headline is a clear, straightforward one, announcing that the article is about European culture. But it is also a somewhat surprising one, since it is the USA, we are told, which give Europe its common culture. This creates expectancy. We want to know more and want to read the article.
What seems most interesting at first is that an American article reproduced in a French newspaper is about Europe, not the United States. So we expect an outsider's view of our continent. Besides, the date of publication (2 May 2004) is significant: the day before (1 May 2004) ten more countries entered the European Union, making it a union of 25 member states.
2. – § 1 & 2
– (c)
– thesis + examples
– the cinema/the theatre & music/painting/literature/pop music
1 it is a certain cultural identity
2 the most common cultural link across the region now is a devotion to American popular culture
3 Europeans have tried to reinforce national and regional identities
4 the power of Hollywood
5 Europeans now rarely choose to see one another's films
6 few shows that are not local become commercial hits
7 There is a similar phenomenon in the visual arts.
8 most non-national best sellers come from popular American writers
9 even European pop music rarely crosses the region's borders
10 unless it also communicates culturally, popular taste will become ever more American.
3. This article has no obvious political bias and does not reflect a narrow American point of view. Indeed, in the concluding paragraph, an expression such as "there may also be a price to pay", shows that the journalist is in favour of greater European communication in terms of culture. Similarly, the article does not reveal any obvious anti-Americanism.
However, the article is not a neutral, factual one: it reflects the opinion of the journalist who wrote it. And in order to look at it criti-

cally, a further distinction may well have to be made. American culture is constantly linked to the idea of a "popular" culture in the article ("a devotion to American popular culture", "American popular culture spread...", "popular taste will become ever more American."). So isn't the real difference between culture generally and popular culture? American popular fashion and culture may well be the real common point between the younger generation in most European countries, but when it comes to less popular culture, many French people will still be familiar with the names of European directors outside France (Wolfgang Becker, Almodovar), with that of painters like Francis Bacon or architects like Norman Foster (British) or Herzog (Swiss).

If we look again at the examples given by the journalist, we can see that it is this difference which matters. It is true (paragraph 7) that few Europeans could mention the names of living French, German or Spanish artists, but could they give the names of living American painters? And the American "bestsellers" mentioned in paragraph 8 are all popular thrillers.

We can agree with the journalist that we need to know more about our neighbours' contemporary culture, but isn't the real "danger" the spread of an "easy" form of popular culture, particularly among young people: the culture of jeans, Coca-Cola, soap operas and reality TV.

To conclude, the journalist is right indeed when he says that an American popular culture is now the common point between a number of European countries, and is probably better-known than their own varied cultures, but this is giving the world "culture" two very different meanings.

I 3. Analyser un texte littéraire

Réponse: Metaphor: 6 – Simile: 2 – Metonymy: 3 – Synecdoche: 8 – Hyperbole: 1 – Apostrophe: 11 – Anaphora: 12 – Oxymoron: 4 – Paradox: 10 – Chiasmus: 5 – Understatement: 7 – Euphemism: 9

1. (a) metaphor (b) comparison (c) metaphor (d) metaphor (e) comparison

I 4. Analyser un texte de fiction

1. Voir tableau ci-dessous.

2. a. (3) – b. (2) – c. (4): second paragraph and (1): first paragraph. – d. (1)

I 5. Analyser un poème

1. 1. sonnet – 2. Visual poem – 3. Nursery rhyme – 4. ballad

2. love: above – rough: tough – fine: mine/pine – woe: know/no – face: pace

3. A. alliteration – B. alternate rhymes – C. onomatopoeia – D. couplet rhymes – E. assonance – F. eye rhyme

	Point of view of a character	Outside point of view
First-person narrative	(1) Carver: the man's point of view (I expected) (4) Salinger: the boy's point of view (I don't feel like going into it)	
Third-person narrative	(3) Carver: Al's point of view (As Al saw it...)	(2) J.Austen: we know what goes on in both Bingley's and Darcy's minds. (He was haughty, reserved and fastidious/Bingley was sure...)

4 hale and hearty (alliteration)/wear and tear (rhyme)/kith and kin (alliteration + assonance)/first and foremost (alliteration)/sink or swim (alliteration + assonance) /safe and sound (alliteration)/spick and span (alliteration)

5 (c) (a) n'a que 4 pieds et n'est pas un pentamètre. De plus le premier pied est un "trochee". (b) a un rythme iambique mais n'a que 4 pieds.

6 (a) vers 1 et 3: "trochees" ; autres vers: "iambs" – (b) "iambs" dans les vers 2, 3 et 4. Dans les vers 1 et 5 l'accent est sur hick/dick/dock.

II 1. Conseils pour décrire et analyser un document iconographique

1 *In the foreground/On the right* is an Earl/(*below* his right hand)/*Opposite* him sits the young woman's father/*Behind* the two of them, *in the background/Between* the two fathers and the window/standing *behind* his master, *in front* of the window/the alderman's agent, *to the left* of him/
On the left of the picture, sits the bride, *between* her future husband, on *the left* and a lawyer, on *the right/On the left*, the bridegroom/*behind* the bridegroom/*In the bottom left-hand* corner, below the bridegroom/On the walls, in *the background/at* the top/and *underneath* it, on the left, St Sebastian. In *the middle* of the four paintings...

2 1. The woman is holding a spanner in her right hand. 2. She has a raccoon in her lap (*sur ses genoux*). 3. She is wearing skating shoes. 4. There are no chessmen on the red and black chessboard. 5. A bottle and a glass are floating in the air above the chessboard. 6. There is a blackbird in the husband's dressing-gown pocket. 7. One end of a piece of string is tied to the husband's hand; the other end is tied to his wallet on the carpet, below his wife's armchair. 8. Scissors are used as candlesticks on the mantelpiece (*manteau de cheminée*). 9. There are no figures on the face of the clock, but it says "April Fool". 10. There are ducks flying in the room above the husband and wife. 11. The man wearing a bowtie in the picture above the chimney has his hands coming out of the picture. 12. The zebra is coming out of the frame (*le cadre*) in the top right-hand side corner. 13. There's a fish jumping out of the water in the staircase in the top left-hand corner. 14. There's a tap on the left-hand side of the chimney. 15. There are two milk bottles instead of flowers on the plant in the foreground.

II 2. Analyser une peinture ou une photographie

1. C – 2. H – 3. A – 4. D – 5. G – 6. F – 7. E – 8. B

II 3. Analyser une publicité

an airline
people who love adventure
humour
an original idea / the viewer's curiosity

II 4. Analyser un dessin humoristique

1 A. 2 – B. 6 – C. 4 – D. 8 – E. 1 – F. 9 – G. 10 – H. 3 – I. 5 – J. 7 – K. 1

2 2. 3 - B

II 5. Analyser un tableau ou un graphique

1. growing – 2. continuing – 3. early – 4. more – 5. less – 6. more – 7. less – 8. sharp – 9. both – 10. higher – 11. pronounced – 12. evenly

III Traduire

Avant toute traduction

1

Source, auteur, date…

Extrait de roman. Si vous connaissez l'auteur, Raymond Chandler, vous savez qu'il est américain et auteur de romans policiers qui ont pour cadre les milieux urbains corrompus et pour héros le détective privé Philip Marlowe.

Who? Where? When? What? Why?

Un majordome *(butler)* conduit Philip Marlowe, le narrateur, auprès d'un vieillard *(General)*. La scène se passe dans une serre *(greenhouse)*.

Organisation du texte

Le texte suit la progression de Philip Marlowe jusqu'au général (cf. les expressions en bleu.)

Temps

Il s'agit d'un récit où alternent une série d'actions (→ passé simple en Français. Ex : "we went through that") et des descriptions (→ imparfait en Français. Ex : "The plants filled the place…)

Point de vue/modaux

Le narrateur est Philip Marlowe; c'est son point de vue que l'on a dans tout le texte.

Ton/registre

Bon niveau de langue. Le ton est détaché, les faits présentés sans commentaire direct.

Procédés stylistiques

Comparaisons étranges et inattendues dont il faudra garder l'originalité en Français. (cf. les passages en rouge.)

The path took us along to the side of the greenhouse and the butler opened a door for me and stood aside. It opened into a sort of vestibule that was about as warm as a slow oven. He came in after me, shut the outer door, opened an inner door and we went through that. Then it was really hot. The air was thick, wet, steamy and larded with the cloying smell of tropical orchids in bloom. The glass walls and roof were heavily misted and big drops of moisture splashed down on the plants. The light had an unreal greenish color, like light filtered through an aquarium tank. The plants filled the place, a forest of them, with nasty meaty leaves and stalks like the newly washed fingers of dead men. They smelled as overpowering as boiling alcohol under a blanket.

The butler did his best to get me through without being smacked in the face by the sodden leaves, and after a while we came to a clearing in the middle of the jungle, under the domed roof. Here, in a space of hexagonal flags, an old red Turkish rug was laid down and on the rug was a wheel chair, and in the wheel chair an old and obviously dying man watched us come with black eyes from which all fire had died long ago, but which still had the coal-black directness of the eyes in the portrait that hung above the mantel in the hall. The rest of his face was a leaden mask, with the bloodless lips and the sharp nose and the sunken temples and the outward-turning earlobes of approaching dissolution. His long narrow body was wrapped – in that heat – in a traveling rug and a faded red bathrobe. His thin clawlike hands were folded loosely on the rug, purple-nailed. A few locks of dry white hair clung to his scalp, like wild flowers fighting for life on a bare rock.

The butler stood in front of him and said: "This is Mr. Marlowe, General."

The old man didn't move or speak, or even nod. He just looked at me lifelessly. The butler pushed a damp wicker chair against the backs of my legs and I sat down. He took my hat with a deft scoop.

Then the old man dragged his voice up from the bottom of a well and said: "Brandy, Norris. How do you like your brandy, sir?" "Any way at all," I said.

Raymond Chandler, *The Big Sleep*, 1939.

❷ 1. ❶ – 2. ❷ – 3. ❷ – 4. ❷ – 5. ❶ – 6. ❸ – 7. ❶ – 8. ❸

2. Conseils généraux pour la traduction

❶ 1. Le roi Edouard VII a régné après Richard Cœur de Lion. 2. Il me restait deux livres, ce qui ne suffisait pas pour faire seize kilomètres en taxi. 3. J'ai pris le *Times* et *Le Songe d'une nuit d'été* pour lire dans le train. 4. Au musée Victoria & Albert, il y a plusieurs tableaux de Sir Peter Lely. 5. How long will it take to drive from Dover to Edinburgh?

❷ 1. Qu'il se soit, lui, excusé, c'est tout à fait extraordinaire! – 2. Ils pensaient, il le savait bien, qu'il avait la solution. (la traduction proposée serait correcte s'il n'y avait pas de virgules en anglais.) – 3. Il est sûr qu'elle viendra. (Elle est sûre de venir = *She is sure that she will come.*) – 4. Le chat nettoya l'assiette en la léchant. (Le chat lécha l'assiette propre. = *The cat licked the clean plate.*) – 5. L'athlète entra dans le stade en courant. (… courut dans le stade = *ran in the stadium*) – 6. Il dit ensuite qu'il n'y avait pas de danger dans l'immédiat. (Il continua à dire.. = *He went on/kept saying*) – 7. Je n'ai pas grande opinion de sa nouvelle pièce. (Je ne pense pas souvent = *I do not often think about…*) – 8. Elle connaissait déjà le livre, ce qui est très bien. (… le livre qui est excellent: pas de virgule avant *'which'*).

3. Utiliser le dictionnaire

❶ 1. 4 – 2. la première – 3. on – 4. La fenêtre grince quand on l'ouvre. J'ai mis du céleri râpé dans ma salade. Il y avait des bûches dans la cheminée. Sa voix affectée me tape sur les nerfs.

❷ (a) teə – (b) tɪə – (c) teə

❸ (a) tearful – (b) torn – (c) tearing

❹ (a) Le bas de ton pantalon est déchiré. (b) Elle n'arrivait pas à s'arracher à ses amis. (c) La pièce était vraiment mélo./C'était une pièce à faire pleurer dans les chaumières. (d) Ils partirent en trombe pour suivre le taxi. (e) Il a été obligé d'en parler à sa mère et il s'est fait bien attraper. (/Il s'est fait sonner les cloches.) (f) Il est tiraillé entre son amour et son devoir. (g) Ils ne mirent pas longtemps à démolir sa théorie.

❺ a. for – b. back – c. for - by – d. from

4. Les procédés de traduction

❶ (1) transposition (2) emprunt (3) étoffement (4) transposition

❷ (1) Le vieillard avançait en traînant les pieds derrière elle. (2) La balle passa près de lui en sifflant. (3) Mes pots de géranium ont été emportés par le vent. (4) *He swam across the Channel.*

❸ (1) Elle était jalouse et surveillait son appartement pour voir si d'autres femmes y venaient. (2) Tous les trains à destination de Londres auront du retard. (3) Il appela le chien en sifflant. (4) Ils font des provisions de bois en prévision de l'hiver.

❹ (1) Il se contenta de hocher la tête. (adverbe → verbe)

(2) Elle me regarda et sourit. (groupe prépositionnel → verbe)

(3) Dès l'ouverture du magasin, la foule s'y précipita. (verbe → nom)

(4) *Her name is Lila.* (verbe → nom)

❺ (1) À votre santé ! À la vôtre ! (2) Il était heureux comme un roi. (3) À quelque chose malheur est bon. (4) *You're welcome.*

5. Quelques réflexes : version

❶ 1. FA (confiance) – 2. non – 3. FA (difficile) – 4. FA (passer sous silence) – 5. FA (prédisposé à) – 6. non – 7. FA (démissionner) – 8. FA (raisonnable) – 9. FA (minuscule) – 10. non

2 1. On la disait très ferme. 2. On lui dit d'être très ferme. 3. On pense qu'ils ont quitté le pays. 4. Les jupes se portent très longues cet hiver. 5. Il appela sa secrétaire et se fit apporter le dernier rapport.

3 1. Il ouvrit la porte d'un coup de pied. 2. Il descendit la rue en boitant. 3. L'eau entrait à flots. 4. Il s'est enroué à force de parler.

4 1. Ils suivirent plusieurs couloirs pour arriver enfin devant une porte fermée à clé.
2. Elle tomba dans la neige et abîma sa jupe, ce qui lui rappela ses jeux d'enfant.
3. Il me dit que j'avais de la chance d'avoir hérité d'une telle maison.
4. Il entendit quelqu'un l'appeler et reconnut la voix de Dan.

6. Quelques réflexes : thème

1 After weeks of preparation, everything was ready for D-day the night before. On the next day, he got up at six...
He's been getting up at six since he started working in Nancy.
He always gets up at six in the morning.
I've read a lot of books – I love it/I love reading. (pas de mention de temps)
I read a lot of books when I was in hospital. (emploi du prétérit car l'action est située dans le temps.)

2 (1) get – (2) would have been able – (3) is believed to – (4) would

3 He had, when packing, forgotten the card they had given him.
He sometimes went to the park.
She took a bottle of brandy from a cupboard.
With a lot of gestures, he explained what had taken place.

4 (1) can – (2) must – (3) must be working – (4) can't – (5) should – (6) might – (7) may (8) have to

5 1. He cycled round the town. 2. The bus drove past us without stopping. 3. He managed to sneak into the house. 4. He ran back to help the child. 5. He limped off.

6 (1) into – (2) about – (3) at – (4) in – (5) through – (6) out of

IV S'exprimer correctement

1. Les verbes be, have et do

1 1. It's raining. 2. He's very old. 3. She's afraid. 4. She's between thirty and forty. 5. He's at the office every morning. 6. I think they're right.

2 1. There are 2. There was 3. There used to be 4. There should be 5. There must be

3 1. impossible 2. How much money have you got? 3. impossible 4. You've got to spend less money. 5. They haven't got a swimming pool. 6. impossible

4 DO: 1. i – 2. g – 3. h – 4. b – 5. a – 6. f – 7. e – 8. d – 9. c
MAKE: 1. g – 2. a – 3. f – 4. e – 5. c – 6. i – 7. d – 8. h – 9. b

2. Phrases affirmatives, négatives, interrogatives, exclamatives

1. When did you buy it? 2. How will you come? 3. Why can't you wait? 4. Whose idea was it to give this party? 5. How much did he give you? 6. What should he have done two years ago?

3. Tags, reprises, réponses brèves

1 1. shouldn't they? 2. didn't she? 3. had they? 4. wouldn't they? 5. hadn't they? 6. are they?

2 1. "The price of petrol keeps rising." "So does that of gas."
2. She might have problems, and so might her husband.
3. " I can't bear hypocrites." "Neither can I."
4. "The UK (United Kingdom) is preparing a new immigration law." "So is France."
5. "I never entered a pub when I was in England." "Neither did my sister, but I did."

3 1. I think so – 2. I don't believe so – 3. they 'd love to – 4. so I understand – 5. I'm afraid not – 6. So it seems.

4. L'impératif

1. Don't smoke in here! 2. Do keep quiet (will you?)! 3. Let's go for a walk in the park. 4. Let's buy this record for his birthday, shall we? 5. Let's not be (/ Don't let us be) too critical.

5. Les temps

Le présent

1 1. non – 2. We often play bridge together. – 3. A cedar tree grows very slowly. – 4. non – 5. I never get up before 10 on Sundays!

2 1. are going/'re going – 2. are/'re always watching – 3. does not/doesn't wear - likes – 4. is watering - think - looks – 5. Does this pen belong – 6. are you running - always run – 7. Do you want - I don't think - I'm thinking

Le prétérit

1 jumped – ran - tried - pushed - chose - took - threatened - shut - struck - took - left

2 1. They'd rather (they would rather) you arrived early. 2. Martha thought it was time her son left home. 3. I wish he invited me more often. 4. I wish I were as rich as my cousin! 5. He'd rather his friend told him the truth.

3 1. was washing – saw 2. washed – returned 3. caught – were you doing 4. read – woke up – were performing

Present perfect

1 1. already – 2. recently – 3. ever – 4. just – 5. not yet

2 1. "I've never seen *Star Wars*". "I saw it last year, during the summer holidays." 2. "I've finished my revisions!" "But you said that last week!". 3. The economic situation improved after the new president was elected, but it has recently got worse. 4. I went sailing a lot when I was at school, but it's the first time (that) I have windsurfed.

3 1. 've been playing – 2. 've played – 3. 've come – 4. 's been walking – 5. 've watched – 6. 's been watching

DEPUIS

1 1. since – 2. since – 3. for – 4. for – 5. since

2 1. I haven't been to the swimming pool since it reopened. 2. I have loved snails ever since I had some at your place. 3. Their house has been flooded for a week. 4. I read the book three months ago. 5. I haven't read anything for three months.

PAST PERFECT

1. came - had been painting - were – 2. have been driving - haven't had - left – 3. had been rising - chose – 4. had invited - had ever seen – 5. was born - grew up - has made up his mind

I 6. Les modaux

CAPACITÉ

1 1. could skate – 2. can ou could - can ou could – 3. Can you hear - can't speak – 4. could not/couldn't - could have written – 5. was able to repair – 6. could see

2 1. You could have apologized. 2. Every night, I can hear my neighbours take their shower. 3. How could I improve my work? 4. I wasn't able to close the window this morning. Can you help me? 5. I don't know if I'll/I will be able to come next week.

PERMISSION

1. Could we borrow your mobile phone? 2. Mobile phones are not allowed in the museum. 3. Dad, can I have the car tonight? 4. He has been allowed to go out on his own since his birthday. 5. You can/may take these chairs: I have others.

DU POSSIBLE AU CERTAIN

1 1. It can't be eight o'clock. 2. He might have accepted if we had asked him. 3. They must have told her the truth. 4. He may resign. 5. They might have taken refuge somewhere. 6. We should have a sunny day tomorrow. 7. It will be/It must be the pizza... 8. She's bound to/sure to succeed. 9. She is sure that she will succeed.

2 1. may/might – 2. must have left – 3. couldn't have reached – 4. may/could take – 5. must be revising.

L'OBLIGATION

1 1. must – 2. had to – 3. have to – 4. didn't have to – 5. musn't – 6. will have to

2 1. I had a through train, so that I didn't have to change. 2. Shall we have to cook in the chalet? 3. The doctor says you must wear your glasses all the time. 4. School starts again on Tuesday, but we have to be there on Monday to get our books. 5. My computer broke down yesterday, and I had to stay at the office to wait for the repair man.

LE CONSEIL

1. ought to have taken off – 2. should tell – 3. should lower – 4. should have decided – 5. ought to drive

LES CONDITIONS

1. were - would be – 2. would have asked – 3. sent – 4. rings – 5. had not inherited – 6. would give

WOULD, USED TO, BE USED TO

1. used to living – 2. used to – 3. would always – 4. not used to walking – 5. get used to – 6. did you really use to have

PARLER DU FUTUR

1. are just about to leave – 2. will buy – 3. is to take place – 4. are dining out – 5. is going to stop – 6. was to have flown – 7. will love – 8. 's laying

HAD BETTER – WOULD RATHER

1. Hadn't you better see a doctor as soon as possible? 2. I'd rather he hadn't gone to live abroad. 3. I'd rather pay more taxes than have such public transportation. 4. They'd rather you sent them an e-mail. 5. You'd better look at the road instead of looking at me.

7. Verbe + préposition ou/et particule

1. in-back – 2. back – 3. out – 4. off – 5. down – 6. off – 7. away – 8. out

8. Le nom

LE PLURIEL

1. There was a strange species of bird on the roofs and among the leaves. 2. I've damaged my tights going down the stairs. 3. The police have arrested the air hostess and the whole of the crew is now on strike. 4. He has a lot of cattle and about a dozen sheep. 5. The two men had their hands hidden in the pockets of their trousers.

DÉNOMBRABLES ET INDÉNOMBRABLES

1. The news is not good. There is more and more flu (/There are more and more cases of flu) in the village. 2. If you go to the market, can you buy pork, fruit and half a pound of butter? 3. I made a short trip to London, for I was hoping to find a job there. 4. Tomorrow, we'll move out the luggage and the furniture. 5. The information he gave me has helped me to find some work/a job.

9. Les articles

◆1 1. A man survived an 18-storey fall from a Cape Town hotel room and was well enough to call out to rescuers. Nicholas du Plooy broke his arm, a leg and injured his neck on Tuesday when he landed on the roof of the hotel's reception, his fall apparently broken by metal roofing sheets. (*The Times*, April 23, 2004)

2. Television for parrots has been launched to help bored birds to pass the time. The World Parrot Trust, based in Hayle, Cornwall, has produced what is believed to be the world's first DVD for birds. Polly Vision, 80 minutes of images of wild parrots preening, feeding and flying, has been released as part of World Parrot Day on May 31. (*The Times*, May 22, 2004)

3. An £80,000 boat designed by Malcolm Barnsley, a Southampton engineer, to be the world's fastest has been launched. Sailrocket will challenge the speed sailing record in Weymouth. She can reach more than 50 knots (57.5 mph), nearly twice that of a competition yacht. (*The Times*, April 24, 2004)

◆2 1. He is a surgeon and works in the hospital three times a week. 2. He stayed in the sun without a hat and has a headache. What a pity! 3. Do the ghosts of the dead sometimes come back to see the living? 4. Jean Brun, an engineer in Lille, claims that mobiles can be dangerous. 5. We will have the opportunity of talking to Professor Barton during lunch.

10. Les quantifieurs

(UN) PEU DE / BEAUCOUP DE

1. many - a lot – 2. so many - much – 3. too much - too much – 4. little – 5. Many - a few – 6. Many - few – 7. A little - too many – 8. How many - how much

SOME, ANY, NO

1. any - someone – 2. some - any – 3. anyone - any – 4. some - some – 5. anything - no – 6. none - any – 7. Anyone - some – 8. no - any

PARLER DE DEUX ÉLÉMENTS

1. I hate both mustard and vinegar. 2. Both John and Mary can drive, but neither of them has ever owned a car. 3. I can neither cook nor sew. 4. Both of his school reports were poor. 5. How can you both work and listen to music at the same time?

11. This et that

1. this - that – 2. that - that – 3. This - that - This - that – 4. that - This/that - that – 5. this

12. Les pronoms

1. They accuse each other of lying, and I don't know what to do to help them. 2. That plumber of mine doesn't do his job well, and

he calls himself a professional! 3. I've had my windows changed, but my neighbours have kept theirs. 4. He does not wash, gets up at 3 and talks to himself. 5. A friend of mine has hurt himself going down the stairs.

I 13. La traduction du français « on »

1. They tried to enter through the window. 2. We tried to enter through the window. 3. Ever since the statue was stolen, we have locked the church in the afternoon. 4. I was told (/They told me) to fill in this form. 5. And if we went to the cinema? They have *Jaws* on at the Odeon. 6. In life, you can't always choose.

I 14. Génitif, nom + of + nom, noms composés

1. Tess's clothes – 2. her silk dress – 3. the president's secretary – 4. the letters of the unemployed – 5. Japan's veto – 6. yesterday's news – 7. the Paris opera – 8. a music lover – 9. Paul's old credit card – 10. the most beautiful girl in the world.

I 15. L'adjectif

❶ 1. long-haired–2. poorly-paid/badly-paid/ low-paid – 3. moneymaking – 4. an often-quoted – 5. tight-fitting

❷ 1. interested - interesting – 2. frustrating - boring – 3. worried - worrying – 4. surprising - surprised

❸ 1. It's a delicious home-made apricot jam, which is similar to the one my grandmother made. 2. In that painting by Breughel, the blind lead the crippled. 3. She is too careful an employee to have made such a mistake. 4. You don't like the young, but the young people I know are very well-mannered. 5. Chapter 3 begins with the description of a poorly-dressed drunken woman. 6. The Scots and the English are British, but the English people with whom I stayed last month did not like the Scots.

COMPARATIF ET SUPERLATIF

1. the simplest - the best – 2. less polite - the better – 3. the more surprised - least/most friendly – 4. the elder - the more/less handsome – 5. harder - the worst – 6. The farther - the less/more likely

I 16. La dérivation

1. actress - stardom – 2. runner - outruns – 3. simplify - misspelling – 4. overdressed/ underdressed - foolish 5. careless driver – 6. dirty - drinkable - harmful – 7. selfishness - saddened – 8. underestimate - possibilities

I 17. Le passif

❶ 1. I was taught that such behaviour is rude. 2. The new job was offered to George and... 3. I was lent the money I needed by Susie. 4. He is called a liar by everyone. 5. ... lunch was being served. 6. I think these old trousers should be thrown away.

❷ 1. They were attacked in the street. 2. I'm phoning you while my car is being repaired. 3. They were shown/showed the contract by the lawyer. OU: The contract was shown/ showed to them by the lawyer. 4. Apple-pie can be served with ice-cream. 5. His request has just been refused.

I 18. Le discours indirect

1. The boy told his mother that when he was older he would be a doctor. 2. She exclaimed that there couldn't be a leak, that (/as) she'd had the car repaired two months before. 3. He wondered where she had hidden the money. 4. She declared that she loved it there, and that she was going to stay until the following month. 5. Joanna said that she was just phoning to tell her mother that she might be late, because her car wouldn't start. 6. She advised him not to be late for his train, as it wouldn't wait for her. 7. She told him that he should get himself another suitcase and that

they could go and buy one the next day if he wished. 8. Peter said that Granny had always been fond of pets, so that they must get her a dog.

I 19. Les propositions relatives

1. in which – 2. which – 3. who – 4. whose – 5. which/that/Ø – 6. which – 7. that - about which. 8. whom

2 1. Here's the painting which/that/I (had) talked to you about. 2. They've stopped producing this shampoo, the sales of which had gone down. 3. This book, a few pages of which are damaged, cannot be sold. 4. Here is all that you will need. 5. The passer-by whose bag had been stolen was furious.

I 20. Les formes V + -ing / V (to) + V

Verbe + -ing ou to + verbe

1. selling - not to do – 2. giving him - spending - for him to grow up – 3. to stop - to walking – 4. buying - being caught – 5. for them to come back - leaving - to take care – 6. decorating - to do – 7. to help me (to) get back – 8. to take - new immigrants from entering – 9. giving - working – 10. to see - to buy

Make, have et get : traduction de « faire faire »

1. I'll have the bedroom redecorated. 2. The music was so loud that he couldn't make himself heard. 3. In the army, he'll be made to obey. 4. They grow leeks in their garden. 5. I had my secretary say that I was not in. 6. The city has just had the castle restored.

I 21. Verbe/adjectif + that

1. I suppose (that) he's going to resign now. 2. Her friends had insisted that she should stay (/ that she stay) for a few days. 3. They demanded that they should be (/be) given their money back. 4. It's a pity that they should not have met earlier. 5. It's normal that you should be (/are) angry.

I 22. Les adverbes

1 1. They arrived late last night in Norwich. 2. They finally tried to lift the vase carefully. 3. She is very/extremely tired; however, she is also very/extremely happy to be alive. 4. He could almost distinguish the tower although it was quite far away. 5. He seldom jogs in the park these days. 6. Honestly, have you ever seen such behaviour! 7. He too feels pretty disappointed./He feels pretty disappointed too. 8. "Are you comfortable enough?" she often asked me.

2 1. You are not yet 16 and you can't see this film. 2. No sooner had I opened the door than I heard a strange noise/Hardly had I opened ... when I heard... 3. Let's wait. It's not yet warm enough. 4. Have you ever been to Glasgow? I no longer go there these days.

II S'exprimer correctement à l'oral

1 a 'suspect to sus'pect an 'insult to in'sult ba'lloon bi'ology bio'logical phi'losophy o'pinion consti'tution 'precious 'industry in'dustrial mathe'matics re'publican 'demonstrate dis'criminate ca'reer 'democrat demo'cratic democrati'sation a 'rebel to re'bel 'comedy co'median

2 I could never have done it. <u>Could</u> you?
"We'll come <u>for</u> lunch then." "No, not for lunch, after lunch."
"I've lost my keys. Do you know where they <u>are</u>?" "Yes, they're in the kitchen."
<u>That's</u> not what I said. I said that he should have called before he came.

V Découvrir la culture

Quelques différences entre l'anglais britannique et l'américain

1 1. He left his truck in the parking lot and took the elevator to his friend's apartment.
2. Have you got suspenders I can wear with this tuxedo!
3. I've never had an automobile and can't tell the hood from the trunk.

2 1. He had his favourite meal of steak and chips, asked for the bill and left.
2. When she was in the toilet, she realized she had left her handbag in the boot.
3. We'll take a taxi to go to the town/city centre.

INDEX

D

V

W

Y

Z

Imprimé en France par Mame Imprimeurs à Tours (08032156)
N° de projet : 10149390 - Dépôt légal : mai 2008